25 YEARS OF

DEER

& DEER HUNTING

THE ORIGINAL STUMP SITTERS MAGAZINE

Credits:
Front and back cover photos by Charles J. Alsheimer

Published by

krause
publications
The World's Largest Hobby & Collectibles Publisher

700 E. State St. • Iola, WI 54990-0001

Please call or write for a free catalog of publications. The toll-free number to
place an order or to request a free catalog is (800) 258-0929,
or use our regular business number (715) 445-2214.

Library of Congress Catalog Number: 2002105757
ISBN: 0-87349-502-0
Printed in the United States of America

Dedication

In the late 1960s, Jack Brauer and Al Hofacker set up a deer hunting camp in northeastern Wisconsin. They called themselves "The Stump Sitters." Their common goal? To constantly learn more about North America's greatest game animal. From those humble beginnings, Brauer and Hofacker forged ahead and eventually founded the first newsstand magazine devoted to white-tailed deer. Thanks, guys. Your never-ending quest for practical and comprehensive deer hunting information not only made generations of hunters more successful, you also made us better stewards of the land.

Contents

Foreword

It's hard to believe, but a quarter-century has passed since two Wisconsin men made their dream of "deer hunting for a living" come true.

In the mid-1970s, Jack Brauer, an insurance salesman, and Al Hofacker, a teacher, decided they loved white-tailed deer hunting so much that they'd quit their jobs and start a club — and later a magazine — devoted to their hobby. The magazine, *Deer & Deer Hunting*, was not only an instant success, it helped build one of today's most successful North American industries.

When the first issue of *D&DH* rolled off the press in 1977, skeptics said it would never last. White-tailed deer hunting was too small of a niche, claimed the naysayers.

How wrong they were. Today, economists estimate that people spend more than $15 billion a year to hunt white-tailed deer.

Although *D&DH* was nearly an instant success in Wisconsin, co-founder Jack Brauer deflects much of the magazine's national success to Debbie Knauer. Knauer, who joined *D&DH* in 1981 as its its one-person advertising sales department, later became publisher — a position she held for nearly 20 years. Knauer now heads the crafts division at Krause Publications, *D&DH's* parent company.

"Debbie had a grander vision for producing a magazine for a national audience," Brauer said. "She took our magazine to steps I would have never taken it to." In fact, Knauer was one of the main forces behind expanding *D&DH* to its current format, and she was critical in developing the annual *Whitetail Calendar* and the *Deer Hunters' Almanac*. She was also instrumental in *D&DH's* work with respected groups like the National Bowhunting Education Foundation and the Archery Manufacturers and Merchants Organization.

Today, *D&DH* is led by publisher Hugh McAloon, an avid whitetail hunter from Oshkosh, Wis., who joined Krause in 1984. Although he worked primarily with the company's sports collecting division for many years, McAloon helped convince Krause executives to pull the trigger on purchasing *D&DH* in 1992.

"We thought it would be a natural extension to our business," McAloon said, noting that Krause already had three outdoors titles — *Turkey Hunter*, *Trapper & Predator Caller* and *Wisconsin Outdoor Journal*. "Besides, in the publishing business, it's not often that you get a chance to acquire the No. 1 publication in its field. This was an opportunity that we couldn't let slip away from us."

Krause didn't hesitate, and the rest, as they say, is history. With talented employees and cutting-edge computer technology, Krause allowed *D&DH* to solidify its position as a newsstand powerhouse. Now printed nine times per year, *D&DH* has an average distribution of more than 225,000 copies and attracts 464,000 readers per issue (includes readers who share copies with family and friends).

As they did in the beginning, readers literally absorb every issue. According to an independent research study, the average *D&DH* reader spends more than *three hours* reading each issue. Now that's hard-core!

From its inception, *D&DH* always attempted to provide deer hunters with a diverse blend of articles about white-tailed deer and the deer hunting of them. The book you're holding includes a sampling of some of those memorable articles and photographs, including contributions by Leonard Lee Rue III, Charles J. Alsheimer, Richard P. Smith, Rob Wegner, Kent Horner, John J. Ozoga, Bob Zaiglin, Greg Miller and many more.

I hope you enjoy this book as much as I enjoyed writing, compiling and editing it. And here's to hoping the next quarter-century brings equal prosperity for the future of white-tailed deer and deer hunting.

— *Daniel E. Schmidt*
Editor, Deer & Deer Hunting
Iola, Wis., Feb. 22, 2002

Introduction

Deer & Deer Hunting magazine was not the product of a grandiose plan developed by a publishing house for a group of investors. Rather, the magazine evolved day-by-day, month-by-month and year-by-year under the direction of deer hunters eager to acquire comprehensive and practical information about white-tailed deer and deer hunting techniques — the type of editorial no one else was publishing for deer hunters.

Jack Brauer, publisher, and Al Hofacker, editor, founded *Deer & Deer Hunting* almost by accident in 1977. Then, in 1979, they became acquainted with Rob Wegner, another ambitious and serious deer hunter. Wegner became a minority partner and brought to the magazine his experience in writing and expertise in the history and philosophy of the sport of deer hunting.

But the history of this magazine began, albeit inadvertently, well before the first issue appeared in mid-1977. In the late 1960s, Brauer and Hofacker were members of a deer hunting camp in northern Wisconsin who called themselves "The Stump Sitters."

The Stump Sitters' deer camp consisted of about a dozen deer hunters who hunted only during the gun deer season, with the exception of Brauer and Hofacker who also hunted deer with bows and arrows. As avid bow-hunters they thirsted for, but could not find, in-depth and factual information about white-tailed deer. Unable to locate the type of information they desired, the two men began studying deer year round, using movie cameras to document deer behavior.

In the early 1970s, members of The Stump Sitters' deer camp went their separate ways, but Brauer and Hofacker continued to scout, film and hunt together at every opportunity.

In early 1974, they were asked to give a brief talk and show some of their films to a group of elementary school students. Their presentation was well-received and soon several invitations to speak came from other schools and sportsman's organizations. Sensing a need for and an interest in these presentations, Brauer and Hofacker worked hard at improving them. From 1974 through 1980, the men took their "Stump Sitters and The World of the Whitetail" program across the Midwest, making as many as 70 presentations per year. They stopped touring in 1981 because *Deer & Deer Hunting* had grown so large that it required their undivided attention.

The original premise of having deer hunters conduct amateur research worked, and several articles in the early years reported the findings. In fact, one article attracted the attention of professional deer researchers and led to a cooperative research project between the University of Wisconsin-Stevens Point and the Stump Sitters Whitetail Study Group.

It became evident, however, that it was impossible for members of the Study Group to satisfy their thirst for information by conducting their own deer studies. Furthermore, readers preferred scientific research. Although such information was readily available, the founders realized it took a lot of time and effort to "boil down" scientific information and present it in a context that most deer hunters could comprehend.

For those reasons and more, the Stump Sitters Whitetail Study Group was phased out, and *Deer & Deer Hunting* was allowed to blossom into the the magazine that still thrives in today's competitive newsstand marketplace.

Today, *Deer & Deer Hunting* possess a mystique unlike any other outdoors magazine. Avid readers not only devour every printed word, many of them save every issue. It's that type of devotion that prods the magazine's staff to constantly strive to make each issue better than the previous one.

We know you'd expect nothing less.

GETTING STARTED
1977 TO 1981

From Stump Sitters
to Magazine Publishers

BRIAN LOVETT, WITH DANIEL E. SCHMIDT

At some point, most deer hunters realize their sport is much more than a quest to bring down an animal.

It's the pounding heart when a thick-necked buck visits a nearby scrape. It's the shed you find in spring along a well-used deer trail. It's the sting of snow or rain on your face while vowing to stick it out another hour. It's the hunting journal that slides down your lap as you fade off to sleep on a cold February night.

It was this desire that spawned *Deer & Deer Hunter* magazine, and that quest continues to drive this publication on its 25th anniversary.

Of course, the product you now find on the newsstand is quite a bit different from those of years past. The record shows that the magazine's first issue was published in 1977. But it was actually born in the Oconto County deer woods of northern Wisconsin in 1969. Its origins trace to a hunting group called "The Stump Sitters." A shingle outside the group's hunting shack carried that name, and it followed two of the men through their career in the "deer business."

Al Hofacker and Jack Brauer were those two members. Although they were the group's only archers, they considered themselves deer hunters first and foremost — not gun-hunters, bow-hunters or muzzleloading hunters. They reasoned that their first love was hunting deer. It really didn't matter what tool they used in the woods.

Upon graduating from a Chicago college, Hofacker returned home before stepping into a job. With some time on his hands, he headed to Oconto to do some bow-hunting. Brauer, a next-door neighbor Hofacker had known since childhood, was also at the cabin. The two men spent the fall "chasing deer around with our bows and arrows," as Hofacker put it.

They continued to hunt together in the years that followed. But both of them shared a problem: They could find little in-depth information on white-tailed deer. Undaunted, they began watching and studying deer year-round, taking careful notes and incorporating their observations with data from scientific journals.

Hofacker says the motivation was simple: "We just had a deep interest in deer. We wanted to become more familiar with the animal. You had to work a little harder for a deer in those days. When you brought one home back then, it was really something."

Hofacker and Brauer did most of the early field work on their own,

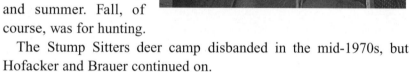

Above: Soon after Al Hofacker transformed his pickup truck into a "company vehicle," he and Jack Brauer, right, took their "Stump Sitters and the World of the Whitetail" show on the road.

Below: Although the Stump Sitters deer camp had about a dozen members, the most serious hunters were, from left, Brauer, Jim Pegel and Hofacker.

although other hunters sometimes accompanied them. They spent a lot of time in the woods each winter, and somewhat less time in spring and summer. Fall, of course, was for hunting.

The Stump Sitters deer camp disbanded in the mid-1970s, but Hofacker and Brauer continued on.

"Most of the guys in our deer camp were not serious about the sport," Brauer said. "They were more social deer hunters, so we made a camp rule that you had to spend 400 hours a year in the woods to

remain a member of the deer camp. That rule eliminated the nonserious hunters and left me, Al and Jim Pegel. Once we started doing programs, we had to throw money in the pot to buy equipment and to travel. Jim couldn't afford this, so he asked to be 'out' of the Stump Sitters. That left me and Al."

Hofacker and Brauer logged thousands of hours of field observations and shot countless reels of 8 mm movie film. Along the way — sometimes by design, sometimes not — they learned a few things about deer. In 1974, they were invited to share some of their knowledge with a group of elementary school children. Other invitations followed, and they soon found themselves on the lecture tour. From 1974 through 1980, they traveled around the Midwest giving their presentations, titled "The Stump Sitters and The World of the Whitetail." In one year, they gave as many as 70 presentations.

Early in their road tours, they learned that the deer hunter's quest for information went beyond seminars. They sensed a demand for a publication that dealt specifically with whitetails, much in the way that other magazines dealt with specific game or fish.

"At that time there were no other deer- hunting magazines in the marketplace," Hofacker said. "So we thought we'd give it a try. We knew nothing about the publishing business, but were confident we knew a little bit about deer and deer hunting."

At the time, Hofacker and Brauer did some writing and worked some sport shows for a now-defunct magazine. At some of the shows, they put out a sign-up sheet for hunters interested in a deer hunting magazine. A small mailing list resulted.

In an effort to satisfy the desire for practical information about deer, the men formed the Stump Sitters' Whitetail Study Group. Hunters collected information and sent it to Hofacker and Brauer, who then analyzed and compiled it. Much of the information was published in *Deer & Deer Hunting*, which was sent to study-group members.

The first issue, published in July 1977, resembled a newsletter more than a magazine. It was merely an 11-by-17-inch piece of paper folded in half, and it had a distribution of about 1,500 copies. Hofacker and Brauer produced most of the first few issues from Brauer's basement, including the writing, design and layout.

"It was a rather crude looking affair," Hofacker said. "But it got

Certificate of Recognition

"In recent years, professional biologists have often been at odds with hunters over deer management priorities and programs. Most biologists have struggled to reach hunters with information on population dynamics and the basis for hunting programs. The magazine *Deer & Deer Hunting* has effectively filled this communication gap and serves as an intellectual bridge between biologists, managers and hunters. The gamble in developing this publication style and content was great, yet the niche that has been filled is a unique one. Clearly, this was not to be a 'me and Joe' hunting magazine, but rather, a publication about the biology, ecology, management, and hunting of the white-tailed deer. It is, without a doubt, the best magazine on white-tailed deer (perhaps on any wildlife species) published for public distribution.

"The first magazines were primitive by today's standards, but the theme was effective and growth rapid. The editors sought and encouraged articles by professionals and have been most cooperative in publishing technical information, while still including informative articles on deer hunting as a sport. Hunting articles focus on the art and science of hunting; respecting deer as a biological species is a dominant theme. The more professional articles are generally written for lay persons, but with the inclusion of scientific terms and arguments permits scientists who work with deer to reach a large reading audience, much larger and very different from the audience reached through professional journals.

"The Northeast Section of The Wildlife Society is proud to recognize the magazine *Deer & Deer Hunting* for its unique and substantial contribution to the wildlife management professions, to the hunters who participate in management programs, and to the species that has at once been the nation's greatest conservation story, as well as the species evoking the greatest controversy. The high educational standards of *Deer & Deer Hunting* magazine are unmatched in the natural resource publishing industry, and we hereby honor the magazine and its staff with the 1987 Northeast Section of The Wildlife Society's Certificate of Recognition."

better with each issue."

Embarking on the venture was a little frightening, Hofacker said. Neither he nor Brauer had a background in publishing or journalism. Even their writing experience was limited. Nonetheless, the newsletter caught on.

The publication grew and eventually evolved into a magazine. Hofacker said the content of early issues was strikingly similar to those of today, with a heavy emphasis on deer biology, behavior and management. The magazine strives to be, practical, entertaining and sometimes controversial.

Knowledge about deer behavior, of course, directly affects hunter success. And information about deer management is also important to hunters, Hofacker said.

"Anything to do with deer or the hunting of deer is within reach of what we published," he said. "Our interest (went) beyond the where-to-go and how-to articles. And we aren't bashful about publishing different viewpoints on the same subject, even when we don't agree."

Soon after the magazine started, Brauer — previously an insurance salesman — went into the deer business full time. Hofacker, previously an electronics technician, joined him in 1979. During that same year, a deer hunter named Rob Wegner became a third partner.

"The best part about it was doing something you enjoyed," Hofacker said. "By June 1979, the three of us were full time, and we were still doing the seminars, in addition to publishing six issues of *Deer & Deer Hunting* each year."

Hofacker and Brauer handled the seminars for adults while Wegner took care of those for school children. The workload, however, became hectic. Eventually, the men sat down and made some tough decisions on the magazine's future. The Stump Sitters' Whitetail Study Group — which was effective in the publication's early years — was phased out, as were the seminars. Hofacker said it became obvious that members of the group couldn't get enough verifiable information about deer from their own studies. Also, a great deal of technical and in-depth information was becoming available from professional wildlife biologists, university professors and graduate students.

At that same time, Hofacker and Brauer incorporated Stump Sitters Inc., forming the corporation that publishes *Deer & Deer Hunting* magazine.

The magazine began to take off in circulation, content and advertising during 1981, Hofacker said. By 1982, its circulation was more than 30,000.

"Debbie Knauer kept telling me that we really wouldn't know if the public would accept our magazine unless it was on newsstands," Brauer said. "So I went and talked to our local magazine distributor, and worked out an arrangement whereby they would distribute the magazine in the northern half of Wisconsin and the U.P. of Michigan. If that was successful, then we would try national distribution."

Finally, in 1985, the magazine was distributed nationally on newsstands, and it has grown steadily since.

While many facets of the magazine underwent change in the first few years, some features remain basically unchanged since their inception. One example of this is the "Deer Browse" section of the magazine, a regular department which appeared for the first time in the sixth issue. "Deer Browse" consists of short items and photographs reporting incidents of unusual deer behavior and the experiences of deer hunters. As well as being the longest running regular department, it remains one of the most popular parts of the magazine.

In 1982, the "Readers Recoil" section was added to the magazine in response to increased feedback from an ever-growing number of readers. "Readers Recoil" became so popular that sometimes the editors received more comments about the "Readers Recoil" section than feedback pertaining to feature-length articles.

Not all the letters published were complimentary. In fact, many readers strongly criticized the editors' choice of articles. Rather than discard these letters, the editors published them. According to Hofacker, he knew deer hunters were an opinionated lot, and it would have been an injustice to silence the naysayers by not publishing their views. After all, *D&DH* was a magazine published by deer hunters for deer hunters.

Left: *D&DH* has always prided itself as a lone drummer, and the editors have never worried about offending anyone — even if the topic wasn't deer hunting. That attitude was evident outside the magazine's Appleton, Wis., office in 1989 when first-round draft choice Tony Mandarich was involved in a salary dispute with the Green Bay Packers.

Below: Jack Brauer spent a minimum of 400 hours each year hunting whitetails with gun, camera and bow and arrow. Think about that for a moment — that equals four hours a day, five times a week for 20 weeks!

Study Group is Educating Thousands of Deer Hunters

RICHARD P. SMITH, NOVEMBER 1980

Minutes after legal shooting time on opening day of Wisconsin's gun-deer season, a shot was fired from young Doug Brauer's stand. Moments later, Al Hofacker sent a bullet down the barrel of his rifle at a buck. That's a typical beginning for deer season here at the Stump Sitters' hunting camp.

The Stump Sitters' Whitetail Study Group is an organization of deer hunters throughout North America who are interested in learning information about whitetails that can be applied to their hunting with guns, bows and cameras. Jack Brauer and Al Hofacker from Appleton, Wis., are the founders of the organization. Doug is Jack's son.

Jack's stand was within 100 yards of the location where his son sat, so he hurried over to see if Doug connected. The excited boy explained that a forkhorn appeared unexpectedly and ran off when he shot from his tree stand. Doug said he must have missed the shot because he only had a neck shot. Nonetheless, the party searched the area just to be sure. The boy was right. In fact, it was later learned that the buck was the same one Hofacker shot at. Even though both hunters missed, they both at least had opportunities at tagging an antlered buck that morning, which isn't common in today's deer woods.

In fact, if the odds had tipped in the hunters' favor that morning, three of the four Stump Sitters club members would have had deer hanging by noon on opening day. Simply having the opportunity for that type of success is outstanding no matter where you hunt whitetails. How can one group of hunters find such great success? Although quality land is certainly one reason, proper stand placement is the overriding factor.

Years of research on deer movements, which included hunting time, enabled Brauer and Hofacker to select stands where they would be most likely to see bucks. Some of their findings will probably come as a surprise to many whitetail hunters. For example, in the early 1970s, they found that scrape-hunting was a waste of time on their northeast Wisconsin property. This specialized form of stand-hunting involves posting within sight of one or more scrapes made by rutting bucks.

After spending countless hours hunting over scrapes, the two men decided to conduct their own rudimentary research project to determine if their suspicions were correct. Using Super 8 movie cameras

Editor's note: Although researchers conducted extensive studies on white-tailed deer behavior in the 1950s and '60s, their scientific conclusions were often of little value to everyday deer hunters. That's part of the reason why Al Hofacker and Jack Brauer founded Stump Sitters — they wanted to create an outlet where serious deer hunters could share information, and, in turn, learn more about whitetails and the hunting of them. When *Deer & Deer Hunting* was only three years old, Michigan outdoor writer Richard Smith visited the Stump Sitters deer camp in northern Wisconsin. This never-before-published article explains how Hofacker and Brauer fused their love for whitetails into *D&DH*, North America's first magazine devoted to deer hunting.

Above: The Stump Sitters got started by lecturing to grade schools and membership organizations. Here, Al Hofacker explains the differences between white-tailed deer and mule deer to a group of grade-schoolers in Appleton, Wis., in 1976.

and cable releases, they monitored scrapes for long periods.

The cameras were rigged with windshield-wiper motors and 12-volt batteries. This allowed the cameras to expose one frame of film every 12 seconds. At that rate, a 50-foot film cartridge would last 12 hours. Cameras were positioned near fresh scrapes.

Over nine days, the cameras recorded much buck activity. However, nearly all of the activity was at night. The men also learned that young bucks made frequent scrapes, but never in the same spot.

After reporting their findings to the study group, Hofacker and Brauer watched as the mail poured in. Hunters were amazed by their project, and the findings soothed fears that other hunters were "doing something wrong" when hunting near scrapes because they experienced similar results.

In fact, the study sparked a mini revolution among rut-hunters.

"We use scrapes and rubs as a means of identifying the area being used by bucks," Hofacker said. "From there we get back to that same old question, 'What are the deer eating?' Then we find trails leading to and from feeding areas in locations with a lot of scrapes and rubs, and position our stands along those trails."

The men soon learned, however, that their study couldn't apply to all hunting situations. They also heard from many successful scrape-hunters. They welcomed the diverse reports and shared them with study group members. Eventually, Hofacker and Brauer decided to solicit similar studies from the members. To learn more about white-tailed deer and deer hunting from a hunter's perspective, the men devised observation sheets and distributed them to study group members. Members were asked to record all deer observations and document each sighting by recording the date, time, wind direction, direction of deer movement, hunting methods used and prevailing weather conditions.

"There is a lot of misinformation and myths about deer," Brauer said. "A lot of hunters are being misled. That's why we started trying to gather useful information, and the study group developed from there."

Although most data is gathered during the fall hunting seasons, some is collected during every month of the year. Many study group participants "hunt" deer year-round with cameras, or simply observe them regularly.

Hunters are obviously interested in the cooperative learning process because membership in the organization continues to grow. Results obtained from data sheets, as well as articles on hunting techniques and deer hunting experiences, are distributed to Stump Sitters members via a bimonthly magazine aptly titled *Deer & Deer Hunting*. Much of the information contained in this magazine can be applied directly to deer hunting. Some of the more interesting findings, for instance, relate to weather conditions that are best for deer activity and how availability of various foods affect deer movements.

I often thought whitetails would be more active during daylight hours when it's cloudy or overcast. This is not true according to thousands of Stump Sitters data sheets. According to the group's data, the best days for deer activity are those with a clear sky, little or no wind and temperatures 5 to 10 degrees below the seasonal average.

Hofacker said there is usually an "explosion of deer activity" on ideal days that follow long periods of lousy weather. For example, four days or more of heavy rain, snow or strong winds usually reduce deer activity. However, when the bad weather passes, deer will be out in droves, and hunters who are afield at the same time should see plenty of action.

Stump Sitters' findings also confirm that deer are more active than normal preceding a storm. However, Brauer and Hofacker said this is more often true when snow is involved.

Food availability can also have a dramatic effect on deer movement, according to study group information. In fact, members report that whitetails will abandon one food source for another. Hofacker and Brauer first documented this behavior in the early 1970s when they observed a herd of whitetails that fed regularly in an alfalfa field in summer. The herd included seven bucks, and the men could easily identify each buck because they observed them daily for several months.

When archery season approached, the deer vanished. In fact, in the week leading up to opening day, no deer visited the field. Study-group members eventually located the deer in a woodlot nearly 2 miles from the alfalfa field!

Why had the deer abandoned the field? Well, the woodlot was home to a good stand

Above: Some new products of the late 1970s seem ancient when compared to what's available today.

Below: *Deer & Deer Hunting*'s earliest subscription premium was the Stump Sitters patch. Many hunters — now "seasoned" veterans — still wear the patch proudly on their hunting jackets.

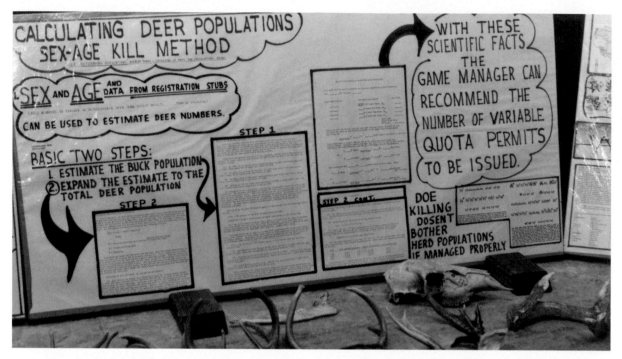

of oaks, and the trees had just started dropping acorns. This change forced the deer to change their feeding habits.

Another time, Hofacker installed an electronic trail watcher on a well-used deer trail in a woodlot. Hofacker buried a sensor in the trail so he could record every time a deer walked over it. Deer activity was fairly constant for several weeks, then it suddenly stopped. Curious as to why deer activity ceased, Hofacker examined the area and learned a nearby farmer had recently cut an alfalfa field. The freshly cut field attracted deer like a magnet and caused them to virtually abandon the woodlot. For the next two weeks, deer fed regularly in the cut field. Then, nearly as suddenly as before, they abandoned the field and returned to the woodlot.

Although scientific researchers documented such deer behavior

Above: Although the Stump Sitters worked hard to dispel many commonly-held myths on deer management, many hunters in the 1970s — as they do today — thought game managers issued too many antlerless permits.

Right: Anyone who's remotely familiar with the deer hunting industry's roots will recognize this face. Tink Nathan's famous buck lure gained acceptance by hundreds of thousands of whitetail hunters in the early 1980s.

many years before the Stump Sitters, never before had it been presented in a popular medium. With *Deer & Deer Hunting* magazine, hunters can now learn more about deer behavior from such hands-on studies by other deer hunters.

Besides providing practical and comprehensive information for white-tailed deer hunters, the Stump Sitters also try to dispel myths about deer and deer hunting. It seems that myths often take on lives of their own and pass from one generation to the next.

For example, in-the-field observations by Stump Sitters members have dispelled the following myths:

✓ Only bucks snort.

Thousands of data entries show this is simply not true. In truth, both bucks and does snort, or "blow" air through their noses as a warning to other animals.

✓ A deer is not wounded if it runs with its tail up after being shot.

✓ A deer is wounded if it runs with its tail down after being hit.

Study group members have proven these long-held beliefs to be incorrect. Although some members reported observing tail-down behavior among wounded deer, they agreed that this behavior is more of an exception rather than a rule. As a result, members agree that a deer's "tail language" cannot reliably indicate if a deer has or hasn't been wounded.

The Stump Sitters are also uncovering interesting information on hunter behavior. For example, data sheets indicate that many hunters get stuck in a rut of hunting the same way every day, season after season. In this case, Hofacker and Brauer learned that many low-success hunters continue to fail because they use the same stand for each hunt and hunt it the same way each day. Thanks to this study group finding, such hunters can identify their problem and break out of their rut by adopting slight changes in their tactics.

While the Stump Sitters Whitetail Study Group founders have accumulated a lot of facts on deer and deer hunting, they will be the first to admit they don't have all the answers. As we enter the 1980s, Hofacker and Brauer know more myth-breaking facts will be revealed about white-tailed deer. They also know more questions will arise.

That's OK with them. As long as there are questions, they'll spearhead the effort to answer them. And they'll use their new magazine, *Deer & Deer Hunting*, to spread the word.

Above: Al Hofacker's meticulous notes on deer behavior and research trends formed the nucleus in which *Deer & Deer Hunting* built its unique editorial content.

Below: One of the most memorable ads from *D&DH's* early days plugged Damart's long underwear. The ad ran in various forms throughout the 1970s and '80s.

How Hunters & Researchers Fulfilled Leopold's Prophecy

ROB WEGNER

*D*eer & Deer Hunting's greatest contribution to white-tailed deer research and deer management lies in making professional literature available to the general public. This is as true today as it was in 1977. The job wasn't always easy, but Al Hofacker, Jack Brauer and I thought it was our duty to produce a magazine that legendary conservationist Aldo Leopold would have found interesting.

A deer hunter himself, Leopold believed the scientific community had a lot to learn from hunters, and that cooperative efforts between hunters and wildlife professionals could benefit everyone.

Here's a glimpse at the deer research break-throughs that *D&DH* helped popularize over the past 25 years.

1977 to 1982

Deer & Deer Hunting was destined from its inception to be a different sort of hunting magazine. Structured around a grass-roots study group of deer hunters, members contributed data-sheet information from in-the-field observations of white-tailed deer. The editors returned that data to deer hunters in the form of well-written articles that included in-depth graphs, charts, tables, figures and illustrations. Reprints of research articles from state agencies appeared in the pages of early issues, and the editors worked hard to summarize and popularize scientific information on the natural history of deer and how that information applies to successful deer hunting and management. Professional biologists soon started contributing articles on their own field studies on whitetails.

In July 1979, the magazine published its first in-depth, professionally written feature, "The Deer Hunting Ethic: A Right or a Privilege?" complete with 20 references, including the works of Aldo Leopold and *Ortega*, plus the legacy of *St. Hubert*. It was clear *D&DH* was not to be a "me and Joe" affair. By publishing deep-digging, scientific references that supported research articles would become the magazine's distinctive trademark.

In October 1979, the academic journal *Cynegeticus: A Publication Devoted to the Interdisciplinary Study of Hunting* published an in-depth piece on the Stump Sitters. In that article, "The Stump Sitters: Leopold's Prophesy Fulfilled?" the author noted "the magazine's greatest contribution to white-tailed deer research and deer management lies in making professional literature available to the general public."

Later that year, the Stump Sitters negotiated with professors Jim Hardin, Neil Payne and Charley White, from the University of Wisconsin at Stevens Point, for a cooperative research project that included computer evaluation of deer data collected by the study group. This led to the monitoring of the relationship between white-tailed deer activity and environmental factors. The results were published in *D&DH* and the *Journal of Wildlife Management*.

The project eventually resulted in a master's thesis entitled, "Characteristics of Hunter-Collected Data on White-tailed Deer Movements and Environmental Conditions," completed by deer hunter/biologist Scott Hygnstrom on April 29, 1983. The Stump Sitters provided Hygnstrom with data on whitetails from 30 states and one Canadian province, including 33,026 hours of observation that produced 10,121 deer sightings. Hygnstrom found the study group members were most effective at seeing deer on days with clear skies, light or calm winds and no precipitation.

I joined the Stump Sitters in Fall 1979 when Brauer and Hofacker hired me to collect, summarize and disseminate technical information on deer and deer hunting. By 1980, professors of deer management such as Kirk Beattie began writing articles for *D&DH* – helping put deer hunters and deer managers on the same page.

On the literary side, the bylines of such great naturalists as T. S. Van Dyke, Theodore Roosevelt, Aldo Leopold, Sigurd Olson, William Moneypenny Newsom, Leonard Lee Rue III, John Madson, George Mattis and Edmund Ware Smith appeared in the magazine, contributing to a rich blend of literature, science and personal experience.

In October 1981, *D&DH* published an editorial essay, "Crippling Losses and the Future of American Deer Hunting," which generated hundreds of letters to the editor. Although the article generated much controversy in the hunting community, it spurred the owners to adopt a policy not to cave to special interests or political pressures. As a result, *D&DH* soon became known as the magazine that wouldn't shy away from publicizing hotly-debated topics.

What's more, deer research wasn't limited to the magazine's featured articles. In fact, the editors found ways to incorporate new and fascinating information in all departments, including "Rue's Views" and "Deer Browse." In fact, the theme of including odd stories about whitetails in "Browse" started with the December 1981 issue when the editors borrowed an article about the 52-point "Hole-in-the-Horn" buck from a 1945 issue of the *Journal of Mammalogy*.

Below: Wasp Archery was one of the first companies to manufacture broadheads for on-the-go bow-hunters. This ad, from the early 1980s, explained the benefits of a replaceable-blade broadhead with a three-point locking system.

1982 to 1986

By 1982, the magazine's distribution — the number of magazines printed per issue — was 20,155, and the editors found themselves drawing even more heavily on material from the scientific community. One of the highlights was the article "In Velvet," which appeared in the August 1982 issue. For perhaps the first time ever, scientific insights on antler growth from the scholarly minds of men like Sir William Macewen, A.B. Bubenik, Bernard Stonehouse and George Wislocki were presented in a context that could be easily understood by everyday deer hunters.

In the October 1982 issue, deer researcher Scott Hygnstrom summarized his findings on the effect of environmental conditions on deer movements based on Stump Sitter data. He asked how many deer hunters hunt in the rain and observed, "I frequently read articles describing the virtues of hunting in the rain, but what are the deer doing while it rains, snows, sleets or hails? Researchers generally agree that during periods of rain, deer activity decreases. The results of the Stump Sitter/Stevens Point study reinforced the findings of previous researchers on this question."

As Hygnstrom continued his research, other researchers such as Dave Samuel of West Virginia University, Valerius Geist of the University of Calgary and Scott Craven of the University of Wisconsin at Madison also began writing features on such diverse topics as lessons deer teach us, and the overabundance of deer in certain areas. Professors Robert Jackson and Robert Norton from the University of Wisconsin at La Crosse also shared their now-famous research of the "five stages of hunting." Other important contributions were made by professor Jim Applegate of Rutgers University, who also invented the board game "Oh My Deer" in an effort to teach hunters responsible deer management.

In February 1984, Hofacker and I traveled to Little Rock, Ark., for the 7th Annual Meeting of the Southeast Deer Study Group. This trip would have a profound impact on deer research for the magazine. This meeting provided an important forum for sharing research, management strategies and discussions of problems related to deer management. I continued making this annual pilgrimage for the next decade, and in the process collected, synthesized and disseminated deer research to the general public through *D&DH*.

At the 1984 meeting, Hofacker and I met professor Larry Marchinton, who presented the keynote address on "Dogs, Deer and People in the South." That presentation eventually appeared as a fea-

Above: In 1983, Rob Wegner followed professional deer researchers as they used telemetry equipment to track the movements of deer along the banks of the Wisconsin River.

ture article in *D&DH's* August 1984 issue. These classic deer meetings opened many doors for future articles and new associations with researchers from across the country. Over the years, the association allowed *D&DH* to cultivate its reputation as the only hunting magazine devoted to science-based whitetail information.

In the Fall 1984 issues, Craven continued his four-part series, "So You Got A Deer," and New Jersey deer researchers Bob McDowell, Jim Applegate and Bob Lund waxed eloquently on the challenge of maintaining quality deer herds and maximizing human benefits with a continually declining open space.

By the end of 1984, the magazine's distribution reached 54,535.

In 1985, Wisconsin deer researcher Bill Ishmael contributed several articles on urban deer problems, and analyzed the increasing interest in muzzleloading. Professors Robert Jackson and Ray Anderson also continued to share their new research findings on what makes the deer hunter tick. Later that spring, Brauer and Hofacker announced that *D&DH* was offering a $2,000 grant to support a research project entitled, "Deer Use of Corn in Agricultural Areas."

However, the most time-consuming project in 1985 revolved around crippling losses among bow-hunters. The topic was intense, to say the least. In fact, I recall having many phone conversations with Hofacker that lasted well beyond midnight. We agreed the topic needed intense scientific research and not the casual observations of a couple individuals.

Our efforts resulted in an in-depth piece written by Hofacker that was published in the June 1985 issue. "Crippling Losses: An Update" covered 10-full pages, without ads, and included 10 more references in addition to the 40 references cited in the October 1981 issue. By accessing the University of Wisconsin's 34 libraries in Madison, we uncovered every scrap of information that existed on the topic. Unfortunately for us, many of the studies were flawed. In fact, the truth on crippling losses wasn't realized until 1995, when Jay McAninch, then a researcher for the Minnesota Department of Natural Resources, oversaw a ground-breaking wounding-loss study.

The study, written as a master's thesis by Wendy Krueger, revealed that nearly 90 percent of all deer shot by bow-hunters eventually go home with the hunter. This conclusion debunked the long-standing myth that bow-hunters crippled more deer than they killed.

D&DH followed its June 1981 crippling loss update with a 19-page article in the August issue. The controversial topic took on a life of its own, spurring some nasty letters to the editor. However, cooler heads prevailed, and readers

Below: The whitetail industry experienced many highs and lows during the last 25 years, and few of those early companies weathered the storm. Summit Industries was one of the exceptions. A leader in tree stand technology for parts of four decades, Summit grew into an industry powerhouse.

THE BEST.

The Ultimate Treestand

SUMMIT
SPECIALTIES

P.O. Box 786 • Decatur AL 35602
For Brochure Send $1.00
Dealers Welcome

still respected what we were doing with *D&DH*.

One letter of praise came from professor Aaron Moen, a highly respected deer biologist from Cornell University. It was dated June 5, 1985.

Dear Editor: Your magazine is, in my opinion and I'm sure others too, about the finest vehicle for communication with the hunters that can be found anywhere. Your emphasis on knowledge and research findings lends credibility to its content, and the lack of advertisements for alcoholic beverages lends quality to the recreational aspect of hunting.

With the magazine gaining national acceptance, 1986 proved to be a major highlight. With issues spanning as many as 148 pages, the names of well-known deer researchers like Geist, Moen and John Ozoga graced many pages. While Ozoga analyzed artificial feeding in '86, Moen introduced his new computerized deer management model, "The Modern Deer CAMP," and also wrote articles on rubs and fawn behavior. While Geist examined how deer communicate, *D&DH* field editors wrote essays on leading deer researchers like Bill Severinghaus, Lou Verme and Al Brothers.

The August 1986 issue contained one of the most in-depth articles ever printed on buck rubs, "White Scars of the Deer Forest." The article spanned 14 pages and included magnificent deer photos, figures and charts. The nation had never seen such a detailed and technically oriented presentation of deer behavior. That was followed by one of the most dynamic deer-research pieces ever assembled: "Buck Movements & Hunting Pressure," that was published in the October 1986 issue. This 20-page article featured dramatic blurbs, scientific charts and spectacular photos by Judd Cooney, Mike Biggs, Jeanne Brakefield and Leonard Lee Rue III.

The editorial frenzy reached a climax as the magazine's first decade came to an end. Hofacker's 22-page "On the Trail of Wounded Deer — The Philosophy of Waiting" was an in-depth research piece that could have served as a master's thesis in and of itself. At the same time, Geist continued to analyze threats to wildlife conservation, Ozoga reviewed deer-herd dynamics and Moen examined crippling losses with his computer at Cornell University while using *D&DH* survey data.

Steadily, more research-based articles came in from deer biologists across the country, including several from new field editor Kent Horner, a college professor and regular participant at the Southeast

Above: During the mid-1980s, Rob Wegner moved to Deerfoot Road in the heart of "The Uplands" in southwest Wisconsin, and collecting books on deer research became his passion. Today, Wegner's whitetail library is valued at more than $225,000.

Deer Study Group meetings. Meanwhile, professor Bob Jackson continued exploring the human aspects of American deer hunting, and Aaron Moen explained deer-hunter bias in hunter surveys.

It was contributions like those that marked this five-year period as perhaps the most defining in the history of *D&DH*. It also left readers wanting more. By the end of 1986, *D&DH's* distribution rose to 101,000 — more than five times what it was just four years earlier.

1987 to 1992

By the late 1980s, the popularization of whitetail research was peaking, and *D&DH* led the way.

In the April 1987 issue, professors Karl Miller and Larry Marchinton of the University of Georgia shared their scientific findings on buck rubs. This article broke new ground with hunters because rubs had remained a mystery to nearly everyone outside the scientific community. Miller and Marchinton revealed that, on average, one buck will make anywhere from 69 to 538 rubs annually, with an overall average of 300 rubs per buck. In the same issue, Val Geist examined the concept of sparring and how whitetails use it more for recreation than confrontation. Geist's insights forever changed how serious hunters interpreted such deer behavior.

The culmination of all this in-depth deer research resulted in a national award for *D&DH*. On May 5, 1987, the editors traveled to Boston to receive the honor from the Northeast Section of The Wildlife Society. The groups directors presented the award to the magazine, "For maintaining the highest professional, educational and literary standards while focusing on the deer as a biological species and the art and science of hunting."

Another important research article, "The Scrape," appeared in the December 1987 issue of *D&DH*. With more hunters, especially bow-hunters, interested in using scents while hunting the rut, the editors compiled a 14-page feature that included the latest national research concerning whitetail scrapes. In that same issue, Bob Jackson and Bob Norton explored deer hunting as a social experience and argued that "the day will come for many hunters when bag and shooting opportunities are clearly secondary to the enjoyment derived from hunting with family or just being in the woods with a time-tested partner."

More highlights came from Moen, who examined the dynamics of deer populations, and Geist who wrote another classic essay on "Battle Scars," noting that a buck has to deal with 20 to 30 wounds a year as a result of buck fights. The December issue also included a riveting piece by Dr. Billy Smith of the University of Central Arkansas, who announced

Below: When the compound bow surged in popularity in the late 1970s and early 1980s, many hunters dismissed it as a passing fad. By adhering to high-quality standards, manufacturers quickly proved them wrong.

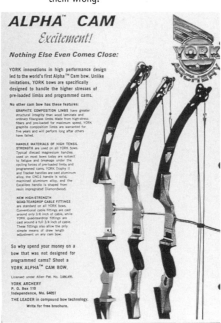

that deer are not color blind and "although it would appear that color is not as potent a stimulus for deer as it is for some other animals, hunters need to be aware of the fact that deer are able to detect color so they can take appropriate precautions."

Amazingly, 1987 had more surprises in store for the magazine. In late December, the publishers learned *D&DH's* distribution had rose to 203,000 — doubling its size from the previous year! Although readers were no doubt attracted to the hard-hitting editorial content, much of the success could be linked to the creative mind of then-advertising manager Debbie Knauer. Knauer, an aggressive business-woman from Door County, Wis., not only helped boost *D&DH's* page count by attracting national advertisers, her tireless efforts helped position *D&DH* as a newsstand powerhouse.

Despite the successes, the editors often worried if they were presenting too much scientific information. Would a preponderance of deer research turn off too many readers? After agonizing over that question for months, the editors queried readers and learned the answer to be a resounding "no!"

After several more months went by, I again posed the question to Al Hofacker. "Deer hunters don't read *Deer & Deer Hunting,* they study it!" he said.

D&DH readers from the late 1980s were also introduced to John Ozoga, the nation's leading white-tailed deer biologist, whose book *Whitetail Country* captured the nation's attention a few years earlier. Ozoga, who would later become the magazine's research editor, is literally a walking encyclopedia of deer research. His work as a deer researcher at the Cusino enclosure in Michigan's Upper Peninsula is considered by many as the most comprehensive ever done on white-tailed deer.

In 1988, Grant Woods, while working on his master's thesis at Southwest Missouri State University, wrote an article documenting how deer use licking branches throughout the year. Until then, many hunters thought licking branches were used only in autumn, in conjunction with scrapes. Woods also explained how licking branches allow whitetails to relay chemical messages. In August 1989, *D&DH* awarded Woods a research grant to study the rubbing behavior of mature bucks at the Mt. Holly Plantation in Berkeley, S.C.

Later that year, William Samuel kept readers informed of deer parasites and diseases, and Aaron Moen explored the question of how long it takes for a deer to die.

In early 1990, Lee Nesbit, a professor of philosophy, provided philosophical research findings on controversial issues such as avoiding the word "kill." According to Nesbit, "any hunter who guiltily converts himself into a phony 'har-

Below: With the bow-hunting industry in its infancy, *D&DH* provided manufacturers with a medium to drum up new business. Revolutionary hunting products like the Redken climbing tree stand were among the first to be advertised in the magazine.

vester' because he thinks it will play better to the nonhunting audience simply gives credence to the anti-hunting propaganda."

In the August 1990 issue, the editors continued tracking wounded deer behavior with a 21-page feature article uncovering the results of 10 new scientific studies (1984 to 1989) and 22 newly found references to the problem.

In 1990 the editors added a regular research column entitled "Deer Behavior," which also led to the columns "Deer Biology" and "Hunter Behavior." During this time, Wisconsin deer biologist Al Cornell continued a long tradition of well-crafted, in-depth reports on all aspects of deer management.

As 1990 ended, *D&DH's* distribution reached an all-time high of 276,771. By October 1991, the field research of Grant Woods on buck rubs ended, and he and Marchinton, Dave Guynn and Karl Miller began writing articles on buck rubs for *D&DH*. They found that small rubs are rarely rubbed more than once; antlerless deer use rubs, and most rub behavior is nocturnal.

Later that year, I began focusing my own research efforts on individual deer camps and clubs, and reported my findings in the "Deer Hunter Behavior" column. This research eventually led to my book *Legendary Deer Camps*, published in 2001 by Krause Publications.

1992 to 2002

Without a doubt, 1992 was the most pivotal year in the history of *D&DH*.

On April 15, Brauer, Hofacker and I sold the magazine to Krause Publications of Iola, Wis., a publishing firm that emphasized quality and editorial integrity. With vast resources and strong national connections, Krause immediately breathed new life into *D&DH*, propelling it from what was, in essence, a family-oriented operation to a business-savvy unit that maintained the vision originally drafted by Brauer and Hofacker.

To keep the magazine true to its roots, Krause maintained *D&DH's* status quo by hiring Knauer as publisher and Patrick Durkin as editor. Under Durkin's guidance, the magazine continued to tap the nation's top deer researchers for insightful articles. What's more, Knauer and Durkin spearheaded a 1993 reader survey that examined tree-stand usage by whitetail hunters. The

Below: The popularization of deer research in *D&DH* culminated in a national award from the Northeast section of the Wildlife Society in Boston on May 5, 1987. Jay McAninch, left, presented the award to editors Rob Wegner, center, and Al Hofacker, right.

result was an award-winning, three-part series that set the standard for tree-stand safety in North America. In fact, it was *D&DH's* survey that revealed that more than one in three hunters have fallen while hunting from high places. The sobering facts revealed in these articles is now used in hunter-education classes across the country. *D&DH* conducted an equally informative three-part series in 1999.

In 1992, *D&DH* also initiated the *Wisconsin Deer Report*, a newspaper that examined science-based deer-management issues from the nation's top deer-hunting state. Unfortunately, the newspaper failed to attract enough readers to justify its continuance.

Above: *D&DH* began a new chapter when it was purchased by Krause Publications on April 15, 1992. Present for the transaction were, standing from left, Giles Heuer, Chester Krause and Rob Wegner, and seated from left, Jack Brauer, Clifford Mishler and Al Hofacker.

In 1993 Krause published Hofacker's anthology *Deer & Deer Hunting*, a coffee-table book that includes some of the greatest deer research articles of all time, including Hofacker's classic, "The Philosophy of Waiting." That was followed up by *The Deer Hunters*, released in 1997 and edited by Durkin. That book includes research-based articles from Woods, Geist, Jay McAninch, Jim Heffelfinger, Larry Machinton, Mickey Hellickson, Bob Zaiglin, Ed Langenau and Walt Hampton

As 1993 came to a close, Woods and his colleagues at Clemson University continued to enlighten the readership with the conclusions of their three-year study on rubs. They found that traditional rubs on aromatic species were used more frequently than those of non-aromatic species.

Ozoga officially became a *D&DH* field editor in June 1994. Since then, his articles have educated deer hunters, managers and scientists on the complexities of deer behavior and biology with in-depth explanations. In 2000, Krause published Ozoga's *Whitetail Intrigue*, which might be the most comprehensive book on science-based whitetail information ever published.

Of course, *D&DH* built its reputation on more than just publishing articles on deer research. In fact, the book you're holding is testament to the myriad ingredients that helped *D&DH* evolve from a newsletter to a well-read and respected magazine dedicated to white-tailed deer.

What's in store for the next 25 years? Nothing but much of the same, I'm sure.

Why I Bleed *D&DH*

CHARLES J. ALSHEIMER

Have you ever sat in a deer stand and tried to figure out why you love deer hunting? Have you contemplated why anyone in their right mind would sit for hours in rain, sleet and snow for a chance to get close to a white-tailed deer? I'm sure that if psychologists tried to analyze the serious whitetail hunter, they would have to re-write their textbooks. An explanation for why we do the things we do would be a fascinating read.

For me, life as an outdoor communicator has been an unbelievable journey. It's been full of twists, turns, potholes and big dreams. I grew up in Eastern "fly-over" country doing a lot of the things rural kids did back then. I loved sports and was blessed to have above-average talent in basketball and baseball. Though I still love both sports, neither can hold a candle to my love for hunting.

The hunting bug bit me at an early age. I was the oldest of five kids (and the only boy) and had a dad who enjoyed deer hunting. I'll never forget my mom waking me up on a cold November morning in 1952 saying, "Charlie, it's time to get up. If you want to go hunting with Dad, you need to get up — now!" I was only 5½ years old.

Before hitting the woods that morning, Dad took me to a diner for breakfast. The small eatery was a favorite among deer hunters, and many were already gulping down eggs and coffee when we arrived. I'll never forget the sight of red-plaid coats hanging on the garment poles at each booth. Some smelled of dairy barns, while others smelled of stale smoke. Amid the aroma of fried eggs and coffee, hunters chatted while they planned their morning hunt — talk about a room full of testosterone, excitement and expectations. This was followed by a morning of tagging along behind my dad in the woods. Although it was nearly a half-century ago, I remember the day like it was yesterday. And, although I didn't realize it at the time, that day was the beginning of my journey.

I also remember childhood moments when my mom occasionally made off-hand comments about the unusual amount of time I spent hunting and pawing through hunting magazines. She was raised in an urban setting 30 miles east of New York City and didn't think it was normal for a youngster to spend so much time on what she viewed as an "odd-ball sport."

My outdoor dreams kept growing as I entered my teen-age years. Instead of going to the library to study science, math or English, I'd read *Outdoor Life* and *Field & Stream*. I loved the out-of-doors and thoroughly enjoyed reading hunting articles.

Back then, my heroes were athletes and *Outdoor Life* shooting editor

Above: Charles Alsheimer was the first outdoor writer to spread the Stump Sitters' message to Eastern hunters.

Jack O'Connor. He was arguably the best-known hunter in the world and a true word-smith. I read everything O'Connor wrote, and to this day find myself still influenced by his words. That's why my favorite deer rifle is a .270, even though I have ballistically superior rifles in my gun cabinet.

My love for deer hunting jumped a level after I graduated high school — even though I couldn't hunt. When I entered the United States Air Force, I knew my life was about to change drastically. However, I kept true to my favorite pastime by dreaming of the day I could again roam the fields and woods. While serving in Vietnam, I bought some camera equipment with hopes of some day using it to photograph whitetails back home. With the camera in hand, I was set for the birth of a dream.

That dream became a reality when I returned home. Then, in 1972, I graduated college and took a sales and marketing job with a large furniture corporation. For the next seven years, I learned the ways of corporate America from Haas Hargrave, the company's vice president of sales and marketing. He instilled in me something far more important than sales forecasts, balance sheets and profit margins.

Haas, a former college football coach, loved the outdoors and was an incredible hunter. However, he had no sons. Our friendship flourished because he knew I was a jock who loved to hunt. Looking back on the time I worked for him, it's clear he was always pushing me toward bigger and better things.

One morning in March 1979, Haas walked into my office and said, "When you're off the phone come into my office, I'd like to talk to you."

I remember getting off the phone and sitting there for a moment wondering why he wanted to see me. When I walked into his office, Haas told me to close the door and sit down.

Before I could say anything, he slid a magazine across his desk and said, "Take a look at this."

I can remember looking at the cover and reading the words *Deer and Deer Hunting — The Stump Sitters Report #10*. I thought to myself, "What in the world is this?"

Before I could speak, Haas said, "Look at Page 6." After giving me a few moments to digest the column that began with the headline, "Help Wanted," he continued. "I picked this up on my trip to Milwaukee this week and thought of you as I was looking at it. It looks like it's a new magazine. You know, with your knowledge of deer hunting, you should consider responding to their request for writers. I believe you're the kind of person they're looking for, and you have the ability to write for them."

I looked at Haas over the opened pages in my right hand and said, "Do you really think so?"

"I really do," he said. "And in the long run I think you'd be a whole lot happier doing something you love rather than marketing and selling furniture the rest of your life."

I took Hargraves' lead and wrote to *Deer & Deer Hunting*, not really expecting anything would come of it. However, a few days later I received a letter from *D&DH* co-founder Jack Brauer. Brauer said he liked my resume and hunting background and asked if I'd give him a call, which I did. The next thing I knew he and co-owner Al Hofacker asked if I'd be willing to write articles on topics they would select.

The rest is history.

Over the next 14 years, the relationship I forged with Brauer and Hofacker is one I'll forever cherish. They were true visionaries and the epitome of what dedication, honesty and integrity are all about. They birthed my outdoor career and gave me the wings that have allowed me to pursue what I've come to realize is one of the greatest jobs on earth. God only knows where I would be today if a corporate executive had not bought that copy of *D&DH* while on a business trip. I get goose bumps when I think of how it came together, but there's more to the story.

As I write this in April 2002, it's only a few months until my 25th anniversary as a *D&DH* contributor. I don't know where the years have gone, but it seems like only yesterday that I got Brauer's letter.

There were no specialty magazines when I began this journey. In fact, *Outdoor Life, Field & Steam* and *Sports Afield* were the only significant magazines on the market when it came to white-tailed deer, and those publications only printed limited articles on whitetail hunting. This isn't to say there weren't writers penning deer stories. Larry Koller, Ben East and John Wootters were household names to serious deer hunters, and I knew I didn't have enough background or ability to even carry their ammo boxes.

However, Brauer and Hofacker saw something in me I didn't. I can still remember an afternoon in July 1981 when Brauer, Hofacker and Rob Wegner hooked up with me on a conference call to see if I'd consider becoming one of *D&DH's* first field editors. It was an awkward phone call for me because I didn't know why they wanted me to be a field editor when, in my opinion, far more knowledgeable whitetail writers were available. However, they were persistent with their offer, and I accepted. I recall being so overdosed on adrenaline that I hardly slept a wink for two days. Although my field editor status began in Summer 1981, it wasn't until the September/October issue that Richard P. Smith and I were unveiled as the magazine's first two field editors.

In the years that have passed, my career as a writer and photographer has flourished. During this time, I've had hunters, other writers and even a few editors ask me why I've remained loyal to

Below: Alsheimer incorporated scientific information into his hunting tactics long before it was vogue. This photo accompanied the November 1979 article he wrote for *D&DH*, "The Rut: A Scientific Approach."

Above: After joining *D&DH* as a field editor in 1981, Alsheimer helped conduct hunter-based research projects for the Stump Sitters.

*Editor's note: Alsheimer's "The Journey" won first place in the magazine categories of two contests: New York State's Outdoor Writers Association "Excellence in Craft" contest, and the Outdoor Writers Association of America's "Family Participation" contest.

one magazine for so long. Honestly, there's no one answer. Several factors make *D&DH* one of the loves of my life. Let me explain.

There are firsts in everyone's life — firsts that help shape who we are. I've had a lot of them. In the outdoor-career category, *D&DH* was my biggest first. We all need a foundation for our careers, and *D&DH* was mine. Brauer and Hofacker gave me my first break in this business when no one else had a clue who I was. To most, I was the guy with the last name nobody could spell or pronounce. Growing up on a farm, I learned farmers are loyal people. Most never forget who helped them along the way. Because of my upbringing, my loyalty to the magazine has remained rock solid.

In those early days, I realized Brauer and Hofacker were special. They respected my abilities and often asked for my opinions on what types of articles readers would enjoy. I'll never forget the many long phone calls I'd get from Brauer. He'd often begin by saying, "I'd like to pick your brain." In short, he wanted me to offer "my two-cents," and then write about it. Later, editors Pat Durkin and now Dan Schmidt kept this philosophy in place and frequently brainstormed with me on *D&DH's* editorial direction. They've thought enough of me to involve me in the thought process, and for that I'm extremely grateful.

A small thing that meant so much to me in my early years was the way *D&DH* embraced my desire to incorporate my son, Aaron, into my articles. Few publications allow writers to personalize articles by including firsthand hunting accounts of family members. *D&DH* has always marched to a different drummer on this topic, and the reward has been readers who not only relate to the articles, but readers who continually renew their subscriptions. The editors not only allowed me to write about my experiences with Aaron through pieces like *The Journey** (August 1995) and *Life Cycles* (August 2001), but they encouraged it. I believe the family's role in holding hunting together is critical, and Hofacker, Durkin and Schmidt have been true visionaries in this regard. Blood runs thick when it comes to family, and in my case, their encouragement afforded me an incredible transfusion.

I've had several chances to "jump ship" over the past 20 years, including a lucrative offer to pen a regular whitetail column with a high-profile publication. It was very tempting, but I told the editor "thanks, but no thanks." Why? *D&DH* had treated me so well for so long that — even though it took me a few days to decide — my loyalty won out in the end.

When I think of *D&DH,* I think of the tradition and passion that's wrapped between the covers of each issue. The writers and readers are first-class. Aside from *D&DH* being the first magazine devoted to white-tailed deer, much more sets it apart from other publications. The magazine is unique because it intertwines hard-core research with reader participation and observations.

I've written for some of the best and biggest outdoor magazines in this country, and I know of no other that cares more about what its readers think than *D&DH.* One example is the scrape survey Durkin asked me to conduct in 2001. In the survey, I asked *D&DH* readers to respond to questions on whitetail scraping behavior. The response was impressive. I knew much about the kind of people who read the magazine, but after the survey I had a far greater appreciation for the seriousness of those who take time to buy and read each issue. As I learned in the '70s, *D&DH* is a magazine for serious hunters, and it was good to have this reinforced by the survey. I count it an honor to serve the readership.

One of my favorite quotes is, "The greatest things in life are not things. The greatest things in life are experiences and relationships." I often think of that as I reflect on the years I've been writing for *D&DH.* The magazine has given me many of the things one would expect, including a career. However, what stands above all else are the experiences and relationships I've enjoyed. The relationship I've forged with *D&DH's* founders and editors have been great. Brauer, Hofacker, Durkin and Schmidt are all serious whitetail hunters from rural America who have an innate ability to know what other deer hunters want in a magazine. Because their backgrounds, desires and values so mirror mine, the chemistry we've had through the years has made the trip very special.

Winston Churchill once said, "We make a living by what we get, but we make a life by what we give."
Under the editorial leadership of Brauer, Hofacker, Durkin and Schmidt, *D&DH* gave me more than I could ever have imagined. I doubt they realize it, but along the way each has helped make my career as the magazine's Northern field editor a special blessing.

My blood type might be O positive, but when I bleed — figuratively anyway — there's a *D&DH* logo somewhere in the flow.

Below: Alsheimer is as active in the deer woods today as he was 25 years ago. He killed this impressive 9-pointer while bow-hunting near his home in western New York in 2001.

Got a Question?
Ask Leonard Lee Rue!

Q: I recently returned from a hunting trip in northeastern Colorado. I was hunting for mule deer near the South Platte River. Although this is a plains area and mule deer are considered more of a foothills species, some really large muley bucks have been taken in this area. The thing that surprised me was that, although I have hunted this area several times, I'm now seeing more white-tailed deer. This was not the case several years ago when I first hunted there. Are whitetails forcing the muleys out?

J.L. Wheeling, W. Va., December 1986

A: White-tailed deer numbers are definitely increasing in eastern Colorado. In fact, whitetails are increasing both their range and numbers in most Western states and Canadian prairie provinces. Whitetails are moving up the river drainages of the South Platte, the South Republican and the Arkansas rivers. The brushy river-bottoms provide the whitetail with the cover it needs to thrive and survive. Although mule deer used to frequent these bottoms, as whitetail numbers increase, the muleys move to open areas. Today, there are more whitetails than mule deer along the South Platte. Hunters, however, annually take more mule deer than whitetails because muleys are more visible in their open areas.

The lopsided harvest helps expand the whitetail's range. Not only have whitetails become more numerous, some of them are huge. In 1978, Ivan Rhodes tagged a monster buck in Yuma County near the Bonny Reservoir. It is the first whitetail from Colorado to ever make the Boone and Crockett record book. It scored more than 182 B&C typical inches.

Editor's note: *By writing about this up-and-coming whitetail herd, Rue helped spark a hunting revolution in Colorful Colorado. More hunters booked trips to the state after learning about its incredible white-tailed bucks, and, from 1990 to 2000, 84 Colorado whitetails were accepted into the Pope and Young Club's record book, and 17 were accepted into the B&C record book.*

Q: You claim that deer prefer to feed on plants in soil that has been fertilized so they can obtain trace minerals. How do they know which plots have been fertilized?

Anonymous, December 1983

Editor's note: *Leonard Lee Rue III has authored more than 35 books and 1,200 magazine and newspaper articles. His roots with D&DH go back to the very beginning. After contributing photographs for the first six years, he started writing his popular "Rue's Views" column in 1983.*

Above: No discussion on *Deer & Deer Hunting's* history can take place without mentioning Leonard Lee Rue III. His "Rue's Views" column still ranks as one of the top-read items in the magazine.

A: By taste, deer can easily discover fertilized land. Soil fertilized by different substances imparts slightly different flavors to the vegetation that grows in it. Any enrichment of the soil usually produces an enrichment of the vegetative growth, making the fertilized vegetation grow taller, more abundantly and usually darker in color than the same vegetation growing on unfertilized soil. I became aware of these taste differences as a kid back on my family's farm. We had a large orchard that was used as a nighttime pasture for cows and horses. The manure from these animals constantly enriched the soil, and the vegetation was always much heavier where it grew on the previous year's droppings.

Even after a year, I could see enough remnants of the manure to determine which droppings had been from a cow and which were from a horse. The cows would eat the lush vegetation that grew in the horse manure, but would not eat the plants that grew in the cow manure, and vice-versa with the horses. We didn't always have enough manure to completely cover all our fields, so we covered as much of the land as possible each year. The following year, we started with the land that received no manure the previous year. We also applied lime and phosphorus to the manure in the cow stable to cut down on odor and also because it was good fertilizer. So, we were adding minerals to the land when we added the manure. I soon noticed deer would always feed on the fertilized manured section of any field. All animals instinctively know that they need minerals and trace elements in their diet. This is why many mammals, including deer, chew on bones and antlers.

Q: Will a mature buck breed does in the same area where it makes primary scrapes? Also, do bucks have specific areas for breeding?
A.J., Endicott, N.Y., December 1984

A: Wild sheep have specific areas where all the males, females and young congregate every year before the breeding season. Dominant rams battle over ewes as each one enters her estrous period. Elk congregate in traditional areas where a dominant bull gathers cows into a harem, and he protects them from other bulls. In some regions, moose gather in breeding groups where the dominant bull does most of the breeding.

White-tailed deer are different. They do not have a specific area in which they gather to breed. While searching for receptive does, each buck constantly travels over a greatly expanded breeding range. A buck might make many primary scrapes in an effort to advertise his presence to does and other bucks. A buck's home range is typically one to two square miles. During the rut, that range can be expanded to as much as 12 square miles. As a result, a buck might not revisit an individual scrape for several days.

When a doe enters estrus, she will be anxious to breed. In these situations, the doe will actively seek a buck. This can involve a doe visiting a primary scrape and "advertising" her presence. If the buck happens to pass through the area at the same time, breeding might occur at or near the scrape. Remember, this is possible — not likely.

Q: Many years ago I attended a seminar at which you spoke. The subject was white-tailed deer hunting. You spoke about a "joy stick" as the best buck hot spot. I have spent many hours scouting each season since that seminar, but cannot say I ever found what I call a joy stick.

During this season's scouting, I found what I would say has to be a "joy stick." Can you provide more information so I can confirm my discovery?

C. S., Bethpage, N.Y., June 2001

A: I think I know what you're talking about, but it's not a "joy stick." Years ago, I often lectured on a whitetail phenomenon called a "licking stick."

A licking stick is usually a 1-inch diameter green sapling that has been broken off about 30 inches above the ground. Bucks break the sapling by hooking it with their antlers. Occasionally — rarely — I have found deer using a dead sapling or upturned root as a licking stick, but these usually break off too easily. Deer want a resilient stick.

Below: Leonard Lee Rue, right, was a popular speaker when *D&DH* took its whitetail show on the road. Shown here in the early 1980s, Rue answered questions from hunters while *D&DH* co-founder Al Hofacker looks on.

Deer use licking sticks to deposit scent. A deer might lick or rub its forehead on the stick, but the most common use is done by bucks when they rub their ears and antler bases against the stick. In fact, bucks rub these sticks so vigorously that it's amazing they don't rub the hair off their skin.

Bucks usually deposit scent on the stick by licking it for several minutes, then rubbing it for several minutes. They often repeat this process for quite a while. I believe that hunting over a licking stick is more productive than hunting over a scrape because deer of all ages visit licking sticks.

Most hunters don't find licking sticks because they're seldom found near rubs or scrapes. In fact, I have never seen the ground disturbed near a licking stick. Licking

Above: During a visit to the Stump Sitters headquarters in Appleton, Wis., Leonard Lee Rue III reviews an issue of *Deer & Deer Hunting* with publisher Jack Brauer.

sticks are seldom found near well-used deer trails. I find them scattered along oak ridges, made by deer while they're searching for acorns. The only indication that they are licking sticks is that all of the bark will have been scraped off the top 8 inches of the stick. In that regard, they're kind of like rubs — the exposed trunk can be seen for quite a distance.

Q: When hunting whitetails, how high should I place my tree stand?
N.O., Easton, Pa., April 1986

A: The height of a tree stand must be determined by the amount of hunting pressure. Under normal conditions, a stand placed 12 feet above the ground would be above the regular sight plane of a deer. Twenty years ago, Eastern deer did not look up, although Western deer did because some predators, such as cougars, often attack from elevated positions. Today, Eastern deer are subjected to far more predation from trees — in the form of deer hunters. Facetiously, I say our Eastern deer are wearing their hoof tips off falling over rocks because they are always looking up into trees. In areas of average hunting pressure, I would suggest placing your tree stand at a height that's comfortable for you. Twenty feet is plenty high for normal situations, and 30 feet or higher is ideal for hunting high-pressured deer.

Editor's note: *Although Rue's advice was sound, it no longer applies in today's age of deer hunting. As today's hunters realize, the height of a tree stand is less important than how well it's camouflaged. What's more, with the tremendous advancements in scent control and stand technology, many successful hunters rarely place their stands higher than 25 feet. In fact, New York's Charles Alsheimer rarely places his stands higher than 17 feet. A hunter will experience more success if he hunts at a height that's comfortable for him, while paying attention to wind direction and natural camouflage.*

Q: Do twin bucks ever grow big racks? I say they don't. Am I wrong? West Virginia has a lot of spikes, and I think those should be thinned out so other bucks can grow larger.
L.M. Reedy, W. Va., June 2001

A: Yes, you are wrong, and in more ways than one. I have raised some pairs of twin bucks in which each produced 10-point racks that scored in the 160s.

If you are concerned about a father/son relationship you are wrong there, too, as all farmers and now deer ranchers, breed their biggest, best males to produce the best offspring possible. Sperm from some gigantic breeding bucks now sells for as much as $1,500 a shot to be used in artificially impregnating superior does. We are producing bigger, better bucks through genetics.

Inbreeding is not a problem when you're talking about wild deer. A dominant buck might breed his daughters and even his granddaughters, but this is not a problem. In New Jersey, as many as 80 percent of the bucks are killed each year. The state also has a liberal deer hunting season whereby a hunter can, theoretically, tag more than 120 deer per year! Hunters in New Jersey must shoot a doe before they can take a buck.

There's little chance a yearling buck would breed his mother, aunts or sisters, because almost all yearling bucks disperse from their birthing area. Most of those young bucks leave the area voluntarily, but those that are reluctant to go are driven from the area by their close female relatives before they reach 14 months of age. These young bucks would also be intimidated by dominant bucks.

If you have a lot of spikes, as is true of many areas with high deer populations, it's not the result of inbreeding — it's the result of having more deer than the land can support. Spikes are the result of the herd not getting sufficient, high-protein food that's needed to produce big antlers. Thinning out the spike bucks will only help if you also thin out the does to reduce your total deer population. This will give the habitat a chance to recover.

Q: Can deer really be called?

G.G., Tom's River, N.J., June 1986

A: Yes, deer can be called. Several companies make terrific deer calls. Deer make many different sounds that are not only vocal but include snorts and the stamping of their feet. Most manufactured calls imitate the grunt, snort and bleat. Rattling antlers are also considered a type of call.

Both does and bucks snort, and they make two different snorts. The most common is made by the deer with its mouth slightly open.

Below: A preponderance of spike bucks in a deer herd is not an indication of inbreeding. Although other factors also come into play, spikes are usually the result of the herd not getting sufficient, high-protein food that's needed to produce big antlers.

Above: Leonard Lee Rue III grew up hunting whitetails on his family's farm in New Jersey, where he has fond memories of deer hunting's simple pleasures, such as muzzleloading buckskin apparel.

This snort, which is an alarm signal, is made when a deer blows air from its lungs through its mouth. This snort alerts every deer that hears it, but how deer react to it varies. In fact, the alarm snort often arouses a deer's curiosity and causes it to investigate.

The second snort is made when a deer blows air through its mouth and nostrils. This creates a much higher-pitched, whistling sound. You would not want to imitate this call, because it literally blows away every deer in the area. This is the paramount warning call, and other deer seldom question it.

The bleat is another call that all deer make. Often associated with fawns, the bleat often sounds like "blat" when made by older deer. A fawn's bleat is somewhat higher-pitched and is similar to the bleating of a lamb. Does make a much-lower bleating call, and mature bucks often make a raspy, low-toned call similar to that of an old ram.

Another call is the grunt, which is made by bucks and does. This call stimulates a deer's curiosity. Grunting will not necessarily scare away smaller bucks because, although they may not want to get into the battle, they are always anxious to see one. Grunting is an exceptionally good call to use while hunting.

Editor's note: *Although deer calls predate American Indians, modern deer calling did not gain great acceptance until the 1980s. Companies like Haydel's of Louisiana, Woods Wise Products of Tennessee and Quaker Boy of New York were among the first companies to mass-produce white-tailed deer calls.*

Q: Is there such a thing as a swamp deer or a mountain deer? If there is, what's the difference?
Anonymous, October 1983

A: Deer do live in swamps and mountain ranges, but there's no such thing as the "swamp bucks" that old-timers often say live troll-like existences in remote swamps. That said, let's examine the differences between whitetails that live in swampy regions and mountain ranges.

There's no physical difference between deer that live in these habitats. Take either one and put it in the other's habitat, and there would be no difference. I have heard hunters claim that swamp deer have longer hoofs than mountain deer. While it's possible that mountain deer wear off their hoofs more quickly by walking on rocky terrain, the hoofs are not genetically longer. A deer's hoofs grow continuously throughout its lifetime, as do our fingernails. In fact, hoofs and fingernails are composed of the same material — keratin.

Q: Do white-tailed does also use a buck's scrapes?

Anonymous, February 1984

A: On only one occasion have I seen a doe use a scrape that had been made previously. Friends living in the South inform me they have seen does urinate in buck scrapes on different occasions. What is not generally known is that when a doe enters estrus, she will actively seek out a buck as he will hunt for her. On two occasions while watching captive deer I observed estrous does attempt to mount a buck. I have seen this same behavior among dairy cows. In fact, you might have seen the results of such attempted mountings, but didn't know what you were looking at. When the hair on a buck's back and hindquarters is scuffed up, it is usually the result of these attempted mountings.

Q: I often take my wife and sons for a drive through our area to observe deer. Most of the deer we see are feeding in fields, on the golf course or on lawns at the edge of town. I only see deer browsing on twigs during winter. Is the whitetail considered a browser or a grazer?

J.O., Wayland, Ky., August 2000

A: I agree that deer feed more on farm crops and grasses than on browse. However, I believe deer are basically browsers that are often forced to eat farm crops and grasses in absence of quality browse.

A deer's favorite food is acorns, but it also favors berries, apples and other fruits and mushrooms. A deer prefers forbs and broad-leafed plants over grasses, even though it will eat a lot of grass. Legumes — such as alfalfa, clover, trefoil and soybeans — are also avidly eaten by deer. In short, deer are opportunistic feeders. However, I believe they will feed most heavily on browse when given the choice.

CARVING A NICHE
1982 TO 1986

Rendezvous at Lone Popple

RANDALL P. SCHWALBACH, AUGUST 1986

The native people of the far north, the Inuit, were some of the greatest hunters ever. They were also great storytellers and philosophers. In studying the stories handed down from generation to generation, one encounters an Inuit saying about the "roundness of life." The saying expresses an abstract thought with grace and simplicity. As a modern hunter, I like to use that Inuit expression to help understand a lesson taught to me by a lone popple tree.

My acquaintance with this lone popple began long ago. I hunted from it back when I didn't know much about deer hunting. The tree rose out of a bedding ground of willow and canary grass. To the south, it overlooked a field of goldenrod sparsely studded with mature tamaracks, so my stand resembled a bleacher seat at a giant chessboard — the size of a football field — where the tamaracks were the pieces in a game being played by the gods. Possibly Diana was taking on Orion.

I liked the view best on an October morning just after the sun rose, when the frosted tips of the goldenrod sparkled like jewels, and the smoky gold of the tamaracks was at its peak. That was the time of the day — in the ever-changing light — when the gods made their moves.

I never went to this deer stand in September, for that is when I concentrated on the oak woods. And I never went to the lone popple in December because it was too exposed to the wind. The lone popple was my stand for the middle of the season, maybe because the first time I ever went there was in late October, and I thought I should stick to some kind of symmetry in my hunting. At the time, I had been stumped by the lack of deer movement shortly before deer went into their rutting frenzy. Where were they? It seemed to me that a mysterious place might solve the mystery.

In truth, the lone popple did not solve the mystery, and I had poor luck there in late October. However, there was still something about the place that I liked. When the firearms season arrived three weeks into November, I stuck with the lone popple. Nine days passed without a buck sighting, but that didn't dissuade me from my friendship with the tree. I visited it in spring, when the world was soggy and geese flew overhead. I didn't go to sit for any length of time, just long enough to see how the chess game was progressing. Satisfied that it was a healthy match, I rambled onward.

Whenever I visited the lone popple, hunting became secondary. I knew that — sooner or later — I would have a memorable sighting from that stand. I didn't try to force it. When the time was right, it would happen.

It was 11:30 a.m. on a Sunday in mid-November, the last day of the early

bow season. I had missed a forkhorn earlier that morning, and — satisfied that I had my chance — I headed for the lone popple so I could nap in the sunshine. When the wind wasn't blowing, it was a good place to nap because the sun seemed to reflect off the goldenrod at a perfect angle to the crotch of the popple, which made a good natural stand. The crotch was also good because I could lean back and put my feet up on another limb, as if in a reclining chair. My view of the world from this position was unparalleled, but the warmth of the sunshine made it hard to keep one's eyes open. I remember thinking about how Jim Corbett, the famous hunter of man-eating tigers in India, used to sleep in the tops of trees with good crotches, and my last thought was that I was glad there were no tigers here.

The noon whistle from the town seven miles away roused me to attention, though I still didn't open my eyes. My ears were primed, however, and five minutes later I heard the unmistakable ticking of antlers in the brush. As I opened my eyes, an 8-point buck strode into view. He moved steadily, his eyes glued to the field, into which he quartered from the bedding area. Although I was less than 15 yards from him and poorly camouflaged, I slowly assumed a shooting posture without spooking the buck.

When he was 25 yards away, I sent an arrow flying. The broadhead sliced the air just below his rib cage, and the unscathed buck took one great leap, shook his head, and trotted off to a nearby creek bottom. It's amazing how a small drama can be flawlessly recorded in one's memory.

This past year, I ended my archery season in early October by taking a mature buck in the oak woods. I spent the rest of the season hunting with my camera. Fortunately, my hunting partner still had a tag. That allowed me to live vicariously through his hunts.

On the morning of the last day of the early archery season, my buddy missed a shot at a forkhorn. On that day, something prompted me to visit the lone popple at midday. It was as if the decision was made outside my being. The full significance of this occurred to me only recently.

I had not yet climbed the popple that season, and it felt good to be back. It was good to find the old tree still standing, and good to feel the warmth of the sunshine on my face as I nestled into the reclining position that the crotch afforded.

The noon whistle sounded in the distance, reminding me of the day when I missed the big buck. I was falling asleep in the pleasantness of my reverie when the sounds of swishing grass brought me back to reality. A large buck was moving at a steady pace through the goldenrod in front of me. Although he was 50 yards away, I instinctively brought my camera up and snapped several frames as the buck moved confidently forward. After he was gone, I took a moment to observe how the chess game was coming, then hiked back to the cabin for lunch.

As I contemplate the similarities of the two November days which occurred years apart at my lone popple, I ponder not only the coincidence, but also the greater significance of man's relationship with nature through the sport of deer hunting. What seems most remarkable is deer hunting teaches us not only lessons of the woods, but offers clues to the greater meanings of life. Men throughout the ages have pondered these same thoughts, such as the Inuit hunters who spoke of the "roundness of life."

I must visit the lone popple more often. Somehow, it helps me understand.

ABOUT THE AUTHOR
Randall P. Schwalbach became a contributing editor for *D&DH* in April 1986. Over the next five years, he also served in the associate editor position. His "mood" articles were favorites among *D&DH* readers.

Deer Hunting in the Adirondacks

CHARLES J. ALSHEIMER, OCTOBER 1984

The beauty of North America is the complex variety God mani-fests to us through natural wonders. Oh, what a land, with its rolling hills, dense forests, meandering river bottoms, flat grassy plains, and grand mountain ranges! Except for a few areas, this piece of Eden, sandwiched between the Atlantic and Pacific oceans, is home to the white-tailed deer. Whether you live in Maine, Georgia, Texas, Illinois or Alberta, the whitetail is a universal subject to those who love the outdoors.

Many "experts" profess to know where the best white-tailed deer hunting can be found, yet few mention New York's Adirondack Mountains in the same breath with other more popular areas. Perhaps this is because very little is known about deer hunting in this remote corner of New York, even though Europeans have hunted deer there since the mid 1800s.

The name "Adirondack" was not given to the area until 1838, when Ebenezer Emmons, chief geologist for the state topographical survey, named it. Before then, the only peo-ple known to have spent much time in this formidable mountain region were the Algonquin Indians. Unfortunately, we know little about their activities because they left no recorded history.

Even today, the splendor and hunting potential of the Adirondacks receives little attention. In traveling to the Adirondacks to research this essay, I was puzzled why so little is known about Adirondack deer hunting.

Actually, the Adirondack area carries the official title of Adirondack Park. Within the boundaries of the park one becomes aware of its immense size and potential to hunters. No doubt this will surprise many, but Adirondack Park is the biggest park, state or national, in the United States.

To quote from Lincoln Bennett's *The Ancient Adirondacks*: "The Adirondack Park, covering some 9,475 square miles, comprises a green and blue mosaic of ancient mountains, more than 1,345 lakes with names (and hundreds without names) and millions of acres of hardwood and evergreen forest, the whole iridescent tapestry is cross-stitched by roads and embroidered with small hamlets, villages and towns." Also, within the park are 46 mountains approaching or exceeding 4,000 feet high. The park includes 6 million acres of land within its boundaries, known as the "blue line," making it larger than

Above: Adirondack hunters of yesterday were rugged individuals who went the extra mile to hunt bucks.

Yellowstone, Yosemite, Grand Canyon, Glacier, and Olympic national parks combined. To put it another way, the park is about the size of Vermont.

Unlike the National Parks, however, privately owned land lies within the Adirondacks, nearly 3.7 million acres. The balance of the park is state-owned as the Adirondack Forest Preserve. The land remains protected under controversial Article XIV of the New York constitution, which states, "The Adirondack Forest Preserve cannot be leased, sold or exchanged. Nor shall the timber thereon be sold, removed or destroyed." In other words, it will be kept forever wild.

The recreation value of this outdoor mecca didn't evolve until around 1866, when W.H.H. "Adirondack" Murray wrote *Tales of the Adirondacks*. With the Adirondack wilderness only about 200 miles from the most densely populated part of the United States, New York City, the elite came in droves. Resort hotels sprang up throughout the Adirondacks to cater to fashionable city people. In addition, lumber companies moved in, realizing there was a fortune to be made from the Adirondack's hundreds of square miles of unbroken forests. Along with this influx came market hunting for deer and other game.

Because nearly all of the Adirondacks consist of unbroken wilderness, the market hunters and guides used two methods to bring down whitetails: jacklighting from boats, and driving deer with dogs. It is difficult to ascertain which came first, but at any rate, both methods were very successful throughout the Adirondacks before the turn of the century.

As lumber operations boomed, the deer population exploded with the emergence of second-growth timber. The peak deer population in the Adirondacks occurred around 1890, but the high numbers severely damaged the winter range through overbrowsing. With the Adirondack deer herd at an all-time high and the winter range over-browsed, the stage was set for nature to deal the whitetail a cruel hand. During Winter 1892-93, the Adirondack's deer herd received a severe blow when heavy snows and the resulting starvation killed large numbers of whitetails. At the time, writer Wellington Kenwell stated that about 250 deer died around Indian Clearing on the south branch of the Moose River in Hamilton County, N.Y.

Bad weather, market hunting and unlimited seasons all affected the Adirondack deer herd. Before 1886, there had been no bag limit in the Adirondacks, but in that year, the season was established from

Aug. 15 to Nov. 1 with a bag limit of three deer per person. In 1892, this was reduced to two deer, and deer hunting with dogs was outlawed. Then, in 1897, the state prohibited jacklighting in the Adirondacks.

These season and bag-limit changes were not without controversy, however. Hounding and jacklighting were popular hunting methods before the turn of the century. With literally hundreds of lakes and many elegant resort hotels in the Adirondacks, the guide boat was king. With a good pack of dogs and a knowledge of the waterways, guides could easily satisfy their clients' needs.

One man who objected to jacklighting was Theodore Roosevelt. At age 15, Roosevelt went to the Adirondacks in hopes of killing his first white-tailed buck. Edwin Reid, who wrote of Roosevelt's hunt, said, "Roosevelt's first attempt at jacking or fire-hunting, as it was also called, was no success. The deer ran as Teddy shot and missed. So instead of bagging a deer that night, he shot a large owl which was perched on a projected stub. Innocently and quite conceivably, Teddy mistook its two glaring eyes for those of a buck standing in the water.

"The next night, Teddy made the grade of a 'deer jacker' by killing a 'yearling buck still in the red.' But, he did not feel triumphant about this feat, even if he was just a lad and this was his first deer kill. He admitted he was 'glad to get it' at the time but was also aware of feeling never to repeat such an unsportsmanlike act."

Accounts such as this brought an end to the hounding and jacklighting era in the Adirondacks as the 20th century began. With the 1900s came modern methods of deer hunting. The Adirondack guide still catered to those wishing to bag a big white-tailed buck, but now the setting was different. Driving, still-hunting and floating remote rivers during daylight in a canoe became the preferred ways to bag a buck.

Magazines like *Harpers Weekly, Journal of the Outdoor Life*, and *American Sportsman* wrote about many such hunts in the Adirondacks. Some deer camps were shown as nothing more than wall tents pitched in a mountain clearing, while others showed log cabins nestled beside some unknown stream with smoke curling from the cabin's chimney and deer hanging from a pole.

While wading through the files of the Adirondack Museum Library at Blue Mountain Lake, a feeling of nostalgia set in as I thought of how grand the 1920s Adirondack deer-camp experience must have been. Though there are still some guides and hunting lodges in the Adirondacks, things are a little different today.

First, today's Adirondack herd is not as abundant as com-

Above: These Adirondack deer hunters scored on three mature bucks while hunting the Cold River area in 1980.

pared to the late 1800s. Unfortunately, man doesn't manage the deer herd —Mother Nature does. For the most part, the Adirondack deer herd rides a roller coaster. When mild winters prevail, the herd increases, only to crash during severe winters, which happens quite often in this rugged North country. With nearly half of the 6-million-acre tract under the "forever wild" clause, most of today's Adirondack forest is climax timber, which offers little deer browse during harsh winter months.

Ted Smith, the Adirondack's senior wildlife biologist for New York's Department of Environmental Conservation, told me, "The central Adirondacks is tough hunting because of the 'forever wild' situation. Because of the harsh winters, there is a reduced yearling frequency, but there still are older-class deer throughout the Adirondacks. So we know there are some nice trophy deer there."

With less-than-adequate habitat in many areas of the Adirondacks, the deer population density doesn't come close to approaching other areas of the Northeast. This is vividly illustrated by the fact some areas of New York support up to 25 deer per square mile of deer range, while some areas of the Adirondacks might only support eight to 10 deer per square mile.

This being the case, most deer hunters who might like to hunt the Adirondacks choose, instead, to go where there is a larger deer population. Another reason deer hunters think twice about hunting this region relates to its remoteness. One person, who I consider an outstanding deer hunter, told me of his experience. "I always wanted to hunt the Adirondacks, and when I finally got my chance, my entire deer hunt was spent fearing I'd get lost. I spent more time looking at my compass than looking for deer."

Unquestionably, the Adirondacks is one piece of rugged real estate, but for those who know what they are doing, the rewards are great. Some of the heaviest white-tailed bucks in North America run these mountain ridges. Men like Jim Massett of Bridgeport, N.Y., and Dick Johndrow of Ticonderoga, N.Y., made quite a reputation for themselves with the big Adirondack bucks they killed. Using physical stamina they developed in nonhunting months, both men learned the Adirondacks intimately in the late 1970s and early

1980s. Both were long-distance runners, and they ran daily to stay in shape for hunting season. When hunting season arrived, they hunted the most remote areas of the Adirondacks.

Massett used to scout his hunting area during summer while fly-fishing for trout, and then set up a base camp in early fall. When the rut came, he and his friends hunted the mountains around the camp. Massett told me that many of the bucks he killed had probably never seen a human, and most were more than 7 years old.

Another group of Glens Falls, N.Y., hunters became very well known throughout the Northeast for the large Adirondack bucks they killed. The group, known as the Horn Hunters, went to their remote Adirondack deer camp when the rut was in full swing and hoped for good tracking snow. Their deer pole and monstrous bucks were testimony to what roamed the ridges.

But you needn't be a mountain man to hunt the Adirondacks.

Peter Lemon, a commercial photographer from Long Lake, N.Y., has seen his share of success. He usually doesn't hunt far from home, but he tries to hunt where there are no other hunters. He does this by using a canoe to get to his hunting grounds, then still-hunting remote areas. Over the years, he has killed some very respectable bucks. As we sat in his home talking about Adirondack deer hunting, he shared some very interesting observations.

"I've been hunting in the Adirondacks for 30 years," he said in 1984, "and the beauty of the Adirondack deer-hunting experience is the terrain. It's so varied. You can hunt the mountaintops — and some do so very successfully — or you can hunt the swamp edges with its hemlock and thick undergrowth. Deer hunting here is the experience. Being able to canoe across the lake in the early morning hours to get to your hunting grounds is far more enjoyable to me than getting out of a car, slamming a door, and rattling things around. It's the experience that sets this place apart.

"I've hunted whitetails in Maine, Wyoming and the Catskills (New York's other mountain range), but I haven't found anything to compare to this country. And the animal itself, well, I'm convinced that the most handsome whitetails come from northern Michigan, Maine and here. They have heavy shoulders, massive necks, are gray and have a lot of character. Also, if more deer hunters took to those mountaintops, record rack after record rack would be produced."

As New York State Big Buck Club records attest, many whopper bucks come from the Adirondacks each year, with usually at least one Boone and Crockett qualifier — despite minimal hunting pressure. It makes one wonder what other buck might be out there.

Not all areas of the Adirondacks produce equal numbers of large-racked bucks. By far, Essex County is the best area, followed by St.

"I ALWAYS WANTED TO HUNT THE ADIRONDACKS, AND WHEN I FINALLY GOT MY CHANCE, MY ENTIRE HUNT WAS SPENT FEARING I'D GET LOST. I SPENT MORE TIME LOOKING AT MY COMPASS THAN LOOKING FOR DEER."

"A Successful Adirondack Deer Hunt" the last trip of the Ticonderoga and Chestertown Hunting Club 1906

Above: The caption printed on this postcard reads," 'A Successful Adirondack Deer Hunt' the last trip of the Ticonderoga and Chestertown Hunting Club, 1906."

Lawrence and Hamilton counties.

Two of the largest bucks killed in the region suggest the overall caliber of bucks living there. For example, Lime Avery killed a 180-class buck in Hamilton County. Strangely, the buck was killed while still in velvet.

Another top Adirondack buck was killed in 1953 by Herb Jacquish. An 8-pointer, it scored 179 B&C points. Jacquish killed this buck in the Schroon Lake region of the Adirondacks when he was just a teen-ager.

Through the use of deer check stations, the DEC monitors antler size by age. Because of the primitive make-up of this region, antler growth is not equal to other parts of the country for bucks in the yearling to 5-year-old classes. Most Adirondack yearling bucks grow only spikes, and a 3.5-year-old buck usually doesn't carry impressive headgear. But the uniqueness of these mountains is that many bucks live 5.5 to 9.5 years, allowing them to grow large racks. During the 1983 season, Adirondack bucks sampled were 4.5 years old and had an average of 8.21 points. The 5.5-year-old bucks averaged 8.36 points; 6.5-year-olds, 9.5 points; 7.5-year-olds, 9.2 points; and the 8.5- to 9.5-year-olds, 9.6 points. To put it another way, age and the harshness of the winters mean a great deal in the Adirondacks.

Unlike other areas of New York, the Warrensburg office of the DEC also monitors dressed weights of those bucks coming through their check stations. Stumvoll stated that during the 1983 season, 3.5-year-old bucks averaged 162 pounds dressed; 4.5-year-olds, 178 pounds; 5.5-year-olds, 188 pounds; and 6.5-year-olds, 183 pounds.

To hunt this region, you needn't know the mountains intimately. It's important, however, that you do a little groundwork.

There are other ways to hunt this vast mountain region. Smith suggested that familiarizing yourself with the region is the first step. Many deer hunters from around the country do this by bringing their families to the Adirondacks on vacation in summer. He said that after you've located an area you want to hunt, you can gain additional information through topographical maps that can be purchased locally or by writing to the U.S. Geological Survey.

Smith also noted that forest rangers can play a big part in helping hunters find good hunting areas on the 2.7 million acres of state land. After a hunter narrows down where he wants to hunt, the ranger can provide a wealth of information.

With more than 1,300 lakes dotting the Adirondacks, canoes continue to be a popular means of getting to prime hunting grounds. Many successful deer hunters, like Peter Lemon, rely on canoes to get them where they are going — areas inaccessible by other means. One word of caution is in order, however. Because of the area's high winds, a hunter should know what he's doing before crossing many of the Adirondack lakes.

Because the Adirondack gun season opens earlier than in many other parts of the country (late October), most of the deer hunting pressure occurs during the first 10 days of the season. But the best hunting arrives later in the season when tracking snows come.

The rut can vary in the region, but is generally in high gear about Nov. 10. Though most of the hunting pressure occurs during the first two weeks of the season, the four largest harvest days throughout the Adirondacks were opening day with 7.5 percent, Nov. 12 with 6 percent, Nov. 18 with 4.7 percent, and Nov. 13 with 4.5 percent. As you can see, although the largest single-day harvest is on opening day, better hunting opportunities occur during the mid-November rut.

It has become quite evident to me that more and more serious deer hunters are considering Adirondack Park for deer hunting. Guys like Jim Massett and groups like the Horn Hunters turn their dreams into reality in this unbroken wilderness. They find that they don't see a lot of deer, but the quality of what they do see is outstanding, not to mention the country they see in the process.

William Chapman White, writing in 1954, said of the Adirondacks, "None (other state or national park) has the unique development that is Adirondack history. Few have thriving villages right next to state woods and a permanent population that lives year-round with the woods at the back door, setting a pattern of life unique in America. It is that inseparable connection between the Adirondack woods, open on all sides, and the Adirondack people that make the area what it is."

I might add that few places in America offer the deer hunter so much. Whether it's the dipping of a canoe paddle in the water on the way to a remote hunting ground, the spiral of pungent smoke rising from the deer camp chimney, or the smell of cedar in the thick forest swamps, the beauty of it is the experience. It is the memories that make a Adirondack deer hunt unique.

ABOUT THE AUTHOR

Charles J. Alsheimer has been a *D&DH* contributor since 1979 and a field editor since October 1981. Over the years, his articles and photographs have won numerous national awards.

Whitetails
& Cornfields

ROB WEGNER, DECEMBER 1985

"Look at the stalk," that great nature writer Hal Borland wrote. "Sturdy, economical, efficient. It stands braced on its roots. It is of quick growth. Its long, broad leaves are so arranged that they catch rain and dew and funnel it down where it is needed. As a plant, it is very near to perfection. It silks out, as we say, with vastly more silk than is needed, just so each kernel on the incipient ear can be properly fertilized. It tassels out, with a pollen-bearing apparatus that's ideal for its purpose. And it concentrates its yield, a big quantity of useful grain, in compact form. It ripens and is an almost perfect storage crop. It is packed with nutrient for man or beast."

No wonder man has spent endless time improving the nutritional value of this marvelous plant, and that the whitetail searches it out with such great intensity.

Both white-tailed deer and corn were indigenous to North America at the time of its discovery. One can scarcely imagine what the exploration and development of America would have been like without them. In fact, corn and white-tailed deer formed the bridge over which English civilization crept. As one of the leading white-tailed deer foods of this country, corn (*Zea mays*) today grows in greatest abundance in the East and the Prairies.

Whitetails frequently use this distinctive American cereal in ways that do not conflict with man's interests: They eat waste corn after the farmer harvests the fields, and they bed during the day among the cornstalks, which provide them with excellent cover before the harvest. Whitetails use corn, however, in ways that directly conflict with man's interests: They peel back the tight husk of the ear on standing corn and meticulously strip the cob, kernel by kernel, to the tune of millions of dollars each year. Between October 1983 and September 1984, 47,000 Wisconsin farmers alone (55 percent of Wisconsin's 86,000 farmers) reported deer damage to their cornfields. University of Wisconsin researchers estimated the value of this damage at $20.6 million, or $438 per farm.

Whitetails most frequently use cornfields when the corn reaches 3 to 4 feet in height. The most frequent damage results when they nip off the tops of the stalk and pull out the developing whorl. Wildlife biologist John Calhoun of Illinois describes what happens: "The animal usually takes one bite, drops the stalk, and moves on. Where this occurs on scattered stalks, the corn can be pollinated from surrounding plants and little permanent damage is done. If damage is over a large area, and the nipping is done immediately before the tassel emerges, the corn might not form a good ear. This sort of damage is usually very local, however, and is usually caused by some unusual circumstance such as in fields near a refuge, in areas where high water has forced large numbers of deer out of the lowlands or where farmers have allowed deer to go too long unharvested."

In Iowa, corn constitutes the most heavily utilized food item in the annual diet of the whitetail — it consists of 67.7 percent by weight, 39.7 percent by volume, and is eaten by 84.4 percent of Iowa's deer. In Kansas, corn and sorghum make up 53 percent of the total volume eaten by whitetails. In Ohio, corn ranks as the second principal food eaten by whitetails in frequency, but first in weight. In Illinois, whitetails use corn in a manner that far exceeds their use of wild foods. In southern Wisconsin during autumn, the monthly volume of corn in the whitetail's rumen averages 24 percent. In west-central Minnesota, corn consists of 37.7 percent by volume of the whitetail's diet, and remains the most frequently damaged field crop in the state. In Nebraska, corn remains the preferred white-tailed deer food, especially in fall and winter. In summer, corn silks provide whitetails with a tasty treat as well. In the Midwest in general, cultivated crops such as corn and soybeans represent 41 to 56 percent of the foods eaten by white-tailed deer on agricultural ranges.

Many questions remain unanswered with regard to the whitetail's use of corn and cornfields. Do whitetails prefer waste corn to standing corn? Will they leave their home ranges to search for standing corn? If so, how far will deer move out of their normal home range? Will this movement be daily, or will deer reside near the cornfield? How much waste corn will a deer consume? How much unpicked corn will a deer consume? Can we truly estimate corn damage caused by deer? How much corn damage will farmers tolerate? Do whitetails prefer to feed on the external limits of cornfields? Does any pattern emerge for their use of cornfields? What is the value and cost of corn as a food patch for deer? What effect do autumn tillage systems have on the whitetail's winter abundance of waste corn? How do the answers to these questions affect deer hunters?

To answer some of these questions, *Deer & Deer Hunting* provided a cash grant to the University of Wisconsin in the early 1980s. The school's department of wildlife ecology used the money to help fund a project called, "Deer Use of Corn in Agricultural Areas." It was coordinated by Professor Orrin Rongstad and then-graduate student John Herron.

The researchers obviously knew corn and alfalfa comprised the major portion of the whitetail's diet. However, they knew little about the quantity of corn that wild whitetails consume and how much of an impact

July 1, 1986

Dear Editor,

Just thought I'd pass along part of a conversation I had with a fellow deer hunter last week.

While riding home with his 7-year-old son, Jarrett, he noticed his son was engrossed in a recent issue of *Deer & Deer Hunting*. Jarrett's dad commented to me that he is sure he has a future deer hunter on his hands. I am sure he has.

You're making it tough on all dads and "big brothers." There won't be much for us to teach Jarrett when he reaches the legal hunting age. By then, he will have read your magazine for a number of years, and that's a tough act to follow.

Peter J. Fiduccia
Warwick, N.Y.

deer populations create on cornfields.

The study's purpose was three-fold: Determine how many deer used six cornfields during one winter (1984-85), monitor the amount of corn consumed by deer on a daily basis and follow the movements of 38 radio-collared deer. The project studied the whitetail's use of cornfields by observing one small cornfield and five small food plots. The researchers measured the whitetail's use of corn and cornfields by periodic observations and by track counts after snowfalls. Herron and Rongstad estimated the amount of corn consumed by sampling the corn remaining in each field during the study period.

All six sites were located on the Badger Army Ammunition Plant in southern Wisconsin. The plant occupies nearly 7,000 acres of rolling pasture and farmland. Only 10 percent of it is forested. Previous research indicated the tract supported a healthy herd of 250 to 400 whitetails, depending on the season.

In 1984, BAAP wildlife managers planted five food plots in cooperation with the U.S. Dairy Forage Research Center. These plots, all corn, were .48, .53, .9, 1.61, and 2.09 acres in size. The two smallest cornfields were not included in the study because they produced no corn. Only the .9-acre field received fertilizer and herbicide treatment. Through an agreement with the U.S. Dairy Forage Research Center and BAAP managers, 5.23 acres of an existing cornfield was left standing until April 1985.

Herron and Rongstad monitored deer use of these fields by track counts after fresh snowfalls. This method yielded 15 to 19 observations for each field, concentrated between Dec. 24, 1984, and March 6, 1985. The researchers also determined use of the 5.23-acre cornfield by direct observations. The other food plots were too far from roads to be effectively observed. On March 6, Herron and Rongstad knocked down 839 corncobs in two corners of the 5.23-acre field to see if deer favored these sites. The researchers then counted the remaining ears on April 21.

Herron and Rongstad eliminated two of the food plots (.43 acres and

Above: In a university study, researchers discovered that the average white-tailed deer in southern Wisconsin consumes about two bushels of corn during autumn, or 1.2 pounds per day.

Figure 1.
Corn Consumed by White-tailed Deer
in Four Cornfields in Southern Wisconsin

	The Cornfield	Field 3	Field 4	Field 5
Acres	5.23	1.61	2.09	0.90
No. Stalks	107,304	35,378	43,472	19,696
No. Ears	101,616	8,453	12,042	4,865
Ave. Ear (In.)	7.5	4.9	4.8	4.9
Percent Corn Remaining				
Sept. 1	94.7	23.9	27.7	24.7
Oct. 6	--	17.7	25.5	19.1
Dec. 24	93.7	4.2	11.7	12.2
Jan. 9	92.1	2.7	9.4	5.6
April 21	89.1	2.0	1.0	2.3
Ears Remaining				
Sept. 1	101,616	8,453	12,042	4,865
Oct. 6	--	6,262	11,085	3,762
Dec. 24	100,543	1,486	5,086	2,403
Jan. 9	98,826	955	4,086	1,103
April 21	95,607	708	434	453
Total Corn Consumed				
Dec. 24 to April 1	4,936	778	4,652	1,950
Est. Deer Days	232	172	2,635	404
Ears/Deer/Day	21.3	4.5	1.8	4.8

— *John Herron, "Deer Use of Corn in Agricultural Areas," 1985.*

.53 acres) from the study after observations revealed these plots produced virtually no corn. Figure 1 summarizes the results for the remaining fields.

By the time the study began, the three food plots already showed evidence of use by deer. By counting the remaining ears of corn and the fresh cobs, the researchers estimated the amount of corn present in each field at the beginning of fall. However, they calculated deer use from data collected after Dec. 24. Figure 2 shows the deer use and corn estimates for each field during the study. Field 4 received the heaviest use during the study, with track counts indicating frequent visits by more than 20 deer per night. The 5.23-acre field, hereafter referred to as "The Cornfield," consistently received light use by deer with six out of 16 track counts indicating no visits the previous day.

Here's a look at each field's activity data:

Field 3. This 1.61-acre field received the lightest deer use of the three plots. Throughout fall, a radio-collared doe regularly used this cornfield during the day, and frequently bedded in the cornfield in the evening. Located at the corner of an alfalfa field and surrounded on three sides by an abandoned field, Field 3 was about 350 yards from the nearest road, hidden from view. Its distance from wooded cover (160 yards) probably accounts for the low use it received.

A comparison of the amount of corn consumed and deer use for the season indicates deer consumed 7,745 ears of corn in fall. During the study period, deer consumed 778 ears, or 4.5 ears per deer per day. This

Figure 2.
Deer Use and Corn Yields of
Four Cornfields in Southern Wisconsin

	Sept. 15	Dec. 24	April 21	Deer-Days*
Field 3	8,453	1,486	708	635
Field 4	12,042	5,086	434	2,635
Field 5	4,865	1,103	453	404
The Cornfield	101,616	100,543	95,607	232

*Study period: Dec. 24 to April 21

— John Herron, "Deer Use of Corn in Agricultural Areas," 1985.

number remains partly offset by the fact corncobs in Field 3 were uniformly small, averaging 4.9 inches long.

By Jan. 9, only stunted ears of less than 3 inches long remained.

Field 4. This field received heavy deer use, with an estimated 45 deer living within a half-mile. This field was adjacent to woods and a mowed grass field. By the end of December, at least eight deer used this plot daily. Use increased steadily throughout winter, peaking by Feb. 12 when 68 deer visited the cornfield in the evening. Undoubtedly, some of the deer tracks counted represented multiple visits by individual deer. By March, use dropped to about 12 deer per night. Use peaked once more following a snowfall on March 30.

Comparing the amount of corn consumed with deer use for the season indicates deer consumed 11,608 ears of corn during fall, or 4.4 ears per deer per day. This number is also partly offset by the small size of ears in the field, with an average size of 4.8 inches. During the study, deer consumed 4,652 ears, or 1.8 ears per deer per day. This number remains undoubtedly low because many deer probably visited the food plot twice an evening in late winter, so each deer was probably consuming closer to 3.6 ears of corn per day.

Field 5. This field was the smallest of the food plots. It was adjacent to a small patch of woods. Tracks indicated that most deer using this plot approached it from the northeast. In fact, deer use of Field 5 showed a different pattern than the other fields, averaging 12 deer per night at the end of December, and increasing to about 20 deer per night during the first week of January. From then on, use dropped continuously to about two deer per night in March.

In Field 5, deer consumed 4,412 ears of corn in fall. This number also remains partly offset by the small ear size — an average of 4.9 inches. Data collected between Dec. 24 and Jan. 9 indicate deer consumed eight ears per deer per day.

The Cornfield. The results of this 5.23-acre field surprised us. Despite being the largest field studied and having an abundance of corn, it received the lightest use. The Cornfield was part of a larger 9-acre field with the outer rows harvested. Eighteen to 24 rows of harvested corn

Figure 3.
Corn Consumed by One White-tailed Deer

	Sept.	Oct.	Nov.	Dec.	Total
Days (number)	8	31	30	21	90
Food Eaten (pounds)*	40	155	150	105	450
Volume In Corn (percent)	14	15	37	20	24
Corn Eaten (pounds)**	6	23	56	21	106
Standing Corn Eaten (percent)	100	80	10	0	--
Standing Corn Eaten (pounds)	6	18	6	0	30
Waste Corn (pounds)	0	5	50	21	76

*Assuming 5 pounds of food eaten per day
**56 pounds per bushel

— *Charles M. Pils, et al., "Foods of Deer in Southern Wisconsin," 1981.*

surrounded the standing corn. The harvested portion showed no evidence of deer use during the entire study.

Daily deer use of The Cornfield fluctuated from zero to 10 deer from the end of December to early February, averaging about two deer per visit. Deer consumed 4,936 ears of corn in this field, averaging 21.3 ears per deer per day. These were full-sized ears, 9 to 10 inches long. This result was alarmingly high, and researchers were uncertain where the error occurred. A count of stripped and partially consumed ears also indicated deer consumed about 5,000 ears during fall and winter. Herron and Rongstad also sampled two transects across The Cornfield to see if deer favored the outer rows. While the results have not been tested statistically, it appears that four samples of the outer 120 stalks indicate that less corn remained in the outer rows than in the rest of The Cornfield, suggesting deer prefer to feed on the external limits of cornfields. This was only one of several valuable insights we learned from this study. We also concluded standing corn doesn't represent the only way to provide mass quantities of food for wintering whitetails. Farming technology, particularly in the harvesting of grain, provides deer — and wildlife in general — with a great deal of waste corn. Automatic corn pickers miss many ears. In fact, Wisconsin DNR researchers estimate waste corn represents 5 percent of the total crop, or about five bushels (280 pounds) per acre.

In a study conducted in central Illinois, Richard Warner studied 71 cornfields. In 1981, he estimated waste corn in untilled, harvested fields at 384 pounds per acre, compared with 40.5 pounds per acre in intermediately tilled fields, and 3.3 pounds per acre in plowed fields. Warner concluded the amount of waste corn in untilled fields doubled since the early 1940s, despite modern technology.

While studying the dynamics of waste corn and its nutritional quality

on the Southern High Plains of Texas in southeastern Castro County (1979-1982), wildlife researchers observed a corn-crop loss of 3.7 percent, with a waste of 324 pounds per acre. Tilling of harvested fields removed 77 percent of initial waste, whereas deep plowing and hand salvage removed 97 percent and 58 percent, respectively. While changes in the nutritional quality of waste corn remain unknown, we do know standing corn has a high Vitamin A content and 9.9 percent protein (Figure 2). Corn, however, is deficient in the amino acid lysine, and it isn't a good single-source of protein.

Only one study examined corn consumed by deer in terms of pounds per day. In studying the food habits of white-tailed deer in southern Wisconsin in 1981, Wisconsin DNR researchers estimate that one deer consumes approximately two bushels of corn during the autumn months, or 1.2 pounds per day (Figure 3).

The story of whitetails and cornfields reaches its ultimate conclusion in the Corn Belt, a region of fertile, well-drained soils throughout Iowa and parts of Illinois, Indiana, Ohio, Missouri, Kansas, Nebraska, South Dakota and Minnesota. In this region, corn occupies approximately 50 percent of the cultivated land and produces about 80 percent of the nation's corn crop. This region also produces some of the nation's largest whitetails, both in antler dimensions and body weights. In fact, Minnesota's Carl J. Lenander shot one of the largest bucks of all time while hunting in a cornfield in 1926. His buck weighed 402 pounds dressed, and 511 pounds on the hoof!

Venison from corn-fed deer never remains untouched at my deer shack. It seems to take on a deeper and richer red color than venison from deer living exclusively on browse, and it certainly tastes sweeter to me. Indeed, the sweet taste of venison tenderloins from a corn-fed deer, together with roasted sweet corn and a glass of fine wine, keep me on the track of whitetails in the ripening, waving cornfields of Indian Summer.

ABOUT THE AUTHOR
Robert Wegner joined the Stump Sitters Study Group as director of research and education in 1980. He eventually became editor, and later a co-owner, of *Deer & Deer Hunting*. After the magazine was sold to Krause Publications in 1992, Wegner became a free-lance writer, specializing in the cultural history of white-tailed deer and deer hunting.

Deer Hunting from a Canoe

RICHARD P. SMITH, JUNE 1983

Deer hunting from a canoe ranks as the ultimate form of still-hunting in my book, and here's why.

It takes a skilled practitioner to creep within easy bow range of a spooky whitetail on foot. In fact, darn few deer hunters possess the skills to do so consistently. However, it's a different story from a canoe. These streamlined watercraft are capable of carrying deer hunters within bow range of whitetails as a matter of routine. The skills necessary to guide a canoe quietly along the course of a winding river are easier to master than what it takes to noiselessly walk along the forest floor. For this reason, most deer hunters should be able to successfully still-hunt from a canoe.

Jim Redmon from Higgins Lake, Mich., introduced me to this interesting still-hunting technique last October. We bow-hunted together and, as his guest, I rode in the bow of the canoe as we drifted downstream with the current. One difference between still-hunting afoot and in a canoe is that the best way to operate from a canoe is with a partner. Solo still-hunting through the forest presents no such problem. On the other hand, deer hunters who like company will appreciate the benefits of sharing a hunt from a canoe.

Teamwork becomes essential when hunting this way, especially with bow and arrow, because it's only possible to comfortably draw when facing one direction. As a right-handed shooter, I could draw and shoot toward the left bank. If we encountered deer on the right bank, it would be up to Redmon to turn the canoe 180 degrees so I could shoot in that direction. As luck would have it, the first deer we saw stood on the right side of the river.

I saw the deer, a doe, standing in a small opening ahead of us and pointed it out to my partner. I riveted my eyes on the feeding whitetail as Redmon used his paddle to turn the canoe without making a sound. Redmon instructed me to draw my bow halfway into the turn so I would be ready to shoot when we swung around.

Before we completed our turn, however, the canoe drifted downstream from the doe, and I no longer had an open shot, so I relaxed and eased my arrow back to a resting position. Redmon's reaction caught me by surprise.

"Draw again," he whispered urgently. "Get ready!"

The reason for his urgency quickly became apparent as my gaze shifted along the bank to a point even with us. There, I spotted a huge

Above: Hunting from a canoe is one of bow-hunting's biggest challenges. The tactic, however, can be deadly for hunting remote-area whitetails.

doe standing broadside, no more than 15 yards away. I started to draw again, but realized an arrow could not penetrate the alders that now screened the doe. Had I noticed the doe sooner, I might have found an opening to put an arrow through from the upstream position.

Later, when we discussed the situation, I discovered why my actions puzzled Redmon. When I pointed toward the deer I saw, Redmon immediately spied the second doe a short distance downstream. Each of us concentrated our attention on different deer, but thought we were looking at the same one.

Although I failed to get a shot at either deer, the incident illustrates how effective floating rivers by canoe can be in putting hunters within easy range of whitetails. It would have been impossible to get as close to those whitetails while still-hunting on foot.

Redmon does most of his float-hunting for deer with his brother, Jeff. Their deer hunting strategy developed as an offshoot of duck hunts conducted in the same manner. As they drifted down various rivers in the Houghton and Higgins Lakes area in search of waterfowl, they frequently saw deer.

Their first deer-hunting effort occurred during the November gun season in 1981. They both received antlerless permits that year and figured float-hunting would be a good way to fill them. Because thick cover lines the rivers they hunt, they started hunting with shotguns using buckshot and slugs, thinking those loads would give them an advantage. The brothers got poor results with shotguns, however, so they switched to rifles.

Jeff missed his first shot at a doe he spotted bedded along the riverbank, but when she stood up, his second round put her down for keeps. On that same trip, Redmon downed a large doe with one well-placed shot.

After shooting a deer, the brothers simply field dress it and load it in the canoe for easy transport to their vehicle. This method of getting deer out of the woods is certainly much easier than dragging them through swamps, up hills and over long stretches of brushy cover.

Redmon said the key to their success during gun season was heavy hunting pressure in the vicinity of the river they floated. This pressure concentrated whitetails in cover along the river where they felt secure. The deer were indeed secure from most hunters, but not the Redmon brothers.

Deer also seek security along river bottoms earlier in fall when bow seasons are open, as the Redmons learned in 1982. They also discovered that visibility along river banks becomes much better in November after deciduous leaves fall and frost kills grass and other vegetation that grows along the river banks. The increased visibility in November makes it easier to spot deer, especially those that are bedded. Optimum visibility occurs when snow blankets the ground.

Rick Powell is another Michigan deer hunter who uses a canoe on some of the state's rivers to hunt whitetails. He waits for a good covering of snow before employing the technique. River bottoms are important wintering spots for deer in this area, which accounts for increased activity in these locations once snow accumulates. Like the Redmons, Powell prefers a rifle for hunting from a canoe during gun seasons. He enjoys some of his best bow-hunting during December.

Shooting a bow and arrow from a canoe can be tricky. More often than not the hunter is moving, not his target. Unless the paddler can quietly stop the canoe, the river current continually pulls the craft downstream. Therefore, it's important for the archer to be at full draw when he drifts into position for a shot. Once the canoe passes an opening, it's difficult to back up without spooking the deer.

Range estimation is just as critical. Hunters constantly encounter new scenes as they drift along. If a deer suddenly appears and offers a shot, a bow-hunter must make a quick and accurate yardage judgment. A miscalculation can make the difference between a hit and a miss.

Bow-hunters who anticipate hunting from a canoe can gain range estimation experience by practicing on targets at unknown distances. Guess the distance, shoot, then check your accuracy by counting the number of paces it takes to reach the target.

Because bow shots are often taken while drifting, string trackers can be a valuable aid. The string would be just as important for finding arrows that miss their mark as helping to trail an arrowed deer. Without a marker, it's easy to lose track of exactly where the deer stood when you shot, as well as your own position, due to movement of the canoe. With a tracking string attached to the arrow, the archer can easily reconstruct a shot after beaching the canoe.

Gun-hunting from a canoe presents fewer problems than bow-hunting, as the Redmons proved during 1981. A person in the bow can aim either right- or left-handed, and shot distances aren't usually far enough to make range estimation with rifles a concern. Gun-hunting from a canoe can also be more productive than other methods, as Redmon proved last November. After failing to connect on a deer during the first two days of the gun season using conventional tactics, Redmon tried a float hunt the third day.

His hunt ended about half an hour into the day. Redmon saw a doe

Above: The most important thing to strive toward when float-hunting is paddling quietly. This is best achieved by floating at a slow, even pace.

standing about 10 feet from the river and dropped her on the spot. Then he enjoyed a leisurely float the rest of the way downstream, seeing 14 more whitetails along the way.

Any river that flows through good deer country and is accessible to the public can provide quality deer-hunting opportunities from a canoe. Areas with high deer densities are best because this increases the hunter's chances of seeing deer. Although many river bottoms in the Midwest, East, South, and West contain habitat that attracts whitetails, only a fraction of the habitat is usually visible along either bank from a canoe. The more deer that live in the vicinity, the greater the odds some of the animals will be visible from the river. It helps, of course, if the cover in river bottoms accounts for a large share of what's available in the area, which might be the case in some locations where there is a lot of farming.

To minimize noise and the need for paddling, float hunts should be planned to travel downstream between two points of access. I recommend using two vehicles, one at the starting point and the other at the end of the float. As an alternative, make arrangements to be dropped off, then picked up later. Hunters should float rivers before hunting season opens to learn how long it will take, as well as whether that portion of the river will even be worth hunting. Some stretches produce more deer sightings than others for a variety of reasons.

Canoes ranging from 13 to 17 feet in length work well for float hunting, provided they are stable. Natural green, brown, or a camouflage pattern helps avoid detection by deer. Canoes in the 13- to 15-foot range are best if it's necessary to carry them any distance to reach the water.

It's a simple matter to learn how to steer a canoe for hunters who haven't had the experience. All steering is done from the stern and can be mastered with a little practice. The paddle is used to push and pull perpendicular to the canoe as well as parallel with the craft for a variety of maneuvers. Individuals who anticipate hunting from a canoe for the first time should float a river or two before the season opens to become familiar with these maneuvers. Canoeing practice can be combined with scouting missions.

The most important thing to strive toward when float-hunting is paddling quietly. This is best achieved by floating at a slow, even pace. Speed isn't any more important when still-hunting from a canoe than on foot. Use your eyes more than your paddle as you move downstream. Rivers with fast currents are not well suited for deer hunting from a canoe because they carry the hunter too fast to carefully scan surrounding terrain for deer If a whitetail is sighted under these circumstances, it would be more difficult to get a good shot than on a river with slow current.

An alternative to float-hunting from a canoe is to use chest waders and an inner tube like the type designed for fishermen. This approach is most practical for gun-hunting because it can be difficult to shoot a bow with a bulky inner tube hanging around your waist when standing in deep water. While this approach would enable hunters to slip up on deer as quietly as in a canoe, and sometimes more quietly, it's certainly less comfortable. What's more, if successful, a float-tuber would face the difficult job of dragging a deer out of a remote area.

As with other types of deer hunting, the best times to float-hunt are early and late in the day. During the rut, any time of day can be productive. I bow-hunted with Redmon in the morning and evening. We saw no whitetails during the morning float, but we observed five in the evening. Some of Jim and Jeff's best floats, as far as deer sightings, have been in the morning. Keep in mind that a stretch of river that fails to produce any deer sightings at one time of day might be crawling with whitetails during a different time period.

In Michigan, canoeists, are required to carry a life vest or buoyant cushion for each person in the craft. It is also illegal to shoot at deer while they are in the water. To be legal targets, deer must be on one of the river banks. Laws vary in other states, so be sure to carefully check the hunting regulations before planning a trip. In fact, some states prohibit the discharge of firearms and bows while in boats and canoes.

Although floating rivers by canoe is the ultimate form of still-hunting for whitetails, this approach is also an aesthetically pleasing way to hunt deer. Hunters can concentrate on their surroundings, freed from worries about snapping twigs, rustling leaves, or brushing against tree branches. Thus, there is a greater opportunity to appreciate the ruggedness and beauty of the whitetail's home grounds.

Simply put, float-hunting is relaxing and enjoyable, even if no deer are observed. What more can you ask of a hunting technique?

ABOUT THE AUTHOR
Richard P. Smith was one of the first deer hunters to join the Stump Sitters Study Group in 1977. A *D&DH* field editor from October 1981 to June 1995, Smith hails from Marquette, Mich. His proven whitetail tactics have educated generations of North American whitetail hunters.

Camouflage:
Sight, Scent, Sound

KENT HORNER, OCTOBER 1984

Deer hunting matches the hunter's stealth against the deer's alertness. The hunter, in attempting to avoid detection by deer, must pay attention to sight, scent and sound.

A hunting partner of mine states that before he parks his vehicle and starts his trek into the woods, he checks these three items for any flaws in his game plan.

"Try to make the deer draw a blank about your presence in the woods," he said. "Camouflage basically includes the lack of sight, scent and sound rendered by the hunter as perceived by the deer through its sensory perceptors."

As I listened to my buddy, I knew he was correct, because he is certainly a successful deer hunter. Simply, finely honed camouflaging techniques help hunters get close to deer. Camouflage 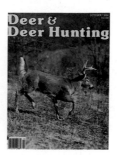 encompasses much more than zipping on a pair of coveralls, although that is a good beginning. Camouflage goes beyond just mimicking plants or landscapes.

Although the whitetail is an extremely alert animal that stays alive by evasive action, its wariness has to stop somewhere. A buck can't, of course, flare its tail and run eternally! Instead, it constantly evaluates the situation and decides if what it senses warrants expending energy. As a result, a whitetail doesn't always run when confronted with various events in its environment. It does, however, remain more alert until it satisfies its curiosity about anything strange in its immediate area.

First, let's check out the whitetail's sight. Naturally, hunters should try to avoid being seen by deer. Consequently, the hunter has two choices: ambushing or stalking his quarry.

At this point, depending on individual preferences, hunting techniques begin to differ. In short, some hunters prefer to sit on stand and some like to stalk or still-hunt. Some combine the two techniques. The weapon the hunter uses plays an important part, too.

For example, the hunter who stalks deer with a bow undertakes a tremendous challenge. However, because the challenge is the driving motive for most deer hunters, the more difficult it is, the better some hunters like it.

Also, to "kick" one's tree-stand 20 feet up a tree and sit there, remaining quiet for several hours in frigid weather takes a lot of mental and physical discipline (and the correct kind and amount of layered clothing to be comfortable and appropriately camouflaged).

Above: To reduce the chance of being scented, the hunter should pay attention to wind direction, morning and evening air current flows and the probability that a deer might scent him through molecular transfer of human scent.

Regardless of how one hunts, the most important point is not to let deer know you're near them. Thus, the hunter should try to blend with the woodland terrain by donning background-colored clothing and being as inconspicuous as possible.

Trebark camouflage is effective in the dead of winter, when trees are devoid of leaves. The gray colors merge with the drab tree trunks in the woodland terrain. In fall, however, color-splotched Vietnam or World War II camouflage patterns are more effective.

Snow camouflage, with alternating white and gray streaks, is effective when the winter forests are covered with snow and shadows. However, that's the only time that a deer hunter should wear white outer clothing. The white flag shown by a deer when startled is a message to other deer to "get the heck out of Dodge!"

Except in snowy conditions, a deer hunter wearing or using any white material negates his camouflage because deer quickly notice white objects.

Regardless of color perception by deer, it's movement that primarily evokes their final response. Deer depend on their own movement — evasive movement — for survival. Thus, although deer are poor at object interpretation, they readily detect movement. Consequently, while on stand, hunter movement should be as slow and deliberate as possible. When a deer approaches the hunter's stand, any movement in the deer's line of vision will almost certainly be noticed. A tree stand raised to about 20 feet gives the hunter an added camouflaging advantage. Remember, the primary concept of camouflage is to cause deer to draw a blank in hunter detection.

Although a deer is half-witted in object interpretation, it's a genius at interpreting scent. The hunter might fool a deer's eyes, but it's a much greater task to remain undetected by the whitetail's sensitive nostrils.

Thus, reckoning with scent is probably the hunter's greatest camouflaging challenge. Hunters can never be completely sure that their scent is entirely masked. They can, however, reduce their odds of being detected because of their scent.

Your approach to your stand is highly important. Another hunting friend of mine is careful not to touch woodland saplings while walking to and from stands. He has told me that after touching a sapling en route to his stand, he once saw a deer come along the trail and spend considerable time sniffing the same tree 36 hours later.

Fox, skunk and sex scents applied to clothing or footwear mix with the hunter's scent. However, these lures also put deer in a state of general alertness, because deer pay attention to other woodland creatures. Consequently, deer do not draw a sensory blank when faced with a hunter doused with such masking odors.

During the rut, however, the hunter might opt to forego a deer's general alertness and aggressively entice bucks with pheromone-based sex lures.

Scenting abilities significantly enhance a deer's reproductive and browsing activities. So, predator detection is not the only reason that deer are experts at the scenting game. It's arguable then, from a species survival viewpoint, just why a deer is so keen in detecting a scent. Predator detection for the deer is not the only long-range benefit derived from the excellent olfactory perceptors in its nose. Finding mating partners during the rut is also critically important for deer survival. Thus, sexual scenting is just as important as predator scenting over time.

To reduce the likelihood of being scented, the hunter should pay attention to general wind direction, morning and evening air current flows and the subsequent probability that the deer might scent him through molecular transfer of the hunter's scent pool. The hunter sitting in a tree stand several feet above the ground tends to keep his scent pool dispersed in air currents above the level of the deer.

However, the hunter lives in an imperfect and fallible world along with his quarry. So, in the run of a hunting day, urine, fecal deposits,

DEER CONSTANTLY DIFFERENTIATE BETWEEN NATURAL WOODLAND SOUNDS AND THOSE THEY THINK REPRESENT DANGER. SLAMMING VEHICLE DOORS, METALLIC BUMPS AND SQUEAKING TREE STANDS CAN FOIL A DEER HUNT QUICKLY.

chewing tobacco, dropped gloves, etc., mix and mingle with deer droppings and other debris on the forest floor.

What can one do? And how do you keep deer from scenting not only you but all the other junk that you tote around in the woods! One can't, entirely. The hunter can, however, decrease his chances of being scented. Here are a few techniques some deer hunters use: shower, using only water without soap just before hunting; while perched for hours in a tree stand, spit tobacco juice in a small plastic bottle that tucks conveniently into one's outer coveralls; if possible, take care of all "personal hygiene" before nearing one's stand (light meals and no caffeine consumption might alleviate "later misery" while on stand); don't throw trash near your stand; while scouting or hunting, try not to handle saplings along the trail; walk to the stand in light clothing and don heavier garments at the last moment before climbing; and, if hunting a scrape, make observations from a distance.

The final aspect of our camouflage system is sound. Deer are unpredictable in their response to sound, at least more so than to scenting. In our modern world, deer become accustomed to a variety of man-made noises. One game preserve I hunt is near a military base that has frequent helicopter traffic. The deer have become used to hearing these overhead noises. However, one sound that will always get a deer's attention is the hunter's cracking of a dry twig.

Since Day 1, large predators have been trying to slip up on deer. Thus, through natural selection, the deer family has been trained to be alert to particular sounds. Deer know that only other large animals can cause that very precise crackle rendered by a dry, snapping twig. The early North American pioneers knew that, too, and reckoned with these cellulose denizens of the woodland lying underfoot.

For instance, in 1841, James Fenimore Cooper in writing *The Deerslayer* has Hawkeye say, "Broken branches are unskillful landmarks, as the least exper'enced know that branches don't often break off themselves ... and they also lead to suspicion and discoveries."

Still, most sounds generally alert whitetailed deer, although they do not necessarily startle them. Deer constantly differentiate between natural woodland sounds and those they think represent danger. Slamming vehicle doors, metallic bumps and squeaking tree stands can foil a deer hunt quickly.

The scuttering squirrels, chipmunks, turkeys, raccoons, song birds and other ani-

mals are frequent noisemakers in the deer forest. Also, falling branches and decaying trees tumble occasionally to the ground.

None of these noises, however, is quite like a snapping, dry twig stepped on by a four-footed or a two-footed predator. And, a deer is the first creature in the woods to know that, because their lives and survival have depended upon their recognition of danger for thousands of years.

Finally, because camouflage tests one's total hunting effort, the hunter's own skills and physical conditioning influence how well he implements this three-pronged camouflage system. Over the hunting season, skill with a bow, muzzleloader and rifle is crucial.

Thus, keeping one's muscles, reflexes and stamina in a state of readiness is not wasted time. An excellent plan, then, is to combine your preseason scouting with walking and improving your general conditioning and skills. For, in the final analysis, these physical attributes might figure into how well you can institute your camouflage system when the moment of truth arrives.

ABOUT THE AUTHOR
Alabama's Kent Horner, above, left, was a *D&DH* field editor for 13 years. Horner was one of the first wildlife professionals to bridge the gap between scientific deer researchers and everyday deer hunters. He is shown here with Richard P. Smith, another long-time *D&DH* field editor.

GLORY DAYS
1987 TO 1991

Buck Fights:
A Photo Essay

BOB ZAIGLIN, OCTOBER 1989

Although deer managers — and hunters — sometimes succeed in releasing a pair of bucks with locked antlers, death of the survivor is usually inevitable. In fact, hunters should never attempt to release locked bucks — such situations are extremely dangerous and can lead to a direct confrontation with the surviving animal.

A common misconception among deer hunters is that bucks engage in all-out fights to earn breeding privileges. Although that can happen, it's rarely the cause of full-blown battles. According to *D&DH* contributing editor Leonard Lee Rue III, rut-time battles most often occur because one buck has invaded another buck's home range. "Bucks seldom fight with other bucks that belong to their own group," Rue wrote in his popular book *The Deer of North America*. "They have associated with one another throughout the rest of the year, and dominance has already been established."

According to John Ozoga, violent dominance fighting differs markedly from sparring and is relatively rare among white-tailed bucks. His research shows that true "push fights" usually occur only between evenly matched bucks that are 3 years old or older.

The bucks shown on these four pages were all free-ranging whitetails that engaged in battles with other bucks during the rut's peak.

Left and opposite page: Bucks might interlock their antlers while fighting more often than once believed. These free-ranging South Texas bucks became locked in combat and died during the 1987 rut.

Right: Although a victor in a battle, this white-tailed buck still "lost the war." During an intense fight, the buck sustained fatal wounds. The author photographed the buck shortly before it perished.

Below: The rigors of the rut often result in gruesome deaths. This South Texas buck likely died after another buck's antler pierced its windpipe.

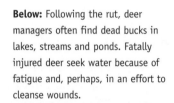

Below: Following the rut, deer managers often find dead bucks in lakes, streams and ponds. Fatally injured deer seek water because of fatigue and, perhaps, in an effort to cleanse wounds.

Right and below: Although researchers have documented fights that have lasted more than 15 minutes, typical fights last only two to five minutes. Fights that result in locked antlers invariably involve bucks of nearly equal size and social ranking.

Doctoring Your Hunt with White Lightning

CHARLES J. ALSHEIMER, OCTOBER 1988

Whenever deer hunters get together, thoughts and ideas flow freely. This past spring, I travelled to Idaho, Montana and Alberta on business, and on several occasions, hunters wanted to know how I hunt Eastern whitetails. The most frequently asked questions were: How do you hunt the rut? What size are racks in the East? How do Eastern bucks react to human pressure? Do scent lures really work? How do you hunt other regions?

The latter is obviously a difficult question — one that requires myriad answers, depending on the particular area. In fact, there are no easy answers. What works in Pennsylvania might not work in Idaho, or vice-versa. Whitetails are creatures of habit, and habitat varies greatly throughout the whitetail's range.

Habit, however, is a common denominator, especially as it relates to hunting rutting whitetails. Today, one subject that goes hand in hand with rut-hunting is the use of deer lures. Because of advertising, word of mouth and mystique, the use and techniques associated with deer lures dominate conversations.

I grew up on a farm in the heart of Eastern whitetail country, and, at the time, the use of deer lures was nearly nonexistent. It's probably safe to say that if a successful deer hunter in the 1960s heard such talk, he would have laughed it off as fantasy. Many things have changed in deer hunting since then, and the use of deer lures represents one of the biggest changes.

How well deer lures work remains a hotly debated subject. While some deer hunters swear they'd never step into a woods without their favorite brand, others laugh off the whole subject as a big, money-making joke.

Frankly, I think it's presumptuous to think all deer lures are foolproof. Up until five years ago (1983), I experimented with many popular brands of deer lures. Some appeared to work, but many gave no indication of working. Then, by accident, my opinion changed.

In October 1982, I heard of a dairy farmer from a neighboring state who killed a record-class whitetail with a bow and arrow. What was unique about this successful bow-hunter was he used the vaginal discharge from his dairy cows as a buck lure. To be more exact, he collected only the discharge from cows in the peak of their estrous cycle.

At first, I found this somewhat humorous, but I decided to give it

Above: According to the author, an overhanging licking branch is the most important feature of a scrape. Bucks and does use licking branches to alert other deer of their presence.

a try. I contacted a dairy farmer/artificial inseminator friend of mine and told him what I wanted to do. Unlike me, he didn't laugh, because he thought the tactic might work. His reasoning was that both whitetails and Holsteins are ruminants, and the natural pheromones of one might attract the other.

Over the last five years, a handful of local bow-hunters in western New York have been using this lure, which I call "white lightning." Actual reactions from white-tailed bucks varied from user to user. However, the bottom line is that if properly used and handled, the lure produces excellent results.

Few of today's hunters understand how to use lures, and too many lure manufacturers seem to be more interested in selling products than educating consumers. Like so many hunters, I used to put the lure on my boots and sprinkle a few drops around my stand in hopes of attracting a buck. Although I still do this to a degree, experimentation taught me a better way to use lures for bow-, gun- and camera-hunting.

For years, I trapped fox and learned scent usage by trial and error. Basically, I discovered the more natural fox scent I could place around a trap, the better my chances of success. This meant I had to not only attract the fox with bait and lures, but also make sure none of my scent remained in the area. This required painstaking efforts, but over time I became quite successful.

The knowledge I gained from trapping spread over into my deer-hunting efforts. In many ways, I hunted whitetails in the same manner in which I trapped, and I enjoyed increased success with each passing year. Now, when I take to the woods during the bow season, I take the same precautions I took when trapping. I wear light-weight, rubber boots, and I never let the boots come in contact with any substance capable of carrying human odor. Consequently, when traveling to a hunting area, I store the boots in a garbage bag until I'm ready to walk to my stand. To keep them clean, I periodically wash them with boiling water. This removes nearly all foreign odors. I also use rubber gloves when handling scents, and I keep my hunting clothes clean and only wear them when hunting.

When I plan to hunt with "white lightning," I make up several lure canisters. First, I punch holes in 35 mm film canisters. Next, I thread a piece of lightweight cord through the holes. This allows me to tie the canisters to branches near scrapes.

Next, I boil the canisters in water to eliminate human odors. After allowing them to dry, I insert three cotton balls into each canister. I do not handle the cotton with my bare hands — I use a sterilized tweezers. The cotton balls act as a sponge for the lure.

I hunted enough areas over the years to know where scrapes will appear from year to year. For this reason, I do not make mock scrapes. My experience indicates certain areas seem to be preferred scraping areas from year to year — at least in the farm country I hunt.

I look for fresh scrapes in early October. Once a scrape is located, I make sure a good licking branch hangs over it. If it doesn't, then it isn't a candidate for hunting. In my opinion, the licking branch is more important than the scrape itself.

Once I find a good scrape, I doctor it much the same way I would a fox set. Using a trapper's trowel, I dig a narrow, 8-inch-deep hole in the center of the scrape. I drop one loaded lure canisters into the scrape and fill the hole with dirt. Careful tamping returns the scrape surface back to its original appearance. I then tie another canister about 6 feet above the ground and above the licking branch. Lastly, I saturate the cotton balls inside the can with more lure. I use an eyedropper to avoid touching the can with my hands. I also deposit a couple droplets of lure into the scrape.

Placing a "scent bomb" a few feet above the scrape might sound contrary to what printed material has always taught. After all, estrous urine should be on the ground, not in the trees, right? Well, I used to think that, but I've observed too many bucks — and does — going after the canister above the branch. Therefore, I no longer think it matters whether the lure is on the ground or above the branch. I've even saturated the licking branch with lure and watched as frenzied whitetails worked over the branch.

To keep the scrape fresh, I replenish the lure above the scrape at least every other day. I also squirt a few drops on the ground so the scent stays in the scrape. By doing this, the estrous scent stays powerful at all times. Replenishing the lure is by far one of the most important aspects of doctoring scrapes. Of course, all of this, including when I hunt, is done while wearing my knee-high, rubber boots. As another precaution, I never touch any branches while in the scrape area, because it's essential not to leave any human odor.

My results during the last five years (particularly the last three) have been amazing. A 9-point buck I bow-killed in October 1986,

UNDERSTANDING WHY A WHITETAIL FREQUENTS A SCRAPE AND WHAT KEEPS HIM COMING BACK WILL HELP YOU UNRAVEL THE MYSTERY OF SCRAPE-HUNTING.

Above: Although secretions from dairy cows had been used by many deer hunters as a buck lure in the early 1980s, Charles Alsheimer was one of the first outdoor writers to master this rut-hunting tactic.

and a heavy-racked buck from last season, which weighed 191 pounds, reacted similarly to my doctored scrapes. During the 1986 bow season, I set out my estrous-scent canisters at a scrape next to a stream. On the morning of Oct. 25, I laid down a scent line where I wanted a deer to walk to give me a good broadside shot. This was done by applying the lure to the soles of my boots.

About two hours after daybreak, I noticed a buck walking through the woods with his nose to my trail and his tail outstretched. At 40 yards, he stopped and made a small scrape, then continued toward me. He stopped about 15 yards away, offering a broadside shot. An arrow behind the shoulder put him down quickly. This buck, like others in the past, responded perfectly to the lure.

One of my 1987 bucks wasn't quite so easy. I had been doctoring a scrape for about a month with very good results. I hunted the scrape 15 mornings in a span from Oct. 15 to Nov. 15, and I lured at least one buck into the area on all but two of those hunts.

Although I saw one dandy buck pass just out of bow range and passed up shots at several smaller bucks, I never arrowed a deer from that setup by the time the bow season ended on Nov. 15.

The next day, I returned to the stand for the opening day of gun season. This time, I didn't have to wait long to get my opportunity. At 8:45 a.m., the same buck I wanted to arrow during bow season walked into the scrape at bow range. A well-placed shot made all the effort and waiting worthwhile.

I'm sure many commercial lures work as well as "white lightning." However, if you want to try the vaginal discharge from a domestic ruminant (cow, sheep or goat), you need to remember a few things.

First, make sure the person who extracts it knows what he's doing. In other words, try not to get any human odors mixed in with the solution. The best, most powerful lure, will be the thick, clear mucous given off by an estrous animal. The thicker it is, the better. The discharge isn't exactly a liquid, so I dilute it with some holstein cow urine. To keep "white lightning" fresh, I store it in a refrigerator. Finally, I discard the mixture after the season. The lure isn't that effective if kept for more than a few months, especially if it comes in contact with air.

What's the most important ingredient to using "white lightning?" Nothing less than woodsmanship! Understanding why a whitetail frequents a scrape and what keeps him coming back will help you unravel the mystery of scrape-hunting. Nothing is foolproof when it comes to deer and deer hunting, and even the best lure won't work every time. However, one thing is certain: Doctoring your hunt with "white lightning" adds a dimension to white-tailed deer hunting that's challenging and exciting.

Above: Although the deer-scent industry was on the cusp of record growth when this article appeared in *D&DH*, Alsheimer's ideas on scrape-hunting helped kick-start the frenzy.

The All-American Deer Drive

ROB WEGNER, DECEMBER 1988

During the early years of our sport, deer hunters employed the deer drive primarily in the South and Southwest. This method of deer hunting descends partially from the English stag hunt and partly from the hunting methods of the American Indians. The English part of the tradition introduces us to the use of horses and hounds; the Indian component gives us the line of standers towards which men drive the quarry. The deer drive as practiced in the Deep South since Colonial times requires not only a quick hand with the double-barreled shotgun, but a firm seat in the saddle. As Judge Caton once remarked, "If the deer hunter returns with a sound horse and a sound body, he may consider himself fortunate." Once the hounds start the deer, the hunters follow them on horseback. Using their knowledge of the whitetail's habits, the hunters strive to gain ground on the deer. By cutting corners and following shortcuts, the hunters thus come to within shooting distance of the fleeing animal.

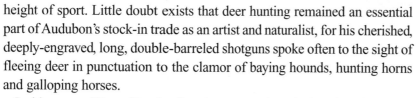

John James Audubon found great excitement in this form of deer hunting and considered it a very agreeable form of outdoor recreation. While we do not generally characterize Audubon as a giant among deer hunters, he greatly enjoyed deer hunting as a sport for many years, particularly the deer drive as customarily practiced in the Low Country of South Carolina with hounds, horns and horses, an activity which Audubon considered the height of sport. Little doubt exists that deer hunting remained an essential part of Audubon's stock-in trade as an artist and naturalist, for his cherished, deeply-engraved, long, double-barreled shotguns spoke often to the sight of fleeing deer in punctuation to the clamor of baying hounds, hunting horns and galloping horses.

In his essay, "Deer Hunting," written sometime during the 1830s and published, oddly, enough in his ornithological biography, Audubon argues that the deer drive, to be practiced successfully, requires great energy and activity, expert rifle shooting, a thorough knowledge of the forest, plus an intimate acquaintance with the habits of deer and how they respond to human pressure. While driving deer, Audubon noticed whitetails frequently retreat from their home range but soon return to their original haunts after the drive ends. In Audubon's day as in ours, hunters designated the drives with particular names such as Crane Pond, Gum Thicket, The Pasture and The Oak Swamp. To his great mortification, his colleagues named one drive after him, a drive where Audubon missed several deer.

In his essay, Audubon reports that men still-hunted, drove, fire-lighted, called, grunted and decoyed deer for recreational purposes as early as the 1830s. In his essay, he gives us one of the most picturesque and enthusiastic descriptions of the deer drive ever penned:

"Now, kind reader, prepare to mount a generous, full-blood Virginian horse. See that your gun is in complete order, for hark to the sound of the bugle and horn, and the mingled clamor of a pack of harriers! Your friends are waiting for you, under the shade of the wood, and we must together go driving the light-footed deer. The distance over which one has to travel is seldom felt when pleasure is anticipated as the result; so galloping we go pell-mell through the woods, to some well-known place where many a fine buck has dropped its antlers under the ball of the hunter's rifle. The servants, who are called the drivers, have already begun their search. Their voices are heard exciting the hounds, and unless we put spurs to our steeds, we may be too late at our stand, and thus lose the first opportunity of shooting the fleeting game as it passes by. Hark again! The dogs are in chase, the horn sounds louder and more clearly. Hurry, hurry on, or we shall be sadly behind!

"Here we are at last! Dismount, fasten your horse to this tree, place yourself by the side of that large yellow poplar, and mind you do not shoot me! The deer is fast approaching; I will go to my stand, and he who shoots him dead wins the prize.

"The deer is heard coming. It has inadvertently cracked a dead stick with its hoof, and the dogs are now so near that it will pass in a moment. There it comes! How beautifully it bounds over the ground! What a splendid head of horns! How easy its attitudes, depending, as it seems to do, on its own swiftness for safety! All is in vain, however; a gun is fired, the animal plunges and doubles with incomparable speed. There he goes! He passes another stand, from which a second shot, better directed than the first, brings him to the ground. The dogs, the servants, the sportsmen are now rushing forward to the spot. The hunter who has shot it is congratulated on his skill or good luck, and the chase begins again in some other part of the woods.

"I hope that this account will be sufficient to induce you, kind reader, to go driving the light-footed deer in our Western and Southern woods..."

Indeed, Audubon's spirited account of driving whitetails through the interior of tangled woods and across hills, ravines and morasses induced many a Nimrod (hunter) nationwide to take up the chase, to drive the white-tailed deer from the woods. The following account narrates what some of the most illustrious deer drives and famous deer drivers, or infamous — depending upon your point of view — have accomplished since following Audubon's inducement.

One of the earliest Dixie deerslayers to respond to Audubon's inducement was William Elliott, a contemporary of Audubon's and a planter of

Above: The deer drive is one of deer hunting's most time-honored traditions. Successful drives require careful planning, and a good drive results in camp camaraderie and close-knit hunting parties.

the noblest South Carolina breed, who carried the deer drive, Southern-style, to its ultimate climax. In his letters to the Charleston Courier signed "Venator," Elliott described his deer-driving adventures, and when he collected these hair-splitting yarns in *Carolina Sports by Land and Water* (1846), the book became one of the classic accounts of the subject, one of the very few outdoor books to remain in print ever since the date of its original publication.

Elliott drove deer along the banks of the Chee-ha River, one of South Carolina's best deer-hunting grounds of its time, with the enthusiastic gusto of starry-eyed generals engaged in sylvan warfare. With hounds and drivers — "whippers," he called them — moving the deer, he spurred his horse on until gaining a position near the deer's flank. Once wounded, whether shot with the double-barrel or struck in the head with the armed heel of his boot, Elliott would often fling himself upon the struggling animal and bury the fatal blade of his knife into the white-tail's throat.

Elliott referred to deer drives as "raids against the deer" in which the hunters would marshal their forces for a week's campaign and use "all the appliances of destruction at their beck." Those "sleek-skinned marauders," as Elliott called them, had to be eliminated, for they were ruining his crops — the beginnings of our modern-day pest-control policies with regard to deer management. Consequently, Elliott waged havoc against deer in general and bucks in particular, especially old, overgrown bucks who had the insolence to baffle Elliott and his boys.

Once spotted, a buck had to be pursued until its death. After watching one of his hunting buddies, a backwoods ruffian named Geordy, finally kill a deer after wounding six, Elliott cried out in one of his wild utterances, "Done like a sportsman, Geordy, one dead deer is worth a dozen cripples. I remember once, your powder was too weak; and next, your shot was too small; and next, your aim was somewhat wild; and one went off bored of an ear; and another nick'd off a tail. You are bound to set up an infirmary across the river, for the dismembered deer! You have done well to kill — let it grow into a habit."

Driving deer became an intense habit of mind: The noise of the shotguns, the aroma of gunpowder, the baying of the hounds and the echoes of the huntsmen's horns set Elliott's heart to pounding and his mind to the issuance of wild utterances as he galloped on through the deer forest. Although he loved his hounds and horses as well as the deer, when the hounds lost the trail, he cursed the laggards of the pack, the cold of nose and the slow of foot. When one wounded buck miraculously escaped into the depths of a rapidly flowing stream after fleeing the hounds and evading buckshot, Wild Willie stood along the shoreline and vented his frustration by hollering at the buck, "Go, thou fool, no better than Napoleon, hast thou known the fitting time to die! The devil take thee, for thou hast needlessly kicked and thrust thyself beyond the reach of a blessing!" And

THE MERE STORY OF THE AMERICAN DEER DRIVE CONTAINS MORE UNIQUE EVENTS THAN ALMOST ANY OTHER ASPECT OF THE SPORT. IN FACT, THE DEER DRIVE REPRESENTS A RICH SLICE OF OUR DEER HUNTING HERITAGE.

with that grotesque verbiage, the Harvard-educated deerslayer spurred his horse and disappeared from the scene of ultimate disappointment only to find partial consolation later over venison steak at the campfire where Elliott decried all bucks as "luxurious rogues and the greatest epicures alive!"

After reading Elliott's spirit-stirring notes on driving deer to their deaths, Thoreau responded by calling the whole affair bloody, wild and barbaric, although he readily admitted that driving deer proved to be the top-ranked field sport of the South. One thing seems certain: It's hard to compare Elliott's deer drives to anything that occurred before or since. Yet, in terms of effectiveness and blood, they do remind us of the bloody deer drives of "Black Jack" Schwartz who reportedly drove an area near the Upper Mahantongo Creek in Pennsylvania with a radius often running in excess of 30 miles. When the shooting stopped and the smoke cleared, it was not uncommon for as many as 198 deer to lay slain on the forest floor.

Many deer also fell as a result of the grandiose deer drives of Walter Winans, one of the most bizarre characters in the history of deer hunting. One photograph in his deer hunting journal records the illustrious presence of 17 horses, 35 deerslayers and 20 dead bucks. His dramatically-staged deer-shooting photos and deer-driving illustrations have to be seen to be believed. Looking somewhat like a retired general of the Boer War, we see this infamous deer driver in formal hunting attire blazing away at deer at point-blank range with his rifle often being fired from the hip. In the photos of his deer-driving journals, we see dying deer suspended in mid-air while clouds of gunsmoke ascend from his highly polished .275 Rigby-Mauser.

After a lifetime of deer driving, Winans reached the conclusion:

"Deer will not be driven; if they think they are being forced, they will break back, however thick the beaters are. The only way to force deer up to the guns is to make them think you want them to go in the opposite direction.

"Instead of being called deer driving, it ought to be called deceiving-deer-into-going-where-you-want-them-to."

Winans frequently posted his gunners behind the beaters with great success and stressed variation in the methods of driving. If the drive would succeed in one way, that was reason enough for Winans for not doing it that way the next time. He soon learned that an old doe often leads other deer out of danger and often, "gets too clever and has to be killed."

Old Walt prepared three ways of driving each tract and planned them to the minutest details to suit different wind directions. When the wind changed, the drive changed immediately. He did not like noise in the deer forest. Consequently, he used a series of signals with flags. He frowned upon the German idea of using small flags on cords or nets (Lappen) as a legitimate way of preventing deer from going where they were not wanted. The big drives that Winans presided over often yielded as many as 30 bucks in one drive, with every gun getting one or more deer.

This type of strategic success in moving deer must have been what George McCormick, a leading sportsman of Flagstaff, Ariz., had in mind when he assembled 55 cowboys on horseback and 70 Navajo braves on foot in an attempt to drive 8,000 deer off the Kaibab, across the Grand Canyon, through the Colorado River and on to the South Rim. This stupendous effort lead by famed outdoorsman Zane Grey and known as the "Great Kaibab Deer Drive" obviously resulted in the biggest deer drive ever attempted in the history of North America. The idea inherent in this drive revolved around moving deer off an over-browsed range instead of controlling the population through legitimate deer hunting. Apparently, the organizers figured the only way to deal with the irrupting Kaibab deer herd was to turn the animals over to the cowboys.

The planners invited Paramount Pictures to film the event, got permission from the U.S. Forest Service and the National Park Service, elicited the help of cowboys and ranchers for miles around and erected drift fences in strategic positions. Early in the afternoon on Dec. 16, 1924, the 125 deer-drive members took their positions. Loaded down with cowbells, tin cans and other noisemakers, the drivers formed a line on foot and horseback. When forest ranger Thad Eburne dismounted and fired his rifle, as Zane Grey recalls in his book *The Deer Stalker* (1924), "the great deer drive was on."

The line moved forward with the Riders of the Purple Sage hollering cattle-driving calls and the Navajos shouting their chants and clanging their noisemakers. In responding to the jangle of cowbells and the melodious Indian yells, deer appeared in the open terrain to investigate. Hundreds of does and fawns started running up the hillsides, but it soon became evident to ranger Eburne that they were traveling in every direction except the one desired by the drivers. Fawns soon

AS MORE AND MORE STATE LEGISLATURES PROHIBITED DRIVING DEER WITH HOUNDS AND HORSES, LARGE, MAN-MADE DRIVES BECAME THE ORDER OF THE DAY. THESE DRIVES PROVED ESPECIALLY SUCCESSFUL IN THE NORTH.

bounded straight for the Indians.

"The deer are moving, but not forward," one cowboy hollered.

More deer appeared as the drive continued. In one grand spectacle, forest ranger Eburne could see as many as 500 deer at a time.

"Bucks, does and fawns, trios and sextets of deer, lines and groups, began to close in on one another," Zane Grey wrote. "The riders responded with a daring and speed that for a few moments augured well for the success of the movement. But the fleetness of the deer outdistanced the horsemen. Two-thirds of that deer herd streamed up the slope, one long bobbing line of gray and white, to pass beyond the riders; and wheeling back along the ridge, they flashed, leaped, darted in magnificent silhouette against the pale sky."

The drivers soon saw thousands of deer stampeding up and down the canyons. Eburne, as Zane Grey recalls, "drank his fill of that beautiful wild spectacle, because he knew he would ever see it again. He doubted if such a sight would ever be seen by any man. Another winter would find most of those deer dead of starvation."

As the drive progressed, the line gradually wavered, becoming disorganized and irregular. To make things worse, a threatening snowstorm soon became a reality. The cowboys now had to fight snow-laden limbs and brush and could not keep up with the running Indians who quickly outdistanced them. As deer reversed themselves and ran through the line of Navajos, they soon ran directly into the horsemen. Many of the drivers soon lost their way and wandered around looking for familiar landmarks. Others, realizing the failure of the whole fiasco, quit and turned back as the temperature approached zero.

According to one observer, no deer were spotted in front of the drivers, but thousands milled around behind them. Out in front of the drivers, the shivering and frustrated cameramen from Paramount Pictures waited in vain to film fleeing deer in a blinding snowstorm, as did the standers who were official deer counters. Before the drive ended and the high-pitched cowboy yells dissipated, six inches of snow had fallen.

This infamous drive sounds more like fiction than fact. Thad Eburne, the main protagonist of *The Deer Stalker*, summarized the colossal failure of this drive when he wrote, "Looks to me like they just won't drive!" Indeed. It was a hard lesson learned: Surplus deer cannot be driven off their home range to prosper elsewhere.

Not all deer drives end as colossal failures. As more and more state legislatures gradually prohibited driving deer with hounds and horses, large man-made drives became the order of the day and proved more successful, especially in the North. The ghost-like single files of flashlights twinkling along the deer trails in white-tailed deer country in the predawn hours became a standard fixture of the annual deer hunt.

Many of these large drives proved very successful. "The Chilson Bunch," for example, that hunted the old Van Wegan farm in the hills of Pennsylvania, reportedly bagged 37 bucks for 42 hunters during one season alone, after four days of methodically driving an area of less than 500 acres!

The big drives of H.O. Lund and his boys at their deer camp near Iron River, Wis., were also highly successful, because Lund meticulously scheduled and planned them well before the smere game ever started. With fresh snow and favorable wind, his 15-man crew set out for the deer woods. The old man's instructions were explicit:

"Keep the wind in your right ear. Walk slowly, and keep your eyes peeled. There are bucks in these woods with horns the size of rockin' chairs!"

Lund insisted that the drive be slow, methodical and quiet until the final shoot-out. "Why bang away at a spooked deer, high-tailing it like the hammers of hell for the next county, when you could connect with one that was loping along?" he reasoned.

The finale of a Lund deer drive took only about 10 minutes. With final landmarks coming into view, drivers knew all hell would break loose. Wigs Lund saw it many times.

"The rifles of the men posted would open up from all sides and the cannonading would sound like the siege of Vicksburg," Wigs wrote. "We connected, and hung up many the buck on The Big Drive."

The results of the shoot-out would frequently appear in the Iron River newspapers. According to one account, young H.O. Lund finally shot his first deer after 30 days of deer driving and 200 rounds of ammunition.

Deer hunters across this land will do whatever necessary to enhance the success of deer driving. In fact, some hunters will even try to scare 'em to death! For example, when Henry Milliken, a tall and lanky deer-slayer from the woods of Maine, failed to shoot deer on his annual deer hunts, he employed a one-man drive with three standers posted at strategic spots in the swamp. On the east side of the swamp, where deer frequently gave standers the Houdini-slip, he placed a line of cedar-built scarecrows dressed in red hunting clothes and handkerchiefs laced with a strong dose of Wild Root hair tonic. The deer-scaring contraptions looked unusual and ludicrous, but they worked, as deer abandoned their usual escape routes!

While most of us have probably participated in the deer drive in one form or another, not all hunters agree with Audubon's interpretation of the drive as an exciting and very agreeable form of recreation. In fact, some states today prohibit the deer drive. No matter. The mere story of the American deer drive contains more unique events and colorful characters than almost any other aspect of our sport. It's filled with odd situations, strokes of graceless luck and humorous anecdotes. What's more, it represents a rich slice of our deer-hunting heritage.

Uncertainties in Deer Hunting

KENT HORNER, AUGUST 1989

A lot can go wrong on a deer hunt. Nature's woodland variables and the whitetail's evasive ability make deer hunting a sport of uncertainties.

You never know just how and when a white-tailed deer will approach your stand, or even if it will at all. The deer's approach is uncertain even with the hunter's best scouting efforts. I long ago quit making predictions about any white-tailed deer hunt.

Early in the archery season, I have watched whitetails follow the same woodland trail at practically the same minute for several days. Then, suddenly during gun season, I couldn't even "buy" a deer sighting. Therefore, when making bets on certainties in the deer woods, one should lay down his small change first!

Compounded with the unpredictability of the whitetail are other uncertainties of the hunt: misfires, misidentifications, becoming lost, misjudging distance, getting stuck on back roads or in bad weather, encounters with snakes and wild dogs and other dangerous elements. However, hunters must accept these uncertainties, because, if nothing else, they make good stories.

An enjoyable part of hunting is listening to the stories told by hunting buddies, because we can learn from others' misfortunes. An unsuccessful, fouled-up deer hunt might become inordinately humorous, especially when retold in an embellished camp tale, but we should also remember some uncertainties involve hunter safety. These should never be taken lightly.

Greek writers told us 2,500 years ago that tragedy and comedy are closely related in the human psyche. So, hunters tend to abstract misfortunes, uncertainties, and dangers when telling tales.

What follows are documented accounts I've experienced in my years of deer hunting. I've omitted names to spare embarrassment for unsuspecting souls. Hopefully, the lessons they learned will help you avoid the same pitfalls. Remember, these stories are 100 percent true.

Episode 1: This past season, I was relaxing in my home when a hunting buddy pulled into the driveway with his old pickup truck. I soon learned he had just killed a buck.

"Come hunting with me tomorrow," he said as I stepped outside. "It's an either-sex rifle hunt. We'll both get a deer for sure. I saw 11 deer today and killed this one."

How could I refuse? Being assured of bagging a deer, I rousted out

Above: Always know the weather forecast before heading out to your stand. Unexpected rain or fog cannot only ruin a hunt, it can hinder your ability to navigate when darkness falls.

of bed the next morning at 2:30 a.m., tossed my hunting gear into my friend's truck and joined him for the two-hour drive into the wilderness recesses of Tennessee's Cumberland Plateau. After parking the truck, we climbed aboard his all-terrain vehicle and drove two miles farther, negotiating rugged limestone ledges along the way.

Result: Well, we hunted from dawn to dusk and didn't see a single whitetail. After the hunt, we got the pickup truck stuck and were forced to pull it out with the ATV. In the process, my friend fell and stuck an arrow-sharp limestone rock deep into his left hand. After suffering hours of intense pain, he wound up in the emergency ward of the hospital. Pure debacle.

Episode 2: While standing beside his ATV loaded on a truck, a hunter sees a white-tailed deer at a distance. The hunter quickly shoulders his .30-06 and fires at the whitetail.

Result: In his excitement to bag a deer, the hunter fails to notice his rifle's muzzle isn't clear. The shot takes out the ATV's gas tank. The hunter later told me that his ears rang for 30 minutes from the point-blank concussion. Luckily, the gas tank didn't explode.

Episode 3: In the flatland swamps of southern Alabama, a hunter borrows a farmer's horse in hopes of hauling his whitetail back to camp.

Result: After several minutes following the blood trail on horseback, the hunter dismounts and ties the horse to a tree. After following the trail on foot, the hunter eventually becomes lost in the nondescript swamp that's covered with canebrakes and briars. Unfortunately, he also loses the horse, which is still tied to the tree.

After hours of stumbling around in the swamp, the hunter finds his way back to the farmer's house. Although he's thoroughly embarrassed, the hunter tells the farmer about the lost horse. The farmer tells him not to worry and that thirst and/or starvation should cause the horse to eventually break its reins and find its way back to the farm.

Episode 4: A buddy took careful aim, shot, and flattened an Alabama buck that was 350 yards away. I know the distance, because I personally stepped it off while two of my buddies loaded the deer into the back of a pickup truck.

Previous to this display of marksmanship, the same hunter had the following experience while hunting from a 10-foot-high tripod stand overlooking an open field. A deer walked up from behind him and stood directly underneath him. He saw the deer, and pointed his rifle straight down, peered through the scope, viewed a field full of deer hair and fired.

Result: Besides acting completely unsafe, my buddy missed the deer cleanly. As they say, "haste makes waste."

Episode 5: Steve Powell, a medical doctor from Florida, relayed this account as we shared a hunt near Selma, Ala. While bow-hunting in another state, Powell watched as two mature bucks walked into bow range. Nocking an arrow, he readied himself to draw on one of the bucks.

Result: A house cat lurking in the weeds suddenly spooked both bucks, and they sprinted for cover. One wonders whether this solitary cat — not generally a formidable deer predator — was stalking the deer or Powell.

Episode 6: A hunter is sitting in a permanent tree stand overlooking woodland breaks and a small field of corn and soybeans. Near dark, that magic time for bucks, a dense fog starts rolling in. To make sure he can still see through his scope, the hunter shoulders his rifle and aims at a pine stump about 50 yards away. The view is fine. However, the hunter, not realizing he had taken the gun's safety off, accidentally trips the trigger.

Result: The .30-06 blasts the pine stump. Later, under interrogation from other members of the hunting party, the hunter confesses that he shot the pine stump by mistake.

The other hunters quickly and unanimously agree they preferred not to associate with any deer hunter who shot at pine stumps instead of deer. Consequently, they revoke the man's hunting club membership.

Episode 7: A bow-hunter walks back to camp after an unsuccessful hunt. Stopping on the trail, he decides to change out of his coveralls.

Result: A buck suddenly appears and walks within bow range. The hunter — wearing nothing but his socks and longjohns — slowly nocks an arrow, aims and releases. The arrow hits its mark, but the buck whirls and bounds into nearby cover.

Still clad in his socks and underwear, the hunter immediately takes up the blood trail. He hopes the arrowed deer only ran a short distance. It didn't. The whitetail's trail takes the hunter over hills and hollows.

Fearing he'll lose the deer, the hunter presses onward. The deer finally succumbs. Now, still clad only in socks and longjohns, the hunter totes his kill back to camp.

Episode 8: A deer hunter liberally douses himself with raccoon cover scent. Then, desiring to hunt from a ground blind, he sits at the base of a tree atop an 8-foot-high bank that overlooks a rambling creek. He knows a big buck lives in the area.

Result: Zeoring in on the scent, a bobcat approaches the bank and gets ready to pounce on the "raccoon." Acting in self defense, the hunter quickly places an arrow through the cat.

Along the same line, a champion turkey caller once related to me that while he was using a turkey call in a ground blind, a fox slipped in from behind a tree and bit him on the finger!

Episode 9: A deer hunter has a rancid-smelling coat with a deep-pile fur collar. Each hunting season, the hunter "conditions" the fur collar with doe urine. The coat is so foul-smelling that his wife makes him place it in a bag and keep it in the freezer during the off-season.

During the rut, the hunter takes the coat out of the freezer, thaws it, applies some more doe urine, puts it on, and heads for the woods.

"You just wouldn't believe what all follows me through the woods," the hunter said as I hunted with him in Alabama. "But I really have to be alert. Once a buck all but straddled me from behind before I could react and get a shot off."

Episode 10: A gun-hunter is perched in a two-piece climbing stand about 20 feet high in a tree when a whitetail appears and walks to the base of the tree. The hunter, who is not wearing a safety harness, shifts his body in hopes of getting a shot at the deer.

Result: The hunter's movement causes him to lose his balance and fall from the stand. As he falls, he grabs wildly at the stand, causing him to suffer severe cuts on his hands. Luckily, the man survives the falls without any other serious injuries.

Episode 11: A hunter descends from his portable tree stand just as a heavy fog settles into the woods. Instead of taking his usual route back to camp, the hunter opts to follow a logging trail that he passed on the way to his stand that morning. He assumes the trail is a short-cut back to camp.

Result: The unfamiliar trail seems to go on forever, and it subdivides several times. After following it for a while, the hunter realizes he is completely lost. With the fog getting thicker, the hunter decides to stay still and holler for his hunting partner. After an anxious wait, the

ALTHOUGH ACCIDENTS CAN AND DO HAPPEN, SERIOUS DEER HUNTERS STRIVE TO MAKE THEIR MISCUES MINOR ONES. THE BEST DEER HUNTERS CAN SHAKE OFF THESE SLIP-UPS AS MERE FODDER FOR STORIES TOLD AROUND THE CAMPFIRE.

hunter is relieved to hear his buddy's ATV approaching in the distance.

Episode 12: A hunter sees the "brown side" of a deer at about 100-yards through the woods. He aims and fires.

Result: The hunter shoots another hunter's rifle butt. This blatant misidentification obviously begged for a tragic woodland misfortune. Such incidents cannot be called "accidents." What's more, hunters who make such careless mistakes should forever lose their hunting privileges.

Episode 13: A hunter climbs a tree with a portable stand while carrying his loaded rifle over his shoulder.

Result: The unfortunate hunter drops the rifle. The rifle's butt hits the ground first, causing the gun to fire a round back at the hunter, killing him. Yes, this really happened.

Luckily for most serious deer hunters, miscues are only fodder for stories after the hunt. However, it would seem from the above episodes that today's deer hunter is somewhat of a rough-and-tumble-character. Historically, that's how we've been portrayed.

When I hunt I want to hoot and holler a little bit. If I couldn't do that, I'd quit hunting. At the same time, there's a serious side to hunting that I also take to heart. From examining mistakes made by others and myself, I can become a better hunter, prepared for uncertainty.

The white-tailed deer has evolved over eons to evade predators within a small home range. The deer is an escape artist, a woodland Houdini. The whitetail's keen abilities, combined with nature's many other uncontrollable elements — and human nature — ensure deer hunting will always have plenty of uncertainties to fill our modern need for adventure.

Above: When hunting unfamiliar areas, be sure to let someone know where you'll be and how long you'll be hunting. Don't trust your instincts to lead you back to camp.

A Sense of Order

RANDALL P. SCHWALBACH, OCTOBER 1987

The drive from my home in a large city to my hunting retreat upstate begins on a four-lane, interstate highway. As my truck hums along with the flow of traffic, mere feet from the guardrails, concrete pillars and steel light posts that give order to the maze of the city's arteries, I try to remember that not all the world is like this. Some of it remains green and pleasing to the eye, and some of the earth is soft and resilient underfoot.

As the interstate becomes a two-lane, state highway and the traffic begins to thin, I start to relax and unwind. This transition continues as I leave the highway for the county trunk, then the town road, then the back road and onto the sandy lane with two ruts that ends at the head of a foot path. The path leads to a small cabin guarding an oak and aspen highland on the edge of a willow swamp.

By the time I swing open the cabin door, bring my gear inside, start a fire in the woodstove and put on a pot of coffee, I start to feel as if I had never left this place. I guess I haven't, for this is where my heart has always been. The ritual continues as I remove hunting clothes from a plastic bag that also contains a now very dry and brittle assortment of leaves, grasses and twigs.

I hang the clothes outside for a brief air-wash while I take a sponge-bath to purge my body of city smells. I think of Ishi, the last of the Yana people, who bathed in a mountain stream each morning before he went hunting. Although my bath is contained in an enameled wash-basin, I feel a kinship to the great Indian hunter.

Dressed in camouflaged clothing, I paint my face with a few streaks of brown and gray. I then inspect my broadheads before placing my hunting arrows into the quiver. Finally, the longbow is strung, the cabin door is closed behind me, and I take the trail to where the deer live.

The trail grew over during the course of the summer, despite my attempts to suppress the jungle with a weed trimmer and lawnmower back in June. It is thickest in the marsh section, and I know that tomorrow morning, when the dew is heavy, even hip boots won't keep me completely dry.

Approaching the Big Woods, I force myself to slow down. One step at a time, I enter a world of shadows and enchantment, as if I, King Arthur, have stepped into the royal forest. Not wishing to intrude too deeply right now, I choose a ground blind near the trail's entrance. It will serve both as a place of welcome and transition. For now is the time to blend in, not so much in terms of camouflage, but rather in getting synchronized in natural rhythms.

I must not think of tomorrow, or even as far ahead as what I might cook for supper tonight. I must not think of the past, either. I must not think about the journey here by auto, the traffic, the concrete, the hum of wheels. I strive to become one with the present.

As afternoon wanes, a shaft of sunlight filters through an opening and lands on the leather grip of my bow. I am suddenly inspired to draw an arrow and send a broadhead into a rotting aspen stump. Flushed with the plenipotence of a good shot at the imaginary buck, I drink deeply of the rich aromas of ferns, hickory nuts and acorns. In a flash of time, I experience what must be life in its fullest sense.

Soon the chill of the evening creeps up and no deer has appeared. This fact does not make me anxious. I am perfectly content, because I feel accepted here. The season is long, and I know that eventually an antlered deer will come. There's no need to wonder now if I have chosen my stand well. I unstring my bow, but I am not quite ready to leave.

At the eastern edge of the woods, where the trail enters, I wait for a familiar sound. Time seems to have slowed, and I do not feel as

rushed as when I came here. Then, suddenly, the night air is pierced by a shrill cry that crescendos so rapidly I can almost feel the impact of its source — the barred owl. Ready to begin his night, the majestic bird bids the day creatures good luck. I feel a kinship with this owl, a fellow predator, and I am happy to leave these hunting grounds to him.

I do not actually see the trail as I walk back to the cabin at its other end. Instead, my feet feel the way and I hardly even feel confined to this body. Indeed, all is ear and touch. Just sense. No thought. Once I turn and glance at the moon setting over my left shoulder, just above the fletchings of the arrows in my back quiver. It is the only clock I will need while I am here.

After a long day that began elsewhere, I'm physically spent as I roll out my sleeping bag on the mattress next to the wood stove. I undress by the light of a single candle. It is good to feel this kind of tiredness, the fatigue of the body, rather than the mind. I realize that I'm not the same man as when I began this day.

Something changed me, calmed me, refurbished my soul. A sense of order has been restored, and tonight I will not dream. I will sleep the hunter's sleep.

A NEW ERA
1992 TO 1996

A Note of Thanks

JOEL SPRING, SEPTEMBER 1994

Dear Doc,

It seems each autumn I get to see you only a short time to tell you thanks for letting our gang hunt your farm. I leave each year feeling I should have said more. What your piece of land nestled in the rolling hills has meant to me and the rest of the guys (and girls) is more than I could express with words, but let me try.

Your farm gave me my first buck, and my last. It also gave me my first bow-killed buck. I'm not the only one. There's been a steady stream of "firsts" for me and the rest of our gang. First does, first bucks, first turkeys and squirrels. Each new member of our group who comes to hunt your land helps reawaken the excitement of each of our first hunts. In time they'll get to know the magical places and names like Rock Seat and The Beech Tree, The Spring House and Joel's Dog Stand (another letter altogether). They'll learn the imposing woods of The Upper Side and the lonely places on the banks of The Brook, Second Brook and The Back Brook.

For now, these names might seem too simple to the uninitiated, but in years to come the mere mention of The Upper Pasture will conjure up memories of deer and oak trees and frigid mornings.

Speaking of memories, I can remember the first time I sat waiting for the drivers to push through The Bowl, and the way my heart nearly pounded out of my chest when the first of 20 deer burst from the thick pines. My heart still pounds like that. I remember missing my first buck and the sick feeling I felt as one of your neighbors shot him when he crossed onto his property. That sick feeling lasted two years. I remember two years later finally killing my first buck, and the mixture of elation and melancholy that washed over me like a spring flood. That feeling has lasted forever.

I know you've met all of the guys, and they're a good bunch. Seeing them in action on the Bowl Drive or The Pasture or The Pines is a remarkable sight. We work hard, and the drives usually pay off. The spirit of friendship among such a diverse group is as addictive as your deer herd is plentiful. There's always venison for everyone. Not shooting a deer doesn't exclude anyone from taking home meat. When I started hunting, I couldn't really grasp why my father-in-law would always let me sit on the drives and sacrifice his shot at a buck. But as the years wore on, I came to understand it well. I'm to the point where I prefer driving to sitting. I'd rather see people who haven't had much success score on their first doe or buck. I don't know of another sport so entwined with family and tradition and camaraderie.

I've enjoyed the solitary times, also. I remember the first year I set up my bow stand in the old overgrown orchard below your house. I had no sooner sat down than a red-tailed hawk swooped in and picked a red squirrel out of the pines that border the orchard. Even when the deer aren't moving, there's always something to watch. Last year I found the tree where a red fox lives. I was perched above him when he emerged from the hole at the base of the oak tree. (Yes, he's probably the one who has been eating your goslings.)

I remember finding the monster 7-point buck curled up as if sleeping in a hollow between two hemlocks by the Back Brook. I turned him over and couldn't find any wounds. Could it be he died of old age? He was bigger than any other deer I've ever seen running your farm. I guess I'd like to think he just outsmarted us all of those years and died of natural causes. The feeling I had sitting there next to that deer sends chills up my spine even now.

I wonder if I ever told you about the time I tracked a buck I spotted crossing the logging road in the rain, and discovered a fresh set of huge bear tracks on the back ridge. I went to that spot this year — no bear tracks.

The lessons I've learned on your little piece of land in the hills

outweigh anything school has ever taught. I've learned about the sanctity of life and the intricate process of death that makes life so precious. It might sound crazy, but hunting white-tailed deer on your farm has brought me closer to God, too. I've never met the builder, but I've sure seen His work. You've seen the waterfall by the Back Brook. You know what I mean.

Thanks again for letting us on your land each fall. You don't know how much it means. See you in October.

Sincerely,
Joel Spring

One Man's Battle with Lyme Disease

CHARLES J. ALSHEIMER, OCTOBER 1995

I still remember the phone call I received two years ago on a crisp October day. On the other end of the line was a local newspaper reporter who wanted my opinion on the prospects of hunters contracting Lyme disease during the deer season. I can't remember my exact response, but it went something like this:

"I realize Lyme disease is a problem in many parts of the country, but not here in western New York. My guess is that a hunter has a better chance of being hit by a meteor than contracting Lyme disease around here. So, I'd tell your readers not to worry about it. The whole issue is overblown."

Famous last words. My comments returned to haunt me. I ended up being the guy who got hit by a meteor. Less than eight months after that phone call, I found myself in declining health and didn't know why. As you can imagine, I became deeply concerned. America's woods and waters are my workplace, and all my life I've been involved in athletics as a player and coach. I consider myself to be in good shape, especially for a 47-year-old. As a result, I was mystified when my health deteriorated that summer.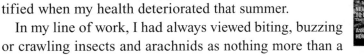

In my line of work, I had always viewed biting, buzzing or crawling insects and arachnids as nothing more than a nuisance. Oh, I always used the necessary insect repellents and protective clothing, but biting bugs never caused me to shy away from a woods, swamp or stream when pursuing my work and recreation. As a serious white-tailed deer hunter and photographer, I should have known better.

At this writing, Lyme disease is pretty much diagnosed clinically. As a result, it often becomes a diagnosis of exclusion. In other words, unless a person has the classic Lyme disease rash and tests positive for the disease in a blood sample, the physician will usually attempt to eliminate other diseases before suspecting Lyme disease as the culprit. For that reason, Lyme disease is often called "The Great Imitator." It produces a wide range of symptoms that mimic nearly 200 other illnesses.

Lyme disease is caused by the bacteria *Borrelia burgdorferi*, and is not difficult to treat if it's diagnosed quickly. Unfortunately, diagnosis remains a big problem and, left untreated, the bacteria multiply and spread quickly, increasing the risk of serious complications. A quote from the book *Coping with Lyme Disease* illustrates this point:

"The diagnostic problems surrounding Lyme disease are derived primarily from the fact there have been no tests that could simply and positively detect the *Borrelia burgdorferi* spirochete, thus confirming Lyme and initiating the traditional therapeutic process."

My bout with Lyme disease had a vague beginning. I had always thought, because of sketchy media reports, that I could only get Lyme disease from certain ticks, specifically the *Ixodes*, or deer tick. Further, I believed that if I were bitten, I would develop a telltale bull's-eye rash around the bite. Neither was the case with me, and, as you'll see, there might be many other ways to contract the disease.

My encounter with Lyme disease probably began in May 1994. During May and June, I was doing a tremendous amount of deer photography on and near my farm. My goal was to capture doe and fawn behavior on film. The photography went well despite high populations of mosquitoes, black flies and "punkies." For the most part, I kept these nuisances in check. Still, despite wearing lightweight hip boots, protective garments, and insect repellents, I took a few hits. One morning, while photographing a whitetail at a stream crossing, I watched as a black fly bit my right wrist. I felt a great deal of self-gratification when I squashed it before it could fly away. By the next morning, the bite had swollen a little and turned red, but it didn't concern me.

Within a week, I came down with a sore left elbow (I'm a lefty) while pitching batting practice to my son's high school baseball team. I've been a baseball coach in various leagues for nearly 25 years, and have pitched batting practice at nearly every practice during those years. I seldom got a sore arm, even when I pitched competitively, so I shrugged it off as old age catching up with me.

A week later, with my left arm still sore, my right wrist and the toes on my right foot started becoming sore. Also, I began encountering a wide range of ringing in my ears. That caused a little discomfort, but I still didn't give it much thought. My concern increased a week later when my right hip began hurting. I didn't know it then, but worse symptoms were coming.

By the first week of June, I found myself getting tired in the middle of the day, so I began taking a 10-minute "power nap" every noon. I awoke from these siestas feeling refreshed and ready to go. Often I would joke with people about these naps, and mention how great they made me feel. As with the sore arm, I figured Father Time's clock was slowing me down.

Then, one night in mid-June, I pulled up to a traffic light and noticed I had difficulty reading the neon sign on a bank next to the intersection. I don't wear glasses, and figured it was merely eye fatigue. After all, during my annual eye exam the previous February, the doctor told me I would have to start using non-prescription reading glasses because of my age. I figured that might be part of the problem.

Unfortunately, within a week of the neon-sign episode, I was having trouble focusing during the day. This condition was especially disturbing because it was affecting my photography. I wondered what on earth was going on. More than once I worried about my future in photography if I couldn't see well enough to use my cameras. Of course, those thoughts were premature, but I had serious concerns.

Slowly, I began to feel like an old man. From mid-June to mid-July, more unfamiliar symptoms began plaguing me. At the end of June, while bush-hogging some of our hayfields, my heart began racing for no apparent reason. I quickly turned off the tractor's power take-off unit, cut back the engine's throttle, and stopped the tractor.

Above: While the deer tick receives most of the blame for spreading Lyme disease, some experts believe any biting, blood-sucking bug — such as the black flies infesting this buck's antlers and ears — can transmit the illness.

I put my hand to my chest, wondering if my heart was going to jump through my shirt. I was scared, but within a couple of minutes the palpitations stopped. Little did I realize that was only the beginning of more episodes.

On Independence Day, I dusted off the bow and began shooting in preparation for the fall. I wanted to go on a bow-hunt for whitetails with the Realtree Camouflage folks in October, and I wanted to be ready. My practice sessions didn't go well. After about three shots each day, my left "pitcher's elbow" began aching. That — coupled with the sore joints, fatigue, blurred vision, ringing ears, and a second bout with irregular heartbeats — greatly increased my concerns.

By mid-July I was battling yet another problem. Without warning, pain began shooting through my thigh and arm muscles. Though these pains lasted only a couple of seconds, I felt as if I were being stabbed with an ice pick. Despite all the discomfort, I was able to function, though I was becoming greatly concerned.

Around the end of July, another new twist developed. I felt quite good for a few days. I still had joint soreness, but my stamina and steady eyesight were returning. I began thinking I might be getting over whatever plagued me.

Unfortunately, the recovery lasted only a few days. I later found out that this short "recovery" is a trait of Lyme disease. Slowly, all of the problems returned except the heart palpitations. In addition, another new problem surfaced: bouts of nausea. The bouts never last-

HGE: A New Tick-Borne Threat

The tick often responsible for spreading Lyme disease also carries a potentially lethal bacteria that has stricken more than 60 people nationwide. Researchers speculated in July 1994 that the disease, called human granulocytic ehrlichiosis, or HGE, was spread by the deer tick, which carries Lyme disease.

It wasn't until 1995 that more cases surfaced. HGE has affected dozens of people in Connecticut, Minnesota, New York and Wisconsin — states with high numbers of deer ticks. At least four people have died from the bacteria. In contrast, federal health officials have yet to document one death from Lyme disease.

HGE, which attacks white blood cells, can produce severe flu-like symptoms, and diagnosing it can be difficult. The most common symptoms include fever, chills, severe headaches and muscle aches. They usually occur one to three weeks after exposure.

"With HGE, you can go from wellness to a really severe, debilitating disease within hours," said Dr. Johan Bakken, an infectious disease specialist from Duluth, Minn.

The illness is easily treated, but responds to only one type of antibiotic, called doxycycline, while Lyme disease responds to several.

To help prevent getting either disease, avoid the carrier: biting ticks and insects. Here are some suggestions:

✓Wear a long-sleeved shirt, long pants and socks when outdoors.

✓Avoid open-toed shoes.

✓Tuck your shirt into your pants, and your pant cuffs into your socks.

✓Wear light-colored clothing to make ticks more visible.

✓Avoid brushing against shrubs and tall grass.

✓Use insect repellents with 10 percent to 30 percent DEET, which has proven effective in repelling ticks.

---

ed more than five to 10 seconds, but they hit once or twice a day.

When August arrived, I got lucky. One afternoon, I was on the phone with Dave Buckley, a fellow outdoor writer from West Valley, N.Y. With our conversation nearly complete, I asked about his wife, Beth. Dave responded, "Oh, much better."

"Better? What's wrong," I asked.

Dave told me Beth had contracted Lyme disease, and was in the final stages of treatment. When he told me about it, I asked to speak with her. After asking many questions about her symptoms and how she was being treated, I said goodbye.

For the next hour, my mind was racing at warp speed. Many of Beth's symptoms resembled mine. She never got a rash from being bit, and neither had I. All I had was a slight scar, still visible, from the black fly's bite. Beth also hadn't tested positive for Lyme disease on her first test.

After doing a little more self-diagnosis, I called Dave and Beth again. I told them of my symptoms and the lack of any Lyme disease rash. Beth was involved in a Lyme disease support group, and urged me to see a specialist. She gave me the address and phone number of Dr. Joseph Joseph, a Lyme disease specialist in Hermitage, Pa., which is 250 miles from my home.

After I hung up, I began doubting my self-diagnosis and basically convinced myself that I couldn't possibly have Lyme disease. In all honesty, contemplating the long drives between our farm and Dr. Joseph's office had a lot to do with my attitude. The next day, however, with all the symptoms still with me, I called a friend who is a general practitioner. He said he was not an expert on Lyme disease or its treatment, and that if I knew a specialist, I should go to him. He also said he could give me the blood test for Lyme disease if I wanted.

With reservation, I called Dr. Joseph and made an appointment.

On Aug. 16, 1994, I made the 250-mile drive to his office. The crazy thing was, I had felt fine the previous 36 hours.

Meeting Dr. Joseph was a breath of fresh air. He was personable and, like me, an outdoorsman. He put me through a battery of tests before we sat down to talk. During our conversation, he grilled me about my symptoms, my line of work and how much time I spent outdoors. About 15 minutes into our conversation, he said: "I don't know what your blood test will reveal, but I've seen enough cases to tell you that you probably have Lyme disease. I'm not going to wait for the test results to start you on medication."

I drove home with a sense of relief. Within a day, I began my oral medication, and felt a major improvement within a week. The soreness started going away and I could see better. But I had a major setback two weeks into the treatment. One morning, while photographing wildflowers, my left knee began hurting. Soon after, I bent over to photograph a low-growing flower and was unable to get up. I rolled over in the dew-laden grass and tried to straighten out my leg. The pain was incredible, but I eventually made it home. My knee was tender for the next two days. I later learned that this pain was nothing more than a "Herxheimer reaction." Herxheimer occurs when the Lyme disease spirochete, while being attacked by the antibiotics, gives off toxins and causes the immune system to react. Not being versed in this aspect of the treatment, I thought the Lyme disease had returned.

I returned to Dr. Joseph on Sept. 17 and, as we talked, he said my first blood test was negative. Still, he was so certain I had Lyme disease that he conducted more blood tests. The second test was different, and proved to me what many medical experts were learning about Lyme disease: Just because the first test is negative doesn't mean the second test will also be negative. Fortunately, Dr. Joseph had begun my treatment a month before the disease was confirmed.

By November, I began feeling like my old self. I believed I had received a new lease on life. I finished my medication on Christmas Eve, and haven't looked back. Not a week goes by that I don't think of the saying, "If you have your health you have everything." No truer words were ever spoken.

I've also thought a lot about the mystery of Lyme disease and the difficulty of getting the right treatment. I was fortunate to find a competent doctor who specialized in Lyme disease. I was also thankful a socialistic system of national health care was not in place when I got the disease. If I would have had to stay within my own HMO for treatment, I wouldn't have been able to see Dr. Joseph.

Lyme disease can probably be contracted from several types of insects and arachnids. Though Dr. Joseph didn't mention it, I have also read where, in theory, Lyme disease could be passed on through blood, milk and other body fluids or in meat that hasn't been thoroughly cooked.

I urge you to be more alert to the symptoms of Lyme disease than I was. I've learned there are about 70 symptoms of Lyme disease that are similar to those of other diseases. I had nearly 20 of the symptoms, and through self-diagnosis, I became fairly certain I had the disease when local doctors weren't so sure. Of course, I didn't have the classic symptoms: I believe I contracted the disease from a black fly's bite, not a deer tick's; I never had the customary bull's-eye rash; and I tested negative for Lyme disease the first time.

I've deeply pondered my disease, its treatment and the role that luck and fate played in my diagnosis and recovery. I'm just thankful I found the right doctor at the right time.

ABOUT THE AUTHOR

Charles Alsheimer was 47 years old when he contracted Lyme disease. Unfortunately, it took him many months before he received a proper diagnosis. Even today, copies of this article rank as the most-requested items by readers calling the *D&DH* office in Iola, Wis.

Tips for the Never-Say-Die Hunter

RICHARD P. SMITH, OCTOBER 1995

I bet the person who wrote the cliche, "If at first you don't succeed, try, try again," was a consistently successful white-tailed deer hunter. Over the years, that philosophy has helped me connect on several bucks, including a pair of whitetails I bagged during the fall of 1993.

The first was a 6-pointer taken at the end of the first week of Michigan's heavily hunted gun season. The second was a giant 10-pointer I shot during the last week of Saskatchewan's month-long firearms hunt. In both cases, most hunters had left the woods before I scored. No doubt, many of the hunters had filled a tag and were satisfied to quit for the year. Most of the unsuccessful hunters, however, had merely gone home, either because they ran out of time, grew weary of deer hunting or figured their chances were slim to none.

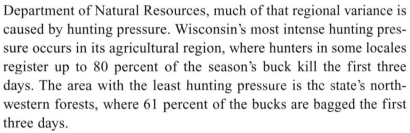

If you look at statistics, you can see why some hunters feel so hopeless after the season's first few days. For example, data gathered in Wisconsin from the mid-1980s through 1990, show that 60 percent to 80 percent of the gun season's buck kill occurs during the first three days, depending on the region. According to Arlyn Loomans, a wildlife manager with the Wisconsin Department of Natural Resources, much of that regional variance is caused by hunting pressure. Wisconsin's most intense hunting pressure occurs in its agricultural region, where hunters in some locales register up to 80 percent of the season's buck kill the first three days. The area with the least hunting pressure is the state's northwestern forests, where 61 percent of the bucks are bagged the first three days.

In some states, the lowest percentage of the kill occurs on the season's final day. For example, in Wisconsin, the percentage of the buck kill that day ranges by region between 2 percent and 2.6 percent, with a statewide average of 2.2 percent. Thanksgiving Day yields the second lowest percentage of the statewide buck harvest at 3 percent.

In general, the percentage of deer killed declines steadily as the season progresses. The biggest drops typically occur after the first and second days, and then blips of activity occur the rest of the season, with Saturdays usually netting the highest harvests.

Loomans said hunting pressure drops off just as dramatically as

Above: No matter what your goals or time limitations, you'll always improve your odds if you hunt until the season ends.

the kill, but detailed information on hunting effort is typically difficult to obtain. The trend is probably similar in other states, but not as dramatic where firearms seasons last longer than Wisconsin's nine-day event. In Michigan, for example, although a dip in hunting pressure occurs after the opening of its 16-day season, a survey found it likely isn't as steep as what's seen in Wisconsin. The year of the Michigan survey, 1985, about 39 percent of the total deer kill occurred on opening day, 11 percent on the second day, 9.3 percent on the third day, and 4.1 percent on the fourth day. Contrary to Wisconsin's experience, the last day was the fourth best day of the 1985 Michigan season, at 6.3 percent.

Although there was a dip in pressure during Michigan's season after the first three days, it wasn't dramatic. The first three days accounted for 13 percent, 12 percent and 10.5 percent of the season's total hunter days, respectively. Pressure remained moderate during most of the rest of the season, with an expected increase on the second weekend. There was just as much hunting effort on the last day of the season as the second Sunday, at 5.7 percent.

Michigan's longer season might tend to distribute the harvest and hunting pressure more evenly after the initial onslaught. If that's the case, we could assume it should work the same way in states and provinces with still longer seasons. That is often difficult to prove, however. Alabama's gun-hunt, for example, starts in late November and ends Jan. 31. Because Alabama's rut peaks in January, I thought a higher deer kill would result in that month.

However, David Nelson, an Alabama deer specialist, said data indicate the harvest trend is similar to other states, with the highest harvest occurring on opening day. He added that smaller harvest peaks occur on weekends and holidays, especially during good weather. Nelson said harvests are driven by hunter participation. The more hunters afield, the more deer are shot.

Despite such trends, I've always found that hunters who remain in the woods after the crowds go home have an excellent chance of success, sometimes even for a big buck. For example, I hunted in Alabama during January 1995, and had chances at a pair of 8-pointers during a week of hunting. I missed the first one because my scope had been knocked out of alignment, but the second buck wasn't so lucky. He was the larger of the two 8-pointers and was the largest buck taken by the camp's hunters during the season. The buck weighed 215 pounds on the hoof. Its heavy rack gross-scored 130 inches.

No doubt, most whitetails get shot each year during the gun season's first few days, which reduces the number of deer available. However, most hunters also go home after those first few days. That means there's less competition for the remaining deer, and that's usually enough to give serious hunters a good chance of getting one. In addition, they're likely to have a high-quality experience. The pace is often slower, more relaxed and less competitive later in the season. It also allows you to explore new areas without stumbling onto other hunters.

I shot that 6-pointer in Michigan's Upper Peninsula in 1993 at a site that was new to me. Because of other commitments, I had no time to scout the area during the preseason. Therefore, I began my late-season hunt by alternately sitting and still-hunting along abandoned logging roads.

Most of the first two days were uneventful. I saw some scattered rubs, scrapes and tracks, but no concentrated deer activity. I spent some time posted near the few scrapes I found, but soon resumed searching for better sites. I saw my first deer shortly before the second day ended as I still-hunted toward my truck.

The small-racked buck was trotting toward me down a logging road. I dropped to one knee as I raised my rifle, but the buck saw me move. He turned broadside and started running by the time I got him in my scope.

My shot missed him cleanly, but I searched the area intently that evening and again the next morning before resuming my scouting/still-hunting routine. After penetrating some new territory, I finally found what I was looking for: two fresh rubs and three scrapes close together. I posted nearby the remainder of the day, but failed to see anything.

However, I wasn't discouraged. Now that I had a focal point, I shifted to stand-hunting. I figured if I posted there long enough, I would eventually see one of the bucks that made the rubs and scrapes. Over the next few days, I discovered the area contained even more fresh rubs and scrapes. After unraveling a distinct scrape/rub line, I began posting downwind. I continued the vigil the next three days without seeing one deer. I was growing discouraged.

But something happened the third day on stand to renew my faith. Snow fell overnight and continued to come down until about an hour after daylight. When I hadn't seen anything by 2 p.m., I took a short walk to see if any deer had moved nearby. I found a set of fresh tracks that looked as if they had been made by a buck. More importantly, it appeared the prints were made after daylight because they contained little snow. If the buck followed a similar course the next morning, I figured I might have a chance of seeing him.

My confidence rose another notch when I left that evening and found three more fresh sets of tracks to the north, one of which

Above: Most hunters go home after the first few days of the season. That means there's less competition for the remaining deer, and that's usually enough to give serious hunters a good chance of killing one.

might have been made by a buck. When I returned before daylight the next morning, I found tracks everywhere. It looked as if one or two bucks had been chasing a doe.

Based on the fresh activity, I was confident of seeing a buck that day. Soon after daylight, I heard a deer behind me to the left at 30 yards. When I shot him, I thought his antlers had eight points, but I soon found this 3-year-old buck had no brow tines. My persistence had paid off! Based on the fact I heard only one other shot that morning, and saw just a few hunters' vehicles on the way home, I knew I was one of the few still hunting by the end of the season's first week.

My brother, Bruce, had a similar experience farther south in an area with a higher deer population. Coincidentally, he had also shot a 6-pointer the day before, and had heard only one other shot that morning. That spot is a perennial producer for Bruce, and because he had faith, he stuck with the stand after several uneventful days.

Weather conditions often have a major impact on deer activity and hunting success. As you know, the weather is indifferent to our desires for good hunting conditions. High heat, pouring rain, heavy snows or high winds can hurt our chances for success.

Although the weather conditions during that Michigan hunt weren't bad, they were far from ideal. The wind blew hard for several days, which generally reduces deer activity. When it stopped blowing on the sixth and seventh days, and the temperature stayed close to freezing, my brother and I scored. The fresh snow that fell in my area didn't hurt, either.

I've found that major storm fronts late in the season greatly boost a persistent hunter's chances. Whitetails are most active before the storm begins and then again after it's over. Three years ago, an approaching snowstorm that hit eight days into my Michigan hunt provided exceptional hunting for the two days preceding its arrival. During the first of those two days, I passed up a 3-pointer soon after daylight and soon saw several does and fawns file by. About 3:30 p.m., a big mature buck with a heavy 8-point rack chased a doe into view, and I dropped him cleanly.

Besides my success, at least two other bucks with notable racks fell that day in Michigan. For instance, Bill Smith and his son, Mark, enjoyed some incredible pre-storm success. Mark shot a 140-class 10-pointer at about 10 a.m., and Bill dropped an 18-pointer that scored more than 210 Boone and Crockett inches!

Persistence is especially important when hunting mature whitetails. If you've set high goals for yourself, you almost always need to hunt longer and harder than normal, which means passing up smaller bucks without regret.

This brings me to the second buck I bagged during 1993, one that required a lot of resolve. I made this hunt in late November, and my goal from the start was to shoot a whitetail with at least 10 points or an exceptional 8-pointer that scored at least 140. I knew my goals were realistic for that area.

Although the province's firearms season had been open since Nov. 1, and many big bucks had been shot, I saw at least one buck each of the four days I hunted, and shot one on the fourth day whose rack had 10 points and an inside spread of nearly 21 inches. I passed up three other decent bucks before getting him. Each of the bucks I let walk were beautiful in their own way, but only by being persistent and passing them up was I able to meet my goal.

No matter what your goals or time limitations, you'll always improve your odds if you hunt until the season ends. On several occasions, I've bagged bucks during the season's final minutes simply by being tenacious and flexibly using information gathered during previous days. If I decide to try a new area or new method, I don't wait until the next season. I adapt my hunt while time still remains in the current season. For example, on windy, stormy days when deer aren't likely to move, stand-hunting can be a waste of time, so I still-hunt or join other hunters to make drives.

Of course, it's not always necessary to modify your tactics or location to score late. I remember a forkhorn I once shot in the season's waning minutes. I had seen him several days earlier and passed him up, hoping for a chance at something bigger. When that hadn't happened as the season wound down, I shot the yearling the next time I saw him.

For that matter, the season's final days are often our last chance to fill antlerless deer tags. Shooting these deer not only secures good meat for the winter, but it represents good deer management. To maintain deer herds within the habitat's carrying capacity, we must often shoot does and fawns. In fact, given a choice, I'll pass up a yearling buck for an adult doe anytime it's legal.

Like any other deer hunting skill, patience doesn't come without practice. Never-say-die hunters aren't born that way. At one time, they probably struggled as much as anyone to stay in the woods when things got tough. But over time, the longer they stayed on stand, or stayed behind after everyone else went home, the more success stories they compiled.

MAJOR STORM FRONTS LATE IN THE SEASON GREATLY BOOST A PERSISTENT HUNTER'S CHANCES. WHITETAILS ARE MOST ACTIVE BEFORE THE STORM BEGINS AND THEN AGAIN AFTER IT'S OVER.

Deer Research: Doe Activity During the Rut

JOHN J. OZOGA, JUNE 1995

If you hunt whitetails during their breeding season — as most of us do — but don't understand the breedable doe's behavior, you could be in trouble. Like it or not, the buck you hunt is at the mercy of the estrous doe.

Or is he?

Plotting out-of-season buck movements, monitoring weather conditions, determining food sources, calculating moon phases, and so on, might be important and can contribute to success. No doubt a host of factors could provide clues about a buck's travel patterns. But all too often the estrous doe is the most potent force in determining a buck's whereabouts, behavior and vulnerability. All your careful plotting and meticulous strategies will likely go down the tube if the estrous doe unexpectedly appears in the wrong place at the right time.

Wildlife managers are also concerned about deer activity, especially during the breeding season, but for different reasons than the hunter. With regard to a deer's welfare, there's a definite relationship between the amount of energy taken in (food) vs. the amount spent (activity). An energy deficit during autumn, for whatever reason, can hurt a deer's physical condition, interfere with reproduction and lower survival rates during the critical winter months.

The rut is characterized by greatly increased movement among all deer, but especially so by bucks. Therefore, the rut demands that deer spend a lot of energy. Sometimes, greatly increased buck activity can be linked to higher-than-normal buck mortality during winter.

Mounting evidence also suggests an energy deficit during autumn can diminish the doe's physical condition and her breeding success. This means the rut's social stress can have the same damaging effects as nutritional stress on deer. Increased social (behavioral) stress can cause increased activity, depressed physical condition, delayed breeding, lower conception rates, increased foraging and damage to the environment. Ultimately, such factors lead to unhealthy fawns or no offspring at all.

Louis Verme and I explored the activity patterns of estrous whitetails more than 20 years ago. Consequently, I was captivated by a recent article in the *Journal of Mammalogy* by Rick Relyea and Stephen Demarais (1994), titled, "Activity of Desert Mule Deer During the Breeding Season."

Using motion-sensitive radio-collars, Relyea and Demarais found activity for mule deer bucks and does increased from pre-rut to post-rut. They also observed that bucks were most active around sunrise and sunset (crepuscular) during pre-rut and post-rut, but that female mule deer shifted their normal daily rhythm from being most active during twilight hours in pre-rut to constant during peak rut, followed by low levels of crepuscular activity during post-rut.

Relyea and Demarais speculated that changes in daily activity patterns of females could be caused by harassment of females by males. In their words, "Assuming our radio-collared females were bred during peak rut and a male could not differentiate a bred female from an unbred female until he approached her closely, pregnant females could reduce interactions with males by becoming less active during times of greatest activity of males and more active during times of lowest activity of males."

Because the behavior of mule deer differs quite markedly from that of whitetails during the breeding season, certain species' differences in activity patterns during the rut are expected. For one thing, white-tailed bucks also move outside of their normal home range, but only during peak rut, not normally throughout the pre-rut to post-rut period as with mule deer.

Most studies show that white-tailed does move shorter distances per day and concentrate their activities on a smaller portion of their range during the rut. During peak rut, females become more

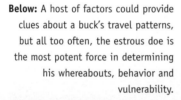

Below: A host of factors could provide clues about a buck's travel patterns, but all too often, the estrous doe is the most potent force in determining his whereabouts, behavior and vulnerability.

active, but tend to crisscross a smaller area. The advantage of this behavior is that the doe's urinary signals are concentrated during the breeding period, thereby enhancing doe-to-buck communication during the doe's short receptive period.

That means whitetails are most active during peak rut because bucks are traveling outside their home range searching for does, and does are walking intensively in a small area to attract bucks. Such behavior ceases after the breeding period.

While monitoring activity patterns of penned whitetails in the early 1970s (using an elaborate array of wiring, microswitches and event-recorders), I accidentally discovered that does became restless and began pacing in their pens shortly before mating. This observation led to a more intensive investigation of doe activity patterns during estrus, which we later published in the *Journal of Wildlife Management* (1975). Ultimately, we used a measure of the doe's activity as a means of predicting estrus. That information proved valuable in other reproductive studies and during some sophisticated studies of blood hormone changes around the doe's estrus period.

Our studies with penned does revealed that a doe will accept a buck only during a 24- to 36-hour period at peak estrus. However, we observed that in the absence of a tending buck, the doe became about 28 times more active than normal one to two nights before estrus. This restlessness coincides with increased ovarian production of estrogen, the female hormone that precipitates a doe's mating urge. In fact, we calculated that one doe walked more than 20 miles the night before she mated. Based on our findings, we theorized that such an increase in doe travel would be adaptive, in that the estrous doe would then more likely find a mate if one were not nearby.

Stefan Holzenbein and George Schwede (1989) tested our theory by monitoring the activities of eight radio-collared does at the National Zoo's Conservation and Research Center at Front Royal, Va. Instead of wandering extensively, however, seven of the does they tracked restricted their movements to core areas of their home range around the time of estrus. Bucks were apparently readily available and quick to locate does as they came into estrus. Presumably, all seven does were bred within core areas of their normal range.

Holzenbein and Schwede concluded that does usually make their location predictable by restricting their movements before becoming receptive, making it relatively easy for a buck to find them. Also, such a concentration of doe activity likely accounts for a buck's tendency to cluster his scrapes in certain locations where he might attract the greatest attention from prospective mates.

THERE'S SOME EXPERIMENTAL EVIDENCE THAT SUGGEST DOES ARE INDEED "MATE SELECTIVE," THEREBY RESPONDING MORE POSITIVELY TO ONE SUITOR THAN ANOTHER.

However, if a doe attains estrus without being found by a buck, she might wander extensively in search of a buck.

Some researchers suggest that estrus among all but the youngest of related reproducing females should be synchronous, because estrus can be induced by male-produced pheromones. If so, it's also conceivable that females compete for the attention of choice mates.

Subordination tends to have a strong suppressor effect on a doe's reproductive performance. Older, maternally experienced does within a clan are most dominant; they also control the most favorable habitat, maintain the best physical condition, and usually breed first. Therefore, if a dominant doe and a subordinate doe come into estrus at the same time, the dominant doe might displace the subordinate and copulate first. If this is the case, subordinate does are more likely to delay mating, more readily mate with a subordinate male, and are more inclined to go searching for mates.

There's some experimental evidence that suggests does are indeed "mate selective," thereby responding more positively to one suitor than another. In our studies at the Cusino enclosure in northern Michigan, for example, we found that does were more receptive to bucks similar to them in age. That is, mature does preferred to be courted by mature, rut-experienced bucks, while yearling does seemed intimidated by the real monarchs.

As researchers Larry Marchinton and Karl Miller note: "The whole process of chasing and courtship is a very visible one that exposes participants to risk from predators, both human and otherwise. This is the only time of the year when white-tailed deer, particularly bucks, forsake cover and put themselves into vulnerable positions."

Marchinton and Miller emphasize that such seemingly neurotic behavior has strong selective values. "It allows the doe to be bred by the most physically superior buck in the area. She dashes around in anthropomorphic terms, making quite a spectacle of herself — so that the local bucks become aware of her impending receptivity and join her entourage, at least until they are displaced by the largest buck. This competition among suitors usually assures that her offspring will be sired by the best buck she can find."

On the other hand, if adult does of a clan regroup during the breeding period, several does might come into estrus in the same general area within relatively few days. If several socially regrouped does come into estrus only a day or two apart, a dominant buck might remain with the clan a few days and breed several does in fairly rapid succession. In such cases, your potential trophy might be pretty well anchored in some distant location for a period of days, leaving you to ponder the reasons for his sudden departure from an otherwise predictable routine.

Keep in mind that many factors can account for differences in the estrous doe's behavior from one area to the next, which might have a strong bearing on buck behavior and hunting success. The timing, length and intensity of the breeding season, as well as the estrous doe's behavior, might differ sharply from North to South in particular. Important factors such as herd density and sex-age composition, which are often determined by the timing and intensity of buck harvesting, will greatly influence the stability and predictability of deer behavior during the rut.

In the North, the rut tends to be short but intense where we also see distinct regrouping of related females during pre-rut, especially in moderate- to high-density deer populations. The North's hunting seasons also tend to be held later, usually during or shortly after peak rut. In contrast, many Southern states have early deer seasons, sometimes resulting in a high buck harvest before peak rut. In some cases, buck harvesting might be so extreme that a buck shortage develops during the peak breeding period. This can produce erratic behavior by estrous does searching for mates.

One thing that has always impressed me about whitetails is their high degree of social order and elaborate communication used during the rut, especially when mature bucks are present. On the other hand, chaotic rut behavior prevails when intensive buck harvesting leaves only yearling bucks to fill the role of herd sires. You'll find that the seek-and-chase style of courtship among yearling bucks differs greatly from the more ritualized soliciting of attention demonstrated by rut-experienced mature bucks.

If you hunt a socially unbalanced deer herd in which mature sires are absent or in short supply, expect the local does to exhibit peculiar behavior during that brief period when they are in rut.

LITERATURE CITED

Holzenbein, S., and G. Schwede. 1989. "Activity and Movement of Female White-tailed Deer During the Rut." *Journal of Wildlife Management* 53:219-223.

Marchinton, R.L., and K.V. Miller. "The Rut." Pages 109-121, in D. Gerlach, S. Atwater and J. Schnell, eds. *Deer*. Stackpole Books, Mechanicsburg, Pa. 384 pages.

Ozoga, J.J., and L.J. Verme. 1975. "Activity Patterns of White-tailed Deer During Estrus." *Journal of Wildlife Management* 39:679-683.

Relyea, R.A., and S. Demarais. 1994. "Activity of Desert Mule Deer During the Breeding Season." *Journal of Mammalogy*. 75:940-949.

Tasty Myths: Is All Venison Created Equal?

RICHARD A. WULTERKENS, SEPTEMBER 1996

"**M**an, was that great venison! You sure could tell it came from a fawn."

"You might as well grind up that whole buck for sausage. The steaks from a big ol' guy like that will be too tough!"

"Of course the meat's not good. You gut-shot that doe, and it took her too long to die."

"Every farmland deer I've eaten tasted good. But those forest deer? They were hardly edible! Talk about a wild taste!"

"Wow, that was a tough steak! Didn't you let your deer hang?"

No doubt you've heard similar comments about the quality of white-tailed deer meat. But how many of the above claims are legitimate, and how many are bunk?

Opinions vary, but I believe the essence of deer meat is this: Venison is venison. That's right, it doesn't matter if you shot your deer in northern Minnesota or South Texas, the meat will taste the same. That's not to say myriad factors don't affect venison's taste before and after a deer is killed, but many strongly held beliefs have little foundation in fact. I would be willing to bet that even a dedicated epicure couldn't tell the difference under controlled laboratory conditions.

Therein lies a large riddle about venison's taste. The factors that affect venison seldom — if ever — occur under controlled conditions. Therefore, even if we could identify all factors, it would be impossible to consistently predict which deer will produce venison with the best taste and texture.

Why? Because even the factors — habitat, weather, food, time of season, wound location, trailing time, individual hunters and individual deer, to name a few — contain too many variables.

Nevertheless, let's examine some factors that contribute to venison's palatability. The more factors you learn to control — to whatever small degree — the better you can enhance the meat's taste and texture.

Let's recognize several truths about taste, starting with ourselves. First, the modern human palate is not discriminating. In fact, its ability to taste is pathetic. Countless centuries of evolution have eroded this sense. In contrast — out of necessity — evolution has enhanced the taste receptors of many species. How? A natural ability to select nutritious foods significantly improves survival.

Above: Although biochemical differences in the sexes are bound to affect venison, it would barely register with the average palate.

Therefore, the taste receptors of most prey species are highly developed. Modern humans, however, have no such need, so more vital aspects of our anatomy have been finely honed, most notably our brains. In fact, most of the five senses have suffered in humans when compared to those of other species.

Our palates have also been deadened by seasonings. The tongues of most North Americans have been so scrubbed by salt and other increasingly potent spices that we have nearly lost the ability to detect subtle taste differences. Nearly everything that's not spiced tastes bland to us. To compensate, we add even more spice to "awaken" our deadened taste buds.

Of course, let's not forget the damage done by smoking or chewing tobacco; drinking alcohol, coffee and chemically treated water; and living in sometimes polluted air and climate-controlled buildings.

The sense of taste also varies by individual. Just as some people see and hear better than others, some taste food better than others. This might be because of lifestyle or genetic make-up, but some of us can sense flavor changes much more acutely than others. And while technology can provide aids for vision and hearing-impaired people, no technological wizardry enhances our tasting proficiency.

Finally, our ability to detect taste differences is affected by emotion and suggestion. For example, preconceived notions about the taste of certain foods affect how we judge their quality. I'm always amazed when people say they don't like the taste of meat from certain wild birds or animals because it doesn't taste like chicken or beef.

They'll ask: "I've never had deer meat. What does it taste like?"

Well, honestly, it tastes like venison. A deer is not a cow. The need to compare one taste to another prevents us from appreciating differences in meats. I'm happy deer taste like deer and not a domesticated creature. After all, if we don't expect a steer to taste like pork, why should we expect deer to taste like beef?

We've also heard friends, family and "experts" discuss how certain factors affect the taste of venison. If we hear that old bucks taste bad, we consciously or subconsciously expect disappointment. If I prepared a roast from a yearling doe and told you it came from an 8-year-old, 230-pound rutting forest buck, I would likely alter your perception of its flavor.

Or would I? Regardless, various factors involving each deer play a role in venison's flavor, including the deer's age, diet and gender. One of the biggest misconceptions about venison is that habitat alone determines its flavor. Although diet affects the taste of meat, I believe the impact of this single variable is of little importance. Others agree.

In writing this article, I interviewed several well-traveled deer hunters. Among them was Charles Alsheimer, Northern field editor for *Deer & Deer Hunting*. Alsheimer said:

"I've killed a lot of deer in different places in North America. And I've heard all the stories, like the guy who says, 'I don't want a big North Woods whitetail because it'll taste like spruce trees. I'll be candid with you: I've hunted Anticosti Island, which is covered mainly by spruce and balsam fir. There is no farmland, and its deer gave me some of the best venison I've ever eaten."

Chuck Kuhns is a biochemist who has done research in human and animal medicine for Smith/Kline/Beecham and other companies. Kuhns said:

"It would take quite an extreme for the average person to detect a difference (based on a deer's diet)."

While Kuhns said high-carbohydrate foods like corn can make venison more palatable, he contends that a deer's diet isn't as important as it is for beef cattle. Why? Kuhns notes that venison lacks "marbling." As a result, its muscle tissue contains little "yellow fat," which is produced by high-carbohydrate food.

Still, others would argue that perhaps some taste-testers haven't traveled to the right places. Greg Miller, a frequent contributor to *D&DH*, said deer he has killed in Alberta consistently produce the tastiest venison.

"Their venison blows everything else away," Miller said. "There's no comparison. It's so mild. My dad has eaten a lot of venison over the past 40 years. I gave him some from one of my Canadian deer, and he kind of wrinkled up his nose,

Below: Venison's flavor hinges on field care. By allowing a deer's carcass to cool quickly, hunters can prevent unnecessary spoilage.

Above: Many factors that affect venison's quality are dictated more by the hunter than the deer. For example, proper field dressing, skinning and processing affect venison more than the deer's diet, age or sex.

like, 'Yeah, right. This is going to be different.' He couldn't believe how good it was."

Miller attributes this flavor to the fact those deer fed heavily on grain crops.

"It's the wheat and the different types of grain they eat," Miller said. "They seem to eat just the right amount of browse to go along with it."

Sylvia Bashline, *Outdoor Life's* food columnist, agrees with Miller. Bashline, who lives in Pennsylvania, said she has detected taste differences between the state's northern and southern deer. The northern deer eat primarily browse, while southern deer often eat agricultural crops.

"My husband and I grew up in the northern part of the state, and all the venison we ever ate came from there," Bashline said. "It was good, but it wasn't terrific. When we moved to the southern part of the state, we were amazed at how good deer could be."

What about the deer's age? I believe it's myth that older deer are so tough and "gamey" that they're inedible. Still, Kuhns said:

"The membranes in an older animal are thicker. Therefore, the meat will be a little tougher."

Kuhns believes that although thicker membranes and the necessary greater muscle density of older animals contribute to the meat's texture, age has little impact on its flavor. Neither does age have enough impact on meat's texture to be noticed by most people.

Neither Alsheimer or Miller give much weight to the idea that older deer taste significantly different than younger specimens. "People look at the big nontypical I have hanging in my house, and say, 'Boy, I bet he was tough.' No way. That was one of the best deer I ever ate, and he was more than 8 years old," Miller said. Alsheimer agrees: "We've gone the gamut. I've had older deer that tasted great, while I've shot some younger does that I thought were a little tough."

In fact, Bashline — a cookbook author — would rather shoot an older deer than a very young one.

"While fawns are good, they almost taste like veal. They really don't have that good venison flavor. I actually prefer a 2- or 3-year-old."

Will a deer's gender affect the venison's flavor? Kuhns said that while biochemical differences in the sexes are bound to affect venison, it would barely register with the average palate. He said estrogen in a doe would likely make its venison less tough, and the venison of a lactating doe would be even more affected.

Kuhns said male androgens (hormones) contribute to beliefs that bucks are more gamey than does. Still, he argues that venison from even a half-starved rutting buck living on his body fat would be indistinguishable from a lactating doe's.

Alsheimer said he has shot rutting bucks, their necks heavily swollen, that tasted great.

Without a doubt, a quick, clean kill contributes more to tasty venison than possibly any other factor, save field dressing. I haven't found anyone who would argue this point. If an animal is killed quickly and bleeds completely, the venison has little chance of degrading. However, poorly placed shots that make the deer suffer and allow it to flee can produce bad venison.

Kuhns notes that several chemicals can actually be toxic, and they can quickly enter the bloodstream of injured deer. This tainted blood is then absorbed rapidly into straining muscle fibers, wreaking havoc on the muscle's cells. Lactic acid, a waste product of oxidation in the cells, will build up.

In addition, the initial adrenaline rush of a wounded, frightened and stressed deer triggers the liver to release glycogen. Kuhns calls glycogen a "high-octane gasoline." It's the same mega-fuel that allows a human to perform extraordinary feats, like lifting an automobile off an injured child. Kuhns said the waste products of glycogen are much worse than those of the standard fuel, glycogen. A glycol infusion dilates the blood vessels, which causes an immediate imbalance in the semi-permeable membranes that make up muscle tissue's membranes. That process allows these waste fluids to leach into the cells, and thus, into the meat.

Kuhns added that the worst scenarios involve gut-shot deer. He also said a hit to the kidneys or the attendant renal artery "would be like dumping sewage treatment material directly into a public water supply." While most of this severely contaminated blood spills into the deer's body cavity, any that gets into the muscle fibers will taint the meat. And, the longer the deer survives, the greater the chance of that occurring.

Therefore, if a goal of every deer hunter is to eat the deer's meat, it's crucial that it be dispatched cleanly and quickly.

Miller relates a telling incident: "A guy going to town during the gun-deer season hit a deer with his truck and killed it. He got out, checked his truck and the deer, and saw it was a fawn that had been wounded. A

Below: Regardless of how cleanly a deer is killed, the animal should be field dressed as soon after the kill as possible. Careful knife work while field dressing is crucial to a clean end-product.

hunter and his buddies tracked the deer to the roadside, and offered the deer to the truck driver because he had smashed up his vehicle. He took it, but he told me the venison was terrible. He had to cook it in a Crock-Pot."

Miller and Alsheimer believe bow-wounded deer suffer less from this phenomenon than gun-wounded deer. They think the tremendous shock and tissue damage caused by bullets put the deer into immediate fright and flight. Bow-wounded deer, however, typically aren't as pulverized and frightened.

"Bow-shot deer often succumb to their wounds with relatively little awareness of pain or danger," Miller said. "They don't get excited."

Alsheimer agreed. "You shoot a deer with a bow and arrow, he doesn't know what hit him," Alsheimer said. "He'll often die within sight of you. What's crazy is I've had them go back to grazing after I shot. I thought I missed, but pretty soon they fell dead."

Another crucial factor affecting venison's flavor is how the carcass and meat are handled, from field dressing, to transporting, to hanging, to butchering and to packaging.

Immediate, proper field dressing allows for quality venison. It's important to evenly and totally cool the meat to prevent spoilage. Too many people botch what should be a simple process by cutting into the stomach, intestines or bladder while field dressing the deer. This can contaminate the body cavity and hasten bacterial growth in

Below: Most venison fanciers prefer the meat be boned, not run through a band saw. Sawing up a carcass can give the meat an "off flavor," which some folks call "aftertaste."

warm weather, which promotes tainting and spoiling. Also, some hunters split the hind quarters and the pelvic bone, exposing this meat to dirt and other debris.

As soon after the kill as possible, the body cavity should be thoroughly rinsed with clean water, regardless of how cleanly the deer was shot and dressed. Alsheimer said he always skins his deer within 24 hours and washes them completely with a hose. Then he wraps the carcass in clear plastic, which clings to the skinned carcass and prevents drying. He's convinced his method ensures quality venison.

Transporting a deer carcass can pose problems, too. Exposing the meat to sunlight, engine heat, flying dirt and engine exhaust lessens your chances of obtaining good venison. Use common sense. If air temperatures are above 40 degrees, consider boning out the meat and packing it with ice inside a cooler. That's assuming, of course, you've already registered the deer and kept the necessary tags and paperwork.

Hanging a deer for several days to "age" it will not enhance the venison unless it's done correctly under controlled conditions. Aging meat is a delicate business, and temperature is critical. Too warm and the meat spoils. Too cold and it freezes too quickly, forming ice crystals that burst muscle cells.

A proper aging temperature for venison must be consistent at about 40 degrees, and not fluctuate more than a degree or two. Hanging a deer from a tree or barn rafters longer than a day or two will probably not do the trick. Only slaughterhouses with large, walk-in coolers are equipped to properly age meat. Another alternative, Bashline said, is to bone or quarter the carcass and store it in a refrigerator for a prescribed time.

What aging accomplishes, Kuhns says, is not putrefaction. If done right, it's merely a softening process. Aging, he said, "allows anaerobic enzymes in muscle cells to help the cell feast on itself." This softens or degrades the membranes to where you can cut the meat with your fork. Proper aging merely changes the meat's consistency, not the flavor, although many argue that texture and flavor go hand in hand.

Above: Most professional processors or self-trained experienced cutters agree to several truths. The first: All fat should be trimmed from the meat before it's eaten or wrapped. This is white fat, or "tallow." Tallow is greasy and unpalatable.

Processing deer provides another opportunity to alter the venison's taste. Most professional processors or self-trained experienced cutters agree to several truths. The first: All fat should be trimmed from the meat before it's eaten or wrapped. This is white fat, or tallow, not the yellow fat referred to earlier. Tallow is greasy and unpalatable.

Also, most venison fanciers prefer the meat be boned, not run through a band saw. Boning the meat not only saves freezer room, but it also improves the meat's taste. Sawing up a carcass can give the meat an "off-flavor," which some folks call an "aftertaste." This occurs when the saw spreads the deer's bone marrow across the venison's surface.

I haven't had a bad-tasting piece of venison since I replaced my bone saw with fillet knives. Keeping the deer's hair off the meat also helps keep the venison pure.

Wrapping the meat in airtight packages and thoroughly freezing it also helps protect venison's taste. Kuhns said 5-mil, high-density polyethylene is the best packaging material because it's strong and prevents bacteria from forming.

The best temperature for long-term meat storage is absolute zero, but that's outside the range of the average home freezer. Kuhns said routine meat storage, with an expected shelf life of six months, requires a freezer temperature of about 25 degrees. The breakdown or ruin of frozen meat is caused mainly by three things: oxidation, poor packaging and enlarging ice crystals that rupture the walls of muscle cells.

By now you can see how many elements affect the taste of venison, which ones can be controlled, and how much misinformation exists. Now it's time to discuss a vital link between venison and its taste: preparation.

Before most venison is cooked, it must be defrosted. The best way to defrost meat is slowly. Kuhns said the condition of the muscles should dictate the cooking method. A good chef always watches how fast thawing meat loses its water/blood. If the venison's membranes are fairly intact, which keeps the juices inside, the meat is a good candidate for roasting or grilling. If the membranes are leaking badly upon defrosting because ice crystals ruptured them, the venison should be used for stew or sausage.

Bashline believes venison should be prepared as simply as possible to let its true flavor emerge. She favors a low-heat, long-cooking approach or a high-heat, sear-it and serve-it medium-rare method. She further encourages few seasonings, preferring the meat's unadulterated taste.

Still, Bashline and most serious venison fans agree on the most common venison-cooking mistake: over-cooking. Because venison is virtually fat-free, there's little to prevent it from becoming dehydrated during cooking, which renders it unpalatable. Most people

Below: Hanging a deer for several days to "age" it will not enhance the venison unless it's done correctly under controlled conditions. In other words, deer cannot be aged properly from a meat pole.

fry, bake or grill their venison so completely that it becomes dry, rubbery and tasteless. As Bashline says, "They try to kill it again — in the kitchen."

Although their supposed intentions might be good — eliminating any possible contamination from bacteria and parasites — they cheat themselves of venison's true taste. Besides, deer meat is probably more pure and free from contaminants than most supermarket meat.

Above: The factors that affect venison seldom — if ever — occur under controlled conditions. As a result, even if we could identify all the factors, it would be impossible to consistently predict which individual deer will produce venison with the best taste and texture.

To be safe, though, Alsheimer and others recommend venison be cooked to an internal temperature of 160 degrees for two to three minutes to kill even the most stubborn bacteria and other nasties.

Some research even hints it's possible, in theory, for Lyme disease to be transmitted through undercooked meat, but it hasn't been proven.

That means no more blood-rare venison.

"It's going to be hard for me to give up my rare venison, the chops and things like that," Bashline said. "It would be as painful as pulling a tooth."

Alsheimer, Bashline and Miller also believe the cook is the ultimate provider of tender, good-tasting venison.

"If you have a guy or gal who really knows what they're doing, that can make a huge difference," Alsheimer said.

Indeed. Most tough meat is more a result of matching a particular cut of venison with the wrong recipe, and most gamey meat is caused by a putz behind the pan.

Any good restaurant-goer knows a good chef can turn even a bad piece of meat into a dish fit for royalty. Unfortunately, most folks don't have the talent or time to transform a scrap of poorly shot and handled venison into gourmet fare.

Good venison depends on a variety of factors, some with far greater consequence than others. If you want your deer's meat to taste good, you must develop a careful, unvarying routine to handle the meat from the time it's part of a living deer to when you're cutting it up on your plate.

Once you've mastered those factors, you'll never again allow myths and misinformation to taint your venison's taste.

ABOUT THE AUTHOR
A seasoned whitetail hunter from the Midwest, Richard Wulterkens teaches creative writing to high school students. He became a regular contributor to *D&DH* in 1993.

Clear-Cut Tactics
for Clear-Cuts

GREG MILLER, NOVEMBER 1996

Although research clearly shows white-tailed deer are mainly browse eaters, many hunters have a hard time believing it. After all, farmland hunters most often see deer in agricultural fields, eating everything from alfalfa and corn to soybeans and wheat.

Still, whitetails can be hard to read. Just because you've seen deer feeding on crops doesn't mean they don't prefer browse such as buds, leaves and other "forest products."

Have you ever watched deer make their way to and from the fields? What were they doing? Chances are they were nibbling on twigs, branches, leaves and brush. In other words, they were eating browse!

While being able to identify preferred browse can be beneficial to those who hunt farmland whitetails, it's more of an asset for hunters who hunt deer in a big-woods environment. That's simply because forest deer typically eat nothing more than browse. After you know what the deer are eating, everything else sort of falls into place.

When I first started hunting the big woods, it was difficult to find browse sources because logging activity was minimal. In my opinion, logging makes big-woods hunting much easier. Today, instead of having to spend time learning what deer are eating and where to find it, all I do is look for a clear-cut. Clear-cuts provide big-woods deer with abundant browse.

Although clear-cuts benefit whitetails, they can be discouraging to hunters. How many of us have made a trip to one of our favorite hunting areas to do some spring scouting only to find the woods we've hunted for years has disappeared? Instead of a wooded expanse of perfect white-tailed deer habitat, all we see are thousands of stumps, a tangled mess of discarded tree-tops and deeply rutted trails. Where you once had difficulty seeing more than 50 yards, you can now see nearly a half-mile. Your favorite corner of the forest is gone!

True, clear-cuts are an eyesore and a reason for discouragement — at least at first. However, given a few years, a clear-cut will become tremendous deer habitat. Clear-cuts create an instant attraction for whitetails. Think about it. As soon as the first tree hits the ground, there's a new, highly nutritious food source available. The discarded treetops left behind by loggers provide deer with succulent and tender browse that, until the trees were cut, was unavailable.

Felled trees can provide several deer with an adequate supply of browse for a long time. In many cases, deer will remain near a clear-cut until other food sources emerge from new growth. Actually, it's a cycle. Felled trees act as attractants in winter and then, just about the time deer are nipping off the last of the discarded tops, other preferred foods begin to appear: first, grass and weed growth, then tender poplar, birch, oak and maple shoots, depending on the region. Suddenly, there's food everywhere.

To better understand clear-cuts, it's important to know how deer use clear-cuts of different progressions. For instance, it's obvious that first-year clear-cuts don't provide the type of cover whitetails require for bedding, even in fair to warm weather. So, although whitetails will frequent first-year cuts daily, these visits will be for feeding only. Deer will seek bedding cover elsewhere.

If hunting pressure isn't too intense, deer using a first-year clear-cut will form predictable patterns. They'll leave their bedding areas and head to the clear-cut just before dark, and they'll remain there until first light. Most deer hunters realize that any time deer get into such predictable patterns, success rates rise.

The best way to unravel deer movements in a clear-cut is to figure out how deer are approaching and departing a first-year cut. Walk the perimeter of the clear-cut and pay attention to all active runways. Your priority is to find the runways that show evidence of buck travel. These runways should be fairly easy to identify because they'll contain numerous scrapes and rubs. Because I prefer to hunt for mature bucks, I'll establish stand sites along buck travel routes where I find the largest antler rubs. If the areas you hunt experience a lot of pressure, I doubt you'll catch a mature buck near a first-year clear-cut during daylight. You would be wise to follow buck travel routes some distance away from the cut before looking for stand sites. How far is far enough? I start by placing my stands several hundred yards from the clear-cut. If I don't see any daylight buck activity after a couple of hunts, I'll move even farther away. I'll keep moving farther into the forest until I see bucks during the day.

Regrowing clear-cuts provide deer with food and cover for up to 10 years. This can create a tough situation for hunters. Instead of having to bed in outlying areas, deer can find adequate cover inside these now-thick clear-cuts. In most instances, they can literally stand up from their beds and start feeding. The hunting problem with this scenario is that deer have no reason to leave the clear-cut. It's much like deer that live inside cornfields until they're cut. And, because visibility in regrowing clear-cuts is seldom more than a few feet, your chances of shooting a buck while hunting from the

THE MOST EFFECTIVE STRATEGY FOR DEALING WITH TOUGH-TO-HUNT CLEAR-CUTS IS TO USE PORTABLE TREE STANDS AND HUNT ALONG THE EDGE OF THE CUT. IT'S ALSO WISE TO PUT IN SOME EXTRA SCOUTING TIME IF YOU LOCATE SUCH AN AREA.

ground are just above zero.

The most effective strategy for dealing with tough-to-hunt clear-cuts is to use portable tree stands and hunt along the edge of the cut. It's wise to put in some extra scouting time if you locate such an area. Don't fall into the trap of locating a productive clear-cut and then blindly placing your stand in the nearest tree.

Before I select my stand sites, I'll scout as much of the cut area as possible. I want to know exactly where the deer feed, bed and travel. I'll also try to find out where spooked bucks will attempt to head back into the cut. Information of this kind can be invaluable for determining precise stand placement.

Unfortunately, proper stand placement in clear-cuts often means going higher in a tree than normal. When gun-hunting a clear-cut, you'll want to be higher than the regrowth, and that usually means you'll have to place your stand 30 feet or higher. A few warnings: This tactic is not for those who have even the slightest fear of heights, nor is it practical when a stiff wind is blowing. Besides being unsafe, hunting high off the ground during windy conditions makes it difficult to shoot accurately. I'm speaking from experience.

The term "clear-cut" is a bit deceiving. Although it implies complete removal of every plant and tree from an area, a clear-cut is usually a well-thought-out operation. Provided loggers followed some practical guidelines, they'll usually leave many trees standing. These "sentinel" trees have played a huge role in my hunting party's success rate on mature bucks.

In most of the logged areas I've hunted, the trees that were left standing were large pine, oak and ash. However, it doesn't matter what species of trees are left standing. As long as some are left, I can almost guarantee deer will frequent the clear-cut.

My brother Mike was the first of our group to take advantage of this aspect of deer behavior. Starting in the mid-1970s, Mike reeled

Above: While clear-cuts can provide ample food for whitetails for several years, the high-quality browse is usually depleted within 10 years.

Above: White-tailed deer visually relate to any tall trees that are left behind in clear-cuts. These "sentinel" trees can be productive stands sites.

off an impressive record of 11 bucks in 11 gun seasons while hunting from a big pine tree that loggers had left standing in a clear-cut. At the time, we believed the pine just happened to be in a perfect spot. However, after studying dozens of similar situations, we now know it was more a case of deer changing their travel patterns so they could relate to that tree.

In snow country, deer have a tendency to relate to large pines. Deer frequent pine sites because they're one place other than roads or snowmobile trails where deer can travel easier after heavy snowfalls. In fact, it's hard to comprehend how much time deer spend under pines. While scouting and looking for shed antlers in spring, I've seen unbelievable instances where layers of deer droppings blanketed the bases of large pines. It's obvious the deer that wintered in those areas spent most of their time under those pines.

For traveling purposes, whitetails relate to sentinel trees long before an area is clear-cut. Therefore, whenever I scout a clear-cut, regardless of its age, my first move is to note all sentinel trees.

An easy way to find sentinel trees is to walk a clear-cut and note well-used deer trails. The trails are almost always original deer trails that follow geographical features. However, clear-cutting activity causes deer to rely on these trails even more. By placing a portable stand in one of these sentinel trees, you'll be able to cover the runways that pass directly under that tree and much of the surrounding area. It's a tactic my hunting partners and I have used to take many bucks over the years.

Trees are not the only things deer relate to. Whitetails in other parts of North America also relate to highly visible structure. For example, I've seen deer in Texas and Canada that related to old windmills as visual signposts. Just like sentinel trees in clear-cuts, the windmills acted as a "waypoint" for deer. Regardless of which direction they came from, just about every one of those deer eventually made their way to the visual signpost.

Mature bucks react similarly to 2- to 10-year-old clear-cuts, spending much time sleeping, feeding and traveling in regrowth areas. And they will use these areas as sanctuaries when pressured. An experience our hunting group had with a big buck nearly 20 years ago comes to mind.

Our group was making a drive through a 6-year-old clear-cut. About halfway through the drive, we jumped a big buck. However, instead of "playing by the rules" and running past one of our standers, the buck circled around and ran out back of the drive. With about 4 inches of fresh snow on the ground, we knew we had ideal tracking conditions. As it worked out, my dad volunteered to track the buck, while the rest of us posted along known buck crossings.

While tracking the buck, Dad noticed something interesting: The more pressure he put on the deer, the more the buck tended to stay away from thick regrowth areas. He traveled into the regrowth, but only for a short distance. Then he would head back into the more open hardwoods. Unfortunately, we were sure the buck would stick close to the thick cover, and we posted accordingly. Of course, we never got into position to ambush the buck.

Since that experience, we've seen several mature bucks display this same behavior. Obviously, most mature bucks prefer to have as much visibility as possible, and the last place they'll be able to see is in a thick regrowth area. So, while they bed, feed and travel in clear-cuts, mature bucks quickly vacate these areas when the heat is on.

Clear-cut areas older than 10 years are less appealing to whitetails. At 10 years, the regrowth is getting to the point where it's no longer providing much food. Second, there's a severe lack of cover in clear-cuts of this age class. Most or all of the underbrush has been choked out by the thick canopy of the now tall regrowth. Although they might pass through these areas, deer usually won't bed or feed in older clear-cuts. When this happens, you would be wise to relocate your hunting efforts to a fresh clear-cut.

The high demand for paper products has meant a steady increase in the amount of logging activity in big-woods environments. Although it's initially discouraging to see your favorite public hunting land decimated by logging, the shock will wear off when the barren land begins to grow anew, and you'll realize how to take advantage of the tremendous hunting potential clear-cuts provide.

ABOUT THE AUTHOR
Wisconsin native Greg Miller disdains gimmicks and supposed shortcuts when hunting whitetails. In fact, he became a big-buck hunter the hard way — by chasing whitetails on public land for more than 25 years. He became a regular contributor to *D&DH* in 1992.

SILVER SEASON
1997 TO 2002

From Buttons to Boone & Crockett

CHARLES J. ALSHEIMER, AUGUST 1999

The Quality Deer Management movement has the attention of deer hunters everywhere. Wherever I go, people want to talk about it. If you were to hear their questions, you would think there's a magic formula for producing record-class bucks.

I'm amazed at the number of people who believe big bucks can be raised from a bag of minerals or clover seed. I'm equally amazed by the number of times I've heard hunters say that age is all it takes to grow a buck of Boone and Crockett standards. In fact, getting a whitetail from the "button buck" stage to the B&C category is a mystical journey that includes complex variables.

As a teen, I believed age and quality food sources were the magical ingredients to producing a 170-inch buck. As I increased my reading, I realized there was far more to the equation. I also realized that even if the equation is defined, it doesn't guarantee a buck will grow B&C antlers.

In 1995, my son and I built a deer research facility on our farm. Since then, I've worked with some of the most knowledgeable whitetail people in North America to learn more about the growth potential of bucks. Their insights, and the results from my research, shed new light on this topic.

It takes four basic ingredients to produce a buck with a 170-inch rack. In order of importance, these ingredients are genetics, habitat, herd management and age.

Despite the explosion of deer knowledge, many hunters still wonder why their areas can't produce record-class bucks. In reality, the environment required to produce high numbers of B&C bucks doesn't exist. Furthermore, even if an area provides the four ingredients, those components must align flawlessly to produce several record-class bucks. Even perfect conditions do not guarantee B&C bucks.

To see how tough it is to raise a whitetail from a fawn to a Booner, let's look at two scenarios — the real world and a controlled environment — to see how various factors affect antler growth.

The real world is any place in North America with free-roaming whitetails. These deer must cope with everything nature and man throw at them. The stress heaped on them often borders the absurd, and in turn, suppresses antler growth.

I believe stress on free-ranging deer is cumulative, and antler growth is suppressed in varying degrees depending on how many stress factors

Above: It's no coincidence that some of the biggest bucks come from fertile-soil regions. For example, the "Grain Belt" of the Midwest contains some of the most productive soil in North America.

are placed on a herd.

Whitetails still deal with environmental stress factors even when human activity is removed from an area. For example, in remote Southern locations, extreme heat and parasites heavily burden deer herds.

In Northern climates, whitetails have an added problem: brutal winters with deep snow and bitter cold temperatures. Winter's stress can severely suppress antler growth, especially when it produces severe over-browsing of deer range by foraging herds.

No matter where it occurs, drought is a major suppressant of antler growth, especially if it occurs during the critical antler-growing season of April through July. Whitetails need large quantities of lush food to produce full-potential antlers.

Insects are another environmental stressor. Swarms of insects not only kill domestic animals, but they also kill deer.

Most deer need nearly 2 tons of food per year to maintain optimum health. For antler growth, it's critical the nutritional composition of food is optimum at all times. Therefore, during the antler-growing season, food sources must be high in proteins and provide essential vitamins and minerals. During the non-antler growing season — fall through early spring — food sources need to be high in carbohydrates to provide deer with high energy levels.

Habitat, and its ability to support a variety of crops and browse species, is another key to antler growth. Bucks grow impressive antlers when they receive a variety of foods. However, these food sources disappear quickly when too many deer are on a property. Therefore, bucks living on overpopulated range won't always grow large racks.

Unfortunately, the food equation cannot be solved by simply planting crops. For example, soil is often overlooked. It's no coincidence that some of the biggest bucks come from fertile-soil regions. For example, the Midwest's "Grain Belt" contains some of the most productive soil in North America. With this in mind, it's easy to understand why the Midwest has produced 61.6 percent of white-tailed bucks entered in the B&C record book through 1993.

A region's deer population is as important as food availability in allowing a buck to reach maximum antler potential. Antler growth suffers when populations exceed the land's carrying capacity.

Dave Griffith and his brother Rick operate a state-of-the-art deer genetic/semen collection operation in Huntingdon, Pa. After years of observing antler growth in their breeder bucks, the Griffiths have made

some interesting conclusions.

"Whitetails are very sensitive to overpopulation and do poorly if there are too many deer," Dave Griffith said. "We've found that if we leave a breeder buck with a group of does from breeding time to fawning time the buck's antlers are almost always smaller the next year. When we remove the buck from the does right after the breeding is over, antler growth doesn't suffer. Bucks — especially top-end bucks — do better when they can be alone or in bachelor groups.

"We know that if bucks are forced to be around too many deer, they'll seldom reach their full antler potential."

A deer herd's sex ratio is a significant suppressant of antler growth, and it doesn't take many deer to skew the odds against bucks.

For example, antler growth suffers in areas that have more than three adult does for every antlered buck. When herds exceed this ratio, the rut stretches to a danger point for bucks, especially mature bucks. A 2-

Above: No matter where it occurs, drought is a major suppressant of antler growth, especially if it occurs during the critical antler-growing season of April through July.

Above: If you add the fierce competitions waged between bucks to the list of stress factors these animals endure the rest of the year, it's easy to determine why free-ranging bucks have difficulty reaching their antler potential.

to-1 ratio isn't bad, but, for maximum growth potential, an area should have only one adult doe for every antlered buck.

The rut lasts about 45 days on range with balanced ratios. However, when the doe-to-buck ratio exceeds three does for every antlered buck, the rut can last 90 days. That's dangerous, because in the North, that means the rut will stretch into winter. In turn, rutting bucks enter this critical period so worn down they can't recover before their antlers begin to grow in April. In such instances, it's not uncommon for mature bucks to die from additional winter stress.

Tom Morgan is a deer breeder from Union City, Pa. Over the years, Morgan has studied how stress affects deer herds.

"Everyone knows that the rut drives a white-tailed buck crazy, and it doesn't matter if the buck is behind a high fence or roaming in the wild," Morgan said. "We've discovered that if you let a buck breed more than 10 does there is a high probability that his body cannot recover before he begins to grow another set of antlers. And, if he's physically behind in April, his antlers will be smaller than the previous year."

Dave Griffith agreed.

"Allowing a buck access to too many does is not the way to go if maximum antler growth is your goal. A buck cannot control himself during the rut, and too many does will drain a buck of everything he has in him," Griffith said. "When a doe comes into heat she takes a buck on a 24-hour ride he can't control. Because he doesn't know when enough is enough, he gets himself into all kinds of trouble — often trouble he can't recover from."

If all those stresses aren't enough, bucks receive another dose of pressure when the rut begins. If you add the fierce competitions waged between bucks to the list of stress factors they endure the rest of the year, it's easy to determine why free-ranging bucks have difficulty reaching their antler potential.

On good range, bucks are rolling in fat when the chase phase of the rut begins. However, during a two-week period just before full-blown breeding, bucks begin to move constantly, searching for estrous does. This non-stop dash to ensure survival of the species involves everything from chasing to scraping and from rubbing to fighting.

Bucks not only expend a lot of energy during the rut, they often do so at the expense of eating. With these things in mind, it's easy to

understand what kind of stress the rut brings to the white-tailed buck's world.

Predation is another stress factor that affects growth potential. Dogs, coyotes, wolves and humans kill hundreds of thousands of deer each year. However, non-contact predation also affects deer.

Non-contact predation includes the mere presence of predators. This stress can cause bucks to grow underdeveloped antlers. Several projects conducted by Aaron Moen of Cornell University illustrate this point.

In one project, Moen studied the effects of disturbance by snowmobiles on heart rates of captive deer. He also studied the heart rates of fawns in response to wolf howls.

The average heart rate of a white-tailed deer varies in different settings. A bedded deer has a heart rate of about 72 beats per minute. Other rates include standing, 86 beats per minute; walking, 102 beats per minute; and running, 155 beats per minute.

In the fawn study, Moen found that wolf howls increased a deer's heart rate to as much as 265 beats per minute. In the snowmobile study, heart rates were as high as 209 beats per minute.

Although it hasn't been documented, hunting pressure certainly has a similar effect on whitetails. Stress on deer can be great in areas with long seasons and high numbers of hunters.

What does this research prove? Well, an increased heart rate increases metabolism, which depletes fat reserves. The bottom line is any form of predation places some stress on whitetails, which can prevent them from reaching their growth potential. By reducing stress associated with the six factors listed above, you can improve the odds of watching a buck fawn grow into a B&C-class whitetail.

Some people might argue that it's impossible to reduce some of the stress factors because of the region they live in. However, today's high-tech age makes those unthinkable goals reality. The answer lies in controlled environments.

Many deer breeders have experimented and discovered what it takes to raise trophy-class bucks. Of course, their work is done behind high fences, where deer are raised in relatively stress-free conditions. To produce big bucks, most breeders become students of genetics, and they meticulously study individual deer for desired characteristics.

"After genetics I look at a host of factors that I have to build on to get full antler potential," Morgan said. "I see habitat as critical. If a buck's environment is not right — it doesn't matter what kind of genetics he has — he will not reach his full potential. So this means controlling and improving everything from natural settings to a balanced diet to eliminating the number of other deer he can interact with to allowing no dogs near the buck.

"I've been in this game long enough to know that if I can't provide a top breeder buck with the best of conditions, I can't expect him to grow the kind of antlers I think he's capable of," Morgan added.

The Griffith brothers employ a similar approach. They use elaborate breeding and handling facilities to keep their top-end bucks calm and comfortable. By catering to a buck's every need and purging stress from the animal's life, the Griffiths produce record-class bucks.

To further reduce stress on their deer, the Griffiths prevent bucks from breeding too many does. For example, their top breeder buck, Goliath, was allowed to breed just five does in 1998. Combined with the stress-free environment, the buck grew a 250-inch nontypical rack.

"To reach optimum antler growth, every white-tailed buck needs to go into a new antler-growing season with a full tank, so to speak," Dave Griffith said. "Think of it this way: A whitetail's bone marrow system is like a fuel tank. If their bone marrow and body condition are not full and in top condition when the sun says, 'Start growing antlers!' they can't possibly reach their full antler potential. So, body maintenance is critical when it comes to antler growth. Removing stress helps

Above: Dogs, coyotes, wolves and humans kill hundreds of thousands of deer each year. However, non-contact predation, the mere presence of predators, also affects deer. For example, in a study of white-tailed fawns, researchers found that wolf howls increased a deer's heart rate to as much as 265 beats per minute.

achieve the results we're looking for."

Despite the fact huge bucks like Goliath are grown in controlled environments, there's no question much can be learned from these deer. Knowing their full potential puts many other things in perspective.

For example, when analyzing various regions for antler potential, I look at how an area stacks up against the six stress factors. If an area is affected by all six, there is strong reason to believe top-end potential won't exist. However, if an area is affected by only two factors, I want to hunt there because I know the area probably holds many big bucks.

That's not to say I'm a trophy hunter. In fact, I believe many hunters put too much emphasis on the magic antler score of 170 — the minimum score for entry into Boone and Crockett's record book for typical white-tailed bucks.

I believe it's unrealistic for hunters to believe they actually stand a chance of killing a buck that big in the wild. I have chased whitetails more than 30 years, and only once have I killed a buck that grossed more than 170 points on the B&C scoring system. In other words, a 170-class wild buck is a freak of nature.

When hunters ask me what kinds of bucks they can expect to see in places like western Canada and Texas, I tell them not to base their goals on what they read in magazines or see on television.

Be realistic and try to find out what the average size is for bucks in a given area. I believe a realistic expectation for hunts in the best deer habitat in North America is 140 B&C. The bottom line is this: Considering all the stress factors that weigh on a deer herd, it's difficult to find 150-inch bucks in the wild. In many places, few, if any, exist.

In fact, research tells us that the 140- and 150-inch bucks living in Saskatchewan, Wisconsin and New York could easily be 160- to 170-inch bucks if they lived in controlled environments. Furthermore, most deer researchers will tell you that heavy stress, be it drought, predators, severe winters or environmental factors, can suppress antler growth by as much as 20 percent.

There's a whole lot more to getting a white-tailed buck from buttons to B&C antlers than meets the eye. In fact, for most bucks roaming North America, it's an impossible or, at best, nearly impossible mission.

Future hunters probably will kill huge bucks that rival the B&C whitetails killed by Milo Hanson and James Jordan. These awesome bucks are a part of the mystery of life, just like 7-foot basketball players and home-run hitters like Mark McGwire. However, is it realistic to think the road from buttons to B&C is a given? Not hardly. For my money, 140 inches is about as good as it gets, even in the better fair-chase areas.

Stress comes in myriad forms, and one thing is certain: It hurts the hat size of every buck in the wild.

THERE'S A LOT MORE THAN MEETS THE EYE TO GETTING A WHITE-TAILED BUCK TO GROW FROM BUTTONS TO B&C ANTLERS. IN FACT, FOR MOST BUCKS, IT'S AN IMPOSSIBLE, OR, AT BEST, NEARLY IMPOSSIBLE, MISSION.

Felled by Firebolts

DANIEL E. SCHMIDT, MARCH 2001

Two central Wisconsin hunters have practiced quality deer management for years without seeing a record-class buck up close. That changed when they stepped into a familiar alfalfa field Sept. 5, 2000, and saw two record-class whitetails.

Unfortunately, the bow season was 11 days away, and the bucks of their dreams were already dead. The cause of death? A single lightning bolt.

The bucks — a 140-class 12-pointer and a 160-class 11-pointer — were found by Lee Larson, a Waupaca County dairy farmer who was preparing to make hay four days after a storm. After realizing how big the bucks were, he contacted two of his friends who are avid deer hunters.

Matt Sullivan was one of the first people to inspect the bucks. After calling *Deer & Deer Hunting's* editorial office to report the bizarre incident, he drove me to the scene.

Although the ground beneath the bucks wasn't charred, burn marks on the deer clearly indicated they were hit by lightning. The larger buck, the 11-pointer, suffered burns to the chest and the side of its head. The hair on the buck's chest was singed almost to the skin.

The 11-pointer had recently shed its velvet, revealing a spectacular rack with forked G-2 tines and intense knurling throughout the beams. The antlers were still stained with blood from when the buck peeled its velvet. Its rack grossed 167 Boone and Crockett points.

The 12-pointer suffered a lateral burn in the middle of its back. The buck's right antler beam was lightly covered with velvet, and the left beam was partially peeled. The rack, which netted 143 B&C points, featured forked tines and widely palmated beams.

Although rare, deer deaths from lightning have been documented throughout North America. In his book *The Deer of North America*, Leonard Lee Rue III wrote that he has seen many photos of deer that were killed by lightning.

"A close friend of mine found two fine bucks that were killed at one time, and in October 1983, Sandford Olson of Marquette, Mich., came across three deer lying together that had been killed by lightning," Rue wrote. "The lightning had burned furrows across their bodies."

That incident occurred a year after two yearling bucks were killed by a lightning bolt in Shawano County, Wis. A landowner

Opposite: Lightning killed these Wisconsin bucks — a 140-class 12-pointer and a 160-class 11-pointer — on Sept. 1, 2000. The bucks were found by Lee Larson, a dairy farmer who was preparing to make hay four days after the storm.

Above: By the time these lightning-killed bucks were found, a predator made off with one of the buck's left legs and hindquarters. A wildlife expert said the lightning likely dislocated the leg at the pelvic girdle, making it an easy target for a predator.

found the bucks lying next to each other on a hill in a field. "You could clearly see the burn marks on the hides," said Tom Bahti, a wildlife biologist with the Wisconsin Department of Natural Resources.

Another incident that clearly showed burned marks occurred in Nebraska's DeSoto National Wildlife Refuge in 1999 (see the accompanying sidebar on Page 25).

Rue also related this interesting anecdote about a lightning strike: "I once saw a huge tree that had been struck by lightning," Rue wrote. "Even the radial roots had been exploded and laid bare. Within a couple of days, deer had eaten all the loosened soil from around the roots, evidently to get the nitrogen that had been concentrated in the roots by the lightning."

What's rare about the Waupaca County, Wis., bucks is they weren't near a fence, tree or any other kind of conductor. They were standing side by side in a 38-acre alfalfa field, about 50 yards from the edge of a hardwood forest. The field lies on a small rise in what is otherwise flat farm country.

The bucks were facing each other, and died with their muzzles about eight inches apart. So, it's possible they were eating during the storm and dropped dead in their tracks from the lightning strike. The deer's preference for nitrogen-fixing legumes such as alfalfa obviously put them in a feeding site that proved hazardous.

Kerry Beheler is a wildlife health specialist for the Wisconsin Department of Natural Resources. She said although the DNR has documented few cases of deer-lightning deaths, it probably happens more often than most people believe. Beheler said the only confirmed lightning deaths to wildlife in Wisconsin in 2000 involved Canada geese, sandhill cranes and English sparrows. In the case of the sparrows, she said 350 roosting birds were killed by one lightning bolt.

"In smaller animals, lightning usually blows off their extremities," Beheler said. "That's not common for larger animals like deer. They're so much larger that their bodies absorb the electrical impact."

Beheler added, however, that lightning often breaks the legs of larger animals. That might have happened in the Waupaca County incident. Although the carcasses weren't found until a few days after the storm, the 12-point buck was missing its left leg and hindquarter. Beheler said that indicates the buck's pelvic girdle could have been shattered from the lightning, making it easier for a scavenger to remove the leg from the carcass.

"Lightning causes massive internal hemorrhaging," she said. "It results in a free flow of blood in the thoracic cavity. In other words, the heart pretty much blows apart because there's so much electrical current running through the body."

Beheler said she's more familiar with lightning strikes to farm animals. She knows of one case where six heifers were killed when lightning struck a nearby tree. "In a group like that, where animals are in close proximity to each other, the lightning can move along the ground and travel from one animal to another," she said.

She added that those instances are rare, and the animals have to be standing within a couple of feet of each other for the lightning to continue its path. Multiple deaths can also occur during storms that include multiple lightning strikes. That might have happened in Waupaca County, because the storm lasted several hours and included repeated lightning strikes.

Sullivan said news of the dead bucks spread quickly, mainly because some area landown-

Below: Matt Sullivan bow-hunts the area where the bucks were killed. Sullivan said area hunters were disappointed the bucks were killed, but added that the sight of the massive racks renewed some landowners' commitment to their quality deer management program.

ers practice quality deer management and are trying to get others to buy into the concept.

"It's kind of surprising to see two bucks of that caliber," Sullivan said. "You might see one or two bucks like that a year, but you only see them once and usually from a distance. It proves there are big deer around here."

Sullivan said the news also renewed the hopes of several bow-hunters. "They're thinking that maybe there's more big bucks out there."

On a disappointing note, a poacher sawed the racks off both bucks a few hours after the photos were taken for this article. Larson's wife confronted the man as he was leaving the field, and was able to get the racks back. A conservation warden confiscated them that evening.

According to Wisconsin wildlife regulations, antlers from naturally killed deer can be seized by the state. The DNR will likely sell the antlers or keep them for educational purposes.

Lightning strikes the earth's surface about 100 times every second, adding up to millions of times each day. Every year across the globe, more than 1,000 people die from lightning strikes. A single bolt can contain 1 billion volts of electricity. That's enough electricity to power a 100-watt light bulb for three months.

During storms, we are advised to stay indoors

Below: These two yearling bucks were standing on the knob of a field when they were struck by lightning in 1982. Notice the burn marks across their necks and backs. The incident occurred in Shawano County, Wis.

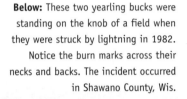

and away from windows. If caught outside, we are told to stay away from trees and avoid open areas. What about deer? Do they know where to go during storms?

Apparently not.

While conducting deer research at Nebraska's DeSoto National Wildlife Refuge in 1999, researchers Scott Hygnstrom and Kurt VerCauteren were alerted to a bizarre situation.

A few days after severe thunderstorms passed through the area, a farmer found the remains of a deer in his soybean field. He called the researchers and told them it had been struck by lightning.

University of Nebraska graduate student Jason Gilsdorf was part of a team that investigated the incident. Upon arriving, he found a 23-by-28-foot patch of dead soybeans scorched by the lightning's intense heat. In the middle of the burned beans were the remains of a 2-year-old white-tailed buck. The buck had been feeding or lying in the field during the storm.

Gilsdorf assumed the buck was struck because it was on the highest point in the area, and the lightning sought the shortest path to the ground.

After sharing the experience with other researchers, Gilsdorf learned lightning also killed several elk on a Colorado mountain in 1999. Also, in 1997, a single bolt of lightning killed six elephants as they huddled together in Kruger National Park in Africa.

ABOUT THE AUTHOR

Daniel Schmidt joined *Deer & Deer Hunting* as the associate editor in 1995. He moved up to managing editor in 1999, and was promoted to editor in chief in 2002.

Do Deer Hunting's Largest Challenges Lie Ahead?

DAVE BEAUCHAINE, JANUARY 2000

Silently, I waited for my heart rate to return to normal. It was a good shot, well within my range, and I heard the deer fall soon after the shot. Still, I fought the urge to excitedly descend from my stand. Instead, I wanted to take a moment to calm down and descend carefully.

As I sat, my mind wandered back to my first deer hunt almost 20 years ago, and I thought how deer hunting has changed for me. Back then, gun-hunting was deer hunting for me, and it was done five hours away on public land in the North Woods. We hunted from the ground in freezing temperatures till noon, went back to the van for lunch, and returned to the woods until dark. Bucks were legal to shoot and does were not, unless you were lucky and drew a rare antlerless permit. I wore a borrowed one-piece suit, two sizes too large, and I rarely saw a deer.

What would those old men in deer camp think about this kind of deer hunting? I lowered my bow to the ground and smiled. Here I am, a scant five minutes' drive from my suburban home, and I'm hunting deer within the village limits. I'm wearing the latest camouflage and shooting a bow and arrows made from space-age materials. I'm also hunting from a commercially made tree stand, I use rattling antlers and grunt calls, and I de-scent everything from my hair to my socks. Beyond that, I scout deer year-round instead of the day before the opener.

Yes, deer hunting has changed, but I often wonder why. That's what led to this article. *Deer & Deer Hunting* recently asked six prominent figures in outdoor communications and wildlife management to help answer that question. Specifically, we asked them to look back over the past 100 years and identify significant accomplishments and events that shaped the deer hunting landscape. In addition, we asked them to forecast the future. What will deer hunting be like in the next 100 years?

Valerius Geist, wildlife researcher, lecturer from the University of Calgary: The greatest accomplishment in the past century is that the United States and Canada got together continentally and generated a system of wildlife conservation the likes of which has no peer. The greatest environmental success of the century is the return of wildlife to North America. Whitetails were virtually nonexistent at the turn of the century. They had been shot down to numbers in total of about 300,000.

Opposite: The compound bow radically changed bow-hunting for the better. It not only spurred an interest in archery, it helped make bow-hunting a legitimate herd-management tool for areas where gun-hunting is not allowed.

> "HOW WE VIEW DEER AND DEER HUNTING IN THE FUTURE DEPENDS ON HOW YOU LOOK AT CHANGE. CHANGE IS INEVITABLE, AND MANY OF US HUNT WITH THE MEMORY OF HOW WE FIRST STARTED."
>
> — JAY MCANINCH

What are they now, somewhere around 20 million, 30 million?

The significance is that we have had a "populace system" of wildlife conservation and management in which Joe Blow could participate. And Joe Blow did participate — enthusiastically.

All the fancy environmental laws of today, like the Endangered Species Act, wouldn't be worth the paper they're written on without that great architecture of conservation that supports all wildlife.

D&DH: How did deer hunting contribute to the success of this management system?

Geist: It played a very important part in the thinking of the fathers of wildlife conservation. They spoke specifically about deer in their speeches. They were making a point by saying, "Wouldn't it be wonderful if deer were abundant again?" Deer were one of the primary concerns in the mentality of those that started the conservation movement.

D&DH: What do you foresee for deer hunting in the next century?

Geist: It will be grim, I'm afraid. The reason why is we are losing the populace infrastructure that politically supports deer hunting. At the same time, we are seeing a growing trend by landowners to privatize and exploit deer for money. This, of course, leads to hunting by only the elite and wealthy — something we are seeing already.

In addition, the anti-hunting and animal-rights movements are really bamboozling the urban population with philosophies — if one can call them such — which have little merit but nevertheless are attractive enough to have emotional appeal. All this stands to reduce the number of hunters, thus reducing the political clout that wildlife has. The two are undeniably linked.

The reason we have turkeys is because we have a lot of turkey hunters and the National Wild Turkey Federation with 150,000 paid members, which raises millions of dollars. There are no such conventions to celebrate white-crowned sparrows or bobolinks — they have no clientele — and they are declining.

Al Hofacker, co-founder of *D&DH*: At the top of the list is the reintroduction of deer and the development of deer-management principles and practices. At the beginning of the century, sportsman and conservation agencies worked together to reintroduce deer to areas where they were basically extinct. In the 1930s and '40s, Aldo Leopold led the way in the development of (wildlife) management. Without these events, there would be no deer hunting today.

The amount of information now available is also important. Several national magazines, shows, seminars, and innumerable books and published materials are available that were written not just by hunters, but by scientists like John Ozoga. I think this has really helped hunters understand their quarry better — its biology, habits and, of course, methods to hunt it.

Opposite: Without the whitetail, hunter numbers would probably be extremely low. Deer are big and exciting, and they evoke the same excitement in hunters today as they did 300 years ago.

Above: Although states like Texas still attract thousands of whitetail hunters each year, regional trends suggest hunting's popularity is shifting. According to a scientific study, only one region — the Midwest — showed an increase in hunters from 1980 to 1995.

Along those lines, I think hunter education greatly improved. Most states made it mandatory for first-time hunters, and it's made the sport much safer. Deer hunters were in the forefront in developing these programs and eventually making them mandatory.

I also believe the compound bow radically changed bow-hunting for the better. It spurred an interest in archery. It really came into existence in the early 1970s, and interest in bow-hunting skyrocketed. When I started hunting in 1969, Wisconsin had about 10,000 archers. Today the state has more than 250,000.

D&DH: What do you foresee for deer hunting in the next century?

Hofacker: I'm not optimistic. Privatization of deer hunting land is a problem now and it's going to get worse. This will force many hunters to public land. I believe the day will come in the next century when you'll still have the opportunity to deer hunt, but not when or where you want. We'll see a lottery system for when and where to hunt on public land, but I hope I'm wrong.

I'm also concerned about who will manage deer in the next century. I say that because after 50 years of developing sound deer-management principles, we still have trouble implementing them as effective practices for management.

In Wisconsin, more than 80 percent of our deer management units are overpopulated, and it's not just a one- or two-year phenomenon. In fact, the statewide deer population has been over the fall population goal since 1981 — almost 20 years. I don't know how long that can persist.

If deer hunters don't cooperate with wildlife managers to manage deer herds, someone else will step in. In Michigan, there was a case where the Michigan Farm Bureau filed a lawsuit against the state because Michigan's deer herd was far beyond the population goals and only getting worse. Essentially, they were filing a lawsuit to take control out of the hands of the Michigan Department of Natural Resources. They were making the argument, and perhaps rightfully so, that deer weren't being managed.

Charles Alsheimer, *D&DH* Northern Field Editor: Obviously, the recovery of the whitetail is number one. But what strikes me most is the specialization of the whitetail industry. There used to be three outdoor magazines: *Sports Afield*, *Outdoor Life* and *Field & Stream*. When *D&DH* hit the street in 1977, it was the first specialized outdoor magazine. After that, other specialized magazines, including other deer-specific magazines began to appear.

Other advancements are the introduction of the compound bow by Allen, which prompted the archery world to explode; the urbanization of America, which caused many farms to return to brush and woodlots; and the introduction of camouflage specifically for deer hunters, which made hunting a designer sport. In addition, we saw a technology explosion: Gore-Tex, carbon arrows, fast-flight strings, glass limbs and single-cam bows, and stainless steel rifles with Kevlar stocks.

Another significant factor is that the 1980s were probably the greatest single decade from a financial standpoint. People had disposable income for guns, bows, magazines and hunting trips.

The economy drove the whitetail industry. Baby boomers like myself had money to spend on the sport. The magazines helped fuel it, and *D&DH* was the foundation of that — it was the first one on the block.

D&DH: What do you foresee for deer hunting in the next century?

Alsheimer: Roy Rogers said "Buy land — they don't make it any more." We can laugh about that, but it paints a less-than-glowing picture for the future of the hunting world. People are buying land and putting up posted signs — I happen to be one of them — and limiting the utilization of the land. There simply won't be more places to hunt. Combine that with fractured family structure, divorced parents and single mothers — there's nobody to take kids hunting.

I believe we have seen the mountain top. I believe it was reached in the late 1980s. We're now on the down side of that hill. Because of animal-rights groups and a changing social structure, hunting isn't as attractive or accessible to kids.

I see us going the way of Europe, but maybe not in my life-

Below: If the outdoor industry learns to reach beyond the stereotypical hunting market, participation might increase.

time. You will have to have money or land to hunt, and you will have heavy regulations.

D&DH: Anything bright ahead?

Alsheimer: Hunters will be more concerned with the quality of deer on their land, and they'll be more concerned with what they can give back to the sport. They'll be better stewards of the land.

John Ozoga, whitetail researcher and wildlife biologist: The past 100 years brings us from less than a half-million deer to the current estimates, which I think are almost 30 million. So in essence, the country went from zero deer hunting — although some places like Michigan still had some hunting — to abundance. That whole process was complex, and it is difficult to pick out specific accomplishments relative to deer hunting. Unfortunately, the animal has become a pest in a lot of areas that are out of the hands of hunters.

D&DH: What do you foresee for deer hunting in the next century?

Ozoga: I'm somewhat pessimistic. We will continue to see a trend toward privatization. The deer-as-pest problem is not going away. It's going to be an enormous challenge to manage deer on small private and suburban parcels. On the other hand, the farmland situation — crop damage and high deer densities — stands a better chance of being solved. I think farmers and deer hunters are more compatible in this situation. We might even see quality deer management in these areas.

On public lands — especially federal — we'll see a trend toward biodiversity and probably less tree cutting, and I think deer populations will be affected by that change. I think state lands will follow that trend eventually, but it's going to take a lot longer.

Dick Lattimer, president, Archery Manufactures and Merchants Organization (AMO): The establishment of the Pittman-Robertson fund in 1937 was probably the most important thing that has happened in the history of conservation. It established a federal excise tax on sporting equipment and provides a lot of money every year for some 3,500 wildlife-management projects in 50 states.

The archery excise tax went into effect in 1975 as part of the Pittman-Robertson Act. Since that time, we've sent $288 million into this fund. The federal government gives each state Pittman-Robertson dollars based on a formula so all states are treated fairly regardless of their size and population.

My point is that this is the hunter's money, not federal money or money collected from the American citizens' income tax. This is money the hunters of America agreed to pool to support the fish and game departments' work, not only to benefit deer and game species, but also nongame species.

D&DH: What do you foresee for deer hunting in the next century?

> "THE ESTABLISHMENT OF THE PITTMAN-ROBERTSON FUND IN 1937 WAS PROBABLY THE MOST IMPORTANT THING THAT HAS HAPPENED IN THE HISTORY OF CONSERVATION."
> — DICK LATTIMER

Above: Who will manage deer in the next century? That's a tough question that doesn't have an easy answer. According to wildlife experts, if deer hunters don't cooperate with wildlife managers to manage deer herds, someone else will step in, possibly government agencies.

If the outdoor industry learns to reach out to minority groups for participation, then the future of our sport looks good. If they ignore minorities, then it's not so good because the racial make-up of the population is changing.

D&DH: Have these groups been ignored by the hunting industry?

Yes. I've been attending national meetings in this field for 33 years and seldom do you see blacks or Hispanics. We have to sell our sport to these folks to be successful. If not enough people participate in hunting and not enough hunters buy equipment, we lose Pittman-Robertson dollars, and the states will not be able to run their fish and wildlife agencies. The states get large percentages of their operating budgets from the Pittman-Robertson fund. The keystone of the whole conservation movement is the Pittman-Robertson Act.

Jay McAninch, executive director, Congressional Sportsman's Caucus: As an avid reader of history and a professional biologist, one thing that strikes me is how the white-tailed deer provided for people in the beginning and end of the 20th century.

In 1900, North America was finishing its settlement phase, and deer were a substantial part of the diet for those settlers. Now, skip through the recovery phase and the evolution of wildlife management to the present day. Deer are still providing for us, only they have gone into a broader set of niches where they are providing an up-close-and-personal big-game animal on the doorstep. People can go into urban parks and enjoy watching them. They're common in suburbia, farmlands and most forested areas. Although they began as an important food source, now, in addition to providing some sustenance, deer are probably far more important to the recreational, social and cultural well-being of people in the areas where they exist.

As far as events in the past 100 years, the most significant event was something whitetails did on their own and under the protection of hunters and conservation: they multiplied and filled every niche in the U.S. with unprecedented numbers. In doing that, they made themselves the premier hunting species for the hunter/conservationist.

As we turn into the next century, deer are the animal most young and new hunters are taught to hunt. When I look back to my beginnings, every person I knew learned to hunt squirrels, rabbits and perhaps pheasant and grouse. Deer weren't on our plate. We went deer hunting after we became more experienced. Today, a generation of hunters learned to hunt by hunting the whitetail.

D&DH: Is that a positive thing?

I think it is. Without the whitetail, hunter numbers would be extremely low. Deer aren't just a huntable species. They're big and exciting and they do to people today what they did to people 300 years ago. It is the abundance and allure of the whitetail that has probably kept hunter numbers up in many states. There's no other species that attracts the number of hunters that deer do.

A lot of people don't realize that virtually every state (conservation) agency runs on two types of income: license sales and federal excise tax on hunting equipment. When you look at license sales and excise tax money, and you look at what portion of that comes from deer hunters, you see that deer put the economic fuel into the system.

So really, not only are whitetails recruiting and maintaining hunter numbers, economically, they're putting the bread and butter into state agencies. This money goes way beyond deer. It supports all kinds of wildlife and land management. You take deer out of the picture, and state agencies wouldn't be able to operate, and they wouldn't have much of a budget.

Above: Privatization of deer hunting land is a problem now, and it's probably going to get worse.

D&DH: What do you foresee for deer hunting in the next century?

Change is inevitable, and many of us hunt with the memory of how it was when we first started hunting. We have a lot more hunters out there and I don't see that changing. We'll see a more crowded landscape with smaller hunting parcels. We'll see demands on deer hunters — because of this crowding — to behave more responsibly, behavior that's more compatible with the landscape.

The days of going into the woods and being away from everything are over. Increasingly, deer hunters are going to be in situations where they're going to hear cars and people. If you accept that kind of change — which is going to happen no matter what we do — and adapt to it, deer hunting will not only remain important, it will grow in importance as we find ways for deer to coexist with human populations.

There's no question deer can do it, they've shown that. The question is, can we adapt to it as hunters? If we do, we can demonstrate that hunting can be a public service, provide recreation and be an effective management tool.

If we look at the growing urban and suburban hunting landscape as an opportunity instead of a detriment, deer hunting's future looks good, and it will be a critical component to whitetail survival.

ABOUT THE AUTHOR
Dave Beauchaine was a contributing writer for *D&DH* in 1999 and 2000.

A Fawn is Born

LEN RUE JR., JUNE 1999

It was one of those mornings when the day seemed like it didn't want to get out of bed. The clouds on this early May morning hung low and menacing, and the brightening light had to fight through multiple layers of leaf canopy before it touched the floor of the Eastern broadleaf forest.

Despite the low-light conditions, I knew the morning would be special. The forest would receive new life, and I was determined to capture it on film.

It took some maneuvering, but I finally found her on a small, dry rise down in the swamp. There, among a multitude of skunk cabbage, the white-tailed doe had been in labor for some time.

She was fully dilated and clearly uncomfortable. She kept changing positions — from standing to kneeling to lying on her side — attempting to hasten the process.

The doe was nibbling browse when the clear sack containing her fawn appeared from her birth canal. Soon, about eight inches of the sack protruded, and I could finally see part of the fawn — its front hoofs — exiting its mother.

The birth of a fawn is not a quick procedure. In an effort to drop the fawn, the doe completed a ritual. The doe walked in circles, then laid down and strained. Every few minutes, she stood and repeated the process. Finally, about 20 minutes later, the doe knelt on her front legs and partially raised her hindquarters. Quickly and quietly, the fawn slid out of its mother and landed gently on the forest floor. Almost instantly, the doe stood, turned and started to clean her newborn.

She wasted no time eating the placental sac and licking the blood and fluids that covered her fawn. She then knelt down and continued cleaning her still-wet fawn.

Newborn white-tailed fawns appear dark brown and slick. However, after a few minutes of its mother's meticulous cleaning, the fawn's coat begins to dry, and it takes on a light-brown appearance. The cleaning process also helps distinguish the fawn's white spots — key components in its natural camouflage. A fawn's speckled coat usually blends well with the forest floor. Therefore, unless it moves, a fawn is not easily pinpointed by predators.

Within 10 minutes, the fawn attempted to stand. However, it didn't achieve immediate success. The fawn pushed its rear legs skyward, but its front legs wouldn't cooperate, and it tumbled gently to the

ground. The infant whitetail failed two or three times.

Finally, on shaky legs, the fawn stood on all fours and surveyed its world. Instinctively, its first tentative steps were toward its mother. The fawn was ready to nurse. About 20 minutes after giving birth, the doe lay quietly as her fawn nursed. She had finished cleaning her newborn, but seemed preoccupied.

I was too busy taking photographs to pay attention to what she was attending to. Amazingly, while in a prone position and tending to her first fawn, the doe began giving birth to another fawn. This birth happened so unobtrusively that I almost missed seeing it.

Still prone, the doe proceeded to clean the twin while its older sibling nursed. Then, after a few minutes, the twin crawled toward the belly of its mother in search of nourishment.

The fawns nursed while the doe continued to clean them with her tongue. Eventually, the doe stood and ate the remaining afterbirth. Although she acquired much-needed nutrients from the birthing material, the doe ate it to eliminate scent. This helped keep predators from finding the area. In fact, she even went as far as to clean up the entire area. She ate all vegetation — and even the dirt — on which amniotic fluid had dripped.

By midmorning, the fawns' coats had dried, and the little deer were proficient walkers. By then, they

Above, right, and opposite: The birth of a fawn is not a quick procedure. In an effort to drop her fawn, the doe completes a ritual of sorts. A doe will often walk in circles several times, then lie down and strain. Every few minutes, she might stand and repeat the process.

could nurse while standing.

Although she had taken steps to conceal her fawns, the doe instinctively knew she had to move them away from the birthplace. She led them to a more secluded area about 50 feet away before lying down. For the next couple of hours, she rested, nursed and cleaned the fawns.

As they nursed, the fawns wagged their tails vigorously, and their mother responded by licking their genitals. This stimulated urination and defecation and, therefore, allowed the doe to keep the fawns scent-free. As their thin legs gained strength, the curious fawns explored their immediate surroundings. They didn't go far, staying within an 8-foot radius of their resting mother.

By early afternoon, it was time for the doe to hide her fawns better. She moved them even farther away from the birthplace and hid them about 250 feet apart. This tactic prevented predators from finding the fawns, and it improved the odds of at least one fawn surviving.

Although they got up and changed beds several times a day, the fawns instinctively knew their safety depended on lying still.

For several days, the doe remained in the immediate area, but aside from nursing, she stayed away from the fawns to minimize danger.

The doe came back to nurse the fawns three or four times every 24 hours, often making these visits at night. By the fawns' second or third week, green vegetation supplemented their diet, and by the fourth month, they were weaned.

By growing quickly in their hiding places, fawns gain enough strength in one week to outrun small predators. Within three weeks, they leave their hiding places and rejoin their mother.

From there, the fawns are ready to explore and experience the whitetail world.

Above: Although a doe acquires much-needed nutrients from her fawn's afterbirth, she primarily eats it to eliminate scent so predators won't be attracted to the area. In fact, a doe will even go as far as to clean up the entire area by eating all vegetation and even the dirt on which amniotic fluid has dripped.

Above: With Fawn 1 already nursing, the doe strains to give birth again. In this case, the doe stays in the prone position while Fawn 2 enters the world. The doe then stands, right, and begins cleaning the twin while Fawn 1 nurses.

Below: With their mother's attentive care, these 2-hour-old fawns are thoroughly cleaned and ready to nurse. They're also ready to stand and walk. Although the fawns will explore the immediate surroundings, they don't stray far from their mother.

The Mythical Void in the Chest

JAY MCANINCH, AUGUST 1998

How many times have you heard someone swear to have shot a deer in the chest with a slug, bullet or arrow, but found neither the deer nor signs it had suffered a mortal wound?

"I hit him dead center in the chest and we never found him!" a bewildered bow-hunter once told me. "We tracked him for more than a mile and then lost his trail. I couldn't figure it out, but my friend asked his veterinarian for an opinion. The vet said there's a small spot in the deer's chest where, if you hit it just right, the broadhead won't cut anything vital. That's what must have happened with my buck, because we never found it."

Nonsense.

Is it really possible to shoot a deer in the lungs or chest cavity without killing it? Or is it more likely that the hunter simply assumed the shot hit the chest, but the wound was actually elsewhere? After all, a shot and the deer's response to it happen quickly, often making it difficult to accurately assess a wound's location.

Answering questions about chest wounds requires knowledge of the whitetail's heart, lungs and chest cavity. By learning the detailed functioning of the respiratory and circulatory systems, we can better understand what takes place when a deer is shot in this vital region.

The chest cavity is known as the thoracic cavity, or thorax. The heart, lungs and their network of blood vessels and supportive tissue often overlap and cover nearly every square inch inside the cavity, whether the deer is inhaling or exhaling. This part of the deer's body forms a closed chamber in which the essential gas of life — oxygen — from the outside air is exchanged for another gas, carbon dioxide, a byproduct of the body processes. To perform this exchange, the deer draws air into its nose, trachea (wind pipe) and lungs. The air then diffuses, spreading quickly across tiny membranes, where it comes in contact with the blood stream. At the same time and place, carbon dioxide diffuses back into the air through the lung membranes. The process ends when the deer exhales the carbon dioxide out through its trachea and nose, while the oxygen-rich blood is rushing to all organs and muscles to nourish the deer's body.

The effectiveness of the oxygen and carbon dioxide exchange depends on continually putting large amounts of blood and air into the same area — the chest cavity. The heart, of course, is the pump

Above: The bow-hunter who maintains razor-sharp broadheads invariably increases his chances for shorter blood trails when hunting whitetails.

through which all blood must flow, and the lungs are the sacs through which all incoming air must flow.

The area around the heart holds the body's largest blood vessels, some carrying "used" blood, which contains high levels of carbon dioxide, to the heart. Other large vessels carry "new" blood, which contains high levels of oxygen, away from the lungs and heart. These major vessels have names. The *superior vena cava*, which comes from the head and neck, and the *inferior vena cava,* which comes from the belly and lower body, are vessels that bring used blood into the heart. From there, the blood is pumped into the *pulmonary* arteries (pulmonary means related to the lungs), through to the lungs, and then back to the heart through the pulmonary veins. Finally, the new blood is pumped from the heart out to the body through the *aorta*.

The rate at which oxygen and carbon dioxide are exchanged is related to how fast the air and blood can be spread out and positioned. The exchange occurs within the rapid division of the airways (called *bronchi*) of the lungs, which branch off from the trachea. Deer have 16 divisions in their lungs after the airways' initial branching. The branching occurs a few inches from the trachea, and ends within 8 to 12 inches of the right and left lungs. This incredible network of airways contains millions of tiny air pockets called *alveoli*. If you were to squeeze a fresh piece of lung tissue, the alveoli would scrunch like those plastic packing sheets with air bubbles.

Each air pocket is surrounded by tiny capillaries — the smallest blood vessels — which allow carbon dioxide to diffuse out and across the vessel membrane while allowing oxygen to diffuse into the vessel. This oxygen and carbon dioxide exchange takes place only in the *alveoli*, which are found throughout the lungs. Incredibly, *alveoli* create a huge surface area — about the size of a tennis court, or more than 80 square yards. This huge area ensures the gas exchange occurs within seconds, and that there is an effective interface between the circulatory (blood) and the respiratory (air) systems.

Why did we explain the chest cavity's complex structure and workings? The important message is that the chest cavity is the chamber in which the body's two most important functions are contained: the circulatory and respiratory systems. Further, the chest cavity is the most important aiming point for hunters because it's large and contains vital functions. Although the head, neck and back are also critical regions, they're seldom preferred targets, particularly for bow-hunters.

Based on the description above, it's easy to see why chest-cavity injuries easily damage the circulatory system, respiratory system or both, usually causing death. Almost every square inch of the chest cavity performs a vital function. Therefore, damage anywhere inside the chest cavity will likely hamper vital functions. Once hunters understand injuries to the chest cavity, they can better interpret what's actually happening in hunting situations. This understanding should reduce the loss rate of wounded deer, and allow us to better predict when deer could recover from a hit.

A shot directly to the heart or any related major blood vessel will result in an easily found deer. An arrow, slug or bullet that penetrates the chest wall and tears or breaks a major vessel and/or the heart will disrupt blood flow to the brain and extremities. Large blood loss occurs immediately, and the deer quickly loses consciousness because little blood and oxygen reach the brain. At nearly the same time, massive blood loss causes lung failure, further reducing the blood's ability to renew oxygen for the body and brain.

The notion that deer hit through the heart and/or major vessels bleed to death is essentially true. The damage is so great that the deer dies a quick, clean death. Whether the heart and blood vessels are severed by a razor-sharp broadhead or by a slug or bullet, major damage to the circulatory system will always be fatal.

Below: Hunters who believe a "dead spot" exists between a deer's backbone and its vitals know little about a whitetail's anatomy.

Hunters who shoot a deer through both lungs — often called the "double-lung shot" — usually find the deer. Unlike shots to the heart and major vessels, lung wounds cause deer to lose consciousness and die from suffocation, or asphyxiation. In other words, the deer dies because it's unable to breathe, not because of blood loss. The process of how lung injuries occur and whether they're fatal requires an understanding of the respiratory system.

Above: Good trackers pay attention to details and assume their deer is dead, especially if their arrow, bullet or slug passed through the deer's chest cavity.

The breathing process is based on the inward pressure created by the lungs pulling against the outward pressure created by the chest cavity. The lungs have a natural tendency to contract because of elastic fibers running throughout them. These fibers stretch when the deer breathes in and spring back when it breathes out. If the chest wall didn't pull the lungs outward, the lungs would contract to a much smaller size.

The chest cavity is shaped and supported by 13 ribs that join at the vertebral column (backbone) and the sternum (breastbone). The ribs and sternum provide the chest cavity's outer dimensions. The entire chamber is bound together by the intercostal muscles covering the ribs on both sides. The cavity is closed on the large end by the diaphragm, a large, flat sheath of muscle separating the chest cavity from the abdomen, or stomach area. The small end of the chest cavity is closed by tissue that seals off the junction of the trachea and esophagus and the first rib.

At rest, the chest cavity has a fixed size that is smaller than what we see when field dressing deer. That's because the chest wall is pulled in by the force of the lungs contracting when the deer exhales, and returns to its normal size when the deer inhales and expands its lungs. The chest wall of a living deer is smaller than when the deer is dead because of the lungs' inward pulling forces.

Those inward and outward forces harmoniously oppose each other through a little-known set of membranes that biologists call the *pleura*. The lungs are cone-shaped, with narrow ends and wide bases. Surrounding the lungs is a membrane called the *visceral pleura*. This membrane hugs the lungs' surface, including the gaps between the lungs' lobes and around the root where they join the major blood vessels. Other than where the lungs join at the root with blood vessels, they float freely in the chest cavity.

The *parietal pleura* membrane lines the inner surface of the chest wall, the upper apex of the chest cavity and on the lower end of the cavity, the upper surface of the diaphragm. This membrane covers the inner chest cavity and only joins the *visceral* membrane at the lungs' root. These two membranes form what would look like a double-walled sac if they could be seen from the side. The thin space between the membranes is filled with a film of fluid that lubricates the membranes, allowing them to slide back and forth as the deer breathes. This allows the lungs to move freely and the chest walls to move in and out.

A second, more critical feature of the *visceral* and *parietal* membranes and *pleural fluid* is that they combine to create the forces that link the inward pressure of the lungs during contraction with the outward pressure of the chest wall during expansion. These membranes function like two pieces of glass pressed together with a film of water in between. If you move the glass pieces, they slide easily and smoothly.

When an arrow, bullet or slug penetrates the chest wall and enters a portion of the lung, the parietal and visceral membranes are broken. Once the membranes are cut or burst, they're likely to separate. That's because strong inward pressure from the lungs and equally strong outward pressure from the chest pull apart the membranes. The chest wall suddenly expands to its full size because it is unrestrained by the damaged lungs. As the membranes separate and create a vacuum, air and/or blood is sucked into the space in between.

A *pneumothorax* is the term for air mixing in this space with the *pleural fluid*. A *hemothorax* describes when blood enters this space, and a *hemopneumothorax* describes when air and blood enter the space. When air or blood enters this space, the pressure decreases between the lungs and the chest wall. Therefore, the lungs can no longer expand fully. In most cases, a hit to a lung is fatal because air and blood from the wound cause at least one lung to partially or completely collapse. The degree of collapse depends on the amount of blood or air in the space. In some cases, the pressure can be so great it causes the heart to put even more pressure on the other lung, further restricting breathing.

When one or both lungs cannot fully function, breathing is increasingly difficult. The deer breathes more rapidly, trying to draw in air to compensate for the oxygen loss. Despite the deer's efforts to inhale, its

Below: A deer's chest cavity is pressurized, meaning the slightest wound will cause massive bleeding.

Above: In most cases, a hit to a deer's lung is fatal because air and blood from the wound cause at least one lung to partially collapse. That's not to say the blood trail will always be short. Because wounded deer can cover a lot of ground in a short time, hunters must adopt never-give-up attitudes when trailing wounded whitetails.

lungs cannot expand, and the flow of oxygen-enriched blood is quickly reduced. The deer loses consciousness and dies by asphyxiation. This process occurs more quickly if the deer is running or walking. The key point is that when a lung is damaged, the seal breaks between the *parietal* and *visceral* membranes.

Why is this discussion important? Simply, a deer hit in the lungs does not die of blood loss or hemorrhaging. Most hunters seem to think a hit anywhere in the chest cavity causes internal bleeding and failure of the heart and/or circulatory system. In fact, death can be quicker when the lungs collapse, while the circulatory system remains largely undamaged and the nervous system fully functional. Such situations explain the extensive muscle twitching that occur several minutes after a deer is clinically dead.

So, can a deer survive a chest wound? Yes, it is possible, but it's highly unlikely. Even if heart, lung or vascular tissue aren't damaged — which is extremely difficult to avoid in chest wounds — the deer's breathing chamber can be fatally breached. Generally, a bullet or slug that penetrates the chest wall will tear a large enough opening to at least destroy the *parietal* membrane. When that seal is broken, a *pneumothorax* or *hemo-pneumothorax* occurs. Remember, with either condition, the chest cavity loses pressure, and respiratory failure quickly follows.

Because bullets and slugs will viciously tear, rip and destroy tissue, sealing the membrane hole is impossible. A deer is slightly more likely to survive a chest-cavity hit by an arrow, because the broadhead slices cleanly and only damages what it can cut. An arrow could hit the outer chest wall and not penetrate the intercostal muscles. If the arrow does not cut the *parietal* membrane, the lungs will continue to function normally. The same thing would happen if an arrow glanced off a rib and the rib did not break and penetrate or damage the chest wall. A hunter might see the arrow in the deer's chest but doesn't realize the arrow never punctured the deer's pressurized breathing chamber.

A deer might also survive a wound between two ribs if the arrow penetrates an edge of the chest cavity, misses the lungs, and exits between two ribs on the opposite side. In this extremely remote case, the crucial factors are that the lungs are not injured and the broadhead slices like a surgeon's scalpel. If the lungs aren't injured, the *visceral* membrane would remain intact, which would mean the seal around the lungs would be intact.

Although the parietal membrane would be cut, the broadhead's cutting width, shaft diameter and the speed at which it passes through the chest affect the extent of damage to the membrane. Because modern broadheads cut like razors, the entrance and exit holes could be narrow, perfect slits. That might allow pressure from the intercostal muscles during inhalation to seal the wound. In a short time, blood could coagulate at the entry and exit sites, further sealing the wound.

With the exterior injuries sealed, only a small amount of air or blood would be sucked between the *parietal* and *visceral* membranes. Also, after the source of the blood and/or air was eliminated, the lungs could retain some ability to expand and contract. Slowly, the pleural fluid would replace the air and/or blood and, in time, lung function would return to normal.

Even so, how likely is such an occurrence? Well, shooting a multi-blade broadhead-tipped arrow through the chest cavity without hitting lung or heart tissue is nearly impossible, but if it miraculously happened, the deer could survive. A more likely case, however, is the arrow would nick at least a little lung tissue while passing through the cavity's edge, and cause some damage, which would likely be fatal.

The chest cavity is a large, critical portion of the deer's body, and it will always be the primary aiming point because hits there generally guarantee efficient kills. Only under incredible circumstances can a deer survive such a hit. In fact, survival simply isn't possible if the chest wound is inflicted by a bullet or slug because of widespread tissue destruction, membrane failure, and ultimately, lung failure.

While it's possible to zip a broadhead-tipped arrow though a deer's chest without killing the animal, a bow-hunter probably has a better chance of winning the lottery. Today's razor-sharp broadheads "cover a lot of ground" as they slice through a deer's chest, severing everything in their path. And because little "dead space" exists in a deer's chest, I believe hunters should find a more plausible reason to explain an unrecovered deer. Most likely, they didn't hit the deer where they thought, and perhaps quit searching prematurely.

For those reasons, shooting at the chest cavity remains the best choice for quick, clean kills.

The Oak Grove

DANIEL E. SCHMIDT, OCTOBER 2001

Chipmunks and pine squirrels scurry across the forest floor 20 feet below me as I secure my safety belt to the red oak's trunk and settle in for an afternoon hunt.

This is the only red oak in the corner woodlot. It's surrounded by a few small white pines and dozens of white oaks. Its trunk diameter is 15 inches, and some of the white oaks are more than twice that. No kidding. These babies are huge.

Not many people get excited by trees, but I do. Trees — oaks especially — provide me great deer hunting opportunities. What's more, they give me something to think about when I'm waiting for deer to appear.

Don't read me wrong: I'm not a tree hugger. Far from it. Although I admire them for their beauty and shade, I'm also the first in line to saw past-prime trees into neat 16-inch chunks for splitting. Like deer, trees are a resource that, when managed properly, allow people to further enjoy life by making theirs more self-sufficient. Wood heat feels much warmer than that made by liquid propane, just like self-cut venison steaks taste better than beef sold at supermarkets. Don't ask me why, they just do.

Barring lightning strikes or tornado-like winds, the white oaks around my stand are decades from becoming firewood. The trees are past their prime, but they're still dropping enough acorns to make this place a hub for wildlife activity.

A fox squirrel that lives in the tree behind me works the forest floor like a ball-boy at Wimbledon. It descends to the tree's base, surveys it surroundings, and dashes for a recently fallen acorn. Picking it up in one motion, the squirrel heads for the base of another giant oak before examining its prize.

I'll watch the squirrels and admire the trees for about another hour before the turkeys show up. No doubt about that. They'll be below my stand precisely at 4:30 p.m. Have been every day for the past week. They seem to enjoy these acorns more than the bumper crop of caterpillars in the nearby hayfield.

There will be other visitors, too. I'm looking forward to seeing a familiar pair of noisy blue jays, a pileated woodpecker and possibly the badger that lives in a rock pile at the field's edge. Those critters only occasionally eat acorns, but they seem to love this grove as much as I do.

A forester friend once told me healthy white oak acorns that

escape consumption will germinate shortly after they hit the ground, putting down deep tap roots. The roots become dormant, then resume growing in spring. He also told me few people realize the upward growth of stems and leaves is heavily browsed by deer and rabbits, and the wannabe trees are often browsed for years before they attain enough growth to escape hungry mouths. In some cases, a white oak's root system can be more than a decade older than the tree's trunk.

Even more amazing, he said white oaks can theoretically live 1,000 years or more. Of course, disease, disasters, logging and urban sprawl have made even 100-year-old white oaks rare creatures in today's woodlots.

That's why this grove is so enchanting. I'm guessing, but the acorns that produced the trees around my stand probably fell to the ground not long after Wisconsin became a state in 1848. Who knows, maybe some of that same acorn crop was used as bread meal by settlers, or perhaps American Indians? Probably not, but it's not as far a stretch to believe the wood from those older oaks was made into barrels, ax handles and fence posts.

Amazing, isn't it? Here I'm sitting comfortably in a tree, passing my time waiting for a deer. I worked this week, but that involved sitting at a desk, and staring at a computer screen. I certainly wasn't outside plowing fields, picking rocks or digging ditches. If the people who toiled this land back then would see me perched in this tree, they would think I was lazy or insane.

Or both.

Those thoughts make me more humble about my existence and more thankful for my time in this stand. Some people had to work long, painful hours for our society to progress to the point where it is today. Think about it. As individuals, we no longer need to plant fields so we can eat or feed horses so we can ride to town. Everything might be more complicated than it was then, but it's also much easier. At least physically.

And speaking of change, despite all of our high-tech computers, automobiles, televisions and telephones, some things haven't changed much, including the stunning white oaks in this grove.

The sun is inching toward the horizon when the first deer appears — a yearling buck. It pops out of a distant pine thicket and frolics across the hayfield. Its destination is clear: the oak grove.

Within minutes, the little 6-pointer is in bow range, but I don't draw on him. Despite a predator instinct telling me otherwise, I decide to let this buck live for another day.

Nose to the ground, the buck gobbles acorns at an amazing pace. He doesn't have the capacity to marvel at the intricacies of this circling life process, but he seems to instinctively know these white-oak byproducts are important for his growth.

The buck hangs around until darkness approaches. Then, as quickly as he arrived, he trots back to his bedding area. Removing my arrow from the bow-string, I survey the towering oaks once more. There's still daylight in the field, but the canopy of these impressive oaks has already brought nighttime to the grove.

I'm not saying I want these trees to live forever. They won't, and I know that. I do hope, however, there will be oaks in this and other groves for as long as there are hunters.

Human and otherwise.

WHITE OAKS CAN THEORETICALLY LIVE 1,000 YEARS OR MORE. OF COURSE, DISEASE, DISASTERS, LOGGING AND URBAN SPRAWL HAVE MADE EVEN 100-YEAR-OLD WHITE OAKS RARE CREATURES IN TODAY'S WOODLOTS.

Photography

Daniel Schmidt was named editor of *Deer & Deer Hunting* in January 2002, becoming only the fourth person to hold that title in the magazine's storied 25-year history.

Schmidt fulfilled a lifelong dream to work for *D&DH* when he became the magazine's associate editor in 1995. He has hunted white-tailed deer for nearly 20 years.

This is the eighth book Schmidt has edited in his tenure at *D&DH*. Beginning in 1995, he edited seven editions of the *Deer Hunters' Almanac*, a book that has become an annual staple for professional wildlife managers and serious white-tailed deer hunters.

His writing and photography have also appeared in such magazines as *Turkey & Turkey Hunting, Whitetail Business, Wisconsin Outdoor Journal, Mathews Solocam Bowhunting Whitetails, Advantage Whitetail Spectacular, Realtree Deer Hunting* and *Bass Pro Shops' Outdoor World*.

Daniel Schmidt

Before joining Krause Publications, Schmidt was an award-winning editor and writer for Lake Country Publications in Hartland, Wis. While there, he wrote an outdoors column that appeared in nine southeast Wisconsin newspapers.

Schmidt and his wife, Tracy, make their home in Iola, Wis., the self-proclaimed "Bowhunting Capital of the World."

SECOND EDITION

Residential Lighting

A Practical Guide to Beautiful and Sustainable Design

• Randall Whitehead, IALD

WILEY

Published by John Wiley & Sons, Inc., Hoboken, New Jersey
Published simultaneously in Canada

For general information about our other products and services, please contact our Customer Care Department within the United States at (800) 762-2974, outside the United States at (317) 572-3993 or fax (317) 572-4002.

Wiley also publishes its books in a variety of electronic formats. Some content that appears in print may not be available in electronic books. For more information about Wiley products, visit our web site at www.wiley.com.

Library of Congress Cataloging-in-Publication Data:

Whitehead, Randall.
    Residential lighting : a practical guide / Randall Whitehead. — 2nd ed.
        p. cm.
    Includes index.
    ISBN 978-0-470-28483-4 (cloth)
        1. Dwellings—Lighting.   2.   Electric light fixtures.   I. Title.
TH7975.D8W49 2009
747'.92—dc22
                                                                                                                2008016848

Printed in the United States of America

10   9   8   7   6   5   4   3   2   1

I would like to dedicate this book to my family,

who learned how to put the "fun" back in dysfunctional.

Contents

Contents

Acknowledgments

- My deepest gratitude to Anita Synovec, who held down the fort as I pulled out what was left of my hair while putting this book together. And especially to Steve Rao for absorbing my misplaced frustrations and talking me away from the edge of the abyss.

My appreciation also goes to Judy Anderson, Naomi Miller, Alfredo Zaparolli, and Fran Kellogg Smith. They were my wonderful technical experts, who know how to get an idea across without loading it down with technical jargon. Zany Rumon and Marian Haworth, teachers of lighting design, were invaluable as the eyes of a student, making sure I got the information across without confusion.

I would like to thank Dennis Anderson, the extraordinary photographer, who captured many of the amazing images in this book. He is the artist behind the lens.

I would especially like to thank our team at John Wiley & Sons: Paul Drougas, for being such a great editor, and everyone else who worked with us to make the project a success.

I would also like to thank Clifton Lemon for working so closely with me on this text over the course of many years, and for turning a plain manuscript into readable art.

In the 1990s, "home sweet home" had become the place to be, according to a Roper Reports survey about the preferences of mainstream Americans. People are now spending more time at home, using it to fulfill a greater number of individual and family needs.

Home is a place to socialize, with larger kitchens to accommodate resident and guest cooks, and great rooms for informal parties. More than ever, home is now also a place for work. It is estimated that between 20 million and 40 million people currently do some type of work at home, whether in a separate room furnished as an office or at a desk in the corner of the living room. People also want "home" to mean a safe place, as well as one where they can enjoy the great outdoors in the evening after a hard day's work by extending entertaining into the patio and garden areas.

Throughout all these varied spaces, lighting is essential to making them both enjoyable and functional. Well-designed lighting can transform a glare-filled, shadowy, annoying place into one that is comfortable and flexible, enhancing the occupants' feelings of well-being. Advancements in technology have resulted in the development of specialized tools that simplify installation and help lighting reveal the best aspects of the environments in which we dwell. The designer will learn how to use this technology to visually shape a home to meet flesh-and-blood human needs.

Presented here is a valuable, detailed approach to lighting the home that is unique because it not only explains the how of lighting design but also provides insights into the why behind design choices. The details of the technology of light must go hand-in-hand with aesthetics and the overriding philosophy that lighting is for people. The author, Randall Whitehead, has the advantage of being not only an experienced lighting designer but a master communicator and teacher as well. Read on, and revel in bringing lighting to its full potential in the most important place in all of our lives—the home.

Wanda Jankowski

Author of *Designing with Light*, *The Best of Lighting Design*, and *Lighting Exteriors and Landscapes*; former managing editor-in-chief of *Architectural Lighting* magazine; editor of *Commercial Kitchen & Bath* magazine.

Residential Lighting

● ENJOYING LIGHT

This book is intentionally different from the many books written on lighting design. The emphasis here is on the art of lighting, not just the technical aspects.

Think of this manual as a guide to applied aesthetics. Light is an *artistic* medium. What you will learn is how to paint with illumination, using various techniques to add Depth, Dimension, and Drama (the three Ds), while at the same time humanizing your environments. Remember, you're not only lighting art and architecture, but the people within the space as well. This book will show you how to create rooms that feel instantly comfortable and are flattering to your clients, with the ability to dazzle at the touch of the button.

Today, all architects, interior designers, and other related design professionals need to know at least the basics about good lighting design. Nothing you learn will have more impact on your designs than lighting, because illumination is the "straw that stirs the drink." You give every single object or space in a home its appearance, tone, and impression through how you light it. Yet people still add lighting as an afterthought—"Oh, yes, let's also do some lighting"—after the architecture has been laid out and construction has begun.

This is a huge mistake. Lighting design needs to be brought in as an integral design element, along with all the other design components from the beginning. The lighting budget, too, should be comparable to the other main design elements of the project. Lighting is not just an option; it can make or break your project.

Homeowners need to learn something about lighting design as well, so they will not be lost when making important decisions about their living spaces. There are many architects, interior designers, and contractors who will say they know all about lighting design but have had little training; the homeowners are often left with poor lighting that works against the overall feeling they desired. This book can also be a valuable reference guide for homeowners who want to understand the *language of light*.

All the new technologies of the past decade have increased lighting's importance. Who needed lighting expertise when the only thing available was a ceiling socket and a lightbulb? That's all

There are three elements within each space that need lighting: art, architecture, and people. Think about lighting people first—you must humanize the light.

changed, but people's thinking has not. Fluorescent lighting alone has gone through a revolutionary change and, with energy considerations and construction codes, is now a must for a home. The third radically different lighting technology LEDs (light-emitting diodes) are now available and present a viable and greener option to both standard incandescent and fluorescent sources.

People have also changed the way they live and entertain, often congregating in the kitchen or a *great room*. Inviting people into your home is simply less formal than it was in our parent's generation. Sometimes the house is designed as an *open plan*, where the kitchen, dining room, living room, and family room all flow together. People tend to move more freely from space to space, instead of staying in one room. The new media rooms and electronic control systems have also changed the way people use their homes. People are cocooning more, spending time with family and friends at home. Good lighting design has to take all these evolving needs into account, using the new technical advances to make lighting versatile enough to accommodate everything, while being kinder to the environment.

OVERVIEW—WHAT TO EXPECT

The first half of this book deals with design tools you will need to put together a well-designed lighting plan. The second half explains what to do on a room-by-room basis for single-family homes. Throughout the book you will be given Web sites to visit that show real-life versions of the products that are being discussed. If you see a company you like, add the Web site to the *favorites* list on your computer. If you see a particular product you like, download a PDF into a folder that will serve as your digital reference library.

Remember, it's the aesthetic approach to lighting design that will be stressed. This book is a springboard to your imagination. The possibilities are limited only by your own creative abilities—and, of course, the client's budget.

A guide to reading this textbook: The first time a lighting term is used within the content of this book it will be shown in **bold** *print. This is an indication that a further explanation of this specific term is included in the Glossary at the end of the book.*

Part One

Understanding Light

"Arthur, I think I liked our little nest better before we put in track lighting."

The Functions of Illumination

The new developments in lighting over the last decade have created opportunities for approaches to ways of creating illumination that have only been dreamed of in the past. Lighting technology has greatly evolved from the time of table lamps and track lights, yet many homeowners have not updated their thinking much beyond that stage. According to *Builder Magazine,* "within 10 years of the launch of Energy Star®, U.S. consumers had purchased more than a billion products qualified under the program". More than one-half of the largest U.S. homebuilders currently participate in Energy Star in some way, such as specifying products with Energy Star ratings. Nearly two-thirds of U.S. consumers recognize the Energy Star logo."

The use of energy-efficient products, especially lighting, is not just a fad, it is a necessity. It is time to step up to the plate and make green design an integral part of your work ethic. We can now achieve lighting effects that are as flexible as our lifestyles, energy-efficient with a lower carbon imprint, and less intrusive in remodel situations. Plus, we can often do it within a reasonable budget and without dramatically changing the way we live. At the same time, we can increase the comfort and convenience levels of our living spaces, both inside and out.

Lighting can be a tremendous force in architectural, interior, and landscape design. It is the one factor that helps blend all the elements together. Yet, it has for too long been the second-class citizen of the design world. The results have left many homes drab, uncomfortable, and dark. Often the blame goes elsewhere when improper lighting is the real culprit causing the discomfort. Helping people become aware of what lighting can do is the first step.

Most of us simply accept what light there is within a given space instead of realizing that we can change and improve the situation. The main objective of this book is to create a *language of light* that is easily understood by design professionals, homeowners, and contractors. Once we all speak the same language, then communication is better and fewer mistakes are made.

Light has four specific duties: to provide **decorative**, **accent**, **task**, and/or **ambient** illumination. No single light source can perform all the functions of lighting required for a given space. Understanding these differences will help you create cohesive designs that better integrate illumination into your overall plan.

The following sections explain the four functions.

DECORATIVE LIGHT

Luminaires (this is the lighting industry's term for light fixture) such as **chandeliers**, candlestick-type wall **sconces**, and table lamps work best when they are used to create the sparkle for a room. They alone cannot adequately provide usable illumination for other functions without overpowering the other design aspects of the space. Think of them as the "supermodels" of illumination. Their one and only job is to look fantastic. Another way to visualize them is as architectural jewelry.

Light performs these basic functions: decorative, accent, task, and ambient—the well-integrated layering of the four within each space will create a unified design. "The mark of professionalism in lighting is the absence of glare."—General Electric

For example, a dining room illuminated only by the chandelier over the table can create a **glare-bomb** situation. As you turn up the **dimmer** to provide enough illumination to see, the intensity of the light from the decorative fixture causes every other object to fall into secondary importance (see Figure 1.1). The wall color, the art, the carpeting, and especially the people are eclipsed by this supernova of uncomfortably bright light. No one will be able to adequately see any of the other elements in the room, no matter how beautiful or expertly designed.

By its very nature, any bright light source in a room or space immediately draws people's attention. In the best designs, the decorative light sources only create the illusion of providing a room's illumination. In reality, it is the other three functions of light (task, accent, and ambient) that are actually doing the real work of lighting up the space.

Another common example of poorly done lighting is the overuse of table lamps and wall sconces with **translucent** shades. Filling a room with translucent shades makes the room look like a lamp shade showroom. It is partly because translucent shades, such as those made of linen or parchment, can draw too much attention to them (see Figure 1.2). When incorporating this type of decorative fixture into a lighting design, consider using an **opaque** shade with a perforated metal diffuser fitted on top. This will help direct the illumination downward over the base, the tabletop, and across your lap when you're reading.

Filling a room with only table lamps to provide the main source of illumination is bad lighting design, as it uses only one available light source. The other three functions of illumination must come into play. This is called **light layering**, where a number of light sources are blended together to create a comfortable, inviting, and flexible environment.

ACCENT LIGHT

Accent light is directed illumination that highlights objects within an environment. Luminaires such as **track lighting** and **recessed adjustable fixtures** are used to bring attention to art,

FIGURE 1.1
No matter how striking a decorative fixture is, such as this oval shaped pendant, if there is no other lighting in the room it tends to visually dominate. This is where effective light layering comes into play.

FIGURE 1.2
Here we see the same style of wall sconce, manufactured by Boyd Lighting, with three types of shades. The fixture in the center has an opaque black shade, the fixture on the right has an opaque metal shade, and the fixture on the left has a translucent linen shade. Of the three, your eye is automatically drawn to the translucent shade.

sculptures, tabletops, and plants. Just like any of the other three functions, accent light should not be the only source of illumination in a room.

The museum effect: when art becomes visually more important than people within the space. Even museums now add additional illumination beyond accent light to help reduce eye fatigue by cutting the contrast in the overall environment.

If you use only accent light, you get the **museum effect**, where the art visually takes over the room while guests fall into darkness. Subconsciously, people will feel that the art is more important than they are. Of course, some of your clients may indeed feel that the art is more important than their guests. Their desires must be taken into account, even if they seem to be incorrect. You may be able compromise on a more layered design that provides some ambient light. If not, their guests will just have to try to be witty or profound enough to compete with the art. (See Figure 1.3.)

How many times have you had to sit down or search for an espresso after going through three rooms in a museum? People can get really exhausted when looking at illuminated art next to non-illuminated walls. Even museums are now adding additional illumination beyond accent light to help reduce eye fatigue, thus cutting the contrast in the overall environment. They too are learning the advantages of light layering to counteract the life-force-draining museum effect.

Effective accent lighting thrives on subtlety. A focused beam of light—directed at an orchid or highlighting an abstract painting above an ornate chest of drawers—can create a wondrous effect. If done well, people won't notice the light itself. They will see only the object being illuminated. The most successful lighting effect achieves its magic through its very invisibility. If you see the light source, then there is no magic.

In the movies, if we can tell how a special effect has been achieved, we feel cheated. We don't want to know how it's done, because we want to think it's supernatural. In lighting design, it

FIGURE 1.3
This African mask is being illuminated subtly with a single recessed accent light. By itself it would dominate the room. It must be layered with other types of lighting to be part of a well-integrated lighting design.

Veiling reflection refers to the glare and eye fatigue resulting from overhead light hitting directly on white paper with black print, as if you were trying to read through a veil.

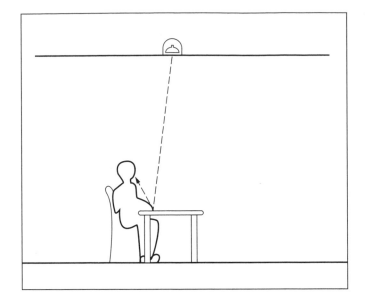

should be no less the case. We want to see the effects of light, but the method needs to remain unseen. This subtlety is what will create a cohesive wholeness, allowing the design, the architecture, the furnishings, and the landscaping to become the focus of a space, not the luminaires or the lamps glaring out from within them.

TASK LIGHT

Task light is illumination for performing work-related activities, such as reading, cutting vegetables, and sorting laundry. The optimal task light is located between your head and the work surface. Lighting from above isn't a good source of task light, because your head casts a shadow onto your book, computer keyboard, or ransom note.

FIGURE 1.4
Veiling reflection (glare) occurs when task lighting is placed directly overhead.

Overhead lighting or incorrectly placed **task lighting** often contributes to what is called **veiling reflection**. It occurs when your eyes try to accommodate the contrast between black print on white paper. This happens when light comes down from the ceiling, hitting the paper at such an angle that the glare is reflected directly into your eyes, causing eye fatigue. Think of it as the mirror-like reflection of a light source on a shiny surface. It may be a glossy magazine page or any matte surface that has markings of shiny ink, pencil lead, or other glossy substance. Veiling reflection is a way of describing the resulting brightness that washes out the contrast of the print or picture. The term comes from an uncomfortable situation where you are trying to read something while wearing a veil (see Figure 1.4).

Another related term is **photo-pigment bleaching**. When you try to read a book or a magazine outside, sometimes the brightness of the sunlight on the page makes it difficult to read. You end up moving to a shaded spot or tilting the magazine until the sun isn't hitting it directly.

A reflective surface is always a reflective surface, which means you can't eliminate glare if you are focusing light onto a mirror-like finish. What you can do is redirect the glare away from the normal viewing angle. That's why light coming in from one side or both sides, instead of directly overhead, is more effective: It directs the glare away from your eyes.

Ambient light is the soft, general illumination that fills the volume of a room with a glow of light and softens the shadows on people's faces. It is the most important of the four functions of light, but it is often the one element that is left out of the design of a room or space.

Portable tabletop luminaires (this is what everybody but lighting designers call table lamps) with opaque shades often do the best job for casual reading, because they direct the light better and don't visually overpower the room when turned up to the correct intensity for the job at hand. You may be thinking, "That's fine and dandy for some Euro-chic interior, but what about my Louis XVI library?" Well, a **Bouillotte lamp** (see Figure 1.5) does a great job of task lighting, as does a **banker's lamp** (see Figure 1.6). **Fluorescent** or **light-emitting diode (LED)** linear lights are also a good source of task illumination when mounted over a work surface with a shelf above or in the kitchen with the fixture mounted under the overhead cabinets. Incandescent versions are not energy-efficient and can get very hot. You will learn about the differences in the types of lamps that are available in Chapter 3. As we go from room to room in Section Two, you will get more examples of properly placed task lighting.

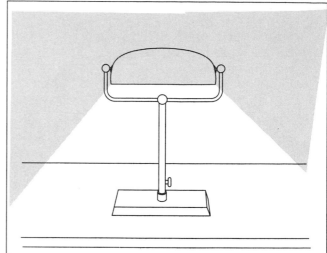

AMBIENT LIGHT

Ambient light is the soft, general illumination that fills the volume of a room with a glow of light and softens the shadows on people's faces. It is the most important of the four functions of light, but it is often the one element that is left out of the design of a room or space.

The best ambient light comes from sources that bounce illumination off the ceiling and walls. Such luminaires as opaque indirect wall sconces (see Figure 1.7), **torchères** (floor lamps), indirect **pendants** (see Figure 1.8), and **cove lighting** can provide a subtle general illumination without drawing attention to the source. You could call it the **open-hearth effect**, where the room seems to be filled with the light of a roaring fire.

Keep in mind that filling a room with table lamps does not provide adequate ambient illumination. These are decorative fixtures that can double as task lights when needed, but they cannot provide ambient light, although they can provide **ambience**. This is what helps people form an impression of a space. Using them alone in a space creates blobs of uncomfortable illumination that overpower the environment. Let these portable luminaires be a true decorative source, creating welcoming little islands of light instead. As mentioned earlier, using opaque shades and perforated metal lids can turn these luminaires into more effective reading lights. Utilizing other sources to provide the necessary ambient light lets the decorative luminaires create the illusion of illuminating the room without dominating the design.

The inclusion of an ambient light source works well only if the ceiling is light in color. For example, a richly hued eggplant-colored ceiling in a Victorian dining room or a dark wooden ceiling in a cabin retreat would make indirect light sources ineffective, because the dark surfaces absorb most of the light instead of reflecting it back into the space.

One viable solution to this situation is to lighten the color of the ceiling. Sometimes the best answer to a lighting problem is to alter the environment rather than change the luminaire. Instead of the whole ceiling being painted in a dark color, how about a wide border in that color

FIGURE 1.5 (left)
A Bouillotte lamp is a traditional tabletop fixture that provides excellent task lighting in a traditional setting.

FIGURE 1.6 (right)
A banker's lamp is another traditional-style fixture that provides good task light while blending into a more traditional setting.

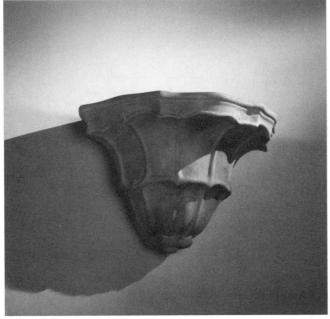

FIGURE 1.7 (left)
This is an example of an opaque wall sconce, by Sirmos Lighting, that offers ambient light from a shape that appears to be an architectural detail.

FIGURE 1.8 (right)
This modern pendant, the Zsu-Zsu made by Artimede, offers good ambient illumination along with a decorative element. It comes in three sizes and is available in both incandescent and fluorescent versions. You will learn more about the advantages of fluorescent lamps in Chapter 3.

with the rest of the ceiling done in a cream color or similarly light hue? A wooden ceiling could be washed with a light-colored opaque stain, giving it a more weathered look without taking away from the wood feel itself, as simple painting would.

If you or your clients are dead set against changing the color, luminaires such as the ones shown in Figures 1.9 and 1.10 will provide their own reflective surfaces. If you were faced with a situation like this where a lighter-colored surface is not an option, a possibility would be to use a luminaire that essentially provides its own ceiling.

Using a traditional chandelier or pendant with a hidden **halogen** or fluorescent source could complement the design while adding a subtle layer of ambient light. Sometimes luminaires can be multifunctional, providing either task and decorative light or task and ambient light from the same fixture.

One such luminaire has been out on the market for many years. It is a metal-shaded pendant generally known as a **RLM** fixture (Figure 1.9). It has a white-painted interior fitted with a **silver bowl reflector lamp**. A silver bowl reflector lamp is a bulb that is coated on the top of the glass envelope to project light toward the base of the bulb. The illumination from the reflector lamp is then bounced off the inside of the shade itself, instead of the ceiling, to provide an adequate

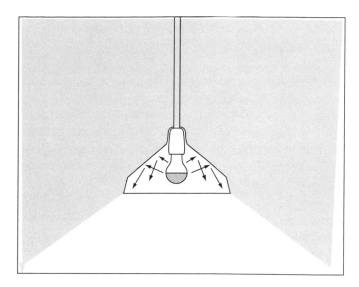

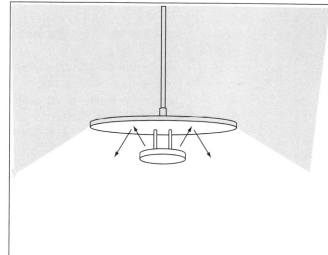

level of ambient light. This a good type of fixture to use when you want to create the illusion of a secondary ceiling level in a vaulted space to create a more human scale to a room. There are more modern versions of the RLM, such as the one shown in (Figure 1.10). The halogen source fitted within an integral reflector bounces light off the dish-shaped reflector and down into the room below.

There are many ways of getting ambient light into a room. Ambient light, just like the other three functions, should not be used by itself, because you end up with what is known as the **cloudy-day effect**, where everything in a given space appears to have the same value, without any depth or dimension. Here again, ambient illumination is only one component of well-designed lighting. Light layering is always the way to go.

LIGHT LAYERING

As mentioned earlier, lighting design is successful when all four functions of light are blended together within a room to create a fully usable, adaptive space. Good lighting draws attention not to itself but to the other design aspects of the environment.

Once you have a good understanding of these functions of light, you can decide which are needed for a specific area. An entryway, for example, desperately needs ambient and accent light but may not need any task light because no work is going to be done in the entry. However, there may be a coat closet that would need some task-oriented illumination.

What we often see is a house lighted for entertaining only. Many of the high-end design magazines show this type of lighting design. It has a very dramatic, glitzy look. Every vase, painting, sculpture, and art deco ashtray glistens in its own pool of illumination. Yet the seating areas largely remain in darkness. What are these people going to do for light when they want to go through the mail, do their taxes, or put a puzzle together with their family or friends? High

FIGURE 1.9 (left)
An RLM fixture coupled with a ceramic bowl reflector lamp provides a wide splay of ambient light without relying on the reflective qualities of the ceiling itself.

FIGURE 1.10 (right)
A more modern version of an RLM fixture, such as the "Spectro" by Boyd Lighting, uses frosted glass or a white metal to bounce the indirect light down into the room.

drama is fine for special occasions but not so great for day-to-day living. You wouldn't want to wear a tux or an evening gown every day, would you?

Also, you should know that the photographers for design magazines often use supplemental lighting specifically for photographing the rooms. Those lights won't be there when someone is living in the house, and the effect won't be nearly as wonderful as it seems on the printed page. What it does do, however, is give people a false sense of what type of illumination recessed **downlights** alone can provide. When it is the only type of lighting that exists, rooms appear smaller and people look older than they really are. On the other hand, if you layer the light properly, it can have all the benefits of Botox without the pesky injections.

This doesn't mean that you should eliminate accent lighting. Just don't make it the only option. Simply putting ambient light on one dimmer and accent lighting on another provides a whole range of illumination-level settings. The additional layers of decorative lighting and task lighting complete the design.

As you become more sophisticated about what lighting can do, you then have the knowledge to give yourself and your clients what they want and what they need. If, once the project is finished, someone walks in and says, "Oh, you put in **recessed lighting**," If they walk in and say, "You look great!" or, "Is that a new painting?" then you know the lighting has been successfully integrated into the overall room design.

• THE BOTTOM LINE

Light layering is the key to effective lighting design. It is the true art of lighting.

The Color of Light—
Painting with Illumination

● COLOR TEMPERATURE

Color temperature and **color rendering** are two of the most critical aspects in understanding how light and interior design are intertwined. The technical definition of color temperature is as follows: "As a piece of metal (black body) is heated, it changes color from red to yellow to white to blue-white. The color at any point can be described in terms of the absolute temperature of the metal measured in degrees of **Kelvin**. This progression in color can be laid out on a color diagram and now can be specified." What the heck are they saying? It would seem that those engineering geeks have been cooped up in the lab too long and have forgotten how to speak plain English.

What does it really mean? The bottom line is this: All **lamps** (remember, this is the correct term for lightbulbs) emit colors. That color affects the colors you choose in your design. Understanding this interrelationship could dramatically alter how you select your color palette for any project.

Color temperature is a way of describing the degree of whiteness of a light source. Color temperature is measured in the Kelvin temperature scale (often abbreviated as 'K'). Sources that produce a bluish-white light have a high color temperature, and those that produce a yellowish white light have a low color temperature.

Understanding color temperature means unlearning your concept of temperature in terms of heat. An oven that is heated up to 5,000° Fahrenheit would be very, very hot. In terms of color temperature, 5,000° Kelvin is very, very cold. The higher the number in Kelvin, the cooler the color of the light. The lower the number in Kelvin, the warmer the color of the light. Try to think of **daylight** as "freezing" and incandescent light as "hot." A little confused? Don't worry—once you've finished this chapter, you'll have a clearer understanding.

DAYLIGHT

Let's start with the sun. If you were handed a box of crayons and asked to draw the sun, what color would you choose? Most people would choose a deep yellow. In reality, sunlight is a yellow-white light. It looks yellow compared to the blue sky around it. Daylight is blue-white, because it is a combination of sunlight and bluish light from the sky. Yes, it is true that in the early and waning hours of the day, there is a golden glow that occurs as the sun nears the horizon and is filtered by the atmosphere. But this is not what we are talking about when we refer to color temperature. So just get that out of your head.

Blue-white light is best for reading true color. That's why when we want to determine the true color of a carpet sample, a sweater, or a bad dye job we run over to the window. You will hear the term **daylight fluorescent**, meaning that this lamp comes close to the color temperature of daylight. However, the proportions of colors that make up this blue-white light may be significantly different from the proportions in true daylight, so the color rendering may surprise you. If you expect a warm, sunlight-yellow color of light from these lamps, you will be very disappointed. The color will be much closer to that of cool white fluorescents, as in the greenish glow of a subway terminal, than a lazy summer's day as dusk approaches. It's great for color matching, but not so good for skin tones.

Color temperature is a way of describing the degree of whiteness of a light source. Those sources that produce a bluish-white light have a higher-degree color temperature, and those that produce a yellowish-white light have a lower-degree color temperature.

DAYLIGHT VERSUS ARTIFICIAL LIGHT

Have you ever gotten dressed before the sun was out or picked out an outfit in a closet with no natural light and then looked down later in the day and realized that what you thought was navy blue was really black, or that two reds you chose didn't really go together? You mentally blame yourself for not being careful enough or being too sleepy at the time. The truth is that under incandescent light (which is the light source in most closets), the colors shift so dramatically that you couldn't tell the difference between navy blue and black, white and yellow, or blue-red and orange-red. Trading your incandescent light source for a good color-rendering daylight fluorescent source will allow you to choose your colors more carefully. Please note, though, that the color of this light is not particularly flattering—so it's best not to entertain guests in your closet (see Figure 2.1).

Why do we all rush to the window when selecting a color? Because we want to see the real color. This is the correct thing to do—daylight does the best job of color rendering. The quality of light is intense and includes the complete color spectrum, so in daylight your material will be able to reflect its own special hue of the spectrum. However, because many of us get dressed before the sun has risen, using an artificial source of daylight is the next best thing.

COLOR RENDERING INDEX

All other light sources get rated on their ability to show color hue as compared to daylight itself. This is called their **CRI** rating (**Color Rendering Index**). Daylight is the best, so it gets a 100 (a 100 percent score). The closer the other sources come to daylight, the higher their scores on the CRI. An 85–90 rating is considered pretty high (see Figure 2.3).

FIGURE 2.1
The colors of the clothes in this closet are best rendered when illuminated with natural daylight or a fluorescent source that is close to the color temperature of daylight.

How does this affect your design practices? Looking at your samples in daylight is fine for daylight situations, but it can be totally inappropriate when choosing colors for nighttime or interior settings without any natural light.

Much of the time designers use incandescent sources (including halogen), which can be thousands of degrees warmer than daylight. Under incandescent light, color selections will shift tremendously. White can go to yellow, red can turn to orange, blue shifts toward green, and grays can turn to tan. Then all your hard work and hours of color selection are down the drain. The bottom line is to make sure to select colors and show your colors to clients under both natural light and the artificial light source you will be using at night so that they will see how these colors can dramatically shift. Most people think that daylight and incandescent light are the same color. This couldn't be further from the truth. They are almost at opposite ends of the **color spectrum**. This difference will greatly affect how these colors are interpreted.

Take a look at Figure 2.2. It shows how some sample lamps compare in terms of color temperature. At the top of the chart, you will see incandescent and **fluorescent** lamps, which give off a warmer (yellowier) color. At the bottom of the chart are the more blue-white sources of light, such as daylight and full-spectrum fluorescent, which are very cool colors. Incandescent, fluorescent, LEDs, and **high-intensity discharge lamps** (**HIDs**) come in many colors. In Chapter 3, you'll get more detailed information on the various lamps that are available.

Rule of Thumb: The higher the Kelvin rating, the whiter (cooler) the color of the light will be; the lower the rating, the more yellow (warmer) the color of the light will be.

FIGURE 2.2

A sampling of Lamp Color
Specifications. Courtesy of
G.E. Lighting, Nela Park.

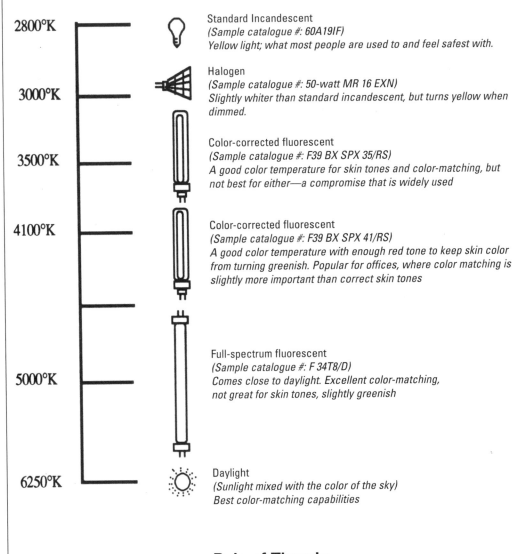

A Sampling of Often Used Lamps and Their Color-Temperature Ratings Measured in Degrees of Kelvin (K°)

2800°K

Standard Incandescent
(Sample catalogue #: 60A19IF)
Yellow light; what most people are used to and feel safest with.

3000°K

Halogen
(Sample catalogue #: 50-watt MR 16 EXN)
Slightly whiter than standard incandescent, but turns yellow when dimmed.

3500°K

Color-corrected fluorescent
(Sample catalogue #: F39 BX SPX 35/RS)
A good color temperature for skin tones and color-matching, but not best for either—a compromise that is widely used

4100°K

Color-corrected fluorescent
(Sample catalogue #: F39 BX SPX 41/RS)
A good color temperature with enough red tone to keep skin color from turning greenish. Popular for offices, where color matching is slightly more important than correct skin tones

5000°K

Full-spectrum fluorescent
(Sample catalogue #: F 34T8/D)
Comes close to daylight. Excellent color-matching, not great for skin tones, slightly greenish

6250°K

Daylight
(Sunlight mixed with the color of the sky)
Best color-matching capabilities

Rule of Thumb:
The lower the number, the warmer the color of light.
The higher the number, the cooler the color of the light.
Reds and peaches look better under a warmer color temperature, while blues and greens look better under a cooler color temperature.

Lamp	CRI (approx.)	Color (approx.)	Whiteness	Colors Enhanced	Colors Greyed	Notes
Warm White	52	3000	Yellowish	Orange, Yellow	Red, Blue, Green	—
White	60	3450	Pale Yellow	Orange, Yellow	Red, Blue, Green	—
Cool White	62	4150	White White	Yellow, Orange, Blue	Red	—
Daylight	75	6250	Bluish	Green, Blue	Red, Orange	—
SP30	70	3000	Yellowish	Red, Orange	Deep red, Blue	Rare-earth Phosphors
SPX27	81	2700	Warm Yellow	Red, Orange	Blue	Rare-earth Phosphors simulates Incandescent
SPX30	82	3000	White (Pinkish)	Red, Orange, Yellow	Deep Red	Rare-earth Phosphors
SPX35	82	3500	Red, Orange, White	Yellow, Green	Deep Red	Rare-earth Phosphors
SPX41	82	4100	White	All	Deep Red	Rare-earth Phosphors
SPX50	80	5000	White (Bluish)	All	None	Rare-earth Phosphors simulates outdoor daylight
Warm White Delu	77	3025	Yellowish Green	Yellow,	Blue	Simulates Incandescent
Cool White	89	4175	White (Pinkish)	All	None	Simulates outdoor daylight (cloudy day)
Chroma 50	90	5000	White (Bluish)	All	None	Simulates sunlight, sun-sky-clouds
N	90	3700	Pinkish	Red, Orange	Blue	Flatters complexions, meat displays, semi-"cosmetic"
PL	-2	6750	Purplish	Blue, Deep Red	Green, Yellow	Plant/Flower enhancement & growth

FIGURE 2.3

Color Temperature Chart. The lower the number in degrees of Kelvin indicates a warmer color; the higher the number in degrees indicates a cooler color.

CRI—Color Rendering Index—A scale that shows how well a light source brings out a true color as compared to daylight.

There are colored lamps, such as red or yellow **LEDs,** and some colors of HID sources, such as **low-pressure sodium**, that are off this scale. HID sources are not normally used in residential design except sometimes in landscape lighting. They are most commonly selected to light mature trees, public areas, or industrial facilities.

A large variety of lamps are available with color temperatures that fall in between the two extremes of the color spectrum. These colors can be good for skin tones and color rendering at the same time, but they are not perfect for either. A little compromise is needed to make the right choice. The purpose of this chapter is to help you refine your ability to make a good choice in terms of color temperature for a particular situation.

Rule of Thumb: The higher the Kelvin rating, the whiter (cooler) the light; the lower the rating, the more yellow (warmer) the light.

HALOGEN EXPOSED

One lamp you hear a lot about is halogen (also known as quartz or tungsten halogen). It is promoted as the "white" light source. This is true when compared to standard household bulbs, but only slightly. Standard incandescent is 2,800° K, halogen is 200 degrees cooler (3,000° K). Also note that halogen is an incandescent source and, like all **incandescent lamps**, becomes more amber as you dim it. So it is only whiter than regular old incandescent when operating at full blast. Yet compared to daylight, it is 2,000 degrees more yellow. That's a huge difference. This means that **white light** is a relative term. Daylight is the definitive white light.

SELECTING COLORS INTELLIGENTLY

So how do you choose colors for a project that will be used in both daylight and evening situations? The answer is actually very straightforward. As mentioned, show your color choices to your clients under the artificial light source you will be using at night as well as a natural daylight source. If you have only daytime meetings, they may be unpleasantly surprised by the way the colors shift at night. Choose tiles, paint, and fabrics in hues that are acceptable in both situations. That way, you end up with a design that looks right both at night and in the daytime hours. If the space you are designing uses fluorescent or LED sources, the color samples should be viewed under the correct color temperature.

The terms **color-corrected** and **daylight** do not mean the same thing. Color-corrected means that the color rendering of the lamp is good to excellent, intended to complement the skin tones of the people and the colors of the surfaces within the space. Daylight means the source is close to the color temperature of daylight, but it does not render skin tones pleasantly.

Many lighting showrooms now have **light boxes** or **color boxes**, which are display cubicles that show a variety of color temperatures and color rendering abilities from a number of different light sources. This is a great way of seeing how the numerous lamps compare to each other. They are normally a series of cubes, painted white inside and equipped with different lamp sources that are switched independently. Holding your material swatches or paint chips inside the cubes, under the various lamp sources, will show you how the colors are rendered and help you choose the correct lamp.

COLOR TEMPERATURE AND PLANTS

Plants love white light. They look lush and healthy under whiter light sources. Unfortunately, most lamps that are used to light plants are incandescent, which, as you now know, has an amber hue. This yellowish light turns the green color muddy, and plants end up looking sickly. What can you do? The answer is to change the color temperature of the light source to a cooler version. Here are some techniques:

1 Have you seen the grow-light bulbs that they sell in hardware stores? These are incandescent sources that have been coated to filter out the yellow wavelengths emitted by incandescent. Replace the existing lamp with a grow-light version. This is a quick fix but not very earth-friendly.

2 Use a **color-correcting filter** to alter the color temperature of the lamp. To make a warm-colored light appear whiter, use a **daylight-blue filter** or an **ice-blue filter**, among other names. They come in sizes to fit everything from **MR11's** to **MR16's** to HID luminaires. You'll learn what each of these lamp terminologies means in Chapter 3, so don't freak out yet.

3 Use luminaires that accommodate fluorescent, LED, or HID sources that come in cooler color temperatures.

Remember that daylight is white light and that moonlight is the same, because it is just a reflection of sunlight. So if you want to create a **moonlighting effect** with your landscape lighting, here again you need to consider not only the color temperature of the lamps but also where the luminaires are located. This technique will be explained in detail in Chapter 15.

COLOR TEMPERATURE AND SKIN TONE

Even though we grew up with incandescent light and are used to the color it emits, it is not the best color for skin because it adds a slightly sallow, waxy cast. A hint of peach or pink in the light is a more flattering light that complements a wide range of skin tones. The color temperature of certain lamps can trick you into buying something that will end up being wrong for day-to-day use. For example, do you have a drawer full of makeup that looked great when it was applied in the department store, but when you got home it was just slightly off? Why do you think this happens? Do you just assume you made a bad choice?

No, it's not really your fault. When those in-store cosmeticians put you in front of that illuminated mirror, do you know what light source they were using? It's halogen! How often are you seen in a totally halogen environment? Almost never! You are more likely interacting with others in a daylight situation or an evening situation with standard incandescent lights. That's why the colors seem wrong. You need to select makeup under a light source that matches the environment in which you will be seen.

A knowledgeable store employee will explain the difference in color temperature between daylight situations and evening situations. Then he or she may recommend two sets of makeup—one for day wear (the office, the park, boating, etc., when you are seen in a color temperature around 5,000° K) and one for evening wear (theaters, restaurants, singles bars, etc., when you are most likely seen in a color temperature around 2,800° K). You, as an informed customer, will

A light box is a series of cubes painted white inside and equipped with different lamp sources that are switched independently. Holding your material swatches or paint chips inside the box under the various lamp sources will help you in making the correct lamp decision.

look at yourself in daylight and incandescent light to see how that particular shade of lipstick really looks. Don't trust the mirror lights! Go to the window with a hand mirror.

• THE BOTTOM LINE

1 Be sure to look at all surface colors (carpets, walls, furniture, etc.) under the lamp type and color temperature specified, as well as daylight.

2 Warm color schemes should use a lower Kelvin source, while cool color schemes need a higher Kelvin source.

3 Remember to let your clients see your material selections under both natural and artificial lighting conditions so that there will be no surprises or disappointments when the project is installed. Yes, this is being repeated for the third time. So take the hint—this is important!

Choosing the Correct Lamps

• LAMPS, A.K.A. LIGHTBULBS

Welcome to the fascinating world of lamps. As you have now begun to understand, this is the lighting industry's term for lightbulbs. That's why we call table lamps "portable luminaires," just so we don't confuse ourselves. So from this point on, when you see the word "lamp," think "bulb."

In just the last ten years, a broad spectrum of lamps has been developed or refined that we can incorporate into our designs. We now have options that are good for the design and the environment at the same time. Still, you must understand that there is no one perfect lamp. Even though there are thousands of lamps to choose from, you will find that there will be favorites that you use again and again because they work well for your particular style of lighting design. As in interior design, there are few absolute rules—only guidelines for selecting colors, creating furniture layouts, and developing other aspects of the design process. The same goes for lamps and luminaire selections. We can offer guidelines, but what you ultimately do will come down to your skills as a designer.

Getting to know the various properties of the lamps that are available will help you in selecting luminaires, since the choice of lamp will determine your choice of luminaire. After all, it's the lamp that provides that all-important illumination. Often luminaires are designed around new lamps that are introduced by the lamp manufacturers.

Terminologies for light output from lamps or light fixtures can be confusing. A lot of terms get thrown around, such as *foot-candles, candelas, lux, lumens*; what's a designer to use regarding light in a room? One measurement says one thing; information regarding a fixture says another. A multiplicity of terms does not make understanding lighting terminology any easier for homeowners or professionals. The following are the official definitions, which don't do much in the way of clarification. Maybe lighting is supposed to be mysterious.

All lamps fit into four categories: incandescent, fluorescent, high-intensity discharge (HID), and light-emitting diode (LED).

SI (Systeme International d'Unites) is an international system of measuring base units and derived units for science. This includes measurements and terms used in lighting that were standardized in 1948. Up to that time, a variety of standards for luminous intensity were in use in various countries, based on the brightness of the flame from a "standard candle" (candlepower).

Foot candle is a *non-SI unit* (not in common usage after 1948) of luminance, but it is still in fairly common use in the United States. This unit measurement of luminance is equal to 1 lumen per square foot, which originally referred to a candle burning 1 foot away from a given source. Because lux and foot-candles are different units of the same quantity, it is perfectly valid to convert foot-candles to lux and vice versa.

Candela (symbol: cd) is the *SI base unit* of luminous intensity (power emitted by a light source in a particular direction) weighted by the luminosity function, a standardized model of the sensitivity of the human eye to different wavelengths. The candela is the modern definition of candlepower.

Lux (symbol: lx) is the *SI unit* of illuminance and luminous emittance. It is a measure of the intensity of light, a standardized model of human brightness perception.

Lumen (symbol: lm) is the *SI unit* of luminous flux, a measure of the perceived power of light. Luminous flux is adjusted to reflect the varying sensitivity of the human eye to different wavelengths of light, which differs from radiant flux, which is the measure of the total power of light emitted. Lamps (lightbulbs) are rated by lumens per watt. This is important to know when comparing one lamp to another. The number of watts does not determine how bright a lamp is; lumens per watt determines this.

So, what they are basically saying is that the terms foot-candle, candela, lux, and lumen are all pretty much the same thing. It all stared with candles and has advanced to LEDs to brighten our world.

All lamps fit into four categories: incandescent, fluorescent, high-intensity discharge (HID), and light-emitting diode (LED). On the horizon is a new type of lamp called ESL (Electron Stimulated Luminescence) which could change everything.

INCANDESCENT LAMPS

Incandescent lamps are what we are most familiar with. This group includes the standard household bulbs you have been screwing into light fixtures your whole life. They come in many sizes and shapes, as well as wattages and voltages beyond the standard household bulb.

Cracking the Code

You can tell a lot about an incandescent lamp from its name. Let's start with a plain-vanilla household bulb. A standard 100-watt version is called a 100A19 IF120V. The *100* refers to the wattage. If you wanted a 75-watt version, the first number would be 75. The *A* refers to the shape of the lamp (in this case the *A* stands for "arbitrary"). The chart below gives some of the most used abbreviations. The *19* refers to the diameter of the lamp. All lamps are measured in increments of 1/8 inch. So our standard household bulb is 19 eighths of an inch, or 2 3/8 inches in diameter. The *IF* stands for "inside frost," and the *120V* means that it is a 120-volt lamp. This is **standard house current** (the voltage of the electricity that runs through your house).

Here's another example: 75R30SP120V. The first number, *75*, specifies wattage. The *R* stands for "reflector," and *30* tells you that the glass envelope is 30 eighths of an inch in diameter. The *SP* stands for "spot," and the *120V* refers to the voltage. To see how it looks in a lamp catalog, look at Figure 3.1.

So, just to review: The first number indicates wattage, the letter(s) indicates the shape of the lamp, and the second number is the diameter, measured in eighths of an inch. The next letter or set of letters indicates the coating, and the last number indicates the voltage (see Figure 3.1). A sampling of shapes of the most commonly used incandescent, fluorescent, and HID lamps is shown in Figure 3.2.

Here are some abbreviations you should get to know, which are used on a daily basis in the world of lamps:

A = Arbitrary

IF = Inside frost

SB = Silver bowl—the crown of the lamp is coated to reflect light up

G = Globe—a lamp with a round envelope, like a ball

T = Tubular—a lamp with a tubular envelope, like a hotdog

R = Reflector—a built-in reflective surface that helps control the spread of light

ER = Ellipsoidal reflector—focuses light more precisely than an R-type lamp

PAR = Parabolic aluminized reflector—a lamp with a glass envelope of very heavy glass that controls its light **beam spread** using an integral reflector and lens

MR = Mirror reflector—a halogen lamp using faceted mirrors to control the light pattern

S = Sign—a lamp for use in signs, normally longer lasting than standard lamps

Lamp Bases

Along with wattage, shape, and size, base designations are also important. The base is the part of a lamp that makes the connection with a socket. A household bulb has a screw-in base, also known as a standard base or an Edison base. An MR16 lamp, a very popular low-voltage lamp, has a **bi-pin** or **bayonet** base.

A candle-shaped or flame-tip lamp can have a medium base or a **candelabra base**. Just to make things more difficult, European countries use different-sized bases than the United States. When selecting a luminaire, knowing what type of lamp fits into it is important (see Figure 3.3).

FIGURE 3.1

A sample excerpt from the
GE lamp catalog

Watts	**75**	—
Order Code	**38207**	*It is important to use this five-digit code when ordering to ensure that you receive the exact product you require.*
Description	**75R30FL**	*This information includes the lamp's burning position. It also includes the abbreviations BDTH (Burn lamp in Base Down To Horizontal position) and BU (Burn lamp in Base Up position only). Also shown in this column is packaging information (48PK, Carded, tray, etc.)*
Volts	**120**	*Each lamp's voltage is listed.*
Case Quantity	**24**	*Number of product units packed in a case.*
Filament Design	**CC-6**	*Filaments are designated by a letter combination in which C is a coiled wire filament, CC is a coiled wire that is itself wound into a larger coil, and SR is a straight ribbon filament. Numbers represent the type of filament-support arrangement.*
Maximum Overall Length	**5-3/8 (136.5)**	*Maximum Overall Length in inches and millimeters.*
Light Center Length	—	*Distance between the center of the filament and the Light Center Length reference plane, in inches and millimeters.*
Rated Average Life Hours	**2000**	*Average Life Hours figure represents the lamp's median value of life expectancy.*
Initial Lumens	**900**	*Initial Lumens figure (in lumens) is based on photometry of lamps operated for a brief period, at rated volts. Mean lumens: Also listed in Fluorescent and HID sections.*
Additional Information	**Reflector Flood Inside Frost**	*Typical application and/or other important information.*

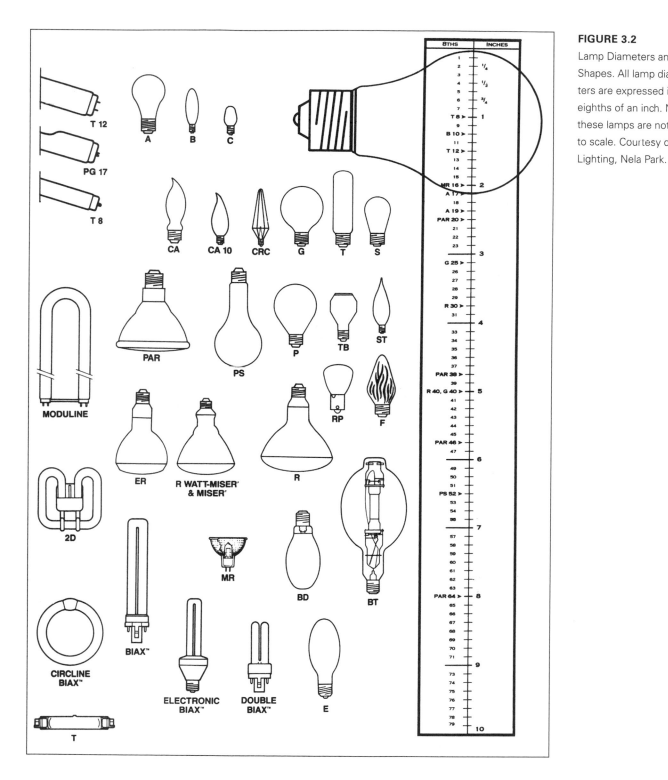

FIGURE 3.2
Lamp Diameters and Shapes. All lamp diameters are expressed in eighths of an inch. Note these lamps are not drawn to scale. Courtesy of G.E. Lighting, Nela Park.

FIGURE 3.3
A sampling of lamp bases. As you can see, lamp bases come in a wide variety of shapes and sizes. The lamp base must match the socket in the fixture. Courtesy of G.E. Lighting, Nela Park.

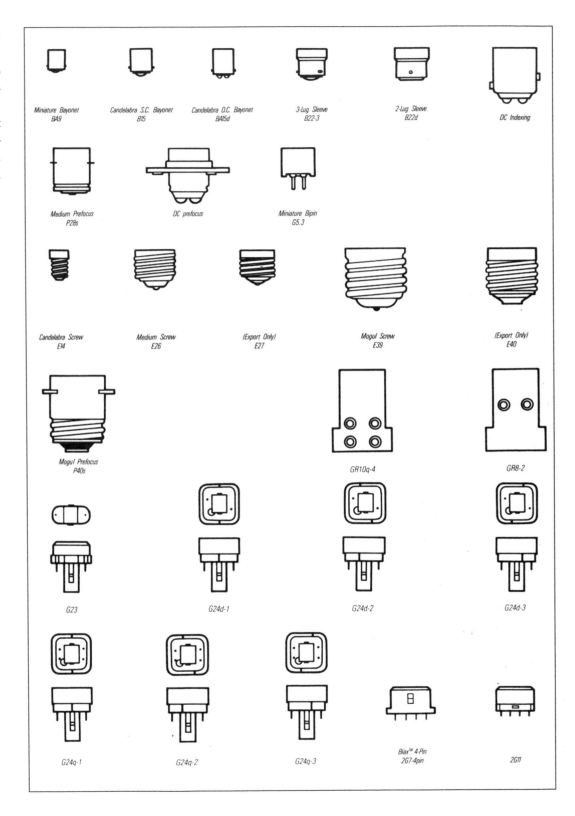

28

The fixture manufacturers will tell you in their catalogs or on their Web sites which lamp(s) fit into a particular luminaire.

Which Lamp to Use?
Often you have a variety of lamps that will fit the same luminaire, so it will be up to you to decide which lamp will work best for your purposes. This will come from experimentation more than from anything you will read. Go to lighting showrooms where they have recessed luminaires or track fixtures installed to see what the various lamps do. Check how bright they are, how tight or diffuse the beam spread is, and what color quality of light they produce. When you are working for a design professional or out on your own, manufacturers' representatives will come to your office to show you the latest models in their lines. There are often trade shows that will show luminaires and lamps, such as Lightfair International (www.lightfair.com). This tradeshow happens every year, alternating between New York City and Las Vegas. It is a fantastic way to see lighting components from a lot of manufacturers in one location.

Lamp Filaments and Hum
A chart of filaments (see Figure 3.4) is shown here just as a point of information. Don't go crazy trying to memorize filament styles. You get what comes with a particular lamp; you would never have to specify a filament type. In the lamp specification guides, the type of filament is usually noted. The main thing to think about with regard to filaments is potential hum. Some lamps hum when they are dimmed. Some manufacturers offer lamps where the filament is attached to a central stem to keep it from vibrating. It is this vibration that causes the lamp to emit a sound. These lamps are often referred to as **rough service** lamps and are readily available; you just need to ask for them by name.

Another approach to reducing hum is to select a lamp with a thick glass envelope. Usually the hum can't be heard through the heavier glass enclosure. It is often the lamp's interaction with a dimmer that increases the tendency to hum. This aspect will be addressed more fully in Chapter 6. For an easy way to help eliminate hum, use a **double-envelope halogen** instead of standard incandescent lamps. Two companies that make them are Westinghouse and Osram (see Figure 3.5).

Voltage Choices
Voltage is also important when you are specifying a lamp. Many lamps come in multiple voltages: 6V and 12V for small lamps, 110V for residential, 130V for "rough service" (these bulbs tend to last longer than 110V lamps because they are operating at less than full brightness), and 220V to 240V for industrial or commercial use. If the luminaire is 120V, the lamp also needs to be 120V. If you try to screw a 12-volt lamp into a 110-volt fixture, the bulb will probably explode when the fixture is switched on. This is not good. Since the different-voltage lamps may look alike, always look at the box that the lamp comes in and the lamp itself, where the information is usually printed.

All lamps in the four categories have their advantages and disadvantages. Understanding what those differences are and communicating that information to your clients is a key element to making intelligent design selections.

When specifying lamps for a project, be sure to stay with the same manufacturer for each type of lamp. That way, the color quality will be consistent from lamp to lamp.

FIGURE 3.4
A wide variety of filaments are being used today. This is a good sampling for reference purposes. The sturdier the filament is, the less it will hum when dimmed. Courtesy of G.E. Lighting, Nela Park.

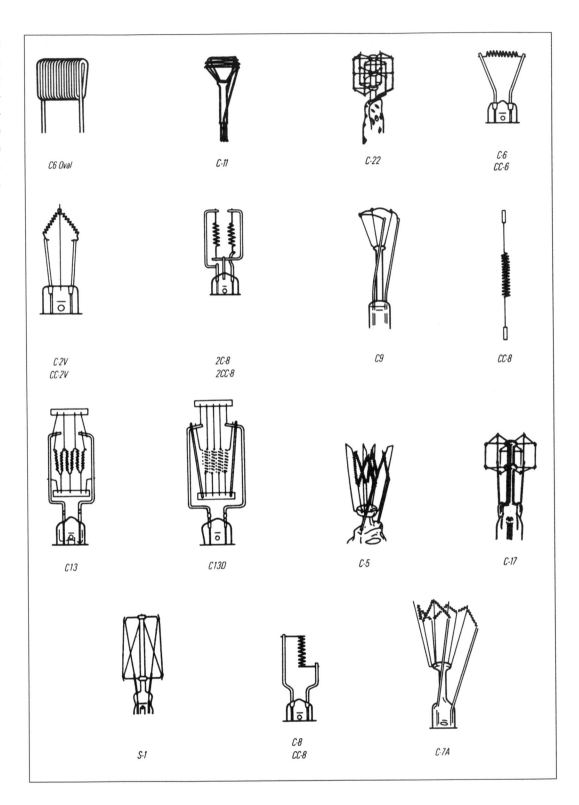

C6 Oval

C-11

C-22

C-6
CC-6

C-2V
CC-2V

2C-8
2CC-8

C9

CC-8

C13

C13D

C-5

C-17

S-1

C-8
CC-8

C-7A

FIGURE 3.5
If standard "A" lamps are humming, a quick fix is to replace these with double-envelope halogen lamps. The thick glass around the well-supported filament eliminates the low-level noise. These particular lamps, made by Westinghouse, come in clear and frosted varieties and in various wattages.

Incandescent Revealed

Incandescent is the type of lamp with which we are all very familiar. It's what we grew up with, and it is the visual image of a household bulb that pops up above a cartoon character's head when he or she gets a great idea. Incandescent lamps are the least efficient of the four categories (see Figure 3.6 to compare how well they do the job of illuminating). They produce more heat than light and are incredibly inefficient. Yet most people are not willing to even consider using other more effective and environmentally friendly options.

The standard household lamp, which you now know is referred to in the industry as an A lamp, has been around since the late 1800s. Incandescent lamps come in hundreds of shapes and sizes and many different voltages. Halogen sources are in reality incandescent due to their structure. They were touched on briefly in Chapter 2 but will be discussed in more detail later in this chapter.

In an incandescent lamp, heating the filament to a visible glow generates light. The hotter the filament becomes, the brighter the light. However, lamp life is shortened by heat. Their glass envelopes are usually clear or frosted but can also be colored to provide a wide variety of hues. A basic incandescent lamp emits a light that is yellowish in color. When you dim an incandescent lamp, the color turns more amber, meaning its color temperature becomes lower. This color shift will dramatically affect the look of objects being illuminated. You must take this into consideration when designing a space. This cannot be stressed enough. A shift in color temperature shifts the color of everything in a space.

FIGURE 3.6
Lamp Efficacy. This chart compares the various lamp categories and their respective efficacies. Mercury, metal halide, and high-pressure sodium are HID (high-intensity discharge) sources. Incandescent gives us the least bang for the buck.

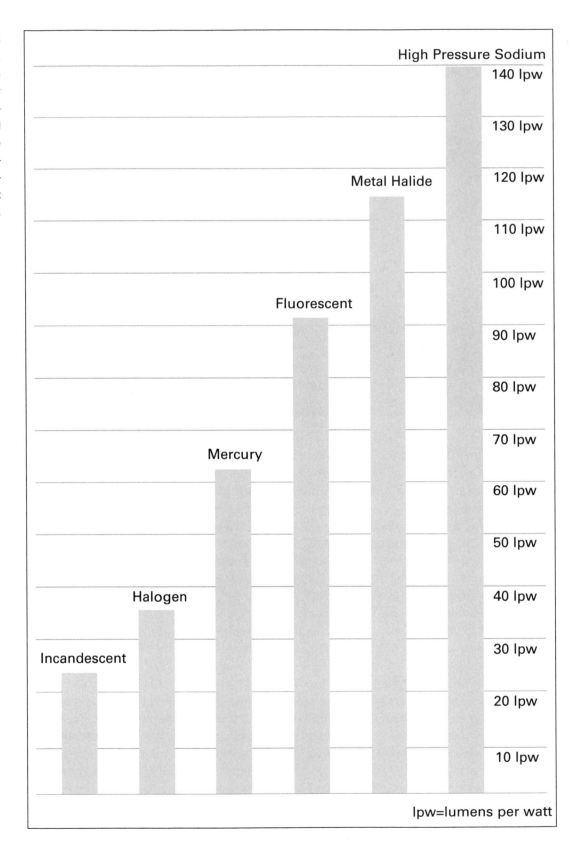

FIGURE 3.6
Lamp Efficacy. This chart compares the various lamp categories and their respective efficacies. Mercury, metal halide, and high-pressure sodium are HID (high-intensity discharge) sources. Incandescent gives us the least bang for the buck.

High Pressure Sodium

140 lpw

130 lpw

Metal Halide — 120 lpw

110 lpw

100 lpw

Fluorescent

90 lpw

80 lpw

70 lpw

Mercury

60 lpw

50 lpw

Halogen — 40 lpw

30 lpw

Incandescent

20 lpw

10 lpw

lpw=lumens per watt

Standard incandescent lamps are:

1 A good point source with good optical control
2 Easily dimmed at a relatively low cost
3 Very versatile in regard to shapes and wattages

There are drawbacks too:

1 Short lamp life: 750–2,000 hours (as compared to 10,000 to 50,000 hours for fluorescents and LEDs)
2 The least efficient of the floor lamp categories (see Figure 3.6)

Yet we love it for that golden glow that takes us back to the time of candles, and maybe even further back, to the days spent in our caves around a roaring fire. Due to concerns over energy conservation and advances in technology, certain lamps have been replaced by newer, more efficient light sources. Yes, this means fluorescent lamps and the newer incandescent colored LEDs. Don't be so quick to brush them off. Today's fluorescents and LEDs are not like the ones our parents or even we grew up with.

It is important to know that the light fixtures you specify can use many of the new lamps now on the market. This is true for fixtures already existing on a project. For example, a 20-watt **compact fluorescent lamp** (called a **CFL**) can replace a 75 A-lamp. They are available as warm-colored screw-in versions that can replace an incandescent lamp in seconds. Many are available in dimmable versions, so you have the full range of light levels that you are used to with an incandescent lamp. These more efficient lamps offer comparable light levels at half to one-third of the power consumption. Even the old 4-foot T12 fluorescents are being replaced by lower-wattage versions in smaller diameters (T8, T5, and even T2 versions) with wonderful and inviting color temperatures. If fluorescent lamps are to be dimmed, make sure they have a dimming ballast.

People need to get over their fear of fluorescents. The moment they see a bulb that looks like swirly soft ice cream, they instantly hate it without even giving it a chance. Try getting your clients—and yourself—to try them out in the garage, basement, closets, and outdoor lanterns first. Once they get used to them, they can move into using them in the kitchen, hallways, living room, and bedrooms. There are even fluorescent lamps that look like flame-tip bulbs for the chandelier in the dining room.

In 1995, certain lamps were outlawed by the Energy Policy Act of 1992 (EPACT), including large-diameter reflector bulbs as well as some cool white and warm white fluorescents. These lamps have been replaced with more efficient light sources. These new sources have found their way into the general market. Now you have to make it your job to try these lamps out.

Note: All low-voltage systems tend to have some inherent hum. That hum comes from the magnetic transformer, the lamp, the dimmer, or any combination of the three. If the transformers are installed in a remote location, then their hum is contained in the attic, basement, or garage space.

HALOGEN

Halogen (also known as **tungsten halogen** or **quartz**) is also an incandescent lamp and might be considered an advanced or improved incandescent lamp. According to General Electric Lighting, "They are just like standard incandescent lamps but contain a halogen gas which recycles tungsten back onto the filament surface. The halogen gas allows the lamps to burn more intensely without sacrificing life."

There is a lot of misinformation about halogen that needs to be cleared up. It is often labeled a "white" source of light. That's a relative term. As mentioned in Chapter 2, it is whiter than standard incandescent lamps by 200° K, but it's 2,000° K more yellow than daylight. That's quite a large difference. Also, it is only whiter than standard incandescent when it is operating at full capacity. When dimmed, it becomes as yellow as any regular incandescent source. You need to treat halogen as basically a warm source of illumination in your design scheme.

Halogens have a number of advantages:

1 Halogen sources tend to be smaller in size than standard incandescent sources of comparable wattage.
2 They produce more light than standard incandescent sources of comparable wattage.
3 They have better optical control than most standard incandescent, fluorescent, or HID sources.
4 Halogens come in a variety of shapes and sizes.

Halogens also have disadvantages:

1 The light yellows when dimmed, as with all incandescent sources.
2 Dimming may shorten lamp life; lights should be turned up full at regular intervals to maximize lamp life.
3 The glass envelope should not be touched without wearing gloves.*
4 They have to be shielded or enclosed in a glass envelope to protect the area around it from its intense heat.

Some other things you should know about halogens:

Beam spreads. With the right reflectors, halogen can produce a wide variety of patterns of light and provide a good punch of light.

Mirror reflector lamps (MR16's and MR11's). Halogens are being made in almost all the shapes and sizes of incandescent lamps, along with a few that are unique, such as MR16's and MR11's. The *MR* stands for "mirror reflector." These particular lamps have been the hot tickets in the lighting world for the last 20 years. Their technology improves with each passing year. Their small size and beam control enable luminaire manufacturers to create a variety of compact fixture styles. Now MR lamps are being made using LED technology, which will in time eliminate the need for halogen versions (see Figure 3.7).

*It is important that you do not touch the glass envelope with your bare hands. The oil in your hands, transferred to the lamp when touched, could create a weak spot on the glass. This point of weakness in the envelope could cause the lamp to explode. If you do touch the lamp, the surface can be cleaned with alcohol. Wearing gloves or using a clean cloth will prevent this problem. A version called **double-envelope halogen** lamps are now available that eliminate this handling precaution, because they have a second layer of glass around them. These are also good to use when humming from a standard incandescent lamp is a problem.

MULTI-MIRROR REFLECTOR LAMPS

MR11's	Wattage	Type	Beam
FTB	20-watt	MR11	10° narrow spot
FTC	20-watt	MR11	15° spot
FTD	20-watt	MR11	30° narrow flood
FTE	35-watt	MR11	8° narrow spot
FTF	35-watt	MR11	20° spot
FTH	35-watt	MR11	30° narrow flood

MR16's	Wattage	Type	Beam
EZX	20-watt	MR16	7° very narrow spot
ESX	20-watt	MR16	15° narrow spot
BAB	20-watt	MR16	40° flood
FRB	35-watt	MR16	12° narrow spot
FRA	35-watt	MR16	20° spot
FMW	35-watt	MR16	40° flood
EZY	42-watt	MR16	9° very narrow spot
EYS	42-watt	MR16	25° narrow flood
EXT	50-watt	MR16	15° narrow spot
EXZ	50-watt	MR16	25° narrow spot
EXK	50-watt	MR16	30° narrow flood
EXN	50-watt	MR16	40° flood
FNV	50-watt	MR16	55° wide flood
EYF	75-watt	MR16	15° narrow spot
EYJ	75-watt	MR16	25° narrow flood
EYC	75-watt	MR16	40° flood

FIGURE 3.7
MR11's and MR16's have a good punch of light for the wattage and a wide variety of beam spreads and wattages.

Figure 3.8
PAR36 lamps. These were
the first low-voltage lamps
to cross over into the residential market.

PAR36 SHAPE LAMPS

Lamp	Wattage	Type	Beam
25PAR36/NSP	25-watt	PAR36	Narrow spot
25PAR36/WFL	25-watt	PAR36	Wide flood
25PAR36/VWFL	25-watt	PAR36	Very wide flood
35PAR36/H/NSP8°	35-watt	Halogen PAR36	Narrow spot
35PAR36/H/VNSP5°	35-watt	Halogen PAR36	Very narrow spot
35PAR36/H/WFL8°	35-watt	Halogen PAR36	Wide flood
50PAR36/H/VNSP5°	50-watt	Halogen PAR36	Very narrow spot
50PAR36/H/NSP8°	50-watt	Halogen PAR36	Narrow spot
50PAR36/WFL8°	50-watt	Halogen PAR36	Wide flood
50PAR36/VNSP	50-watt	PAR36	Very narrow spot
50PAR36/NSP	50-watt	PAR36	Narrow spot
50PAR36/WFL	50-watt	PAR36	Wide flood
50PAR36/WFL/4	50-watt	PAR36	Wide flood
50PAR36/VWFL	50-watt	Halogen PAR36	Very wide flood

Numbered	Wattage	Type	Beam
4405	25-watt	PAR36	Very narrow spot
4406	29.5-watt	PAR36	Very narrow spot
4411	29.5-watt	PAR36	Spot
4414	14.9-watt	PAR36	Oblong spot
4415	29.9-watt	PAR36	Oblong spot
4416	25-watt	PAR36	Ovoid spot
7600	42-watt	Halogen PAR36	Ovoid flood
7606	50-watt	Halogen PAR36	Oblong flood
7610	50-watt	Halogen PAR36	Wide flood
7616	37.5-watt	Halogen PAR36	Ovoid spot

NOTE: All PAR36 lamps listed above are 12 volts.

MR16 and MR11 lamps were originally made for slide projectors, so their catalog numbers often refer to the machinery for which they were designed. They have **American National Standards Institute (ANSI)** letters such as EXN, EXT, and FJX. These are not as familiar as other lamp designations, which, as you now know, correlate to wattage, shape, and size. See Figure 3.8 for a list of MR16 and MR11 numbers and what wattage and beam spreads they represent.

PAR36 lamps. Another group of lamps, made originally for other uses, are PAR36's. The *PAR* stands for "parabolic aluminized reflector" and is available in standard incandescent and halogen varieties. They look like small automobile headlights. Not surprisingly, they were used as airplane landing lights and fog lights on tractors. They too have ANSI designations that don't readily give us information about the lamp, while other PAR36 lamps, produced later specifically for the lighting industry, do have the designations that are readily recognizable.

For example, a 25PAR36 12V WFL means a 25-watt lamp with a parabolic, aluminized reflector that is 36 eighths of an inch in diameter. It operates at 12 volts with a beam spread that produces a wide flood of illumination. See Figure 3.8 for some of the more commonly used PAR36 lamps. These lamps are used less frequently than the MR lamps because they don't last very long and they have a tendency to hum. Plus, they are on the large size.

Here are some straight answers to commonly asked questions about halogen lamps:

What kind of wall dimmer can be used with low-voltage halogen lights?

It's best to use a **dimmer** that is specifically made to control low-voltage lighting. It will say on the dimmer box whether it is specifically designed for low-voltage lighting. Be aware that there are two types of low-voltage **transformers** used with halogen lamps: electronic and magnetic. A transformer is a device that brings 120 volts down to a lower voltage. Make sure you choose a dimmer that is compatible with the system you select. Otherwise, the system may emit an audible hum.

Occasionally, darkening of a halogen lamp may occur when dimmed for a long period of time. If this happens, simply turn on the lamp at 100-percent illumination for ten minutes. The black residue (the result of tungsten evaporation) will disappear. Darkening of the lamp does not affect lamp life.

*All low-voltage systems using a **magnetic transformer** have some inherent hum. That hum can come from the transformer, the lamp, the dimmer, or any combination of the three. MR16 and MR11 lamps hum less than PAR36 lamps. If the transformers are installed in a remote location, then their hum is contained in the attic, basement, or garage space. **Electronic transformers** are quiet because they have no moving parts as do the magnetic transformers.*

What is the light output of a 50-watt halogen desk light with a high-low switch when on low?

The high-low switch cuts the light output approximately in half.

Do halogen bulbs last longer?

The average rated life for a halogen lamp is 2,000 hours. A standard A lamp (remember, this is a regular old household bulb) is rated at a life of 750 hours. Remember that **average rated life** means that on average a particular lamp lasts for the number of hours listed in the lamp manufacturer's catalog or on its Web site. For example, in a hypothetical group of halogen lamps rated at 2,000 hours, after 2000 hours, half of the lamps might be burned out and half will still be working. That's why some lamps seem to burn out right away, while others of the same kind tend to go on forever.

Do halogen bulbs use less energy?

It is important that you do not touch the glass envelope of a halogen lamp with your bare hands. The oil in your hands, transferred to the lamp when touched, could create a weak spot on the glass. This point of weakness in the envelope could cause the lamp to explode.

Not really. The amount of money you'd spend to power a standard 50-watt incandescent reflector bulb (such as a 50R20 lamp) and a 50-watt halogen reflector bulb (such as an MR16) is the same. The difference is that the MR16 lamp can produce a more concentrated beam of light, creating a better visual punch.

Do halogen bulbs use less electricity? Will you notice a difference in the electric bill?

You can cut your energy bill by using smaller-wattage halogen lamps to give a similar amount of light in luminaires that use higher-wattage standard A lamps and R lamps. The big savings come when you switch to fluorescents and LEDs.

Is halogen safe to use in a bathroom? Does moisture affect the bulb?

Yes, it is as safe as any other lamp used in bathroom applications. The National Electrical Code requires that the luminaires be waterproof when located over wet locations. In the lighting industry these are known as fixtures that are "rated for wet locations." In California, bathrooms must be 100-percent fluorescent or LED unless the luminaires are controlled by a **switched motion sensor**

Are halogen bulbs readily available? If so, where?

Lighting showrooms and electrical distributors will carry a ready stock of halogen lamps. Hardware stores and grocery stores carry a limited variety. They also carry lots of fluorescent options as well . . . Get the hint?

How can I determine the width of the beam from various sources?

Lamp and fixture manufacturers have graphs and charts in their catalogs and online to show beam patterns of the different lamps used in their fixtures. The narrowest beam spreads come from the PAR36 VNSP (very narrow spot). The next smallest beam spreads come from MR11 and MR16 spots. Almost all lamp sources can provide a wide beam. It depends on how wide you want it, what type of lamp the luminaire you're using can accommodate, and how far away you are from the object that you want to light. There is no set answer to this question (see Figures 3.7 and 3.8).

How far out from the wall should I locate the recessed adjustable fixtures?

The height of the ceiling and the types of lamp and luminaire being used determine the distance from the wall. Each luminaire manufacturer has charts to show distancing and spacing recommendations for their luminaires.

Look at recessed adjustable luminaires as a good source of illumination for a variety of functions. These can provide accent lighting, wash walls with a soft spread of illumination, or create pools of light to help direct visitors. These fixtures have a lot of flexibility compared to a fixed recessed downlight fixture. People today move their furniture and art around much more than their parents did. The recessed lighting you select needs to be more flexible to match today's lifestyle.

Are there disadvantages to MR16 and MR11 lamps?

The **dichroic** reflectors ("dichroic" refers to a special coating) of some lamps project heat back inside the luminaire itself. This is a special coating. The luminaire must be designed to withstand that heat. Solid-back MR lamps project the heat forward.

Also, the dichroic reflector on some MR lamps can project a colored light out the back. Open or vented luminaires, such as track lights, will allow that color to be projected onto ceilings and walls (this effect is often referred to as "back wash"). Fixtures that are enclosed around the lamp or MRs with a solid reflector won't have this problem. Many MR16's and MR11's are available with aluminized reflectors (solid backs) to help combat the backwash problem.

These dichroic reflectors can often vary slightly the color of the light they project forward. Using one specific company's lamps instead of mixing manufacturers will lessen this problem but may not eliminate it completely. The circle of illumination from some of the tighter beam spreads may also not be consistent. Often, coronas of color and refractions can be seen along the perimeter of the beam of light. The addition of one of the many **spread lenses** or **diffusion filters** that are available can help soften or eliminate this problem. Some luminaire manufacturers include a diffusion filter as a standard part of the fixture.

In the future, we will probably be seeing less and less incandescent light being used for accent and decorative functions. Ambient and task lighting is already falling on the shoulders of fluorescent and LED sources. Even now, most of the holiday lights you buy at Target and K-Mart are LEDs. You may be helping to save the environment without even know it.

FLUORESCENT

Using electricity to energize a **phosphor** coating on the inside of a glass envelope creates fluorescent light. Inside the envelope are droplets of mercury and inert gases such as **argon** or **krypton**. At each end of the fluorescent tube are electrodes. When electricity flows between the electrodes, it creates an **ultraviolet light**. The ultraviolet light causes the phosphor coating to glow or "fluoresce," releasing the characteristic fluorescent light from the whole tube.

Fluorescent lamps come in many shapes that mimic the shapes of their incandescent counter-parts (see Figures 3.9 and 3.10).

The color temperature of the light will vary depending on the phosphors used. Most of today's fluorescents use a blend of three phosphors to give much better colors than what we grew up with. These are call tri-phosphor lamps. Yes, there are still a lot of unflattering fluorescent lamps out there lighting up warehouses and corner stores because they last a really long time.

Ballasts for Fluorescents

FIGURE 3.9 (left)
This R30 reflector lamp, made by TCP Inc., actually encases a compact fluo-rescent within the familiar glass envelope. This lamp will last ten times longer that its incandescent equivalent and comes in both dimmable and non-dimmable varieties.

Fluorescent lamps require a **ballast** to provide extra power to start the lamp and to control the flow of electricity while it is operating. Early magnetic ballasts were partially responsible for giv-ing fluorescents a bad name because they hummed and caused the lamps to flicker. The ballast is usually installed in the fixture **housing,** but in situations where space is very limited, they can be remotely located. Also, some ballasts can operate more than one lamp.

There are two ways ballasts can be manufactured: **pre-heat** and **rapid-start**. Pre-heat ballasts warm the electrodes to a glow stage activated by a starter switch (located on the fixture itself). These are used primarily in small fixtures such as under-cabinet lights. Rapid-start ballasts have a circuit that continuously heats the electrodes, resulting in faster illumination of the lamp. Almost all modern fixtures using 26-watt or higher fluorescent lamps have rapid-start ballasts.

FIGURE 3.10 (right)
Compact fluorescent lamps come in many shapes and styles. They have numerous color tem-peratures and can be either dimmable or non-dimmable. They last ten times longer than a stan-dard incandescent lamp.

There are two variations of the rapid-start ballast: magnetic (the first generation of ballasts), which unfortunately as noted tend to hum and cause lamps to flicker; and electronic (also known as solid-state), which have no hum and make flickering a thing of the past.

Dimming Fluorescents

Years ago, a **magnetic dimming ballast** was very expensive and might flutter if dimmed beyond a certain point. Now, with the advent of new **electronic dimming ballasts**, many of the old prob-lems and negative aspects people associate with fluorescent lighting have been resolved.

For dimming purposes, **solid-state ballasts** (this is another name for electronic ballasts) are the best available and, of course, the most expensive. The dimmable version allows for

90-percent to full-range dimming (depending on the manufacturer), with no hum or buzzing, and you can dim different lamp lengths together. Before, you could only dim all 4-footers or all 3-footers together. The solid-state ballast allows you to dim most lengths together. Chapter 6 will deal further with fluorescent dimming.

The latest technology coming from the lamp manufacturers is the advent of self-ballasted compact fluorescent lamps with screw-in bases that can be dimmed with an incandescent dimmer. A high-priced fluorescent dimmer is not required. One company at the forefront of producing these kinds of user-friendly fluorescent lamps is Technical Consumer Products (www.tcpi.com). This cutting-edge technology will be explained in more detail in the following pages.

Average rated lamp life means that halfway through a test of a certain group of lamps, 50 percent of them are still working and 50 percent are burned out.

Improvements in Color Selection

It is true that early fluorescent lamps were awful, but not now. There were just two colors available in fluorescent for the longest time: cool white or warm white. Cool white gave you a greenish Shrek-like cast, while warm white gave an orange facsimile of incandescent. Their colors were obtained using different phosphor powders. These two choices were (and still are) just poor interpretations of the two ends of the Kelvin color temperature scale. As noted, both these lamps are no longer manufactured in the 40-watt T12 version for the U.S. market. There are new, improved fluorescents out there just waiting for you to embrace them and make them your own. Now there are many alluring colors available in fluorescent. Some are wonderfully creamy peach-toned hues, which are great for skin tones and work well in a residential setting (but not the best for color rendering, just as standard incandescent lamps are not).

You have so many colors to choose from that you can "paint" with light, using a very broad palette. These colors are obtained by coating the inside of the glass tube with a mix of phosphors. Tri-phosphor fluorescent lamps (using a mix of three phosphors) have some of most usable color temperatures for residential use.

Compact Fluorescents

Compact fluorescent lamps have opened up a whole range of uses that were not possible with larger-sized fluorescents. We are seeing them now being incorporated into small-diameter recessed luminaires, wall sconces, pendants, wall-wash luminaires, and many more. This type of lamp is being improved more quickly than any other source on the market (with HID and LED sources running a close second). See Figure 3.11 for the common fluorescent lamp shapes available.

The first compact units on the market had a noticeable hum, did not have a rapid-start ballast, were not dimmable, and had a limited selection of color temperatures. Great strides have been made on all fronts. Today there are rapid-start, quiet, dimmable compact fluorescent lamps in a variety of color temperatures. CFLs are a very energy-efficient source of illumination that can simply be screwed into existing household fixtures, including ceiling lights, table lamps, torchères, wall sconces, and recessed fixtures.

The electronic dimming ballasts at this point are pricey, but they will come down in cost as more manufacturers get into this emerging market. But CFLs' light output, long life, color variety, and energy efficiency make them well worth considering on any project.

FIGURE 3.11

Here are some of the T (tubular) and biax fluorescent lamp shapes that are available. These need a dimming ballast in order to be dimmed.

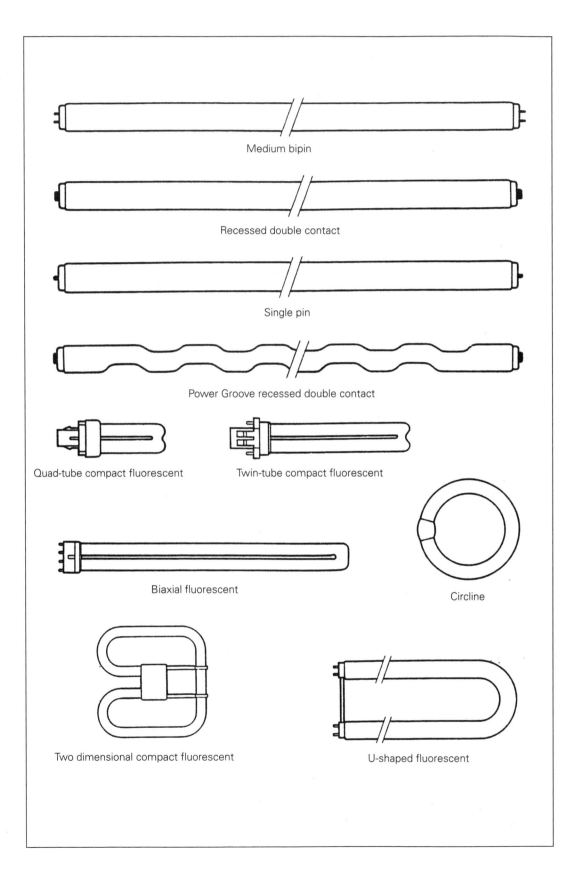

Medium bipin

Recessed double contact

Single pin

Power Groove recessed double contact

Quad-tube compact fluorescent

Twin-tube compact fluorescent

Biaxial fluorescent

Circline

Two dimensional compact fluorescent

U-shaped fluorescent

A newer lamp/socket technology is now taking hold, called GU-24. This is a proprietary socket with a matching lamp that takes CFLs to the next level. It is a hard-wire version of the CFL lamp that meets California's Title 24 requirements. (This will be explained in greater detail in Chapter 5). Its compact size allows it to be installed in most luminaires that currently use a standard incandescent lamp and socket assembly, so manufacturers can offer their lighting products in both incandescent and fluorescent versions without having to reengineer their fixtures. Companies such as Maxlite (www.maxlite.com) are offering a dimmable version of the GU-24 lamps that will make the idea of using fluorescents in the home more palatable to people.

Advantages of Fluorescents

Longer lamp life. A standard household A lamp has an average rated lamp life of 750 hours, while the T8 fluorescent is rated at 22,000 hours! The best that most standard reflector lamps can do is 2,000 hours. A good MR16 gets 3,500 to 6,000 hours, while compact fluorescents are rated at 10,000 hours, a huge difference. It can be especially advantageous when lamps are located where they're hard to change when they burn out—not to mention the energy savings they provide.

Lower maintenance time and cost. Because fluorescent lamps last longer, they need to be replaced less often, saving time and money. Remember that "average rated lamp life" means that halfway through a test of a certain group of lamps, 50 percent of them are still working and 50 percent are burned out. Don't expect all T8 lamps to last 22,000 hours. Some will burn out sooner and some will last longer.

More lumen output. Fluorescent lamps can produce three to five times more lumens for the same wattage used by a standard A lamp. For example, compare the light of a 40-watt household lamp and a 4-foot fluorescent lamp. Both are 40 watts, yet you can visibly see how much more light you get from the fluorescent (see Figure 3.12). Here again, you can see how using fluorescent lamps can produce significant energy savings, because you don't need to use such high-wattage lamps. The newer 4-foot fluorescent lamps with smaller diameters (known as T5's and T8's) provide 40 watts of light output while using only 34 watts of power.

Halfway through its life, a fluorescent lamp may produce 20 percent less light than when it was new.

Cooler source. Fluorescent lamps don't give off as much heat as incandescent sources. So not only will there be savings on air-conditioning, but you won't have the problems of heat damage and fire danger that you may have with high-temperature sources such as halogen. With color-corrected phosphors to equate daylight, fluorescents can make great light sources for closets. They can be installed closer to combustible material.

Color variety. A huge number of color temperatures are available in fluorescent lamps, while incandescent lamps are available in relatively few. So if you need a certain color temperature for a special space or setting, you'll be able to find it more easily using fluorescent lamps.

Dimming. Fluorescent lamps do not change significantly in color temperature when dimmed, as incandescent sources do. When you use fluorescent lamps, you don't have to worry that the whole color scheme will be altered when your client dims the lights.

Disadvantages of Fluorescents

Fluorescents, like all lamps, are not perfect. They too have their drawbacks. Here is a listing of the ones you need to be aware of:

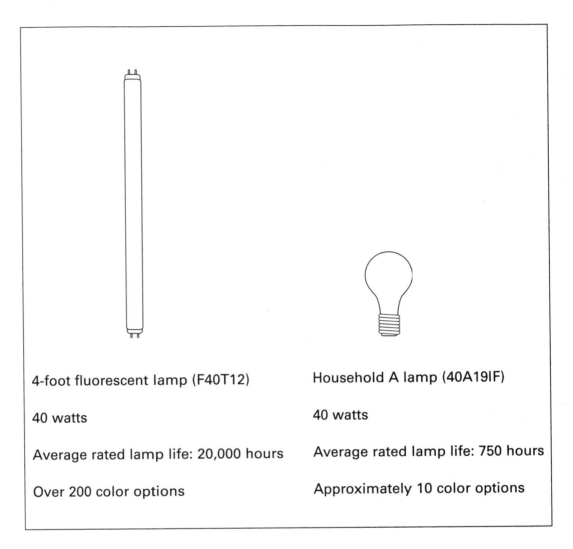

FIGURE 3.12
Here is a comparison between a 40-watt household lamp and a 40-watt fluorescent lamp. The new lower-wattage T-8 fluorescents are even more energy-efficient.

4-foot fluorescent lamp (F40T12)

40 watts

Average rated lamp life: 20,000 hours

Over 200 color options

Household A lamp (40A19IF)

40 watts

Average rated lamp life: 750 hours

Approximately 10 color options

Lamp life and lumen output. Halfway through its life, a fluorescent may produce 20 percent less light than when new. So **relamping** (the lighting industry's term for changing a lightbulb) at that point may be a good practice to maximize the light output for the power consumed. Also the ballast, which is integral to fluorescent luminaires, will still use some power even if the lamp is removed. If you decide to remove half the lamps for purposes of energy efficiency, then the ballast must be disconnected if the energy savings are to be fully realized.

Hum. There are many fluorescent luminaires still on the market that have inferior magnetic ballasts. Be selective—make sure to specify an electronic (solid-state) ballast.

Relative inability to accent. Fluorescent lamps create relatively broad beam spreads of illumination. Through the use of integral reflectors, manufacturers are able to achieve some success directing the light with fluorescent luminaires, such as wall washers for art. They can also be very effective for uplighting trees. There are even compact fluorescents inside reflector envelopes that mimic the directional capabilities of PAR lamps and R lamps. But incandescent and LED sources, such as MR16's, PAR36's, and PAR20's, are still tops in the concentrated-beam category.

Temperature restrictions. A major disadvantage of fluorescents is their difficulty igniting in very cold temperatures. They may start out very dim and take several minutes to warm to full output. Below-freezing temperatures may keep them from igniting at all. Some manufacturers offer fluorescent fixtures that are specially made for colder climates.

Disposal. Fluorescent lamps do have a trace amount of mercury in them, and you must treat them as hazardous waste when disposing them.

FREQUENTLY ASKED QUESTIONS ON COMPACT FLUORESCENT LIGHTBULBS (CFLS) AND MERCURY

Do CFLs contain mercury?

CFLs contain a very small amount of mercury sealed within the glass tubing—an average of 5 milligrams—about the amount that would cover the tip of a ballpoint pen. By comparison, older thermometers contain about 500 milligrams of mercury. It would take 100 CFLs to equal that amount.

Mercury currently is an essential component of CFLs and is what allows the bulb to be an efficient light source. No mercury is released when the bulbs are intact or in use. Many manufacturers have taken significant steps to reduce mercury used in their fluorescent lighting products. In fact, the average amount of mercury in a CFL dropped by the end of 2007, thanks to technology advances and a commitment from members of the National Electrical Manufacturers Association.

What precautions should I take when using CFLs in my home?

CFLs are made of glass and can break if dropped or roughly handled. Be careful when removing the bulb from its packaging, installing it, or replacing it. Always screw and unscrew the lamp by its base (not the glass), and never forcefully twist the CFL into a light socket. If a CFL breaks in your home, follow the cleanup recommendations below. Used CFLs should be disposed of properly (see below).

What should I do with a CFL when it burns out?

EPA recommends that consumers take advantage of available local recycling options for compact fluorescent lightbulbs. The EPA is working with CFL manufacturers and major U.S. retailers to expand recycling and disposal options. Consumers can contact their local municipal solid waste agency directly, or go to www.epa.gov/bulbrecycling or www.earth911.org to identify local recycling options.

If your state permits you to put used or broken CFLs in the garbage, seal the bulb in two plastic bags and put it in the outside trash, or other protected outside location, for the next normal trash collection. CFLs should not be disposed of in an incinerator.

ENERGY STAR-qualified CFLs have a warranty. If the bulb has failed within the warranty period, return it to your retailer.

Prime Uses for Fluorescents

Some situations are particularly well suited for fluorescents:

Ambient light. Fluorescent lamps can do a tremendous job of providing pleasing ambient light. Their soft, even glow of illumination is well suited to providing fill light. The right color temperature and a solid-state dimming ballast can team up for a very usable, flexible, and energy-efficient ambient source of light.

Storage areas. Fluorescent lamps are extremely useful for storage areas and garages. They are an inexpensive way of producing a good amount of illumination.

There are cold-weather ballasts and well-sealed luminaires available that should be used if the project is located in a region with below-freezing temperatures.

Closets and laundry rooms. A color-corrected "daylight" fluorescent luminaire, mounted in the closet or under the overhead cabinets in the laundry room, can provide accurate illumination for color matching. It is like having daylight in these rooms when no natural light is available.

HIGH-INTENSITY DISCHARGE (HID)

This is the third of the four lamp categories and the one that holds the most mystery for designers and architects. But high-intensity discharge lamps are relatively easy to understand and may end up being the perfect lamp selection for a specific aspect of an upcoming project. See Figure 3.13 for HID lamp shapes. The truth, though, is that it's going to be a while before we see HID sources being used much for residential interiors. They are better suited for commercial settings and exterior lighting (both residential and commercial). They are large in size, require a ballast, are not fully dimmable, and have a limited number of wattages.

What Are They?

Inside the glass envelope of an HID lamp is a small cylinder (made of ceramic or quartz) called an "arc tube." It is filled with a blend of pressurized gases. A ballast directs electricity through the tube and charges the gases to produce light. These sources typically have a 10,000-hour lamp life and a very "high lumen output" (this means that for the power expended you get a whole lot of light).

Each kind of HID lamp has its own special blend of gases and produces a different-colored light that falls into these three categories:

Mercury vapor has been around the longest. It produces a silvery blue-green light, which is terrible for skin tones but acceptable for lighting trees. The color can be a little surreal, making trees look ultra-green. A lot of theme parks, such as Disneyland, will use mercury vapor lamps to light up the foliage. It adds a fantasy aspect to the setting.

High-pressure sodium has been the most widely used of the HID sources. Most of the streets in the United States and in other countries are illuminated with high-pressure sodium lamps, which emit a gold-orange light. These lamps too have poor color-rendering capabilities. Trees

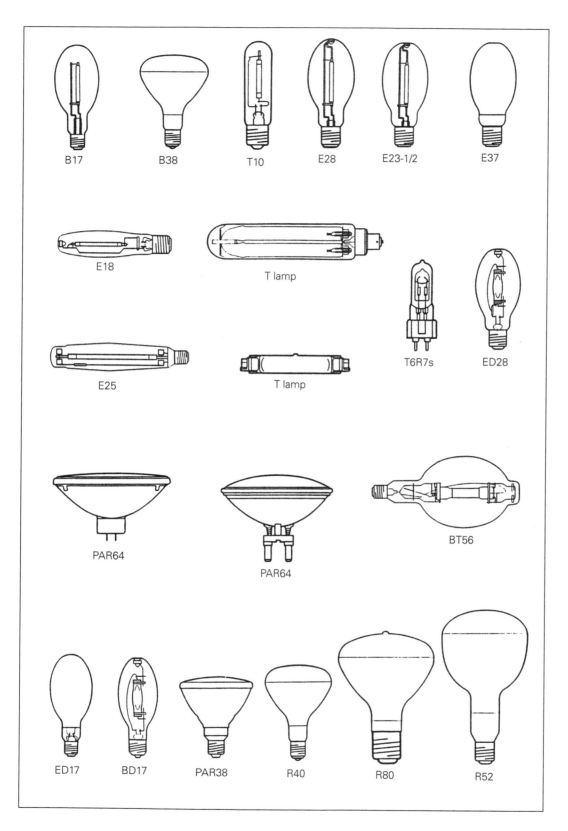

B17   B38   T10   E28   E23-1/2   E37

E18   T lamp

E25   T lamp   T6R7s   ED28

PAR64   PAR64   BT56

ED17   BD17   PAR38   R40   R80   R52

FIGURE 3.13

Here is a sampling of HID lamp shapes. These are rarely used in residential projects.

look dried out and kind of dead; and people resemble the bottoms of copper cookware. Yet brick facades, sandstone walls, and even the Golden Gate Bridge look great when illuminated by high-pressure sodium.

Low-pressure sodium has even worse color quality, which could be described as a gray-orange. This light source gives most colors the same value. For example, cars in a parking lot lit with low-pressure sodium all appear to be the same color. So why is this a commonly requested light source when it has the worst color-rendering ability? Unfortunately, it's in wide use because it happens to have the longest life and highest lumen output. Also, cities that have **dark sky ordinances** require a light source that doesn't overwhelm the night sky.

Metal halide is the newest kid on the block. It is the darling of the HID sources. It produces a light that is the whitest of the four types. It also comes in two very usable color temperatures: 3,000°K and 4,000°K. A special advantage over the other HID sources is that metal halide lamps come in some very small sizes, allowing for more compact luminaires. Many city streets and parking lots are now using metal halide and moving away from high-pressure sodium.

Disadvantages of HID Lamps

One of the main disadvantages of all HID lamps is their tendency to shift in color throughout their lives. They don't all shift the same way, though. Metal halide will shift toward green or toward magenta. This shift differs not only with each manufacturer but with each lamp as well. Mass relamping (which means changing all the lamps at one time) halfway through their average rated lamp life will keep the color as constant as possible. Improved lamps, such as the Phillips Master Colorline™, have a shift that averages plus or minus 200°K over the lamp's life.

Even as you read this, lamp manufacturers are working hard to improve color quality, to reduce the size of mercury vapor and sodium sources, to minimize color shifting, and to extend lamp life.

LIGHT EMITTING DIODES (LEDS)

LEDs are the next big thing in an industry that is always looking for flexible and cost-effective technology. Originally designed to be used as indicator lights in the 1960s for cars, planes, and electronic equipment, this new technology has been creeping into everyday use without us really being aware of it. These long-lasting light sources are now used regularly on commercial projects to backlight signs and displays. Every Target sign you see uses LEDs, not **neon**. Traffic lights are another example of LED technology. These lamps have come a long way from their humble beginnings and now have a proven track record of reliability (see Figures 3.14, 3.15, and 3.16).

The first LED lights were red, followed by green, blue, and yellow. While not originally suitable for general illumination, they worked well as low-power, long-life indicator lights. The last breakthrough was white light, which now comes in a range of Kelvin temperatures and can be dimmed. This development has allowed LED fixtures to be designed for use in residential settings.

LEDs use a completely different technology, coming from the silicon ship revolution unlike incandescent or fluorescent illumination. The technology uses silicon-**diodes** made from two different silicon compounds (silicon/boron and silicon/phosphorus) that are cut into thin wafers,

placed side by side to act as semiconductors. When an electric current of sufficient voltage is applied, a discharge of current is passed from the positive pole of one compound to the negative pole of the other, providing a very efficient transfer of energy that makes light. The LED has small reflectors under the diode that bounce light forward through the epoxy shield that protects it. This technology transfers almost all of the energy directly to light, resulting in very little heat loss. Being a part of the silicon chip revolution, they are also very small in size.

Compare this with incandescent light, which is produced by heating a tungsten wire that illuminates gases in a vacuum. This inefficient method wastes a lot of energy (about 85 to 90 percent), which is thrown off as heat loss, making an incandescent lamp too hot to handle. Fluorescent light is produced by an electron flow between two cathodes, with the light being created by illumination of a phosphorous coating on the inside of a lamp (glass envelope). This technology is a better use of energy because it uses less wattage to produce the same amount of light, the proof being a cooler lamp. The equivalent lumen efficiency of incandescent lamps is 12 to 14 **lumens** per watt, and LED manufacturers have set a goal of 150 lumens per watt by the end of 2012.

White light in LEDs is just on the cusp of development, and good choices for recessed fixtures (to replace MR16 and MR11 lamps) as well as good linear strip lights are now available. LED manufacturers have been very clever in making it easy to switch over to their products by designing light modules that can easily replace existing MR16 and MR11 lamps. They have designed a retrofit that replaces the existing trim and uses the recessed housing that is in place. Two recommended LED companies are Permlight (permlight.com) and LLF (LLFinc.com). Linear track for strip lighting can also be retrofitted. Companies such as Permlight and Axiom (axiompowercorp.com) make LED **festoon** modules that are made to fit into track made by another company. There are also LED screw-in lamps available for portable luminaires, but they do not always meet the current developed standard for incandescent or fluorescent fixtures. Go for the warmer color tones listed as 2,700° K to 3,500° K, which will give the best results in residential settings.

The next big step was to produce white-light LEDs in a range of Kelvin temperatures (2,700° K to 6,000° K). Designers mix orange-based "warm-white" LEDs with blue-based "cool-white" LEDs. Mixing LEDs will help the overall average color temperature so that they can imitate the orange glow of the well-known incandescent Edison lamp (2,700° K) and also have cool-white

FIGURE 3.14 (left)
LED manufacturers, such as Super Bright LEDs, are working hard to create lamps that can replace standard incandescent bulbs. Here are three examples showing various shapes and beam spreads. Notice how the center lamp has fins that function to dissipate the heat and extend the life of the bulb.

FIGURE 3.15 (right)
The "A" lamp on the right is a standard incandescent household bulb; the one on the left is an LED version. Presently the lumen output from the LED version is not very high, but as manufacturers improve the technique, the brightness will increase. The main thing to remember is that a regular "A" lamp converts 80 percent of the energy it consumes into heat and only 20 percent into light. LED technology transfers almost all of the energy directly to light, resulting in very little heat loss.

colors to be more like the MR16 halogen lamp (3,500° K). Dimming LEDs is done by using a low-voltage electronic dimmer such as Lutron DVELV300P. LEDs use a "driver" to down-step the incoming 120-volt direct current to a voltage that is acceptable. A "driver" acts in the same way that a transformer is used for low-voltage luminaires. Sometimes the driver is integral to the LED product that you order. Each company will be able to advise you on the component parts that you will need to successfully install their LED products.

New materials that are both robust and deliver vastly improved efficiency in combination with continuous experimentation, which is human nature, will enable LED technology to reach its full potential in time. Each month, new breakthroughs are being announced.

Consider that Edison experimented with over 900 kinds of filaments before settling on tungsten, which is the one that is still in use today. One of these experiments was a bamboo filament, which worked but did not have endurance. Many of us have been witness to the tremendous advances in fluorescent lighting. It no longer hums, is currently available in a wide range of color temperatures, and can be dimmed. Compact fluorescent lamps are commonly available in small configurations in both medium and candelabra bases to be screwed into portable fixtures.

Luminaires using LEDs can be both highly efficient and long lasting. This ultra-long-life light source lasts a reported 50,000 hours compared to 750 hours for the typical incandescent household lamp. This means only having to change lamps every 7 to 16 years, depending on usage. LED white light qualities and brightness will need to meet and beat the present light source technologies in order to completely replace them, but there are now products on the market that are worth using. They are a "greener" choice in illumination, as they contain no toxic materials in comparison with fluorescent that uses small amounts of mercury.

Problems with LEDs can be "overpowering," which happens when their current limit is exceeded. Technicians must follow wiring instructions exactly, as there is a greater sensitivity to over-driving LEDs if they are not wired properly.

LEDs are great for lighting paintings and textiles because they emit zero UV rays, meaning they won't fade or damage artwork. No UV rays in combination with very little heat make them the most environmentally friendly of the current light sources available.

LEDs are great for lighting paintings and textiles because they emit zero UV rays, meaning they won't fade or damage artwork. They are also the most environmentally friendly of the current light sources available. Although soon ESL (Electron Stimulated Luminescence) may eclpise LEDs in green lighting technology (www.vu1.com).

Caution: HID sources shift in color over their rated lives.

Where to Get More Information

Lamp catalogs are good sources of more specific data on particular lamps. Manufacturers offer a wealth of information, specially compiled to help designers; architects, and homeowners choose the right lamp for a particular need. Most catalogs are available online. The online information tends to be the most current. They are also available through lighting showrooms and manufacturers' representatives in printed form, and sometimes on compact disc. Products are discontinued or added periodically, so it's a good practice to verify information online before making a final specification.

• THE BOTTOM LINE

Understanding the properties of the various lamps in all four categories will also help you choose the correct luminaire. Knowing which lamps work for what you want to create is the main building block for successful and effective lighting design.

Choosing the Correct Luminaires

Being familiar with the many types of luminaires that are available is as important as knowing what lamps should go into them. As you know by now, luminaire is the lighting industry's term for "light fixture." They come in countless shapes and sizes. For the purposes of this book, they will be divided into three categories: portable, surface-mounted, and recessed.

PORTABLE LUMINAIRES

Portable luminaires (see Figure 4.1 for some typical styles) are the ones with which we are most familiar. They include reading lights, **torchères** (floor lamps), and **uplights** (accent lights that are located on the floor behind plants to cast a shadow pattern on the ceiling). If used correctly, they can be a quick fix for a good number of lighting problems. If they are misused, they can visually dominate a room, letting everything else fall into secondary importance (see Figure 4.2). A portable luminaire has a cord and plug and can be easily moved from one location to another.

Please be aware that portable luminaires are just one component of effective lighting design, and for the most part, they should be considered as temporary fixes unless there are no other options.

Humans are naturally drawn to light; it is a part of our physiological makeup. For example, when you are driving down the freeway at night, you are confronted by a steady stream of oncoming headlights. They are glaring and uncomfortable to look at, but don't you look at every pair? When you are designing a room, do you want the linen lamp shades you've selected to be the first thing that people see? Or do you want them to see their hosts, the fantastic art collection, the sumptuous colors you've chosen, and the impeccable furniture selections you've made?

FIGURE 4.1

Typical portable luminaires.
Most can use a screw-in
fluorescent source.

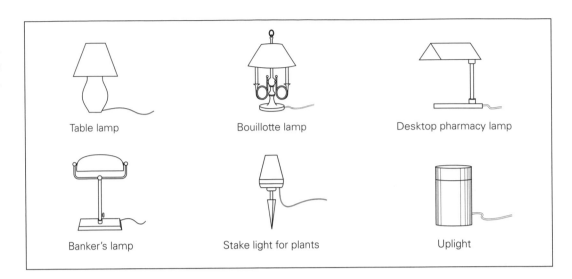

FIGURE 4.1

Typical portable luminaires.
Most can use a screw-in
fluorescent source.

Table Lamps

Table lamps (what the lighting industry wants you to call portable luminaires, even though no one else will) are probably the most overused fixtures in residences. People want this one fixture to perform all the necessary lighting functions: decorative, accent, task, and ambient. The result produces a sea of lamp shades that draw your attention away from everything else.

Table lamps can perform valuable functions if they are selected with care. A luminaire with a translucent shade (linen, silk, rice paper, etc.) works best as a decorative source of illumination. Using a low-wattage lamp (25 watts or less), they create little islands of light that draw people to seating areas and add a comforting human scale to a room.

FIGURE 4.2

Table lamps with translucent shades become the focal point of the room, forcing everything else to fall into secondary importance. An opaque shade would draw less attention.

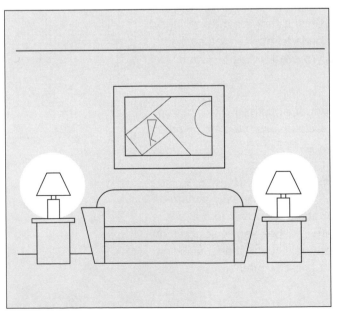

If their primary function is to provide reading light, as mentioned in Chapter 1, consider using an opaque shade of any color and a perforated metal lid, so that the illumination is directed downward onto the table and across the reader's lap. An opaque shade without the lid may cast a hard circle of light onto the ceiling, depending on the lamp being used (see Figures 4.3 and 4.4).

Another consideration is adding a translucent white opal glass or acrylic diffuser on the bottom of the shade. This softens the light and shields the lamps from view. This works very well for swing-arm reading lights that are mounted on a wall next to the bed.

Having these luminaires on dimmers or fitted with three-way lamps (an incandescent lamp that can be switched to 50, 100, or 150 watts) allows some flexibility in light level. This allows them to be both decorative and task sources, depending on the need at the time.

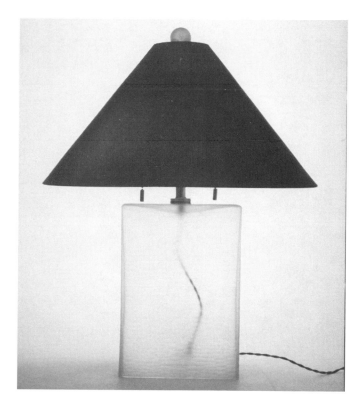

FIGURE 4.3

The black opaque shade on this translucent table lamp, by Donghia, combines two geometric shapes for a positive sculptural effect.

FIGURE 4.4

The white opaque shade on this table lamp, manufactured by Sir-mos, directs your attention to the conical forms of the base.

FIGURE 4.5

A pharmacy lamp with an opaque shade provides excellent task lighting without drawing attention to the light source. A compact fluorescent lamp (CFL) lasts ten times longer than a standard incandescent. It also uses less energy.

FIGURE 4.6

A torchère lamp is a fast, easy way of providing ambient light for a room. Choose one with an opaque shade to prevent it from visually dominating the room.

FIGURE 4.7
Torchère lamps can provide instant ambient light. It is best to select one with a solid shade in order to hide the light source.

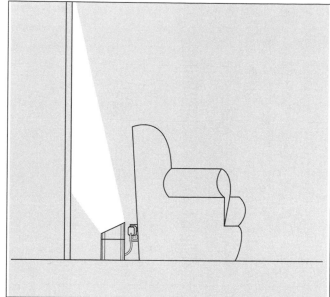

A good alternative would be a pharmacy-type luminaire (see Figure 4.5) with a metal or "cased-glass" (colored glass on the outside and white glass on the inside) shade on a portable floor or table model. Most of these luminaires have adjustable necks so that they can be easily repositioned for the particular height of the person using them. For some examples of these types of luminaires, check out Boyd Lighting (www.boydlighting.com), Phoenix Day Lighting (www.phoenixday.com), and Estiluz (www.estiluz.com).

Selecting a reading light with an opaque shade (normally metal) or a table lamp with an opaque shade (normally fabric with a solid liner) enables it to provide shadow and glare-free illumination. The opaque shade also allows for the light level to be bumped up significantly without drawing attention to the luminaire itself (see Figures 4.3 and 4.4).

Torchères

Another portable luminaire that has been in demand is the torchère (a floor lamp that projects light upward (see Figure 4.6). It is a quick, easy way of providing some ambient light for a given space. Select a luminaire that has an opaque (solid) shade (see Figure 4.7). A translucent shade, such as glass, will draw too much attention to the torchère itself.

Many torchères are available with incandescent sources and integral dimmers, but using a dimmable CFL makes them energy-efficient and still capable of a wide range of light levels. They come in many styles to fit into most interiors, from the very traditional to ultramodern. Some companies to check out are Fine Art Lamps (www.fineartlamps.com), Phoenix Day Lighting (www.phoenixday.com), and Artimede (www.artimede.com).

Uplights

Uplights are another source of illumination for rooms that need some visual texture. An uplight, located behind a tall leafy plant, will cast interesting shadows on the walls and ceiling for a dramatic effect (see Figure 4.8).

FIGURE 4.8 (left)

An uplight behind a plant can help add texture and shadow to a room setting.

FIGURE 4.9 (right)

A series of uplights could do a pretty good job of washing a screen with illumination if lighting cannot come from the ceiling.

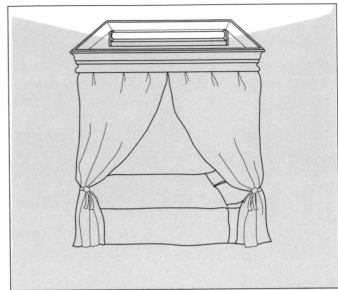

FIGURE 4.10 (left)
A portable accent light on top of a bookcase could do an adequate job of illuminating a painting when budget or ceiling inaccessibility is a problem. A warm-colored fluorescent source would provide a wide spread indirect lighting for a small amount of power.

FIGURE 4.11 (right)
A linear light source on top of a canopy bed could provide some subtle ambient light without immediately revealing the location of the luminaire.

Sometimes, due to existing construction constraints (such as concrete ceilings) or budget constraints, uplights could be used to wash a painted screen with illumination instead of using recessed luminaires or track lighting (see Figure 4.9).

Adjustable Accent Lights

Portable adjustable accent lights are another very flexible solution for highlighting objects without installing track or recessed luminaires. They can be tucked into bookcases or behind furniture to help add some focal points, giving added depth and dimension (see Figure 4.10). Many track-lighting companies make weighted bases that accept their track heads. Ready-made units are also commonly available. For examples look at Halo Lighting (www.cooperlighting.com), Juno Lighting (www.juno.com), and Lightolier (www.lightolier.com).

Where you place your portable luminaire can be a creative endeavor in and of itself. For example, how about using one on top of a canopy bed to provide some ambient lighting for bedroom (see Figure 4.11)? Or what about placing an uplight behind a translucent screen to add some visual interest to a dark corner and some soft fill light for the room (see Figure 4.12)? Portable fixtures work well for rental units, parties, or condos with concrete construction.

Picture Lights

Portable picture lights are available in a variety of sizes to do an adequate job of lighting most pieces of flat art. If you are going to use this type of luminaire, remember to look for the kind that is adjustable from front to back in order to accommodate different frame depths. The battery-operated variety of picture lights, while appealing because they do not require a cord and plug, have a very short life due to the battery. This becomes a maintenance nightmare.

Be aware, though, that picture lights can be harmful to artwork. They project heat and ultraviolet light toward the surface of the art. This will cause paintings and works on paper to yellow and become brittle over time. An art light using an LED MR16 or an LED festoon lamp would reduce the heat generated from other light sources and protect the art from harm. Check out www.fineartlighting.com.

Swags

Hanging fixtures that plug in and are portable are often called **swags**. They utilize one or two hooks in the ceiling, and the cord is sometimes woven through the chain. These were popular from the mid-1960s through the late 1970s and may still be an option if a junction box is not feasible or is placed incorrectly. Stores such as Ikea (www.ikea.com) and Pier 1 Imports (www.pier1.com) have many inexpensive varieties of swag-type luminaires in stock.

SURFACE-MOUNTED LUMINAIRES
Types of Surface-Mounted Fixtures

FIGURE 4.12

Backlighting a translucent screen with a portable uplight is another way of getting some ambient light into a room.

Surface-mounted luminaires are fixtures that are **hardwired** to a wall, ceiling, column, or even a tree. They normally require a junction box, to which they are attached. These luminaires project out from (as opposed to being recessed into) the surface on which they are mounted. These

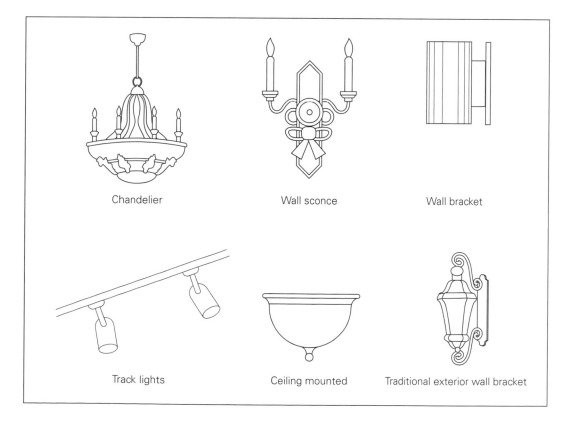

FIGURE 4.13

Even typical surface-mounted luminaires are offering energy efficient lamping options.

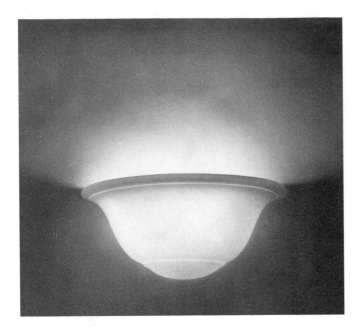

FIGURE 4.14 (left)

A translucent wall sconce such as this alabaster version, by Boyd Lighting, should be used mainly as a decorative element. By creating a perceived secondary ceiling line, fixtures like these can help make a room with very high ceilings appear more human in scale.

FIGURE 4.15 (right)

This arts and crafts-inspired pendant fixture, manufactured by Mica Lamp Company, is both a decorative and an ambient light source. It can be custom-ordered in a fluorescent version to fulfill California's Title 24 requirements when used in a kitchen or bathroom, or for anyone who wants to do his or her part to help reduce energy consumption. If the fluorescent lamps are hidden behind the mica shade, no one can tell that it is fluorescent.

include wall sconces (see Figures 4.14, 4.16, 4.17, and 4.18), chandeliers, under-cabinet lights, and track lighting. (See Figure 4.13 for some typical surface-mounted luminaire types.) Pendant fixtures can double as decorative elements and ambient light sources at the same time. Even in more traditional looks, ambient light can be introduced in a subtle way, such as the mica fixture seen in Figure 4.15.

In older homes the only source of illumination is often a surface-mounted fixture centered in the ceiling of the room. Too often such a luminaire is called upon to perform all the lighting functions for that room. It can be an uncomfortable obtrusive light, often referred to in the industry as a "glare bomb."

Replacing the existing ceiling-mounted luminaire with a **pendant**, an indirect variety of luminaire (as mentioned in Chapter 1's section on ambient light) will help fill the room with soft, flattering illumination. Sometimes simply replacing one surface-mounted luminaire for another can make a world of difference in the quality of light in that space. See, for example, the sconce in Figure 4.19, which is opaque instead of translucent.

Chandeliers are also surface-mounted luminaires. The most common mistake is to let them be the sole source of illumination in an entry, living room, or dining room. Use additional light sources in the room for ambient and accent light, so that the chandelier gives only the illusion of providing the room's illumination.

Track Lighting

Somewhere along the line, track lighting became the easy answer to all lighting design problems. Since it falls into the surface-mounted category, we can address that misconception here.

Track lighting is the solution for *accent* lighting in some situations, such as where there is not enough ceiling depth to install recessed units and in rental spaces, where the clients would like to be able to take it with them. Also, they are appropriate for spaces such as artists' studios, where the lighting must be highly flexible.

Ordinarily, track lighting cannot be a good source of *ambient* illumination, because it is normally mounted on the ceiling. The track heads are too close to the ceiling to produce any adequate indirect lighting. If the track system is mounted on stems that provide adequate space between the track lights and the ceiling, they can provide both accent and ambient light. Should this be the case, use a track head with a lamp that has a wide beam spread to keep the fill light as even as possible.

Track lighting, due to the usual configuration of the fixtures, is typically very directional. Care must be taken not to position the fixtures so that the light beam hits people in the eyes. A light that glares at you is not a good light.

FIGURE 4.16 (left)
This is a more typical sconce with a shade. The perforated pattern in the paper adds an interesting pattern on the wall.

FIGURE 4.17 (right)
The art deco wall sconce was rescued from a demolished movie palace and was reused in a home theater.

FIGURE 4.18 (left)
The sconce we see here goes from standard lighting to functional art. This amazing illuminated sea creature is the creation of Pam Morris of Exciting Lighting.

FIGURE 4.19 (right)
This wall sconce, the Prometheus by Boyd Lighting, could replace a typical candlestick style sconce to add fill light to a room from an existing junction box location.

Track lighting is also a poor choice for *task* lighting. The main reason is that the beam of light produced by the track head is above your client's head, so it will cast a dark shadow onto their book or racing form. The track lighting fixtures are also visually intrusive. If there is another possible way to go, such as recessed lighting, consider taking that approach. If not, there is a technique you can use to help minimize the track's presence. If the space has open-beam construction (a flat or sloped ceiling where the beams are exposed), try to mount the track on the backside of the beams, so that as people enter the room, the beams act as a natural baffle for the track runs (see Figure 4.20). This works particularly well if there are beams or trusses that run parallel to the floor. Some track systems allow you to bend the track into more curvy shapes such as the one in Figure 4.21.

Select a color for the track and the track fixtures that is as close as possible to that of the mounting surface so it will minimize its visibility. Then people will tend to look more at what is being illuminated rather than at conspicuous fixtures on the ceiling. Adding a **louver** or a **snoot** to help shield the light source from view is also a good idea.

Sometimes homeowners or designers specify track lighting because they fear that recessed lighting will be more expensive and wreck the ceiling. That is not really the case. Take a look at the next section for some viable alternatives.

Recessed Luminaires

Recessed fixtures have actually been around since the 1950s. Back then they were square and gigantic, normally 12 to 14 inches on each side. As we moved into the 1960s, they started to come in round versions that were 8 inches in diameter. In the 1970s and into the present, the standard size was 6 inches in diameter, which is still pretty big. Many homeowners who have these existing in their homes don't know what to do with them. There are retrim kits that can turn these existing housings into low-voltage adjustable fixtures that can use MR16's or LED sources; or as we saw in Figure 1.7, they can replace a straight downlight with an LED trim that diffuses the light very well. (See Figures 4.22, 4.23, 4.24, and 4.25.)

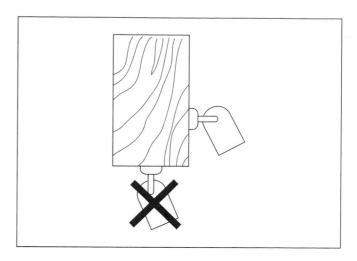

FIGURE 4.20

Mounting the track run on the side of the beam instead of on the bottom allows the beam itself to screen the luminaires from view when people enter the room.

Nowadays designers and contractors are leaning toward smaller-diameter recessed fixtures. The 4-inch-diameter versions are very popular. Here, too, we are seeing some innovations. One is the introduction of square housing instead of the typical round (see Figure 4.26). Another is the ability to retrofit existing 4-inch-diameter housings with LED trim kits (see Figure 4.27).

Sometimes a very shallow recessed fixture is needed to go into a shelving unit or be installed under the overhead cabinets in a kitchen. There is a category of luminaires called "puck" lights that are only 1 inch in depth. Up until recently they were only available with an incandescent source, but now they come in both LED and fluorescent varieties (see Figures 4.28, 4.29, and 4.30).

These puck lights can be surface-mounted or recessed so that they are almost flush with the underside of the casework. They create little pools of light. If a more continuous illumination is desired, then a linear light strip can be used. These too used to just come in incandescent versions, but now LEDs are a ready option (see Figure 4.31).

Some designers like to add a little glow of light at the base of a bathroom cabinet, often referred to as a toe-kick light (see Figure 4.32). It offers enough illumination to get you in and out of the bath safely without turning on an overhead light. They can be hooked up to a motion sensor so they come on automatically when you enter the room. These rope lights now come in LED versions as well as the long-popular incandescent versions.

REMODEL VERSUS NEW CONSTRUCTION

Building a new house from the ground up is not as popular as it once was. Placing recessed fixtures in new construction is easy. All the walls and ceilings are open, so you can see any possible obstructions (see Figure 4.33). Now people are staying in their existing homes and remodeling them instead of moving to larger homes or building new ones. Designers are now finding themselves involved with more remodel projects than ever before. The more of these you do, the more you become accustomed to the problems that are inherent in this

FIGURE 4.21
This custom track system designed by Terry Ohm undulates down the hallway.

Luminaires come in countless shapes and sizes. For purposes of this book, they will be divided into three categories: recessed, surface-mounted, and portable.

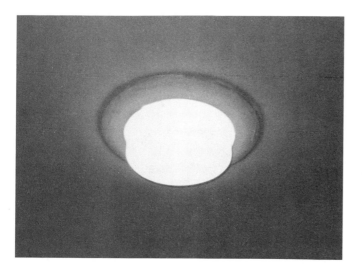

FIGURE 4.22

Standard recessed shower lights often come with a lens that drops below the surface of the ceiling. They tend to be glary and are less efficient, since they use a standard "A" lamp that directs as much light back into the fixture as it does out through the lens.

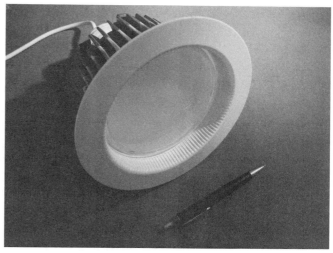

FIGURE 4.23

This 6-inch-diameter retrim kit, manufactured by Cree Inc., can replace an incandescent lamp with an LED source. These kits are made for both screw-in and hardwire installations. The frosted lens helps diffuse the light evenly.

FIGURE 4.24

This 6-inch-diameter retrofit LED trim, by Permlight, had enough lumen output per watt to fulfill California's Title 24 code.

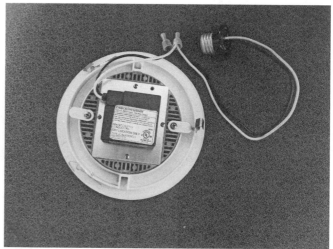

FIGURE 4.25

The backside of the 6-inch-diameter retrofit LED trim, by Permlight, shows how it can simply be screwed into the socket of an existing recessed housing.

FIGURE 4.26
Manufacturers, such as Lucifer Lighting and Number 8 Lighting, are offering square trims for recessed low-voltage fixtures that have 45-degree adjustability.

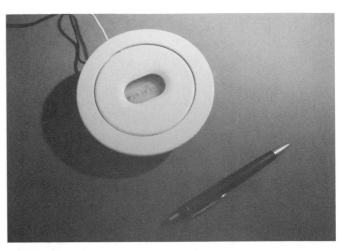

FIGURE 4.27
This 4-inch retrim kit, manufactured by Permlight, allows homeowners to retrofit existing 4-inch downlights with an adjustable LED source. These kits are made for both screw-in and hardwire installations.

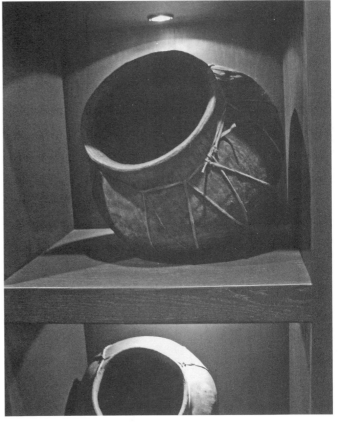

FIGURE 4.28
This LED puck light, manufactured by Lucifer Lighting, is 1 inch deep and 2.5 inches in diameter. It offers a bright punch of light and no UV light to harm light-sensitive materials.

FIGURE 4.29
A pair of LED puck lights works effectively to highlight earthenware pots placed within stacked niches.

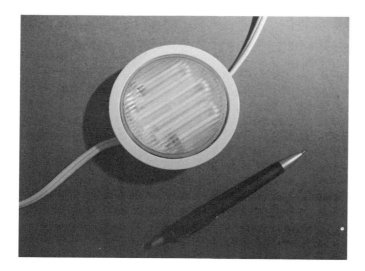

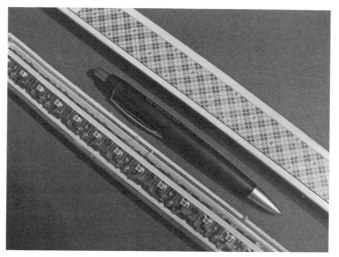

kind of work. What designers may forget is how traumatizing remodeling can be for the homeowners themselves, especially if this is their first remodeling. Part of your job is to get them prepared.

There's no avoiding the sense of invasion that the clients will feel, and how things like plaster dust can literally touch every aspect of their lives. The main thing they sense is loss of control. All of a sudden, they have less power over what is happening around them. This powerlessness, no matter how subconsciously felt, can make them edgy, nervous, and irritable. This is true if you are only adding lighting or the lighting is part of a larger scope of work.

Your job is to give them some sense of control over the process, such as letting them designate which doors the workers should use, what time they can begin work, what time they must stop, where they can park, and which bathroom should be used. You may even go as far as suggesting a private job site phone/fax line and a rented portable toilet to save wear and tear on your clients if the remodel will take a month or more. This is a minor investment that could help offset the psychological problems that inevitably arise on every job.

As a designer, you will come to know how much psychology can be an integral part of your day-to-day dealings with your clients. We are all fearful of the unknown and dislike unwelcome surprises. Informing your clients ahead of time about what to expect and how they can involve themselves will allow the remodel process to proceed as smoothly as possible. In reality, no project is problem-free.

It's helpful to go through the remodel process in your own home to learn firsthand how awful it can be. More than a few relationships have crumbled under the weight of a remodel.

On larger projects, recommend that your clients move out of the space to be remodeled, if it's at all feasible for them to do so. Moving in with other family members, or better yet, finding a short-term rental, will allow them to create an environment that is free from dust, noise, workers, and general chaos. The added cost will be well worth it—in the end, your clients will thank you. Plus, you won't have to deal with them while they're spinning out of control emotionally.

FIGURE 4.30 (left)
There are now fluorescent puck lights being offered, such as this one by Tresco International, 3 inches in diameter and 1.5 inches deep. They are 120: volt and come in two color temperatures: 2,700 degrees Kelvin (close to incandescent) and 5,000 degrees Kelvin (close to daylight).

FIGURE 4.31 (right)
Here we see an LED strip light showing the circuit board containing the diodes on the front. The upper strip shows the backside with an adhesive backing used to install the lighting underneath cabinetry or shelving. This particular product is made by Lucifer Lighting.

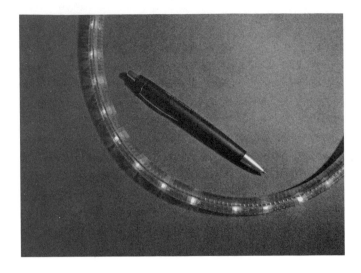

FIGURE 4.32

The flexible rope light, such as this one made by American Lighting Inc., comes in both incandescent and LED versions in both 120-volt and 12-volt options and in many colors.

The following pages contain a checklist of the remodel process, which you can copy and give to your clients at the beginning of the project. Giving it to them in writing is important, because we all have selective memory. Let them ask their questions up front; then help them prepare for the onslaught.

New Construction

Those designers lucky enough to be doing a project from the ground up can still benefit from some advance planning. First of all, incorporate the lighting design into the project right at the beginning—the earlier the better, preferably before the architect has finalized the plans.

Often you come onto the project after the drawings have been submitted to the planning department for approval and necessary permits. Normally the architect has drawn in a lighting plan in order to make his or her submissions comply.

In most cases these are specifications that are called out generically, such as "recessed fixture," "surface-mounted fixture," or "switch," without any manufacturer's names or catalog numbers. Where they are located apply very little to what you will be doing because you haven't yet done the space planning. Put together a furniture layout before trying to lay out the lighting; you can't adequately light an empty space. Knowing the color and reflectivity of the surfaces you are lighting is also very helpful in selecting the right luminaire and lamp combination.

Changes in electrical plans can be made after permit approval without resubmitting the plans. The electrical inspector will simply refigure the permit fee, based on the number of luminaires and outlets installed in the final design. It is important, though, to keep local codes in mind when making these changes. If you have any questions, ask the electrician.

Tools of the Trade

Lighting components and related installation tools for remodel projects have greatly improved to meet the needs of the remodel industry. It used to be that in order for recessed luminaires to be installed into a ceiling, the contractor had to cut a 12-inch square opening in the drywall or plaster and lath, then install **bar hangers** (metal straps; see figure 4.34) to attach the housing to the joists. Next, the contractor would cut a series of holes or channels in the ceiling to run wire from unit to unit and down to the switch. Then a plasterer or drywall contractor had to come in and patch and sand all the holes, followed by a painter.

Presently, many remodel projects can be installed with minimal patching or painting. Here are the components and tools you should be aware of. Some of these were touched on earlier in this chapter. If it is a new construction project, then use housings that are made for new construction. Some states, such as California, require that all recessed fixtures have housings that are made to be in direct contact with insulation, often called **IC cans**. This eliminates the possibility of using remodel housings in California.

Remodel cans. As mentioned earlier, there are housings for recessed luminaires that are specifically made to be installed into existing ceilings. They can fit into a hole that is the same diame-

FIGURE 4.33
In new construction, it is easy to see where the joists are located, allowing you to determine where recessed fixtures can go. In remodel projects, a stud sensor can help indicate where joists are located without opening up the ceiling.

Please note that track lighting is almost exclusively a source of accent light—not ambient or task.

ter as the housing itself. These housings are held in place by using metal clips to attach to the ceiling material, instead of the joists. These housings, also commonly called "cans," come in different diameters. Almost all states allow use of remodel cans, but California outlawed them in 2005. This was for energy conservation purposes. They don't have to be gigantic apertures as in Figure 4.35, but they are still very much the norm.

CLIENT HANDOUT: THE REALITIES OF REMODELING FOR THE HOMEOWNER

At some point you looked around your home and realized it was time for some changes. It's almost inevitable, because most residences require updating as needs and styles change. Remodeling can strike fear into the heart of the most intrepid person. Remodeling has its inherent problems, but most difficulties can be greatly minimized with proper planning and by having the appropriate expectations.

Many of our clients have been through remodeling projects before, but for those of you who have not; we have put together this list of things to expect:

1 *References.* It is my job as your designer to recommend reputable tradespeople. If you have other recommendations or suggestions from friends, neighbors, or family members, I will be happy to interview them.

2 *Contracts.* It is always a good idea to have a contract that spells out what is expected from the designer, contractor, or tradesperson; plus what that person will receive in return, as well as a completion date. This protects everyone involved legally, but more importantly, it serves as a reference to remind all the players what has been promised.

3 *Scheduling.* Since the delivery of furniture, cabinetry, flooring, and light fixtures can be from six to eight weeks or more, the materials should to be selected and ordered before scheduling the tradespeople. Sometimes delivery is delayed. The best option may be to have the contractor schedule the installation after all the fixtures and related components have arrived or at least with a two-week window beyond when materials are expected.

4 *Keep on top of things.* Whether you have contracted with me, as your designer, to oversee the remodeling or have hired a general contractor, it is important that you understand the timetables and check that the work is proceeding as planned. You are a part of the team.

5 *Problems will come up.* Don't let this scare you. It is the nature of remodel projects. If you haven't hired someone to work out the problems as they come up, you will need to deal with them yourself. Some people will have no difficulty with that responsibility; while others would prefer to have someone else oversee the project. A deciding factor might be to look at what you feel your own time is worth. Either way, just be prepared to answer questions when they arise and you will be able to get through your remodel with a minimum of hassle.

6 *Recessed light fixtures made for remodel.* Many recessed fixtures are now made to fit into holes cut into the ceiling and are the same diameter as the housing itself. These round openings can made with a hole saw, which creates a very clean opening in the ceiling. Using this technique, a lot of replastering and repainting can be reduced on the project. In California, though, remodel housings are not allowed by code so new construction housings must be used.

continues

continued

Another special tool called a right-angle drill enables an electrician to feed wires from housing to housing above the ceiling line, so the ceiling can remain intact. Or the electrician can cut a small notch in the sheetrock and run the wiring below the beam. The electrician would then cover the exposed section of wire with a narrow metal plate, and then plaster over the plate to meet electrical **code**.

The more difficult part is to get from the fixtures to the switch locations. That usually involves opening up parts of the wall and ceiling in order to feed the wires through the fire blocking or other obstacles. An electrician specializing in remodel work will keep this opening-up to a minimum. Here again, using this newer technique, electricians have been running the wiring under the joists through a channel cut into the plaster or drywall. Please note that when necessary holes are made, a plasterer or drywall installer and painter will be needed to follow up the electrician's work.

There is also the option of using wireless systems to connect lights to controls. These systems use radio wires to "talk" to the lights instead of wires. These are great for apartments and remodel projects. Some products to look at online are the Radio RA by Lutron (www.lutron.com) and Insteon by Smarthome (www.smarthome.com). This will be covered more in Chapter 6.

7   *Hidden challenges.* No contractor can detect everything that's behind a wall or ceiling prior to starting a project. Sometimes there are factors that necessitate changing light fixtures and switch locations, including obstacles such as additional brace beams, shallow ceiling depths, or ductwork. These occurrences are a normal part of a remodel project, and a certain amount of change should be expected.

8   *Plaster dust.* There are few things more invasive in this world than plaster or drywall dust. Even if the rooms being remodeled are sealed off with plastic sheeting, the dust still penetrates other parts of the house. It is a problem that can be minimized but never eliminated.

9   *Tradespeople in the house.* During the remodel process, you will have a number of people working in your home. It is a good idea to establish house rules that will keep things comfortable. For example, you should designate which one door should be used, which one bathroom to use, and if and when the workers should answer the phone. Remember that they are people too, and sometimes a cup of coffee or a soda is greatly appreciated and goes a long way toward maintaining a good working relationship.

10 *Escape the chaos.* If at all possible; find a temporary housing situation that takes you out of the center of the remodel storm. The investment you make in alternative housing will be worth every cent.

The bottom line: With these things in mind, your remodeling project will go more smoothly. Please feel free to contact your general contractor, your electrician, or me at any time. Continued communication is important in any project.

What designers may forget is how traumatizing remodeling can be for home owners.

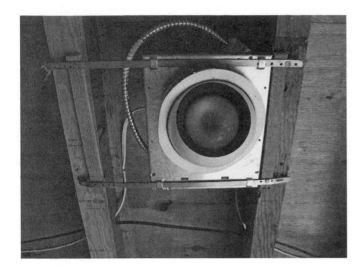

FIGURE 4.34 (left)
In new construction, recessed fixtures use bar hangers to position the housing level with the finished ceiling.

FIGURE 4.35 (right)
Many people are living with existing 6-inch-diameter recessed fixtures from the 1960s, 1970s, 1980s, and 1990s. Instead of removing the fixture entirely, they can be easily retrimmed to use a low-voltage MR16 lamp or a LED source.

The series of **trims** that fit into these housings have edges that are slightly wider than the housings so that they create a finished look for the opening (see Figure 4.36). In any ceiling where insulation might come in contact with the luminaire, the housing code requires the use of an IC-rated housing. These housings are made for direct contact with insulation and are rather large, about the size of a shoe box. They are not yet made in remodel versions, but it may be happening in the future.

Hole saw. When remodel cans first came into the market, the contractors were still using a hand-held saw to make the round openings. This was a less-than-perfect method that wreaked havoc with plaster-and-lath ceilings. They would crack and crumble as the saw moved up and down.

Then a **hole saw** (originally designed to bore holes in doors in order to install hardware) was retooled to cut near-perfect holes in ceilings for remodel cans. It also does a great job of cutting holes in walls for junction boxes (see Figure 4.37). The hole saw is actually a special bit that attaches to a power drill. Good electricians will have various diameters as part of their equipment. Ask bidding electricians if they use them. Those who say they don't could cost your clients plenty in replastering and repainting down the line.

Right-angle drill. Another great twentieth-century invention, this allows the electrician to drill holes through joists above the ceiling line to wire from luminaire to luminaire with little or no opening of the ceiling beyond the holes cut for the remodel cans (see Figure 4.38). This drill comes with a series of 12-inch bits that can be linked together, allowing the electrician to drill up to 4 feet away from the starting position. This can be done from two directions, allowing the luminaires to be spaced up to 8 feet apart without disturbing the ceiling between them.

There are longer flexible drill bits on the market, but the extra length could cause the end of the bit to poke through the new carpeting upstairs, or through the tile floor in the guest bath—just the type of little surprises that should be avoided.

The right-angle drill should be a part of a good electrician's tool collection, but it can be obtained from a tool rental place for a nominal fee of $15 to $25 a day. This is the electrician's responsi-

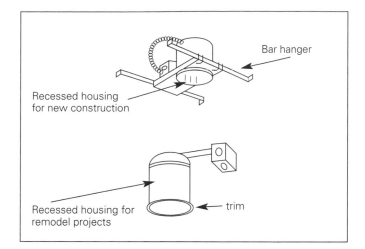

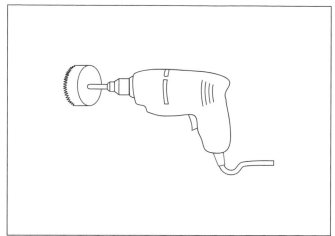

bility. Again, before you hire them, ask the bidding electricians if they have used right-angle drills. The newer method of running the wiring below the joists, which was mentioned earlier, has eliminated much of the need for right-angle drills.

Stud finder. Calm down—it's not as exciting as you may think. The simple truth is that nobody has X-ray vision. So how does the electrician know where to put a recessed luminaire if he or she doesn't know where the joists are located or how they are spaced? Not all joists run on perfect 16-inch centers. Sometimes there is additional blocking to support an upstairs fireplace, bathroom, or heart-shaped waterbed. A stud finder is an electronic device (that senses the density changes in the ceiling) or a magnetic device (that detects nails or screws in the ceiling) to help determine how the joists are laid out (see Figure 4.39). With a chalk line or tape, the joist pattern can then be laid out. If the ceiling has acoustical tile over dense plaster, locating joists will be more difficult.

Wire probe. Once the joists have been charted, the next step is to see if there are any other obstructions that the stud finder didn't pick up (see Figure 4.40). What the electrician should do is drill a tiny hole and insert a wire probe (also called a **fish tape**), which is simply a flexible 1/8-inch-diameter length of wire. The electrician feels around to see if there are any obstructions and also to verify that there is adequate depth for the particular recessed luminaire specified. Sometimes ceilings change in depth depending on what the floor above is supporting.

The bottom line. Understanding how these tools and components work will make you a better director of the work. You'll be amazed at the respect you get from an electrician when you use buzzwords like hole saw and right-angle drill. It's like asking your auto mechanic, "Can you check the timing because the engine is "dieseling"?" instead of, "My car continues to run when I turn off the engine. Can you fix it?"

LOW-VOLTAGE LIGHTING

Many people, including electricians, are confused or intimidated by low-voltage lighting. There are many common misconceptions, which will be clarified in this section. The National Electrical Code labels anything under 50 volts as low voltage. The most widely used systems

FIGURE 4.36 (left)
Remodel cans allow for installation from below the ceiling, often without making a hole larger than the diameter of the luminaire itself. Note: Remodel cans are no longer allowed in California, only airtight housings rated for insulated ceilings (IC cans).

FIGURE 4.37 (right)
A hole saw can make nearly perfect holes in walls and ceilings, even those made of plaster and lath.

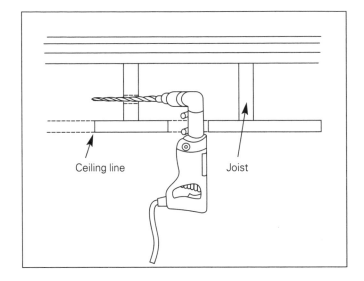

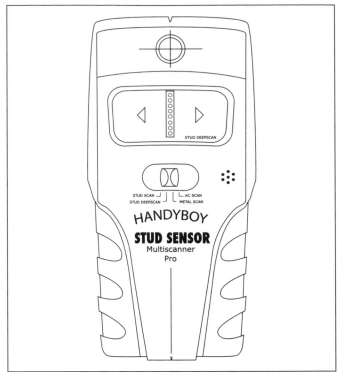

FIGURE 4.38 (left)
A right-angle drill can make holes in joists above the ceiling line.

FIGURE 4.39 (right)
A stud finder helps determine the joist spacing and obstructions by sensing changes in density above the ceiling line.

Ceiling line   Joist

are 12 volts (fixtures and transformers), while 6-volt and 24-volt systems are the next most common. By comparison, line voltage (house current) is 120 volts.

A transformer is used to convert line voltage to low voltage. These transformers can be located within the luminaire (integral) or located elsewhere (remote). There are two kinds of transformers, just like there are two types of ballasts for fluorescents: magnetic and electronic. Magnetic transformers have a lower failure rate but tend to be a little larger than electronic transformers, which are more compact and are quieter.

Advantages of Low-Voltage

Size. Some low-voltage lamps can come in very compact sizes. These tiny lamps allow for fairly small luminaires. These luminaires are easier to tuck out of the way and allow for minimal openings in ceilings. Landscape, track, and recessed luminaires include examples of small fixtures using low-voltage lamps for size advantage. Low voltage lamps can be incandescent or LED.

Beam spread. Low-voltage lamps come in a great variety of beam spreads, from very tight spots of light to wide floods of illumination. Matching a beam spread to the proportions of a particular painting, tabletop, or plant will make it stand out dramatically and help add dimensionality to a room.

Disadvantages of Low Voltage

Transformers and voltage drop. If you choose a remote transformer system, you will experience more voltage drop in the wire from the transformer to the housing, as the distance between them increases. The farther away the luminaires are from the transformer, the dimmer they become. If the distance between luminaires and the trans-formers is too great, it's best to use an additional trans-former so that each luminaire is near a transformer.

The magnitude of the **voltage drop** is directly proportional to the distance from the transformer and to the current, but increasing the size of the cable can mitigate this. If each luminaire has its own transformer, then there is no danger of voltage drop. However, this does increase the cost of materials. Also, remember that code requires that trans-formers are accessible. This is so that if one malfunctions, an electrician can easily reach the problem unit.

Limited wattage. Most low-voltage lamps are available in 75 watts maximum, with a few at 100 watts. This amount

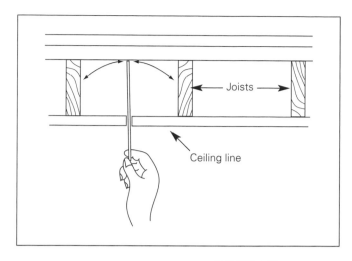

FIGURE 4.40

A wire probe allows the electrician to check if any nonmetal obstructions, not detected by the stud sensor, are in the way of a proposed recessed luminaire location.

of wattage may not be enough to adequately illuminate larger objects, such as tall trees or long walls. The LED versions are not very bright compared to the incandescent versions, but they do emit no ultraviolet light.

Hum. As mentioned, all low-voltage systems have some inherent noise. The greater the number of magnetic transformers, the greater the cumulative noise becomes. Locating the transformer(s) remotely puts that noise in a more out-of-the-way spot. For some people, the hum is barely per-ceptible; for others, it's a constant annoyance. Transformers are not the only potential source of noise. Particular lamps, such as many of the PAR36's, as mentioned in Chapter 3, have their own audible sound. Some dimmers also hum. Choosing components that are compatible will produce the quietest system. Inform your client about potential hum or noise before, not after, installation.

Helpful Hints to Minimize Hum

1 Match the transformers and the dimmers. If you use luminaires that have electronic trans-formers, specify an electronic low-voltage dimmer. If you have magnetic transformers, use a low-voltage dimmer designed for magnetic loads. This helps keep the system from humming.
2 Use a remote transformer system so that the noise is located in the basement, attic, garage, or closet.
3 Specify luminaires that use MR16 or MR11 lamps, to avoid the vibration of PAR36 lamps. The MR lamps tend to be much quieter. Lamp filaments can be a component in the amount of noise produced by a lamp.
4 In using recessed luminaires, make sure to specify a luminaire that has the transformer sep-arate from the housing or with some type of flexible mounting between the housing and the transformer. Otherwise, the vibrations of the transformer may create a resonance in the housing that amplifies the sound.
5 In a room that has hard surfaces, add sound-dampening materials, such as curtains, plants, carpeting, or acoustical tile.

Louvers are designed to help cut glare at its source by shielding the light.

ACCESSORIES

Many optional accessories for basic luminaires are available. Some that can help a particular luminaire do the best possible job of illumination are listed below.

Rule of Thumb: Try to
get the louver as close
to the face of the lamp
as possible. This will
allow for the greatest
amount of illumination.
The farther away the
louver is, the more illu-
mination you will be
blocking.

Louvers

Louvers are designed to help cut glare at its source by shielding the light. Three basic types are available: concentric ring, egg crate, and honeycomb (see Figure 4.41). Check with the luminaire manufacturer for the appropriate louver holder to specify. Some louvers are held in place by pressure.

The concentric ring louver, which looks like a gun sight, was the first one developed and is for the most part pretty useless. The egg crate louver is an improvement over the concentric ring, but it is not the best. The ultimate is the honeycomb louver. They can be made for tiny MR11 fixtures or huge HID luminaires.

Filters

Color filters are available for a majority of the luminaires on the market today. One of the most popular is the color-correcting daylight-blue filter mentioned in Chapter 2. This filter helps minimize the amber hue of incandescent light and produces a whiter light. This whiter light renders art and plantings in a more natural color. Remember, though, that people do not look good under a whiter light, so use this color-corrected filter for objects only, not your clients or their guests.

There are also peach-colored filters, sometimes known as **cosmetic filters**, which are very complimentary to skin tones. Many other filter colors are available as well, such as blue, green, amber, and red. These tend to make a strong statement and should be used judiciously. They also tend to cut down on the amount of light a luminaire can produce, depending on intensity of the color. Companies such as Lee Filters (www.leefiltersusa.com) offer filters in hundreds of colors.

In addition, MR16 lamps are on the market that have a coated fixed lens to produce specific colors. The advantage is that you don't have to buy a separate filter. The disadvantage is that you are committed to that one color. A clear lamp can be adapted to project many colors simply by changing the filter. Try to select **dichroic** colored lenses; they hold up best and give truer colors. Be aware that you may get a rainbow effect at the edges when an MR flood lamp is used.

Lenses

As opposed to filters, lenses are not colored. Instead, they are etched, formed, or sandblasted in various ways to alter the beam spread of a given lamp. Here are some examples:

Spread lenses are pieces of glass that are sandblasted or patterned to widen the overall circle of light produced by a particular lamp. They also help soften the edges of a spread of light. Use these to avoid a sharp cutoff of light.

FIGURE 4.41
The best of the three louver types available is the
honeycomb for cutting
glare at the source.

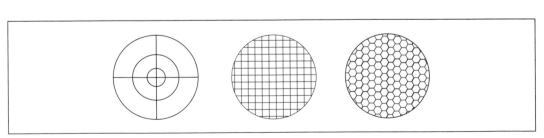

Linear spread lenses stretch a beam spread either vertically or horizontally, depending on how the lens is positioned in front of the lamp. These work particularly well for a rectangular painting or tall sculpture.

Fresnel lenses are holdovers from theatrical lighting. They too help diffuse the light patterns, as does a spread lens. Fresnel lenses are used primarily with recessed luminaires and some track systems.

THE STEPS TO EFFECTIVE LIGHTING DESIGN

Furniture Layout

Your first step, as hard as it may be, is to come up with a furniture layout. Even if the exact design of the sofa or the finish of the dining room table hasn't been finalized, the location is important and greatly affects how your lighting is placed.

This is difficult, but without a semblance of a furniture plan, the lighting will neither complement your design nor be successfully integrated into it. For example, if you are floating a seating arrangement in the center of the living room and plan on table or reading lamps, you must know the location of the furniture and the type of floor covering in order to place the floor plugs in the correct location.

If a client cannot decide on one of your layouts, draw in the floor plugs with a note right on the plan that states "Floor plug locations to be designated upon finalized layout of furniture. See owners or interior designer prior to installation." (See Figure 4.42.)

Another example would be the placement of wall sconces as the ambient light source in a dining room. Their location will affect the placement of art or tall furniture. Will they be placed on either side of the mirror over the sideboard, or will they flank the china hutch? Having a good idea of the size of the mirror or the furniture piece will determine the mounting location of the wall sconces. Also, will the dining room table be centered in the room or centered in the space left after the sideboard is placed? This will determine the optimal location of the chandelier.

As you will soon understand, every design decision is based on a previous design aspect that has been addressed. Help your clients see how integral the furniture arrangement is to the lighting design. Color and style can be decided later; placement is the key.

Elevations

Another important factor is to study the elevations. Check which ceilings are sloped and how high they are. This will help determine which luminaires you use and where to place them. The higher the ceiling, the farther out from the wall the recessed adjustable luminaires need to be placed in order to illuminate the center of the wall, where the art will be displayed.

FIGURE 4.42

The location of floor plugs is determined by the furniture plan and the type of floor covering to be used. This is why it's important to have a furniture layout before implementing a lighting plan, including the size of the area rugs.

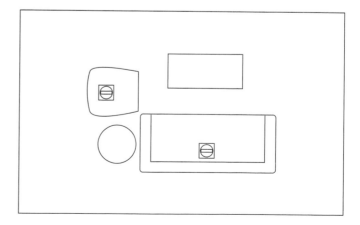

If the art is tall, the luminaires need to be closer to the walls in order to let some illumination reach the top of the piece. If, for example, you have a long tapestry that hangs from the ceiling line, you should use a wall-wash luminaire that more evenly illuminates the full length of the weaving. Manufacturer's catalogs show spacing recommendations based on ceiling heights. Get comfortable using these charts, as they provide very useful information.

Ask Questions

There are no hard-and-fast rules to luminaire placement. It is entirely dependent on what is in the space. The answer to the question "How many recessed lights do I need for a 12-foot × 18-foot room?" requires a series of questions:

1 **What is the room to be used for?** (Some functions require more light than others.)
2 **What is the age of the people living in the house?** (The older we get, the more we are adversely affected by glare.)
3 **How high are the ceilings?** (Tall ceilings allow wall sconces to be mounted higher, so art can be mounted below them.)
4 **Are the ceilings flat or sloped?** (If a ceiling slopes away from the wall you want to light, then a luminaire that compensates for that slope needs to be specified. Numerous manufacturers make them. They are recessed luminaires that have an integral mirror to allow for 90 degrees of adjustment. They are often referred to as a mirror reflector.)
5 **What colors are the walls, ceiling, and floors?** (Darker colors absorb more light, requiring higher levels of illumination.)
6 **Where will the art be?** (Determining the location and size of art pieces helps determine the number of accent lights needed.)

Be Aware of Door Swings

Check the architectural plans to see which way the doors swing. This determines where your switches and dimmers should be located. Don't end up placing them behind the door. This is a common mistake that can be very irritating to the clients once they have moved into their new home. Make sure to have the general contractor or architect let you know if a door swing is going to change. Have the contractor e-mail all the members of the design team when a change is made. It will keep everyone in the loop.

Door swings will affect your furniture placement as well. Double doors that open into the dining room will take up wall space (unless they are pocket doors). This will determine the visual centerline of the wall on which you place furniture and art, which will in turn affect the location of the wall sconces.

Reflected Ceiling Plan

Study the **reflected ceiling plan** (also referred to as an RCP). It will show how the joists run, where the ductwork will go for heating and ventilation, skylight locations, coffered ceilings, exposed beams, and all the other physical aspects that dictate where lighting can be placed.

Specifying recessed adjustable luminaires allows some leeway in placement. You may want a tight spot of light in the middle of a coffee table. A recessed adjustable luminaire can do that without having to be dead center over the table. Also, as mentioned earlier, people move their furniture and art around more today. A fixed recessed downlight has no flexibility, whereas recessed adjustable luminaires can be redirected to illuminate these components in their new locations.

Maintenance

Take into account the accessibility of the luminaire locations you choose. If the owners cannot easily reach a luminaire to change a burned-out lamp, they are much less likely to do it. For example, if you have a 20-foot ceiling in the entryway, don't put a recessed downlight in the center of the ceiling in order to illuminate the foyer table. Use a recessed adjustable luminaire, installed above the balcony railing on the second floor, to facilitate relamping (see Figure 4.43). A long-life lamp, such as an LED, is also advantageous in this situation.

You can also put together a relamping guide for your clients (or the people who will change the lamps for your clients). A binder that shows photographs of specific luminaires and the lamps that go in them will save a lot of trial-and-error time.

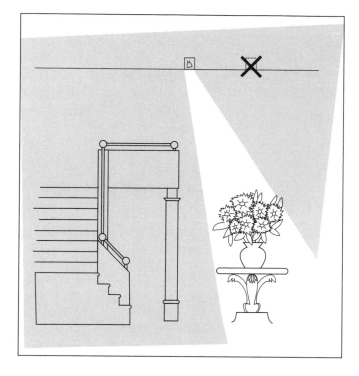

FIGURE 4.43

It's better to locate a recessed adjustable luminaire over the balcony to facilitate relamping from a short ladder than in the center of a 20-foot-high ceiling.

Also, get your clients to buy an extra dozen of each type of lamp to have on hand, and put a snapshot of the fixtures that the lamps go in on the front of the lamp carton or storage box. Using clear or translucent containers will let people know when they are running low on a specific lamp type.

Understanding how a lighting system will be maintained, and using a little foresight in helping your clients to maintain it, will improve your design and your client's long-term appreciation of it.

GETTING MORE INFORMATION ON LUMINAIRES

(See Appendix One for more detailed resource information.)

Now you have a good base of information on which to make your luminaire selections. Try to build your luminaire catalog library, and keep it updated. Lighting showrooms are good places to get catalogs and see new fixtures, and many conduct seminars on new lighting products. Build a rapport with the regional manufacturers' representatives. They are eager to keep you up-to-date on the latest offerings from the companies they represent and can get you samples to show your clients for approval. Collect PDFs of fixtures you use regularly or want to use in the future. You can use these to print out specification sheets for **submittal booklets** or to e-mail to a client or contractor for their approval.

Join organizations such as: the International Association of Lighting Designers (IALD), www.iald.org; the Illuminating Engineering Society (IES), www.iesna.org; or the American Lighting Association (ALA), www.americanlightingassoc.com. These professional organizations

Today people move their furniture around more. A fixed recessed downlight has no flexibility.

give classes and seminars on lighting-related topics. Attending these functions will help broaden your understanding of lighting design and keep your education current.

Subscribe to industry-related magazines, such as: *Lighting Design and Application* (LD&A), www.iesna.org; *Professional Lighting Design North America* (PLD), www.pldplus.com; and *Architectural Lighting,* www.lightforum.com. These are all excellent sources for technical and aesthetic information.

THE BOTTOM LINE

Along with a working knowledge of lamps, a good grasp of what certain luminaires can do will give you the tools you need to create outstanding lighting designs for your clients and for yourself. Remember good design begins at home.

Daylighting—Integration of Natural Light for Green Design Practices

- ## GREENING UP YOUR DESIGN PRACTICES

Homes built today using green building technologies, which lower energy bills, have higher resale values. A survey of the National Association of Home Builders members showed that 87 percent believed green building was important to achieve energy efficiency and stay ahead of their competition. The leading factors triggering firms to expand green building activities were increases in energy costs, utility rebates, and consumer demand.

To reduce energy costs, consider using *daylighting*, a design practice of placing windows, other transparent media, and reflective surfaces so that during the day natural light provides effective internal illumination, heating, and cooling. Energy savings are achieved either from the reduced use of electric lighting or from passive solar heating or cooling. This design ethic can reduce electricity costs by more that 50 percent. If builders have jumped on the bandwagon, don't you think that it is in your best interest to become an advocate for green design as well?

LEED the way

The LEED (Leadership in Energy and Environmental Design) Green Building Rating System is a voluntary, consensus-based national standard for developing high-performance, sustainable buildings. Members of the U.S. Green Building Council representing all segments of the building industry developed LEED and continue to contribute to its evolution. Projects are rated on a point system. There are four levels of achievement (in order of lowest to highest): Certified, Silver, Gold, and Platinum. LEED was created to:

Define "green building" by establishing a common standard measurement.

Promote integrated, whole-building design practices.

Recognize environmental leadership in the building industry.

Stimulate green competition.

Raise consumer awareness of green building benefits.

Transform the building market.

Many Federal Agencies are encouraging or mandating the use of the LEED rating system as a checklist to guide the design and construction process. These agencies include the Department of Defense, the General Services Administration, NASA, the Environmental Protection Agency, the State Department, and the Centers for Disease Control and Prevention, among others. Many states and municipalities are also mandating that their buildings are required to be designed to LEED Certification Standards as a minimum, and some are even requiring LEED Gold and Silver.

There is likely a local U.S. Green Building Council chapter in your area. This is a great way to learn more about sustainable design, and it gives you the opportunity to communicate with design and construction professionals who are interested in using products that would help contribute to achieving LEED certification in their projects. For more information, check the US Green Building Council's Web site at www.usgbc.org.

According to the Nation's Building News Online, "An international study reveals a direct link between the market value of real estate and its environmental friendliness. The study found that green buildings can earn higher prices and attract buyers more quickly; and cost less to operate." Think of green not only as responsible design but also as the color of money.

California's Title 24

California has been way ahead of the curve when it comes to state legislation for energy conservation. The state energy board wrote and helped enact Title 24 as part of California's building code. It affects all aspects of building, including windows, building materials, and especially for the purposes of this book, lighting. Before October 1, 2005, the two areas most affected by Title 24's lighting requirements were kitchens and baths. Now there are mandates that touch most interior spaces of the home as well as the exterior lighting. Listed here are the current requirements, but Title 24 is an ever-changing entity, and it is best to go to the Web site to download the latest version at www.energy.ca.gov/2005_standards/rulemaking/documents/15-day_language/2003-10-21_400-03-001-ET15F.PDF or call the energy hotline at 1-800-722-3300.

Kitchens

The older code required that when entering the kitchen the first switch has to control fluorescent lighting. The new code requires that 50 percent of the wattage must be fluorescent or a light source with an **efficacy** of 50 lumens per watt (some light-emitting diodes are meeting this requirement). For example, this means that for every four fluorescent fixtures (at 27 watts apiece), only one incandescent fixture (at 100 watts apiece) may be installed. The hood light over the stove does not have to be fluorescent.

When calculating wattage, inspectors will always assume that the maximum rated wattage for a fixture will be used. Plus, the high-efficacy fixtures will have to be switched separately from

Natural light is a wonderful source of illumination. Used correctly, it can transform a dark, dreary house into a bright, inviting sanctuary.

any other lighting. One benefit is that there will no longer be a constraint on where the switches are located. Before, the code stated that the first switch leading into the kitchen had to control the fluorescent lighting. Rooms adjacent to the kitchen, such as the breakfast nook, are considered part of the kitchen and must comply with Title 24, if the lighting is on the same switch.

All recessed fixtures must be rated for insulated ceilings *and* be certified airtight. They must also have electronic ballasts. Regarding wattage calculations, track lighting will be rated at 45 watts per linear foot, while a low-voltage rail system will be rated by the size of the transformer. For example a 600VA (volt/amp) transformer will count as 600 watts for the system.

Bathrooms, Garages, Laundry Rooms, and Utility Rooms

All hardwired lighting must be fluorescent or controlled by a manual-on occupant sensor. Every light in the bathroom, powder room, laundry room, and garage will have to be on a motion sensor, if it is not fluorescent. So there goes relaxing quietly in the tub, since you may have to flail around a bit to get the lights to come back on if you still for too long. Also, most motion sensors at present only come in white or ivory, which doesn't bode well for the designer who likes to match switches to the color of the room. Watt Stopper (www.wattstopper.com) is one of the companies working on creating a line of designer colors.

Hallways, Stairs, Closets (More Than 70 Sq. Ft.), Dining Rooms, Living Rooms, Bedrooms, Etc.

All hardwired lighting must be controlled by a motion sensor or dimmer.

Outside

All exterior light fixtures that are attached to the house must be fluorescent or controlled by a motion sensor. Landscape lighting at present is exempt from this requirement.

The trick will be finding non-modern-looking lanterns with a fluorescent source, because very few traditional-looking fixtures have hardwired bi-pin fluorescent lamps as an option. Some lighting companies are working diligently to come up with fluorescent versions that are traditional in appearance. For examples check out Hans Duus Blacksmith (www.hansduusblacksmith.com), Progress Lighting (www.progresslighting.com), and Hubbardton Forge (www.vtforge.com).

Why isn't there a wealth of good-looking fluorescent fixtures? The reason is that these revised fixtures must go through UL (Underwriters Laboratories) testing for the new light source. They normally cost $1,500 per fixture for the testing. This can be an expensive proposition for a fixture manufacturer, especially when it is only one state out of 50 that is requiring such a fixture.

Meeting these Title 24 requirements isn't easy, but unless you will be doing only design work in other states or only noninspected projects in California, then these regulations will be a part of your daily design work. And don't think that California will remain be the only state to mandate energy-efficient lighting.

Daylighting

Daylighting is an all-natural source of illumination that is available to everyone. Making optimal use of daylight can certainly brighten and open up a room or area. Designers should explore the options of daylight in addition to artificial light. Here are some considerations:

Using Windows

Windows are the first option when a designer, architect, or homeowner thinks about getting natural light into a room. Windows do a fine job of providing daylight for rooms that run along the perimeter of the house. It is not written in concrete on either a new construction project or a remodel that that number of windows or their location is set. Sometimes it is an excellent opportunity for the designer, architect, or the homeowner to take a critical look at the existing or proposed window locations. Smaller windows can be made larger and off-center windows can be repositioned to give better balance to a space.

Rooms with little natural light or those that are windowless require artificial light during the day to see. This drives up energy bills. Replacing older windows adds value to a home when more energy-efficient glass is used and window frames are clad in weather-resistant materials. A big selling point to any property is the amount of natural light flowing into the rooms. Plus, more windows offer better circulation of air.

Window Coverings

There is, however, the problem of sun damage (permanent fading and disintegration of natural fibers and woods). The sun's **ultraviolet** (UV) rays eventually harm the furnishings and surfaces within the home. Almost all sources of light damage photosensitive materials, but natural daylight does the most damage.

In a project that will include skylights, consider using the white variety instead of clear or bronze.

Window treatments, such as shades, drapes, sheers, and mini-blinds, do a good job of diffusing the light and slowing down the process of ultraviolet damage. Shutters and blackout shades do a better job of blocking light when it is not needed, such as when the homeowners are on vacation. Quantitative information on recommended maximum exposure to UV light is available in the *IES Handbook* (www.iesna.edu), which is a great source of technical information on industry standards.

Some companies offer a ready-made ultraviolet blocking film that's applied directly to existing windows or you can specify new windows where the UV film is sandwiched between two panes of glass. These companies claim to cut 99 percent of the sun's harmful rays. This sounds very good. What they don't tell you is that any standard glass or Plexiglas® will filter out 98 percent of the ultraviolet light. This is just an additional 1 percent over what standard glass already accomplishes.

Is it worthwhile? Absolutely! If it would normally take five years for the sun to take its toll, the extra 1 percent of UV protection in the film would double the life of your furniture, rugs, and other furnishings. That's a pretty good deal. Remember, though, not only daylight but almost all sources of light also contribute to the damage. LEDs and light traveling through **fiber optics** do not contain UV rays. These two sources are now being regularly used to illuminate light-sensitive materials.

You can't completely eliminate the damage caused by natural light unless you use blackout shades all day, which could be somewhat depressing for your clients. But at least you can slow down the process. Architects often incorporate deep overhangs (eaves) to help control the amount of light coming directly into a window. For new construction they will also look at the placement of the house on the property in relation to what direction it is facing. The south side of a property will always get the most intense light, while the side of the house facing north will get the least intense light. Artists often prefer a north light because it is less intense and relatively constant.

There are manufacturers of shades, both manual and motorized, that can help control natural light to the amount needed. Different types of shade materials can be layered together to offer a variety of options. There are also options for shades to come up from the bottom for privacy and create a kind of **clerestory** (a long, narrow window extending along the top part of a wall), allowing natural light to come in without loss of privacy (see Figure 5.1).

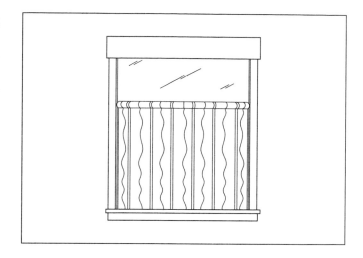

FIGURE 5.1

A shade that raises and lowers from the bottom allows light to come in without loss of privacy.

At night, windows are also wonderful visual portals to exterior spaces, making the inside rooms appear larger. Making good use of windows and exterior lighting can also work wonders in making the exterior landscaping and view a part of the interior spaces. How often have we entered a wonderfully designed interior only to find that the windows are all **black mirrors** at night, where you see your own reflection instead of the view beyond the glass? Exterior lighting will help minimize those reflective surfaces and enlarge the interior at night by visually extending your view out into the landscape. Exterior lighting techniques will be addressed extensively in Chapter 15.

Using Doors

Doors, especially interior doors, do not have to be solid. French doors (they come in many styles), fitted with clear or frosted glass, allow light to travel into the room beyond and though the space, so the natural light is shared with the inner rooms. As long as the glass is obscure, there is no loss of privacy for bedrooms and bathrooms. These are particularly effective for row homes and townhouses where the only natural light comes from the front and the back of the building. This also allows the light in freestanding homes to flow into interior spaces, such as hallways, from the windows along the perimeter.

Using Skylights

The National Association of Home Builders also notes that the demand savings are more important than the energy savings, since daylighting provides energy usage reduction at the most important time—during peak hours, when energy rates are the highest and daylight availability is the greatest. Builders who skimp on skylights do so at their own peril. Today, many homebuyers see skylights as a necessity, rather than as an option. Skylights are like windows, though at night they can become **black holes**. It is a good idea to have some sort of light inside to add a little illumination after the sun has gone down (see Figures 5.2 and 5.3).

Here's another interesting and valuable piece of information: MSN Real Estate reports that "in an effort to attract more female homebuyers, homebuilders are increasingly turning to features like skylights in the bathroom to increase natural light levels. Also, according to the *Hamilton Spectator*, "skylights were selected as the number one option in *dream bathrooms*."

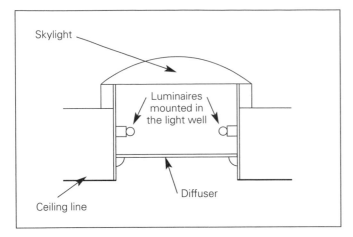

FIGURE 5.2

Lighting in the light well above the diffuser keeps the skylight from becoming a "black hole" at night.

Fortune 500 homebuilder KB Home, for instance, "has partnered with style-icon Martha Stewart to design 900 homes in the Atlanta area, all of which are designed with increased natural light in the bathroom, and plans to eventually take the program nationwide." The U.S. Green Building Council agrees that "energy savings are another selling point for skylights" and that "integrating daylight into home designs can slash interior lighting costs by up to 80% and reduce the need for mechanical cooling during peak rate hours."

Skylights are a great source of natural light but should be used with a few precautions. They come in three standard varieties: clear, bronze, or white. All three varieties can come standard with an ultraviolet inhibitor, or this can be ordered as an option. Although the most popular, clear skylights cause the most problems and result in the most severe sun damage. Here are some of the disadvantages of a clear skylight:

1 The daylight coming through the skylight will be projected in the shape of the skylight. Your clients will be confronted by an intense square, circle, or rectangle of light. The pattern of the sun will eventually be traced on the surfaces of the furniture, floors, and wall coverings.
2 The light coming through a clear skylight will be a hard, harsh light that casts unattractive shadows on people's faces.
3 Clear skylights show dust and dirt immediately—maintenance is a constant problem.

In the case of an existing clear skylight, one solution is to get a pleated or Roman-style shade to help diffuse the light. This is especially good for operable skylights, as the shade can be pulled back to allow for ventilation when needed (see Figure 5.4).

If the skylight is nonoperable, you can install a white acrylic or textured glass diffuser within the light well to help spread out the sun's illumination. If there is enough room in the light well above the shade or diffuser, luminaires can be installed to keep the skylight from becoming a negative space at night.

Properly designed and installed skylights fit well into the energy-saving plan of a home by pulling daylight into dim interior spaces. But, as mentioned, at night skylights can become dark holes in the ceiling. Artificial light can maintain the skylight's place in the lighting scheme. You may have seen track lights or recessed fixtures installed in skylight wells. That idea makes even more sense if you choose an energy-efficient light source.

By directing the light up into the skylight well, you create a soft, even light. This soft, diffuse light flowing from the skylight well can create an interesting focal point, especially at night. Several design elements work together to create the effect. The skylight well should be flared to provide maximum surface area for reflecting light down into the room. Paint the drywall above the fixture with light-colored paint. A semigloss finish also improves the reflectivity. Position the fixture so the lamp can't be seen from the floor, either directly or reflected in the skylight.

FIGURE 5.3
A pair of directional fixtures are mounted on the sides of the light well to provide some artificial light at night. You can also use step lights recessed into the light well walls for a cleaner look.

If a fixture sticks out from the wall, place it near the bottom of the well so it blocks as little daylight as possible. To create the skylight effect with artificial light, the lights in the well will have to be brighter than the room lights. You should put more lighting power into the skylight fixtures or put the room lights on a dimmer.

A fluorescent lamp is the most efficient light source for this application. Select a lamp with a Color Rendering Index (CRI) over 80. If you want to imitate the warmer glow of sunlight, choose a warm lamp with a color temperature of 3,000° to 3,500° K. To achieve a cooler, moonlight effect choose a lamp with a color temperature of 4,000° to 5,000° K.

Track lights can bounce light off of the skylight well or shine down into the room. Track heads and other types of directional fixtures can be purchased with compact fluorescent lamps. If you want to attach a dimmer, you can find compact fluorescents that are compatible, but the price is higher. As an alternative, try low-wattage halogen lamps. They are somewhat more efficient than standard incandescent lamps and work with regular dimming controls. Other surface-mounted fixtures, such as wall sconces, can also work.

If you want beams of light falling directly into the room, you could install recessed lights into the sloped walls of the skylight well. You would have to specify a fixture that mounts in a sloped ceiling. A recessed fixture could also shine into the well from a vertical wall, creating the indirect glow. Most recessed light fixtures can be mounted horizontally to achieve this effect. Many recessed fixtures are available with compact fluorescent lamps. Since most skylight wells are insulated, be sure to find a fixture that is IC-rated and certified airtight.

Don't try to light a glass block wall. It is a translucent product, so light passes through it. At best, you would highlight the grout in between the blocks, which is not the most visually ornate aspect. If the blocks are frosted, then the wall can be directly illuminated.

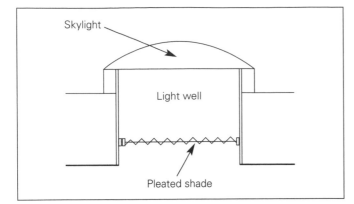

Skylight

Light well

Pleated shade

FIGURE 5.4

A pleated or Roman-type shade, fitted into the light well, will help diffuse the daylight flooding into the room.

USING BRONZE SKYLIGHTS

The same considerations listed for clear skylights also apply to bronze-tinted skylights, which cut down tremendously on the amount of light allowed through. The main concern, though, is not reducing the amount of light but diffusing the light for a more user-friendly illumination.

USING WHITE SKYLIGHTS

In new construction or a remodel project that will include installing skylights, you should consider using white, also known as "opal" or "frosted," skylights (see Figure 5.5) for several reasons:

1 They distribute the light more evenly in a room.
2 They don't project a light pattern.
3 They don't become **black holes** at night.
4 They minimize maintenance because dirt is not immediately seen.

One of the great products on the market are smaller skylights that can be installed easily and use a flexible reflective tubular material to get the natural light from the roof to the room

FIGURE 5.5

A skylight with a diffuse lens softens the incoming light and spreads it out more evenly instead of projecting a beam of light that matches the shape of the skylight.

where the skylight is installed. One company that makes this product is Solatube (www.solatube.com). They also offer an optional light source (incandescent or fluorescent) inside the skylight to keep it from becoming a black hole at night.

Solatube has been used in several LEED-certified projects and is specified in dozens of other projects that are still in design or awaiting certification. LEED also looks at the use of recycled materials. This credit relates to the recycled content of the entire building. Products like Solatube can play a part in this because it uses recycled content in its lenses, fasteners, and trim pieces. The qualification for this is that the project uses materials with recycled content such that the sum of post-consumer recycled content plus one-half of the post industrial content constitutes at least 5 percent of the total value of the materials in the project. There is also a credit available if the project uses a minimum of 20 percent of the building materials and products that are manufactured regionally within a radius of 500 miles.

USING GLASS BLOCK

Glass block (also known as **glass brick**) is a building material that was popular between the 1930s and the 1950s and then fell out of popularity. The postmodern influence of the 1980s brought about a resurgence of its use. Succinctly put, glass block turns walls into windows. The blocks come in clear, patterned, curved, frosted, colored, solid, or hollow varieties. This allows for varying degrees of energy conservation, light transference and varying degrees of privacy. Rooms with little or no natural light could benefit greatly from the installation of a glass block wall, which allows them to borrow light from adjoining rooms with windows or skylights. For more information and examples of applications, go to www.pittsburghcorning.com.

FIGURE 5.6

Glass block appears to be illuminated if the wall behind it is washed with light.

Don't try to light a transparent glass block wall. At best, you would highlight the grout between the blocks, which is not the most visually attractive aspect. The trick is to light the opposite wall. What you end up seeing is the illuminated wall through the glass block. This creates the illusion that the block itself is illuminated (see Figure 5.6). If the blocks are frosted, then the wall can be directly illuminated.

USING MIRRORS

The use of mirrors can be another tool to help make the most of natural light in a space. You can greatly increase the perceived amount of daylight in a room with windows on one side by installing mirrors on the opposite wall. Mirrors can also greatly increase the apparent depth of an area by giving the illusion that the interior extends much farther than it actually does. Cramped areas can become brighter and feel more open.

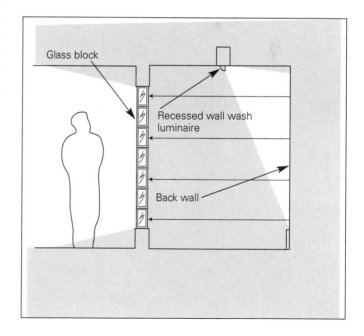

Glass block

Recessed wall wash luminaire

Back wall

WORKING WITH NATURAL LIGHT

Areas such as kitchens and family rooms that are used frequently during the day are prime candidates for maximizing natural light. Closets and laundry rooms that have some source of natural light make it easier to color-match blouses to skirts, ties to suits, and high heels to slacks. Be sure to take precautions to block the natural light when it's not required, as many fabrics, especially silk and wool, are quickly damaged by light.

Don't forget that light colors reflect more light than dark colors. A Navajo White room will make better use of the natural light than one painted a Hunter Green.

• THE BOTTOM LINE

Natural light is a wonderful source of illumination. Used correctly, it can transform a dark, dreary house into a bright, inviting sanctuary during the day.

Controls—Dimming, Switching, Timers, Photosensors, Motion Detectors

Once you have formulated a lighting design, the next step is to decide how to regulate the system or control the lighting design to achieve the desired effect. There are many options, from simple switches to preset multiple-zone/multiple-scene controllers and even the ability to turn on lights from your cell phone.

Every room should have the capability of having light levels for different activities. Different activities will need particular levels of light. A multiple-sconce controller allows the same groups of lights to be dimmed or brightened at various levels by a single control unit (see Figure 6.8). For entertaining, clients will want subtle mood lighting but will need the ability to increase light levels for cleaning. Multiple scene controllers can do this at the push of a button.

The options may be almost limitless, but they need to be matched to the wants and capabilities of your clients. Designing a dimming system that is too complicated leaves the clients intimidated and ultimately frustrated. Try to meet their needs with a simple-to-operate control system.

Also, remember that they are the ones who will be living in the house, so the controls must be logically placed to match their traffic patterns. A common mistake is to locate a majority of the controls at the front door. Most people living in single-family houses in the United States don't enter through the front door. They park in the garage and enter through the garage. This spot should be your starting point. On the other hand, people who live in condominiums do enter through the front door. Each project is different, as are the needs of your clients. Give them options and let them tell you what they want.

> Every room is capable of being viewed and used in multiple ways. Clients may want subtle mood lighting for entertaining, yet also want the ability to increase light levels for cleaning. Multiple scene controllers can do this at the push of a button.

SWITCH CONTROLS

Today, people can put dimmers on most everything, but there are some instances where simple switching is the best choice. Low-activity rooms, such as closets, storage rooms, attics, and

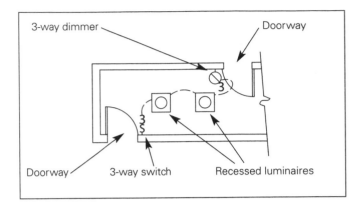

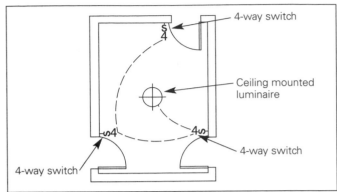

FIGURE 6.1 (left)
A three-way setup means that the lights are controlled from two locations (not three).

FIGURE 6.2 (right)
A four-way setup indicates that there are three or more switches that can turn on a specific light or group of lights.

The mounting of two or more controls side-by-side within one enclosure is called ganging. De-rating is the reduction of the maximum capacity (hood) a dimmer can reliably handle when the side sections (fins) are removed.

pantries, don't need varying light levels and don't require dimmers. If your clients have children or adult loved ones who are on the forgetful side, you might recommend the following alternatives to simple toggle switches.

Three-Way Switching

Three-way switching is a term that confuses homeowners and designers alike. The natural impression is that a light or group of lights can be turned on from three locations, which is incorrect. The correct answer is two locations. Why? Because a single-location switch has two terminals, and a three-way switch has three terminals. It does not refer to the number of control spots.

A four-way switching system allows three or more locations to turn a light or groups of lights on and off (see Figure 6.2). For example, if you have a hallway with a switch at both ends, one of these switches can be replaced with a three-way dimmer to allow for a variety of light levels. The three-way switch at one end of the hall will turn on the lights at whatever level the dimmer at the other end of the hall has been set (see Figure 6.1). In simple three-way setups, you can't put a dimmer at both ends. More sophisticated (and more expensive) systems would allow dimming at both ends.

Momentary Contact Switches

Momentary contact switches (door jam switches) are devices that turn on the light when the door is opened. It's the same way the light in your refrigerator operates. When the door is shut, the light automatically goes out. This works only if the clients, their children, and other household members remember to shut the door completely. Bifold doors don't work well with momentary contact switches because they need to be fully closed to make a good connection.

Motion Sensors/Switched Motion Sensors

Motion sensors turn the lights on as someone enters the room or closet and keeps them on as long as there is movement or for a certain length of time, as preset in the sensor. Some companies make motion sensors with a manual switch (called a switched motion sensor) for clients who plan to spend a great deal of time in a particular room without moving around. For example, if there is a safe in the master-bedroom closet and your clients occasionally review important papers or sort through jewelry there, a switched motion sensor in this location would be advisable. For an example, see Figure 6.3, which shows the CN-100 made by Watt Stopper (www.wattstopper.com).

Panic Switches

Panic switches are switches normally located in the master bedroom that turn on exterior perimeter lights. Nobody wants to run downstairs to the front door when there is a suspicious noise outside at night—most people don't even want to get out of bed. This will also allow the occupants to turn off the outside or entry lights if they are left on inadvertently. A panic switch can also be located in the room of a live-in caregiver, such as a nanny, nurse, maid, or butler.

Half-Switched Receptacles

Half-switched receptacles, also known as "half-hot" plugs, can be a terrific labor-saving device in houses that use a lot of portable luminaires. In a half-switched receptacle, a wall switch activates one of the two outlets and the other outlet is continuously live.

FIGURE 6.3

This switched motion sensor, made by Watt Stopper, fulfills California's Title 24 requirements for bathrooms using incandescent lighting. They are also great for kids' bathrooms and closets.

This allows the clients to plug their table lamps, torchères, reading lights, china hutch lighting, or uplights into the switched receptacles. So instead of the client having to go from luminaire to luminaire to turn them all on or off, they would all come on at the flick of one switch (see Figure 6.4). Items they don't want to be turned on and off, such as clocks, televisions, or stereo equipment, would be plugged into the non-switched receptacles.

Caution: Do not put the half-switched receptacles on a dimmer, because if someone plugged a television or vacuum cleaner into a dimmed receptacle, it could damage the appliance or be a possible fire hazard. This is also a code violation. If your clients want to dim their table lamps, have them purchase luminaires with integral dimmers. If they already have the table lamps, they can be retrofitted with screw-in-type **socket dimmers** (see Figure 6.5) or cord dimmers (see Figure 6.6).

Sound-Actuated Switches

Sound-actuated switches are devices that turn on lights when a noise is made. They are a low-end solution to half-switched receptacles with one inherent problem: If your clients or their guests make noises that are as loud as clapping, they may find the lights turning on and off at an inopportune moment! You have probably seen commercials for "The Clapper" on TV. Now there are much more sophisticated versions of this type of device that work particularly well for shallow closets. Take a look online at the Super Switch Mini Model 01-250 by Novitas Inc. (www.novitas.com).

Timers

Timers are another option for turning lights on and off. Clients who travel or are cautious about security will want their home to look occupied at night. Lights controlled by timers that go on or off at staggered times makes it feel like someone is home. Following are your options.

Plug-In Timers

Plug-in timers are readily available at hardware stores and home improvement centers. You plug them into a live receptacle, and then plug a portable luminaire such as a table lamp into it. Then the device is manually set to switch on and off at specific times. Use a few in the living room

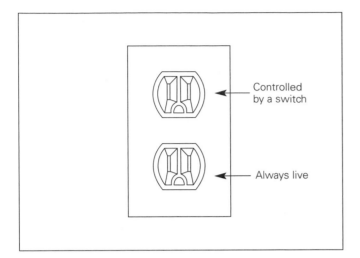

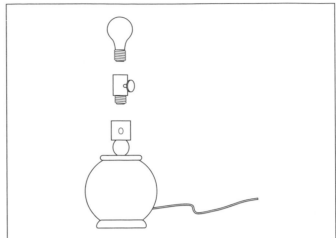

that are set to come on at dusk and go off around 11:00 p.m. Then have one go on in the bedroom at 11:05 p.m. and stay on until midnight. This gives the impression of people being in a gathering spot then going off to bed in a natural progression.

24-Hour Programmable Timers

This type of programmable timer simply turns specific lights on and off at the same time each day. They are available in hardwired (permanently installed) varieties as well as plug-in units. The timer is normally located in the garage. These devices have an override switch, located inside the control box, that allows the homeowner to turn the lights on or off if needed. When these units turn the lights on and off at the same time every day, it is more evident to anyone casing the house that no one is home and that timers are being used.

24-Hour/7-Day Programmable Timers

Another kind of programmable timer allows for different settings each day and gives the option to skip days, for an appearance that seems to be controlled by a person instead of a device. For example, on Monday the lights come on at 7:17 p.m. and go off at 11:33 p.m. On Tuesday the lights come on at 6:50 p.m. and go off at 11:57 p.m. Each day can be a little different. This is great for weekend residences and for clients who travel frequently.

Photo sensors

Photo sensors (also known as photocells or photoelectric cells) are activated by the absence of light. The luminaires come on at dusk and turn off at dawn. Cleaning the photo sensor regularly is a priority. Otherwise, as it gets dirtier, the cell reads dusk as coming sooner, and eventually the lights may stay on all the time. Be sure to locate the sensor in a spot that is free of shade, so that it can detect true dawn and dusk, yet not in the direct path of another light, such as a streetlight, which would cause the unit to "see" daylight all night long and never come on.

Dimmers

Dimmers are a form of control that allows a variable adjustment of light levels (see Figure 6.7). Dimmers come in many varieties, such as rotary, toggle, glider, touch, low voltage, and line voltage.

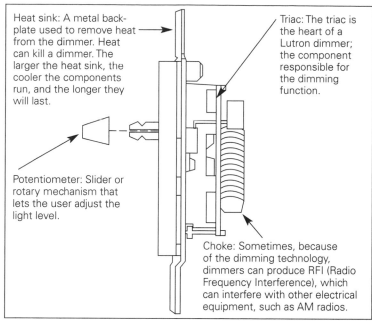

Heat sink: A metal back-plate used to remove heat from the dimmer. Heat can kill a dimmer. The larger the heat sink, the cooler the components run, and the longer they will last.

Triac: The triac is the heart of a Lutron dimmer; the component responsible for the dimming function.

Potentiometer: Slider or rotary mechanism that lets the user adjust the light level.

Choke: Sometimes, because of the dimming technology, dimmers can produce RFI (Radio Frequency Interference), which can interfere with other electrical equipment, such as AM radios.

Here are some points that will help you and your clients make an informed decision:

1   Choose a dimmer that is specifically made for the luminaire type that you are dimming. As mentioned in Chapter 3, use a low-voltage dimmer when dimming a low-voltage system. If the low-voltage luminaire uses an electronic (solid-state) transformer, the dimmer must be electronic as well or there will be an audible humming noise and possible damage to the dimmer or fixture. If the low-voltage luminaires use magnetic transformers, then the dimmer must be magnetic as well.
    Note: Some low-voltage electronic dimmers have only a 300-watt capacity, as compared to a standard 600-watt magnetic low-voltage or line-voltage dimmer. Consequently, you should pay special attention to the number of total watts each dimmer can handle.

2   Be aware of the dimmer's maximum wattage. A normal dimmer is rated for 600 watts. Putting 600 watts on that dimmer requires it to work its hardest. Most manufacturers will provide guidelines for load limits. For example, a Lutron low-voltage dimmer, such as the Skylark SLV600P, can optimally handle 450 watts of luminaires. The mounting of two or more controls side-by-side within one enclosure is called **ganging**. Ganging dimmers decreases their load capacities.

3   **De-rating** is the reduction of the maximum capacity (load) a dimmer can reliably handle when the side sections (fins) are removed. Allow for de-rating when banking dimmers. Dimmers' wattage capacities are reduced when put together in a single box. Dimmers produce heat and need airspace around them in order to work properly. If too many dimmers are put too close together, they will overheat and cause problems down the line. Manufacturers' guidelines will tell you how much load (wattage) a dimmer can handle when two or more dimmers are ganged together. A scored section along each side of the mounting plate or fin is designed to be snapped off for ease of mounting multiple controls in one enclosure.

FIGURE 6.6 (left)

A cord dimmer is a quick way of obtaining a full range of light levels from an existing luminaire.

FIGURE 6.7 (right)

The components of a typical dimmer switch. *Courtesy of Lutron.*

FIGURE 6.8

Dimmer switches come in many varieties. Here are a few for you and your clients to consider. Whichever you choose, stay consistent throughout the house. Don't mix styles.

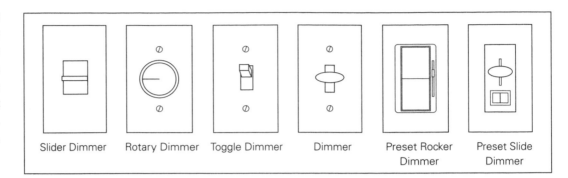

Slider Dimmer Rotary Dimmer Toggle Dimmer Dimmer Preset Rocker Dimmer Preset Slide Dimmer

FIGURE 6.8

Dimmer switches come in many varieties. Here are a few for you and your clients to consider. Whichever you choose, stay consistent throughout the house. Don't mix styles.

4 Choose well-made dimmers. The rotary and toggle-style dimmers commonly available in hardware stores are poorly made. Don't expect much from a $4.95 dimmer; chances are that in six months they will fail.

5 Choose a dimmer style that matches the switch plates being used throughout the house. Some dimmers require special plates that aren't compatible with standard plates for toggle switches or receptacles. Different plate styles in the same house may draw too much attention to an element that should be as low-key as possible. Show your clients the choices available and let them select the style they like (see Figure 6.8).

Wireless Dimming Systems

There are also dimming and switching modules that when plugged into an outlet can then control the devices that are plugged into them from a handheld remote. These devices use a radio signal instead of hardwiring to connect the lighting to the controls. They are inexpensive and relatively easy to install. They do best at dimming incandescent sources and are somewhat limited in their ability to dim low voltage or fluorescent. There are more sophisticated versions of these systems, such as the Lutron Radio RA series (www.lutron.com) that can do almost anything that a hardwired system can do.

FIGURE 6.9

A preset controller, such as the Grafik-Eye by Lutron, allows lights in a room to come on together at different levels called "scenes."

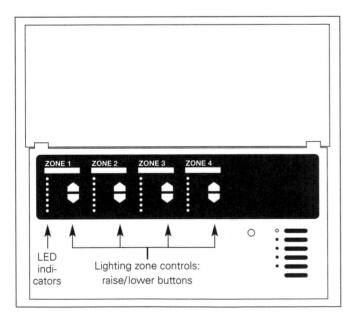

ZONE 1 ZONE 2 ZONE 3 ZONE 4

LED indicators

Lighting zone controls: raise/lower buttons

Preset Dimming Systems

Beyond standard dimmers there are multiple-zone/multiple-scene controllers that allow for a great variety of predetermined light level combinations (see Figure 6.9). These systems, initially very expensive, have come down to a price range that can work within the budget of many projects.

Usually, these controllers are used only for entertaining spaces, such as living rooms, dining rooms, entries, and kitchens. Sometimes the master bedroom is included as well. For loads up to 1,920 watts total in a room, there are a good number of three- to six-channel controllers that fit into a standard four-gang box and use standard wiring. For loads beyond 2,000 watts, a remote booster panel is required. Then the loads are virtually limitless. The cost goes up significantly as more sophisticated components are added. Most of these preset controllers have adjustable **fade rates** that help soften the transition from one scene to the next. This is like the lights dimming in a theater as the play is about to begin.

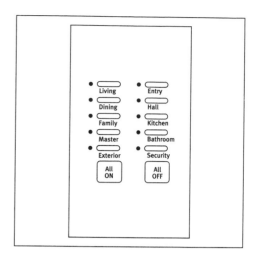

CENTRAL HOME LIGHTING CONTROL SYSTEMS

A logical step in central design was a system that allowed for remote control of the entire house from a few choice locations, such as the master bedroom, the front door, and the door into the house from the garage. Options include turning all the lights in the house on or off, activating pathways of illumination, or turning on exterior **security lighting** (see Figure 6.10).

A controller can override other switching and dimming devices in the house and change your clients' preset light levels. These systems involve complex wiring, so they may be cost-effective only in new construction. Remodel projects may require too much opening of walls and ceilings to justify the total expense. Newer radio-controlled components are making "smart house" systems a possibility for existing homes, because little hardwiring is needed. The controls are activated by radio signals instead of electricity running through the walls.

There are also computer-managed systems called **smart house** or **whole house** systems that allow people to turn on lights, heating, air conditioning, security, and even the hot tub from **LCD** (liquid crystal display) terminals throughout the house. For some, this is the ultimate dream package. They can even control it from their cell phones, but it certainly could scare the nanny if she's home alone. Look online at Lutron (www.lutron.com) and Crestron (www.crestron.com) for examples of these systems.

Again, don't overdesign the control system. A young, hip couple may love these bells and whistles, but older clients or young children may never get the hang of a sophisticated system.

COMMONLY ASKED QUESTIONS ABOUT DIMMING

Do dimmers save energy?

Yes, a fixture on a dimmer uses only the energy consumed.

Does using a dimmer shorten the life of the lamp?

No, heat decreases the life of the lamp. Lower wattage consumption means less heat and longer lamp life. With halogen lamps, it may be necessary to operate them at maximum illumination periodically in order to burn off any black residue, which results from the tungsten evaporation.

FIGURE 6.10

A master control, part of a "whole house" or "smart house" system, allows for activating any of the lights in the house from a central location.

Note: Some low-voltage electronic dimmers have only a 300-watt capacity, compared to a standard magnetic 600-watt low-voltage or line-voltage dimmer. So pay special attention to the number of total watts each dimmer can handle.

Why does the dimmer feel warm to the touch?

This is normal. It is the result of dissipated heat transferred to the fins (a heat sink system) located on the back of the device.

What about feedback from radios or stereos?

With magnetic dimmers some buzzing may occur. Filters are usually installed in the better grade of dimmers. Remote **de-buzzing coils** may be added to a magnetic dimmer to reduce the hum.

TYPES OF DIMMERS
Low-Voltage Dimming

Low-voltage dimmer selection is crucial. Noise from the dimmer and transformer can be greatly reduced if these components are designed to work with each other. The manufacturer's specifications will help you make the correct choice.

It is an industry recommendation that fluorescent luminaires with dimming ballasts should be operated at full capacity for 100 hours before dimming them, in order to break in the system. Some dimming ballasts are pre-cured by the manufacturer prior to being sold.

As mentioned, a common mistake is the specification of a low-voltage dimmer that is not compatible with the type of transformer used in the low-voltage luminaire that it is controlling. Find out the type of transformer before specifying the dimmer. If the information isn't readily apparent in the catalog or online, call your distributor or manufacturer's representative to find the information you need.

Fluorescent Dimming

Dimming of fluorescents has come a long way. As people become more comfortable with fluorescent lighting, their demand for control of the light levels will increase as well. First of all, in order to dim fluorescents, a special dimming ballast in the luminaire must be used.

One of the recurring complaints about early fluorescent luminaires was the incessant hum. Most of this came from magnetic ballasts that vibrate. This vibration may resonate against the metal luminaire housing, increasing the level of the hum. However, the newer electronic ballasts are extremely quiet. When you add a dimmer for a fluorescent luminaire, the electrician will need to run one or two additional wires from the dimmer to the ballast and from there to the luminaire. Fluorescent dimmers require that there be additional wires to carry the dimmed current.

For new construction, this would not be a problem. It is a bit more complicated for a remodeling project—not impossible, just a little more difficult. It's no more involved than adding the additional wiring for a three-way switch. There are some companies that make a two-wire electronic dimming ballast that allows homeowners to replace an existing incandescent fixture with a dimmable fluorescent fixture without having to change the wiring. An example is the Tu-Wire by Lutron (www.lutron.com).

Here are some comparisons between dimming fluorescent luminaires with magnetic ballasts and dimming them with electronic ballasts:

1 Hum is more evident in magnetic ballasts.

2 Both electronic and magnetic ballasts in the moderate price range are dimmable down to 10 to 20 percent of the light output. Magnetic fluorescent dimmers usually have stops that keep users from dimming beyond the 20 percent mark because they flutter at percentages lower than 20 percent.

3 High-end electronic ballasts can have full-range dimming capabilities; in some instances, such as the Hi-Lume electronic dimming ballast by Lutron, they allow for the dimming of unlike lamp lengths together.

4 Fluorescent dimming can be pricey. But considering the savings in electricity, the payback period can be very rapid—usually only two or three years in a typical household. The quality of the components is also a factor. Inexpensive fluorescent sockets can make dimming at low levels inconsistent and cause the light to flutter. Some more reasonably priced fluorescent dimming systems allow for dimming down to 50 percent. For some clients with budget constraints, this may be adequate.

5 Both magnetically and electronically ballasted fluorescent luminaires can be dimmed automatically when tied to a photo sensor. This helps balance the need for artificial light with available daylight, or with use frequency. A home office would be a good candidate for this type of control system.

6 As mentioned in Chapter 3, there are now self-ballasted compact fluorescent sources that can be dimmed with a standard incandescent dimmer. This is the new wave of fluorescent dimming.

HID Dimming

Dimming technology for high-intensity discharge lamps is still in early-development stages. At best, these sources can be dimmed only to 40 percent without shortening lamp or ballast life. There is another system that dims the lamps down to 12 to 15 percent, but this shortens the life of both lamp and ballast. The color shift of dimmed HID sources is generally undesirable.

As with much lighting technology, improvements in HID dimming should arrive in the next three to five years. Like all aspects of your lighting design, involve the clients. Give them their options and help them make an informed decision on how they want to (and can afford to) control the lighting system in their house.

Lighting can make a huge difference in how a space is perceived. The purpose of this section is to get a feel for what lighting can do to a given space, especially the level of illumination. The difference is as clear as day and night.

THE BOTTOM LINE

Designers should review material and installation costs prior to starting the project. Gathering this information will help the clients make informed decisions, especially on control systems. A lighting designer, lighting showroom salesperson, or an electrical distributor can work with you and the contractor to determine the components required and help put the package together. You and your clients will greatly benefit from taking advantage of this type of service.

Remember not to overdesign the controls. They must be user-friendly for the specific client. Each client has a certain comfort level with technology that must be taken into account.

PLATE 1.1

This living room is hardly conducive to conversation or comfort. Visitors would practically have to yell across the room to be heard by the people sitting on the opposite sofa. This space not only needs better lighting, but begs for the confident hand of a good interior designer.

PLATE 1.2

The room takes on a whole new personality when good interior and lighting design are blended. Three recessed adjustable fixtures highlight paintings, plants, art objects, and tabletops, adding a dramatic layer of accent lighting. The center fixture illuminates the coffee table, while the other two cross-illuminate the large painting and offer some fore- lighting of the two ficus trees. The potted plants are back-illuminated with two uplights positioned on the floors behind the containers. A cantilevered ledge, off to the right, hides a linear strip of LED indirect illumination to help soften shadows on people's faces.

PLATE 1.3

The "before" shot of the dining room offers little in the way of any redeeming lighting or interior design. It's as if 1972 had come and gone without the former owners ever noticing.

PLATE 1.4

The dining area is located on the opposite side of the large main room. An enormous hanging fixture, designed by Ingo Maurer, draws guests to the table. This luminaire provides both ambient and decorative light. Two recessed adjustable luminaires, using 50-watt MR16 lamps, offer accent light for the painting and the red metal sculpture in the foreground.

PLATE 1.5

The "before" picture of the wet bar shows a single square recessed fixture that was used to provide the only illumination for the space. This downlighting made the person serving drinks appear as frightening as the wallpaper behind them.

PLATE 1.6

The wet bar area has been transformed into an inviting spot in the main room using a series of three pendant lights that cast a bright red glow. A pair of recessed adjustable low-voltage fixtures highlight the Japanese block prints. Above the cantilever, a run of linear low-voltage lighting, using LED festoon lamps, provides much-needed ambient light.

PLATE 1.8
The "before" picture of the bedroom shows that the former owners were in a bit of a rush to leave the property. Beyond the sliding glass doors, a frightening glimpse of the Astrourf covered patio can be seen.

PLATE 1.7
This master bedroom has become an inviting retreat through good interior design, color selection, and lighting. The ceiling glow comes from a pair of torchères flanking the armoire holding the television. The two reading lights above the bed are individually controlled, recessed, adjustable, low- voltage fixtures. The fixture above the left side of the bed illuminates reading material for the person on the right side of the bed, a positioning that directs light away from the person who is trying to sleep. Each of these fixtures uses a 20-watt MR16 spot to provide a controlled beam of illumination. The backyard area is also illuminated, so that the sliding doors don't become black mirrors at night.

PLATE 1.9 (left)
During the day this stone Fu dog draws little attention to itself.

PLATE 1.10 (middle)
In the evening, he has a yellowish cast when lit with a single 50-watt MR16 spot.

PLATE 1.11 (right)
Adding a daylight blue filter to the fixture brings out the piece's cool stone quality.

PLATE 1.12
Before: The façade of this 1970s-era home has the feel of a bunker. Although the bones of the house are good, anyone can see that this project is ripe for an upgrade.

PLATE 1.13
After: The front yard of the home has been greatly improved with the addition of specimen cacti, succulents, and a new slate façade. But the exterior fixtures, which illuminate the plants and the building, have an amber cast that makes the plants look unhealthy.

PLATE 1.14
The same house with the same fixtures. The one difference is that all of the exterior directional fixtures have been fitted with daylight blue filters to correct the color of light to a more naturalistic hue.

PLATE 1.17

This art niche is illuminated with a series of LEDs that follow the perimeter of the opening. The color of these diodes is yellow, while the niche itself is painted a crimson red. The combination of these two colors creates a vivid orange-red background for the Buddha figure.

PLATE 1.15

This living room is done completely with energy efficient sources. The recessed adjustable low voltage fixtures by JUNO use an LED MR 16 made by Color Kinetics. The photographs are up-lit using a linear LED strip light by Dreamscape Lighting. The woven-wood floor lamp is illuminated from within using dimmable CFLs made by MaxLite.

PLATE 1.16

An arts and crafts style kitchen has lighting that works within the grid pattern that is created by the coffered ceiling. A hanging fixture with four glass shades hangs over the island while four acorn shaped glass shades are suspended at the corners of the ceiling. All these fixtures are made by Metro Lighting and Crafts. Recessed low voltage fixtures by Lucifer Lighting are used to illuminate the surfaces of the island and peninsula.

PLATE 1.18

This entryway has a decidedly 1980s feel. The center fixture is an Art Deco-inspired metal and glass pendant.

PLATE 1.19

The same entryway redone twenty-five years later. Architecturally nothing has changed. The dramatic look results from the introduction of supersaturated color on the walls, new furniture, and lighting. The center fixture has been replaced with a traditional transitional pendant with opaque shades. The new mirror on the far wall is flanked with a pair of candlestick wall sconces. Two recessed adjustable low-voltage fixtures are illuminating the face of the console and the Roman bust off to the left. Even in this very traditional space, a little bit of modern lighting can make all the difference.

PLATE 1.20

This entryway is totally dedicated to drama. The tabletop and artwork take center stage in the space. A layer of ambient light would have helped make family and friends as important as the art.

PLATE 1.21

Here a low-tech solution to produce an interesting effect. A small mirrored ball has been placed on the top of the Indian chest. A single recessed adjustable low-voltage fixture is directed toward the ball to create the star-like pattern on the ceiling. A pair of opaque wall sconces guides visitors from the entryway to the living room.

PLATE 1.22

Guests are welcomed into this grand yet rustic home with a perforated metal star-shaped pendant by Arte de Mexico that casts lush patterns in light onto the walls and vaulted ceiling. A series of torch-shaped wall sconces by Terzani Lighting help add a human scale to the 25 foot tall living room. A custom luminaire constructed from copper tubing and cone-shaped light fixtures, by Lightspann Illumination Design, creates a visual focal point as well as directd accent light for art and table tops.

PLATE 1.23 (top)
This intimate seating area, centered on the fireplace, is a good example of light layering at work. The reveal in the ceiling is uplighted with two continuous runs of LED linear light by Dreamscape Lighting. The pendant fixture by Lightspann Illumination Design offers the decorative element for the space, creating the illusion that it is providing the room's illumination. Recessed adjustable low-voltage fixtures illuminate the tabletop, fireplace façade, and niches, while a single floor lamp provides task light next to the chair.

PLATE 1.24 (bottom left)
A close-up of the chair located next to the fireplace shows a reading light with an opaque copper shade. This fixture provides task light without drawing attention to itself.

PLATE 1.25 (bottom right)
This close-up of one of the niches that flank the fireplace shows a single recessed adjustable low-voltage fixture being used to illuminate the primitive art pieces. The glass shelf allows the light to travel down to the lower objects. Note how the objects have been positioned on the upper shelf to allow light to pass beyond them.

PLATE 1.26

Here in a dining room the existing recessed, adjustable, low voltage fixtures were re-lamped using LED MR16s. These newer versions have a color quality close to that of incandescent (2700 degrees Kelvin), but also come in a slightly cooler halogen color temperature (3000 degrees Kelvin). By using LED MR16s to lamp the recessed fixtures you will be protecting the art from UV radiation.

PLATE 1.28

The original flat ceiling of this master bedroom has been completely transformed. The existing roof line allowed for the ceiling to be raised and beams installed, to create an interesting architectural detail. Each of these newly created coffers where illuminated with a soft perimeter LED light, in addition to 3 pendant-hung art glass fixtures, made by Lightspann. The pendants were fitted with GU-24 dimmable CFLs to help cut down on energy costs and maintenance while the perimeter lighting uses LED linear lights, made by Dreamscape Lighting.

PLATE 1.27
The lighting within the chalet creates an inviting amber glow while the exterior landscape lights, fitted with a daylight blue filter, keeps the conifers looking green and the snow a crisp blue-white.

PLATE 1.29
Creating a balance of light between the interior and exterior of a home can help to visually expand the interior spaces, while adding a layer of safety.

PLATE 1.30

This small dining room benefits from good light layering. The sconces that flank the bay window offer a bit of visually sparkle, while the chandelier, over the table, provides both ambient and decorative illumination. Recessed, adjustable, low voltage fixtures highlight the art while illumination outside expands the view beyond the windows.

PLATE 1.38

In this traditional/transitional dining room an alabaster pendant fixture, made by JH Lighting, produces a good amount of ambient light in addition to giving a soft decorative focal point. The tall paintings are illuminated by recessed, adjustable, low voltage fixtures fitted with linear spread lenses that help elongate the beam spread.

PLATE 1.31

The rear portion of this two-story live/work space has the look of a giant glowing lantern at night. The warm ambient interior light contrasts nicely with the cooler- colored accent light for the garden plantings.

PLATE 1.32 (left)

During the day, this small garden falls mostly into shadow due to the tall buildings that surround it.

PLATE 1.33 (right)

At dusk the garden takes on a decided fantasy-like quality. Here the moonlighting effect comes into play. Shielded low- voltage adjustable exterior fixtures are mounted in the taller trees. The illumination is directed downward through the lower branches to create a dappled pattern of light and shadow.

PLATE 1.34 (left)

During the day the corner of this upper deck falls mostly into shadow.

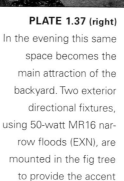

PLATE 1.36 (left)

Here in the daylight the water feature is mostly lost among the lush foliage.

PLATE 1.35 (right)

At night this same corner becomes a delightful focal point. At first viewing it appears that the three candles are providing the illumination. In reality. a pair of shielded directional exterior fixtures provide illumination for the plants and the gargoyle.

PLATE 1.37 (right)

In the evening this same space becomes the main attraction of the backyard. Two exterior directional fixtures, using 50-watt MR16 narrow floods (EXN), are mounted in the fig tree to provide the accent lighting.

PLATE 1.39

A pair of exterior wall sconces, manufactured by Hubbardton Forge, flank the doorway that leads to the garden. Each sconce uses a 9-watt CFL that provides approximately 35 watts of illumination and has an average rated lamp life of 10,000 hours.

PLATE 1.40

This oval pendant fixture, made by Taller Uno, is suspended over the dining room table to help draw people into the space. Recessed fixtures highlight the table setting and center piece while votive candles cast a gentle glow onto diner's faces. The linen shade, fitted with a lens at the bottom, hides the fact that dimmable CFLs are being used.

PLATE 1.41 (top left)

This dramatic pendant fixture, the 'Flotation' by Ingo Maurer normally takes five 100 watt 'A' lamps. Instead five 20 watt dimmable, screw-in CFLs are being used, cutting the power consumption by 400 watts and lengthening the lamp life to 750 hours to 10,000 hours.

PLATE 1.42 (top right)

In this image the "black mirror" effect is used to create this interesting vignette. The Romanesque columns are reflected in the water's surface when the pool lights are turned off. Hidden low-voltage accent lights illuminate the columns and the surrounding oak trees.

PLATE 1.43

As dusk begins to fall, this sensational colonnade gleams against the azure sky. A recessed well light is located at the base of each of the columns to create this impressive effect.

PLATE 1.44

This rather plain entry takes on a dramatic architectural flare when day turns to dusk. The barrel-vaulted ceiling is uplighted with a series of opaque wall sconces that create an intriguing pattern of illumination. Two runs of standard cove lighting would have turned the space into a train tunnel. Instead, this more cost-effective solution creates a much more inviting first impression. The Sconces, made by Justice Design Group, use screw-in dimmable CFL's by MaxLite.

Special Effects

Now that you have worked your way through the basics of lighting design, this chapter will describe some relatively new products and lighting techniques that are beyond standard design.

Homeowners might consider using special lighting treatments that are subtle or controllable enough to be experienced every day. Day-to-day use of specialized lighting such as **neon**, fiber optics, LEDs, and **framing projectors** in residential applications may be too intense or showy for your clients. Commercial spaces can be more adventurous, because people want to be visually transported to a space that has a bit of fantasy to it.

This approach is similar to choosing art that you can live with. A particularly avant-garde painting or sculpture may have an impact initially, but will your clients love it enough to have it as a constant part of their daily existence? Just as in film, music, and commercials, people can get too creative, allowing their creations to outshine the main event. Special-effects lighting can divert attention away from the rest of the space and the people in it. Still, working with your client to make a strong statement is certainly a design option. Some people want a living space that makes guests say, "Wow!"

Usually, lighting works best as part of the background, bringing people's attention to the environment, but rarely to the lighting itself. Designers put together many elements to create an overall effect, including color, furniture, art, plant material, window treatments, and floor coverings. Don't let strong lighting cause other aspects of the design to suffer or take a secondary role in terms of visual inclusion, unless the lighting is to be the central focus. In Figure 7.1, an even backlighting effect does a great job of turning a screen into a 3-D graphic.

As is said in real estate, there are three important things to consider: location, location, location. Since these special lighting effects can have such a strong presence, picking the right place-

ment is a major factor. A glowing visual treat at the end of a long hallway pulls people toward it. These special uses of lighting can help give subtle direction to guests. Art glass is making an appearance as a luminous presence in upscale homes.

The interior entrance gives a first impression of what the rest of the house is like . . . and of the owners. A special effect here can give a great visual clue as to what's in store. Since the entry foyer is not a place where family and guests linger, it is a good spot to consider using lighting with some pizzazz.

Another property of special-effects lighting is that it can give the designer an ability to add dimension to a space. Since the effect is often the strongest visual presence in the room, balancing its light level with the other lighting in a room will help add an intriguing 3-D feel.

Additionally, a visually strong special effect can draw people's attention away from the less desirable elements of a structure, or possibly turn those undesirable elements into a fascinating design look. A room with a jumble of architectural features might benefit from the eye-catching characteristics of a special lighting effect, such as a neon sculpture.

Now apply this concept to an outside situation: An illuminated sculpture could visually allow your client's neighbor's scruffy backyard to fall into the shadows. This involves using the **brightness factor** as a positive aspect of a special effect. As your eyes adjust to the intensity of a neon sculpture, for example, your irises contract to accommodate that brightness. The surrounding area appears to darken considerably, at least as you perceive it. This helps the less-than-pleasant aspects of the neighbor's property fade away into the darkness.

FIGURE 7.2

A framing projector uses a template or series of shutters to "cut" the light to the shape of the art.

FRAMING PROJECTORS

Also known as **optical framing projectors**, these luminaires can focus light to match the shape of the art or table they illuminate. The simpler models on the market use a series of shutters to make the beam of light approximate the size of the art. The more sophisticated units use a custom-cut metal template to match the shape of the art (see Figures 7.2 and 7.3). Ready-made square, rectangular, and circular templates are also available for both high-end and low-end optical projectors. These fixtures come in recessed versions and as track heads. For examples of track versions, take a look at www.lightolier.com (the Dramalux 7645 track head) and www.solux.net. For recessed versions of framing projectors, check out www.wendelighting.com ndwww.phantomlighting.com.

Before MR16's, MR11's, and PAR36's came along, framing projectors were the only way to get a controlled beam spread. Theatrical luminaires had this ability decades ago and still do, but they are simply too bulky for residential use.

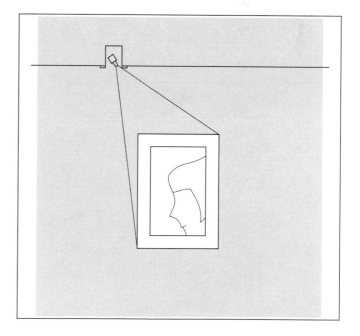

Like everything else that's discussed in this book, framing projectors have their pros and cons. The expensive models do an excellent job of framing the art or sculpture, while the inexpensive models have less precise optics, so the horizontal and vertical lines tend to be slightly convex.

The projectors can cause the art to predominate in the room. This effect can be very dramatic in a museum setting, but it can make people feel like they are of secondary importance in their own homes. A recessed adjustable luminaire without an optical lens, using an MR11 or MR16 lamp, would allow for some light spillage beyond the art piece itself. This actually helps integrate it into the overall design. Framing projectors can be adjusted to soften their focus to create the same effect. If this is the design goal, then using the much less expensive luminaire with a mirror reflector lamp is the way to go. Plus, many framing projectors use expensive, UV-producing halogen light sources that can damage art over time. With the introduction of LED mirror reflector lamps, you can have both beam spread control and UV protection.

Also, framing projectors may need regular adjustments if there is much movement in the building itself, such as kids running around, or if the house is built near a major thoroughfare. An out-of-adjustment framing projector pointed down onto a table can create a disconcerting corona of light on the floor (see Figure 7.3).

FIGURE 7.3

A table that is lighted with a framing projector must stay in its exact position or a disturbing rim of light appears on the floor.

For maintenance purposes, the housing for the framing projector needs to be accessible. That means having a 12-inch-diameter cover plate in the ceiling or installing a trap door in the floor of the room above. If the room upstairs is an accessible attic space, there is no problem, but if it's a bedroom, then carpeting cannot be permanently installed.

If your clients have a very valuable, prestigious piece of art with which they want to dazzle their family and friends, a framing projector would certainly do the trick. Sometimes it's money that helps your client make the final decision. A good recessed framing projector can cost around $1,800, plus the cost of installation. A simpler recessed adjustable MR16 luminaire would cost around $165 plus installation. Surface-mounted framing projectors can cost from $350 on up and are less expensive to install than a recessed luminaire but are visually intrusive in the space.

Lastly, the recessed framing projectors are not very flexible. The lower-priced units do an acceptable job of making a square, rectangle, or circle but usually cannot make irregular shapes. Higher-priced framing projectors can mimic almost any shape but must be refitted with a new custom template if the art is changed.

NEON

Neon has been around for a long time. It was very popular from the 1930s to the 1950s and then began a decline in the 1960s and 1970s. It is enjoying a resurgence of popularity; due mostly to people's refining the art of neon and the more widespread acceptance by architects and designers. Also, the availability of improved transformers allows for a reduction in the noise levels; and easier dimming systems have made dimming more user-friendly. You see the signs everywhere you go in combinations of red, green, yellow, and blue—flashing colors in the darkness of night. Driving around at night would be very different without neon signs. Neon signs tell us when stores are open, and whether or not a motel has a vacancy. They advertise everything from bowling alleys to nightclubs. What would Las Vegas be without its glittery neon signs? This glow is what draws us to neon signs like moths to flame.

In the last 15 years, neon has begun to show up in places other than advertising. Neon artists have begun to use neon glass tubing in sculptures large and small. Some neon artists combine neon art with other media to create one-of-a-kind pieces. Some of these neon sculptures can even light up in sequence as music plays.

Officially, neon in hardwired installations has not been allowed in residences for over 40 years. The **National Electric Code** does not allow systems of 1,000 volts or more to be installed in homes. Neon normally runs in the 3,000- to 15,000-volt range. This is for the issue of safety. Remember when, as a kid, you stuck a fork in the wall plug and got a nasty shock? Or was it your buddy in college? Well, that was 120 volts of electricity. Imagine 15,000 volts coursing through your body. You would be one crispy critter.

Portable neon sculpture is legal and **UL**-listed (**Underwriters Laboratories**—they test stuff out to make sure that it's safe). The main precaution is to make sure that the connections are secure and covered to protect people from the possibility of getting shocked. There is some really great neon sculpture out there in museums and private collections (see Figure 7.4).

Just about everyone is familiar with neon signs, but do you know what makes them glow? Neon is a gas, one of the noble gases in the Periodic Table of Elements. It shares its inert properties with the other noble gases—argon, krypton, xenon, and radon. When electricity passes through these gases, they give off a glow. Neon by definition is a glass vacuum tube filled with neon gas. When electricity is passed through the tube, the gas is excited to produce an orange-red glow. The addition of other gases or phosphors, as well as the use of different-colored tubing, produces a variety of colors. The glass tubing is heated and formed into letters or designs. The overall length and diameter of the tubing determines the size, transformer that is needed. Systems with multiple tubes wired in series require more voltage.

Full-brightness neon, more typically installed in a commercial setting, may be too strong to work comfortably within a residential design. Advanced dimming capabilities now offer a wide range of light levels so that the neon may be more easily integrated into a home setting.

Don't let visually powerful lighting cause other aspects of the design to suffer loss of impact, unless the lighting is to be the central focus.

FIGURE 7.4

A neon sculpture with a plug-in-type transformer creates a strong visual statement.

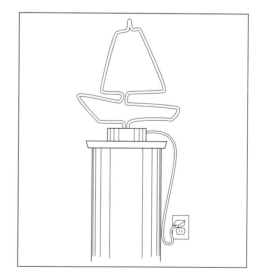

For an added special effect, helium and neon can be combined in a tube to create a curious luminous bubbling effect by using radio-frequency transformers. The bubbling effect is created as radio waves vary.

COLD CATHODE

Cold cathode is a close relative of neon. The tubing is slightly larger (25mm) in diameter than neon (20mm or smaller). Basically, cold cathode is used for illumination purposes, whereas neon is used for signage and as an art form, although there is some crossover. Cold cathode, like neon, comes in more than 30 colors. With cold cathode installations, there are transformers that operate at less than 1,000 volts, which allows them to be permanently installed in residences. Inspectors will want to see a UL label or the label of some other nationally recognized testing laboratory.

In homes, cold cathode can do a wonderful job of indirect lighting behind cove or crown molding. Its small diameter, compared to standard fluorescent lamps, allows a less bulky architectural detail to conceal it (see Figure 7.5). The transformer does have an inherent hum, so it should be located remotely within a soundproof space. The inside of a niche detail could also use cold cathode as its light source (see Figure 7.6). Or it could be used to outline the inside perimeter of a skylight (see Figure 7.7).

Cold cathode technology is now being used to make dimmable and nondimmable CFLs that are much smaller than the typical compact fluorescents. Now you can get long-life flame-tip lamps for chandeliers and candle-type wall sconce that have a lovely incandescent glow. Inside the glass envelope is a tiny coil of cold cathode tubing.

FIGURE 7.5 (left)
Cold cathode can be mounted behind crown molding to provide uplight. (Local codes need to be checked before installation.)

FIGURE 7.6 (right)
Cold cathode can be used to light the inside of a niche. (Local codes need to be checked before installation.)

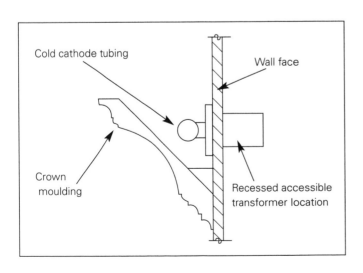

Cold cathode tubing

Wall face

Crown moulding

Recessed accessible transformer location

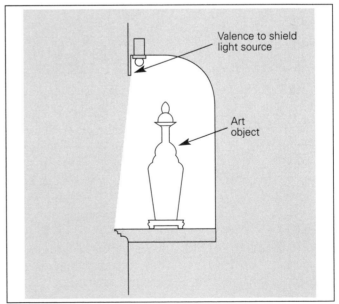

Valence to shield light source

Art object

FIBER OPTICS

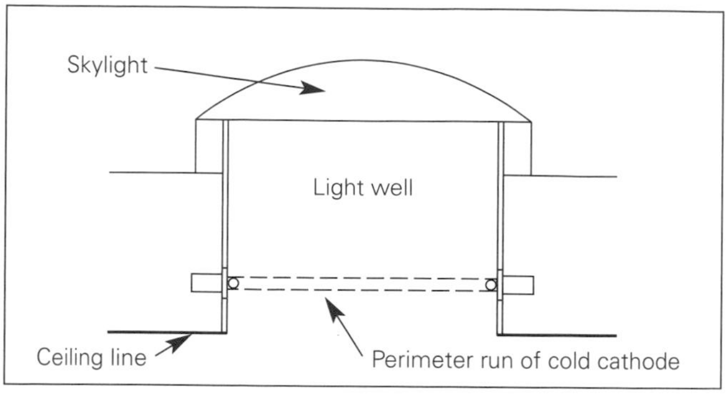

Fiber-optic lighting was the darling of lighting design before LEDs came onto the scene. Illuminated from one end, the light travels through the fiber-optic filament or bundle of filaments in a tube or casing. One variety, called "end-lit" fiber optics, projects an intense light from the end of the fiber-optic run opposite the light source. The other variety, called "edge-lit," illuminates the length of the fiber-optic run. Presently, most fiber-optic runs are illuminated by halogen or metal halide sources, but LED versions are also on the market. Before LEDs came onto the general market, fiber-optic lighting was the only light source that provided illumination without UV radiation.

FIGURE 7.7
Cold cathode can be installed in the light well of a skylight. (Local codes need to be checked before installation.)

A fiber-optic package usually contains two components: the fiber-optic material itself and its source of light, usually called an **illuminator**. The illuminator is a remotely-located shielded box that houses a lamp, a ballast (if an HID source is being used), and a fan (to keep the lamp cool and to help lengthen its life). It can also house an optional color wheel or filter holder that allows the owner to change the color of the light output or allows for a gradual shift from one color to the next. In the 1950s, everyone had a silver metal Christmas tree and a motorized light that passed colored lenses in front of a spotlight on a weighted base. Well, this is just a more refined version of the same principle.

Designers often mistakenly assume that edge-lit fiber optics are as bright as neon and are a viable substitute for neon or cold cathode on a project. This is not the case. While fiber optics and neon can come close to the brightness of neon or cold cathode in certain environments, the true advantages of fiber optics are what they can do better than neon, including flexibility, ease of installation, color-changing capabilities, and low maintenance. These qualities have made fiber optics better suited for many functions usually reserved for other light sources. For examples of fiber-optic lighting products and installations, take a look at www .luciferlighting.com, www.energyfocus.com, and www.fiberopticproducts.com.

Here are the main advantages of fiber optic lighting:

- Increases fire and electromagnetic safety by transporting light rather than electricity.
- Eliminates heat transfer and structural support hardware, simplifying light fixtures, installation, and architectural requirements.
- Reduces ambient cooling system requirements because of reduced heat from light.
- Produces more pleasing light with color change and special-effects options.
- Centralizes maintenance and cleaning, and reduces maintenance and labor costs.
- Can significantly reduce lighting-related energy consumption.

Edge-Lit Fiber Optics

Edge-lit fiber optics can do a pretty good job of approximating the look of a neon sign or sculpture in a darkened environment. The space in which it is being used needs to be relatively dark for the fiber optics to "read" as neon. If there is too much other lighting in the spaces, then the illumination from the fiber-optic run is washed out.

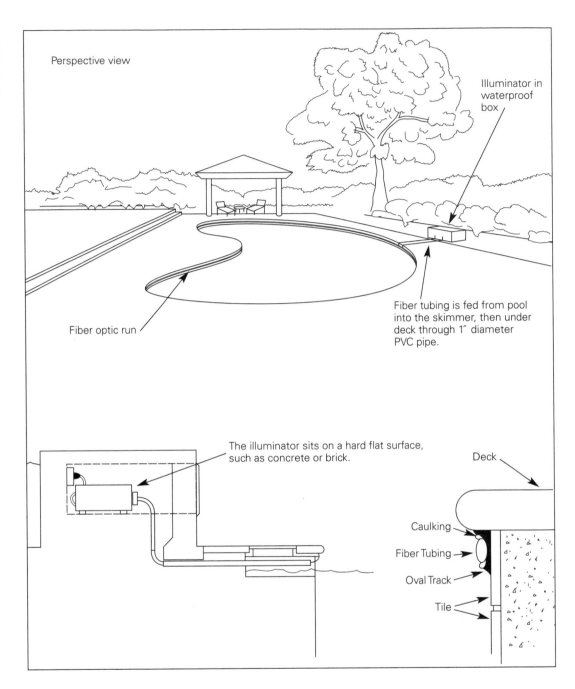

FIGURE 7.8

Fiber optics can be used
to edge-light a pool.
Design concept by
Fiberstars.

Perspective view

Illuminator in
waterproof
box

Fiber optic run

Fiber tubing is fed from pool
into the skimmer, then under
deck through 1″ diameter
PVC pipe.

The illuminator sits on a hard flat surface,
such as concrete or brick.

Deck

Caulking

Fiber Tubing

Oval Track

Tile

One of fiber optic's main advantages over neon or cold cathode is the ability to change the color at will. Red neon will always be red neon. Only replacement of the neon tube will give you a different color, while a simple change of lens is all that is required in fiber optics. LEDs have this same color-changing ability, with a much longer lamp life.

Another advantage of fiber optics is that since there is no electricity actually going through the tube, a fiber-optic run can be integrated into water environments. How about your client's signature or the outline of a giant fish in the bottom of the pool? You can also inset a fiber-optic run into the edge of the client's pool or hot tub for a dramatic effect (see Figure 7.8). You could also

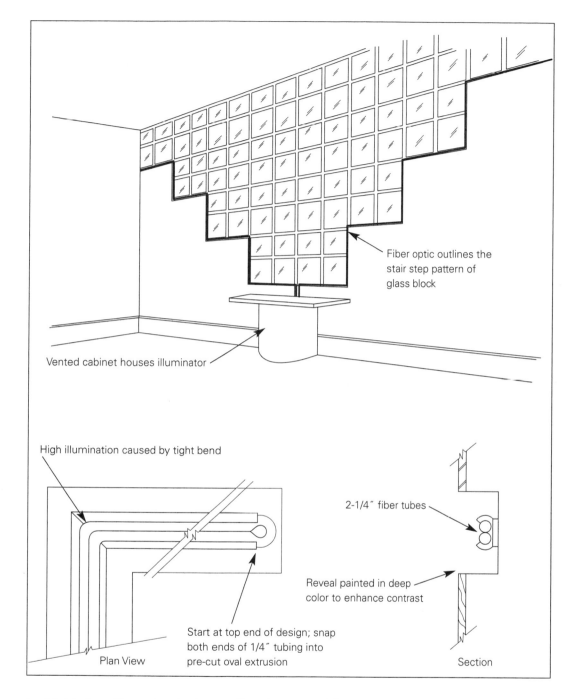

Fiber optic outlines the stair step pattern of glass block

Vented cabinet houses illuminator

High illumination caused by tight bend

2-1/4″ fiber tubes

Reveal painted in deep color to enhance contrast

Start at top end of design; snap both ends of 1/4″ tubing into pre-cut oval extrusion

Plan View

Section

backlight glass tile set in a bathroom floor for a very different type of night-light. If these glass tiles are a frosted white, then inserting a color filter in front of the light source could change the color. You can't do this so easily with LED technology, which is electrified and would need to be accessible when the LED diodes finally burn out.

Fiber-optic runs can also be snaked through walls of glass block to add another dimension to that architectural detail at night. The light source is remotely located in the illuminator, so the homeowner never has to go into the wall to replace the lamp (see Figure 7.9). You could edge-

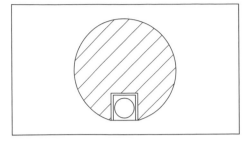

FIGURE 7.10

A sandblasted acrylic handrail glows from within through the use of a fiber-optic bundle running in a channel along the underside.

light a table, a piano, or the steps leading to your client's front door; outline an architectural detail; or create an art piece. If this sounds too over-the-top, then it probably is, but that doesn't mean that someone won't ask for it.

You can consider illuminating a sandblasted acrylic handrail from within by inserting an edge-lighted fiber-optic bundle through the center if it's a hollow straight run. Or you can fit it into a rout on the underside if it's a curved solid rail (see Figure 7.10). Fiber optics can be dimmed, but since the output of illumination can be subtle, dimming is often not necessary. To keep the light level constant throughout length of the run, you should keep the length of a fiber-optic run to 100 feet or less and loop the run back to the illuminator. Optionally, place an illuminator at both ends.

End-Lit Fiber Optics

End-lit fiber optics can perform a variety of interesting functions. For example, single strands of fiber optics can be pulled through a ceiling to create a starry-night effect. The color wheel can do its trick of gradually changing the hue and intensity of those man-made constellations. You could also consider creating the effect of fireflies to a garden on the West Coast, where fireflies don't exist, by hiding fiber optics at different heights in a stand of bamboo. Now, of course, LEDs have taken over this niche market as well. Check out www.fireflymagic.com and www.magicalfireflies.com.

End-lit fiber-optic lighting has traditionally been integrated into display lighting where a remote light source is advantageous for maintenance purposes. Also, because fiber-optic lighting does not emit UV rays, it was considered an excellent source of illumination when conservation of what is being illuminated is an issue. Now LEDs have nudged their way into display cases as well. Like Starbucks, they are popping up everywhere.

LEDs (Light-Emitting Diodes)

LEDs have the "it factor" as a source of illumination for residential and commercial projects. While they are the standard choice to light up instrument panels, clock faces, and dashboards, they have come on like gangbusters to all facets of lighting. Look closely at a newer traffic light—you'll notice a series of smaller points of light instead of one large source of illumination. Since LEDs, especially the colored variety, have an extremely long life (up to 40,000 hours, as mentioned) and wonderfully intense colors, they were a perfect solution for this use.

Now the commercial market is using LEDs to backlight plastic lettering on signage. As mentioned, a lot of what you may think is neon in urban landscapes is really LED technology. Here, too, the intense light and the long life of the source make it a better way of backlighting signage than fluorescent or neon. Neon is fragile and costly. Fluorescent sources have a much more limited lamp life than LEDs, have little flexibility, and don't work well in cold temperatures. LEDs trump most light sources.

The residential market is just opening up for LEDs. The first items to hit the market were backlit house numbers and doorbell indicator lights. These products allowed for the use of the intense colors generally available in LEDs. The new white LED has made them the go-to source for commercial installations . . . and now home lighting as well. What used to be primarily special-effect lighting is becoming the norm.

As far as special-effect uses for LEDs, one popular application in a residence is their use in cove lighting, indirect illumination that runs around the perimeter of a room. The light source is normally hidden in an architectural detail. An LED system with a color changer can create a glow of light on the ceiling that goes from red to blue to green to purple. While this may not be suitable for a dining room application, it would work magnificently for a home theater or media room. It could also be cool under the lip of a platform bed. The white-to-yellow-color-range LEDs would be better for cove lighting living rooms, dining rooms, and bedrooms.

You can also create entire walls of ever-changing light and pattern using LED technology integrated into luminescent panels. Again, while this could be effective for a bar or nightclub, it might be a little too over-the-top for a residential installation—but never say never. For examples of these panels and some installations, go to www.colorkinetics.com. Look at their I-color tile and the I-color module. They have a great steaming video of the Morimoto restaurant in Philadelphia, Pennsylvania (www.colorkinetics.com/showcase/videos/morimoto.htm), which shows the stunning effect of color-changing LEDs.

Another little trend in the use of LEDs is what is referred to as **chroma therapy**, where people can dial in a color through their shower head or the whirlpool jets in the tub to create a hue of illumination that offers them the feeling of peace, calmness, excitement, or even sensuality. The promoters of chroma therapy suggest that color is a sensory experience. Chroma therapy is seen as a branch of holistic healing that uses color to achieve optimal health.

Research has shown that certain colors have measurable psychological and physiological effects on people. For example, warm colors such as red and orange usually act as stimulants and have been shown to elevate heart rates, induce perspiration, and arouse feelings of excitement. Also, studies have shown that people can attach symbolic significance to certain colors, like associating red with love. Cool colors, such as green, blue, and indigo, are thought to be calming, while red, orange, and other warm colors are said to have energizing effects.

Bath fixture manufacturers noticed a growing interest in chroma therapy, and some have offered it as an option in their lines. For examples of tubs, go to www.us.kohler.com and www.jacuzzi.com; for examples of showerheads, go to www.trendir.com/archives/000857.html and www.kzl.en.alibaba.com (Shenzhen Kezhilai Electronics Technology Co., Ltd.). For some people, incorporating chroma therapy into their homes can be as fundamental as choosing paint and fabric colors. Be aware that "the direct link between certain colors and specific psychological or physiological results is tenuous at best," according to Professor Mark D. Fairchild, director of the Munsell Color Science Laboratory at Rochester Institute of Technology in New York. "Surrounding yourself in a color that relaxes you would certainly be a good thing," Fairchild says, "but the degree to which this would be effective or helpful depends on the person's predisposition to the idea." This doesn't keep manufacturers from jumping on the bandwagon, like they did with aroma therapy.

Over the past decade, due to advances in LED technology and for a chance to differentiate themselves from their competitors, manufacturers have broadened chroma therapy's applications,

To keep the light level constant throughout the length of the run, you should keep its length to 100 feet or less and loop the run back to the illuminator. Optionally, place an illuminator at both ends.

such as incorporating it into plasma and LCD televisions. They offer televisions with integrated LED lighting that projects a color of light around the screen that relates to what you are seeing on the screen. They promote it as a way of broadening the sensory experience of TV watching. For an example, go to www.consumer.philips.com and look at the Ambilight.

• THE BOTTOM LINE

Remember, a little goes a long way. Let your project wear one or two pieces of great architectural jewelry—don't empty the whole jewelry box.

Part Two

Using Light

"'Incandescent' is how he thinks, but 'fluorescent' is what I want."

Kitchens—The New Gathering Place

Kitchens have become the new centers for casual entertaining. One reason for this is the change in the way we entertain. It's now more relaxed than it was previously, with a laid-back and interactive feel. Today it's much more likely that guests will gather in the kitchen as the meal is being prepared; often lending a hand while sipping a glass of wine. They are no longer waiting in the living room or dining room to be served.

New homes are being designed by architects and builders to accommodate this change. As a result, the trend is toward **open-plan** houses, where the rooms flow together. The solid walls between the kitchen, dining room, and family room have disappeared. This newly defined space is often referred to as a **great room**.

The impact on lighting design is that the kitchen should now be as inviting as the rest of the house. It too must have controllable lighting levels, so that guests look as good and feel as comfortable as they do in the other parts of the house (see Figures 8.1 and 8.2). This definitely has us rethink some of the lighting methods that have been around for a long time. At first there was the ubiquitous ceiling fixture in the center of the room (see Figure 8.3). Then in the 1970s contractors went to a run of track lights (see Figure 8.4). In the 1980s there was a shift toward using a series of recessed downlights installed in a grid pattern in the ceiling. This was a little better, but by themselves they cast harsh, unflattering shadows on people's faces and your own head still eclipses the work surface.

Sadly, we still see new kitchens, expensive kitchens, with a single source of illumination in the center of the room. Whether this is incandescent or fluorescent, it is essentially a *glare bomb* that provides little in the way of adequate task, ambient, or accent lighting. As our eyes adjust to the glare, the rest of the kitchen seems even darker than it actually is. We see only the light source, and little of the surrounding room.

FIGURE 8.1
A room filled with ambient light helps soften the shadows on faces. The additional layer of fill light is what helps humanize a given space.

Kitchens have become the new centers for entertaining. The impact on lighting is that the kitchen should now be as inviting as the rest of the house.

FIGURE 8.2
A room filled with only recessed downlights casts harsh shadows onto people's faces, placing their features in deep shadow and making their features unattractive.

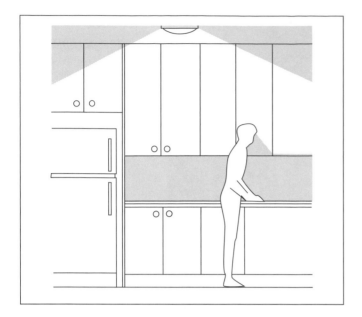

FIGURE 8.3 (left)
The illumination from a
surface-mounted luminaire
in the center of the room is
blocked by one's own body.

FIGURE 8.4 (right)
Track lighting is a poor
source of task light. Clients
will be forced into working
in their own shadows.

As you have learned, there is no single luminaire that can perform all the required functions of lighting for a space. Here, as almost everywhere else in the house, it is the layering of various light sources that creates a comfortable and flexible lighting design.

As mentioned in Chapter 3, track lighting is best used as a source of accent lighting. If you try to use it to light the inside of cabinets or the countertops, your own head can get in the way, casting shadows onto the work surface (see Figure 8.4). The overused surface-mounted luminaire in the middle of the ceiling can cause the same problems.

Under Cabinet Lighting

The first step toward successful light layering in the kitchen is the introduction of lighting that is mounted below the wall cabinets. This type of lighting provides an even level of illumination along the countertops. Since it comes between the work surface and your head, the lighting is much more shadow-free.

These linear task luminaires come in a great variety of styles and lamp sources. What we commonly see is a fluorescent strip luminaire that is mounted at the back of the cabinet. The drawback to this placement is that when people are sitting down in the breakfast area or the adjacent dining room, the light source can hit them right in the eye (see Figure 8.5).

What has been on the market for a while now are linear task lights in incandescent, fluorescent, or LED versions that mount toward the front of the cabinet. They project a portion of the illumination toward the backsplash, which then bounces light without glare onto the work surfaces and out toward the center of the kitchen (see Figure 8.6). This works well when the countertop is a material with a **nonspecular** (not glossy) surface, such as unpolished marble, flamed granite, or man-made surfaces such as Corian by DuPont or a matte-finish plastic laminate.

Lighting designers are often faced with the challenge of lighting highly reflective countertops, such as polished black granite or glossy tile. These shiny surfaces act like mirrors, revealing the

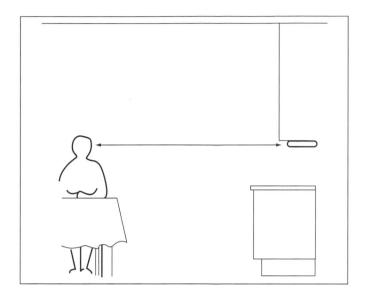 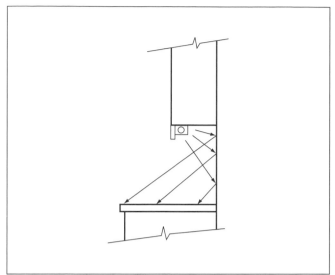

light source under the cabinets. In this situation, a solid reflector could be installed along the underside of the luminaire so that the light is directed only toward the backsplash.

In the worst-case scenario, both countertop and backsplash have a reflective finish, making a true lighting nightmare. If the clients are not willing to choose a surface with a matte finish, then the only solution is to install miniature recessed adjustable luminaires with louvers covering the face of the lamps. Inside the cabinets, a false bottom would need to be created in order to hide the luminaire housings (see Figure 8.7). Luckily, design trends are moving away from high-gloss surfaces in favor of more flat finishes.

Note: The incandescent linear task lights (including halogen and xenon) produce heat and can affect the food stored inside of the cabinet—items such as baker's chocolate can melt. It's a good idea to instruct your clients to store perishables on an upper shelf if heat is a factor. The fluorescent and LED versions produce much less heat.

Under-cabinet lights also come as a mini-recessed or surface-mounted luminaires called a **puck light**. It used to be that puck lights only came in incandescent versions, now they are available in LED and fluorescent options as well. Both Lucifer (www.luciferlighting.com) and Permlight (www.permlight.com) make LED puck lights. Tresco International (www.trescointernational.com) makes very compact fluorescent versions in both an incandescent color and a daylight color. The incandescent color version is better for the kitchen.

GENERAL ILLUMINATION

Ambient lighting plays a very important role in the overall lighting design for the kitchen, just as it does for the other main rooms in the house. It is this soft fill light that helps humanize the space. Note that the color temperature of the lamps in all the lighting used in the kitchen should match, or at least be similar to, the color temperature in other rooms of the house to maintain the visual flow from area to area.

FIGURE 8.5 (left)
Linear task lights mounted toward the back of the cabinet create a distracting glare when people sit at the table.

FIGURE 8.6 (right)
A linear task light mounted at the front of the cabinet bounces illumination off the backsplash and onto the countertop.

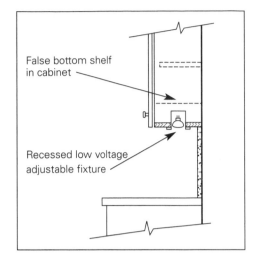

There are a variety of ways to provide ambient lighting. One way, when dealing with 9-foot or higher ceilings, is to install a pendant-hung luminaire or a series of pendants along the centerline of the space. They can be made of an opaque material, such as plaster or metal, or have a more translucent quality such as **alabaster** or **mica**. Not only will they produce a wonderful ambient illumination, but they will also add a more human scale to the kitchen (see Figure 8.8). Before, these fixtures usually used incandescent sources. Now both screw-in CFLs and hardwired fluorescents are available. As long as the color temperature is close to that of incandescent lighting and the lamping is hidden behind a solid or semisolid material, people will be hard-pressed to realize that it is not an energy-guzzling incandescent source.

Another ambient lighting option is to mount linear luminaires above the cabinets, provided there is open space between them and the ceiling (see Figure 8.9). This can be a wonderfully subtle way of producing much-needed ambient light. If the cabinets don't have a deep enough **reveal** on top, a **fascia** (a wooden trim piece) can be added to hide the luminaires from view. You can add a shelf or blocking that is at the same height as the fascia behind the light, to create a potential display area along the top of the cabinet. Without the shelf, the display items would be visually cut off at the bottom (see Figure 8.9). In California, using fluorescent as the indirect light source can go toward the required 50 percent of watts using a high-efficacy light source. While the light source for this indirect lighting can be incandescent (including halogen and xenon) in other states, consider using fluorescent lamps tubes that can be easily and quietly dimmed using solid-state (electronic) dimming ballasts.

If the wall has already been bumped out or soffitted above the cabinets, there is still an opportunity to build a cove or valence detail out of crown molding in which to house an indirect light source (see Figure 8.10).

FIGURE 8.7
The only way to control glare when both the backsplash and the countertop are a gloss finish is to provide cross-illumination from a recessed luminaire mounted inside the cabinets.

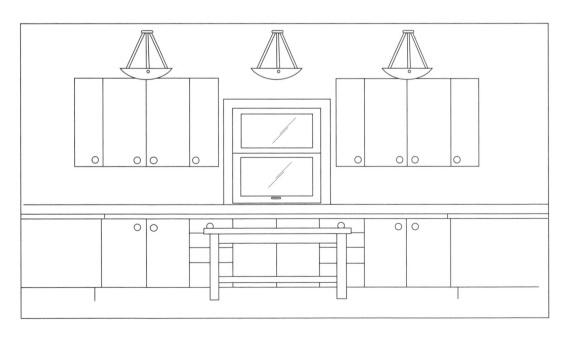

FIGURE 8.8
A series of pendant luminaires can provide a wonderful, inviting ambient light.

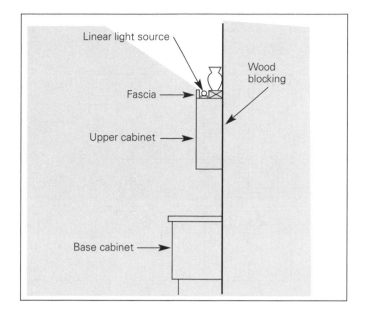

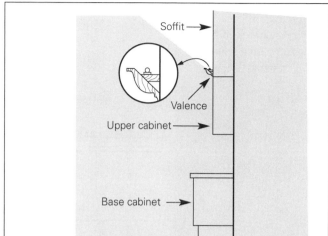

As stated in Chapter 3, California requires that 50 percent of the wattage in a kitchen provide 40 **lumens** or more per watt. Be sure to check local and state codes for building and energy regulations, as these are ever-changing. California is not the only state to have codes that emphasize energy efficiency. The emerging trend is to incorporate energy conservation into building standards throughout the United States.

A less traditional approach to providing ambient illumination would be to install a series of wall sconces on the face of the soffit above the cabinetry, instead of using a crown molding detail (see Figure 8.11). The illumination from these fixtures would not be especially even, but a pattern of light might add some visual interest to a ceiling with little architectural detail.

Skylights can be a great source of general illumination during the day. This is especially true if they are made of a white opal acrylic material or are fitted with a diffusing material (refer to Chapter 5). At night, light sources mounted within the light well can produce adequate fill light (see Figure 8.12), while at the same time keeping the skylight from becoming a *black hole* after dark. Don't let the fact that the kitchen you are designing is on the first floor of a three-story building stop you from installing a skylight. You can still install a faux skylight by opening up a recess in the ceiling (see Figure 8.13) or by using a ready-made faux skylight available from various manufacturers such as the Alter Wave by Lightolier (www.lightolier.com). This will create a feeling of increased height and openness.

FIGURE 8.9 (left)
[Side section] Indirect lighting mounted on top of the cabinets not only produces ambient illumination but could also highlight a client's collection.

FIGURE 8.10 (right)
[Side Section] If the wall is soffitted down to the tops of the cabinet, a valence of crown molding could be installed to house a linear light source.

ACCENT LIGHTING

Your client might have a few art pieces that can stand up to an occasional splash of marinara sauce. They deserve to be highlighted. This helps make the kitchen feel even more like a part of the overall open-home plan. One tasty effect is to dim the ambient and task lights in the kitchen down to a glow, once the party has moved to another area, letting the accented art catch the

FIGURE 8.11

[Front view] A series of wall sconces mounted on the soffit above the overhead cabinets will provide a modern source of ambient illumination.

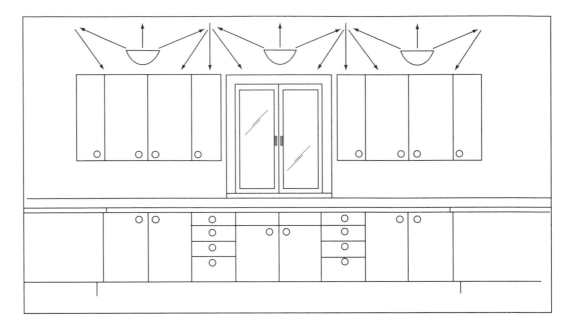

attention. Puck lights can also work nicely inside cabinets with clear or translucent glass panels to provide accent light of the objects within.

What to Consider

Many facets of your kitchen design will determine the way it is lighted. Not only do such variables as ceiling height, natural light, and work surfaces affect the placement or amount of light used, but there are other factors you should consider as well. Here is a checklist:

1   *Color.* Darker-finished surfaces are more light-absorptive. An all-white kitchen requires dramatically less light (40 to 50 percent) than a kitchen with dark wood cabinets and walls.
2   *Reflectance.* A highly polished countertop has a high degree of reflectance and acts just like a mirror. Any under-cabinet lighting will show its reflection.
3   *Texture.* If your end design includes brickwork or stucco, you might choose to show off the textural quality of those surfaces. This is accomplished by directing light at an acute angle onto the textured surface. Luminaires located too far away from the wall will smooth it out (which might be a good idea for bad drywall jobs).
4   *Mood.* Floor plans are more open now. Guests will flow from the living room to the kitchen to the dining room. The kitchen should be just as inviting as the rest of the house. Make sure that there is enough ambient light in the kitchen. This softens the lines on people's faces and creates a warm, inviting glow.
5   *Tone.* The warm end of the color spectrum works well with incandescent light, but cooler colors are adversely affected by the amber quality of incandescent light. Whites turn yellow and reds can turn orange. Make color and finish choices that work well with skin tones and room colors for both day and evening situations.
6   *Code.* In California, designers must conform to Title 24 (the State Energy Commission's requirements for new construction and remodel work (which affects more than 50 percent of the existing space of a kitchen). The code requires that 50 percent of the wattage have an efficacy of at least 40 lumens per watt. Fluorescent and LED fixtures meet these require-

Note: The incandescent linear task lights (including halogen and xenon) produce heat and can affect the items being stored inside of the cabinet. Items such as baker's chocolate can melt. It's a good idea to store perishables on an upper shelf if heat is a factor.

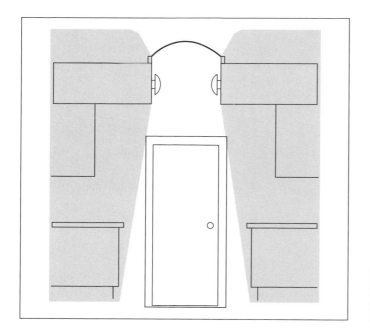 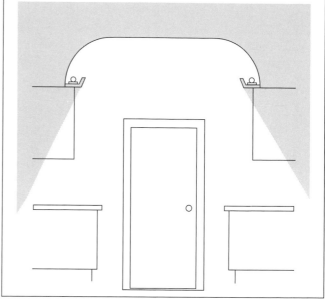

ments. Remember that the fluorescent sources used to meet this requirement must be pronged or hardwired, not screw-in CFLs. Screw-in CFLs, while very handy as substitutes for incandescent bulbs in decorative luminaires, will not count as wattage for the code requirement. In the near future, California will not be the only state with such regulations; most states will be affected. So kiss that incandescent bulb goodbye.

7 *Windows.* Windows that let wonderful light stream in during the day and show off landscaping will become black, reflective mirrors at night unless thought is given to exterior lighting. Outside lighting will visually expand the interior space out into the exterior (see Chapter 15).

8 *Sloped ceilings.* Even if there is enough space above a sloped ceiling to install recessed luminaires, special care must be taken to select units that don't glare. Some luminaires are made specifically for sloped ceilings, while others have a 45- to 90-degree aiming angle to accommodate the slope.

9 *Pot racks.* A pot rack may look just perfect over that center island on the plan, but it's extremely difficult to light a work surface through cookware. If a pot rack is demanded, consider installing recessed adjustable luminaires to cross-illuminate the counter surface of the island or position them above the center of the rack. Still, the shadows cannot be eliminated, so having the option of increasing the ambient light is a way of combating the glare.

10 *Door swings.* Make sure that switches are on the wall of the unhinged side of a door. Otherwise, your client will have to reach around the back of the door to turn on the lights. Have the contractor inform you of any swing changes that occur during the installation process and all the design team members so that you can make sure that the design works in the end.

11 *Bring in a ringer.* Just as interior designers and architects are pulling in kitchen specialists on their projects, those specialists are now turning to lighting experts to make the projects glow. Since the lighting consultant specializes only in lighting, he or she has a vast library of information and knowledge relating solely to light and lighting products. The consultant can turn out a quality design in a short amount of time, saving the kitchen designer's time and ultimately reducing the client's cost.

FIGURE 8.12 (left)

[Side Section] Light luminaires mounted on the inside of the light well can help provide ambient illumination for the kitchen at night.

FIGURE 8.13 (right)

A faux skylight can be created to provide "daylight" even if the kitchen is on the first floor of a three-story building.

Of course, many aspects of this checklist apply to other rooms in the house, so feel free to refer to the list as you go from area to area.

THE BOTTOM LINE

A successful kitchen design is a foot in the door and may be an introduction to do the interior design work for the rest of the client's house (and their neighbor's house).

Entrances—Setting the Tone

Just as you judge people by your first impression upon meeting them, you judge a home by what you see and how you feel as you come into the entry. This makes it doubly important to set just the right mood and tone. The correct lighting is crucial to how people will respond, as well as where their attention will be drawn.

Outside, as evening guests approach a house, the lighting should provide an eye-catching, welcoming feel, as well as security and safety. You will also need to give specific cues showing which way to approach and enter. Be sure to illuminate the house number. Chapter 15 discusses illumination for the outside in more detail.

Inside the home, don't rely on a single decorative fixture (see Figure 9.1). Ambient illumination should surround the entry with welcoming light. Fill light is especially important in this area (see Figure 9.2). People need a gentle glow of illumination to help them feel at ease in new surroundings. This complimentary light also allows the homeowners to look their best when greeting people. Good ambient light in the entry will help transform what is often an awkward moment into a more comfortable and enjoyable encounter. Entry lighting can also energize a person's impression of a home. Highlighting a dramatic painting, sculpture, or architectural detail can help guests feel at once welcomed and impressed.

People respond to what they sense, not always to what is real. A room can be made to look large, airy, and open when the reality may actually be quite the opposite. Too often an entrance in a home is restricted in space, but with lighting and related design techniques, the space can be subtly transformed into a vastly more welcoming place.

> Too often, a foyer in a home is restricted in space, but with lighting and related design techniques, the space can be subtly transformed into a vastly more welcoming place.

ILLUSION

Not all lighting solutions directly involve the use of luminaires. Mirrors, for instance, can be used to create the illusion of greater space or more light. Mirroring on a wall can make a room appear to expand in size. Mirrors will keep wall areas located farthest from the windows from falling into darkness or seeming less important. In the 1980s, the trend was to mirror the entire wall. Now designers are using large framed mirrors that match the size of windows or doorways. Mirroring the backs of bookshelves, display cases, or niches create the illusion of a room beyond and helps reflect light back into the space.

Entries come in all shapes and sizes. Lighting can help you redefine the envelope of the space. Do you want the entry to look larger or more intimate? Do you want a look that dazzles or a look of homey comfort? How about a combination of both? It is possible. For example, in a cramped entry area, you can often use illusion and lighting to "steal" part of another room. In addition to using mirrors, you might consider installing glass blocks or directing an accent light onto a sculpture, flower arrangement, or painting in an adjacent area, such as a hallway, to visually make it a part of a smaller entry.

Highlighting adjacent stairways that flow into in an entry area can provide additional opportunities for expansiveness. Illuminated, they make the room seem larger and provide another focus for the guests' attention upon entering the home. Lighting a painting mounted on the wall along the stairway or illuminating plants or a sculpture on a stair landing can also help a small entry assume the appearance of a grander entrance hall.

CONTROL

Switching and dimming systems can take the same entry that was made to look huge and dramatic for a big party or event and instantly transform it into a cozy and intimate greeting area for small, friendly gatherings. Lighting can—and should—be that flexible.

With an integrated dimming system, your clients can create whatever kind of setting they would like. There's nothing wrong with making the house seem foreboding when uninvited guests stop by, or having the lights go to full brightness when it's time for guests to depart. Review the section on preset dimming systems in Chapter 6 to get a better handle on the idea of creating lighting "scenes."

Lighting that is directed toward the ceiling helps open up a space and makes it feel larger, and at the same time friendly and inviting. Illumination pointed down onto the floor makes an entry seem smaller because the darkened ceiling feels lower. Adding accent light to a darkened space creates highly dramatic settings. Accent light layered with ambient light provides a friendly environment with a bit of visual punch. Positioning the accent lights for the particular art piece is critical (see Figures 9.3 and 9.4). You want the light to enhance the piece, not overpower it or distort it. Make sure that the beam spread of the accent light fits the art it is highlighting. If the light is too tight, it creates a hot spot (see Figure 9.5). Sometimes, directing the accent light at a more acute angle can add texture and dimensionality to the object that it is lighting (see Figure 9.6).

Too often entries end up looking unintentionally dark and uninviting, even if elegantly decorated. Usually it's because the addition of ambient light has not even been considered. Either it was omitted entirely or the walls and ceiling may be too dark in color for indirect light to be reflected and diffused effectively throughout the space.

If the ceiling is not adequately lit, the space seems small; and beams, coffers, moldings, ceiling frescoes, and other design components lose their potential to be marvelous welcoming details. Lighting architectural details well gives people something to engage their interest as they enter, and helps enlarge the feel of the room by expanding the space visually upward. For parties, entrances can serve as auxiliary gathering spots when they are properly lit for people's comfort.

Rule of Thumb: Mount opaque-bottomed wall sconces above eye level, normally 6 to 6½ feet above the finished floor. This applies to 8- or 9-foot ceilings. When you are working with a higher ceiling, the luminaire can be mounted higher.

PLANNING

It's essential that you take lighting needs into consideration at the beginning of the design and construction stages, because additions later will cost much more than adding appropriate lighting touches at the front end of a project. A common approach to lighting an entry is to install a decorative luminaire, such as a chandelier, in the center of the ceiling as the only source of illumination (see Figure 9.1). As a result, everything else falls into secondary importance. This one luminaire draws all the attention. Plus, your clients, as they greet guests, will end up in silhouette, which does not give them a flattering appearance. This should not be your only piece of lighting design but a part of the layering process. This is when light layering comes into play. For example, think about installing a source of ambient light so that an existing chandelier can be dimmed to a subtle sparkle (see Figure 9.2).

FIGURE 9.3
The direct overhead lighting for this seated Buddha causes its facial features to fall into shadow. If the fixture had been located more in front instead of directly over the piece, much better illumination could have been provided for the sculpture.

FIGURE 9.4
This wooden sculpture is successfully illuminated from above because the recessed light fixture is located slightly in front of the art instead of directly on top of it.

Try not to place down-lights over seating areas. They cast hard shadows onto people's faces, making them look older.

FIGURE 9.5 (left) The two low-voltage accent lights that are being used to illuminate this modern piece of woven wall art have beam spreads that are too small to adequately illuminate the piece. They should have more of a flood-type lighting than hot spots of light.

FIGURE 9.6 (right) The metal door benefits from the raking effect of the accent lighting. It adds a tremendous amount of texture and dimensionality.

Note: The bottom of an entry or hall pendant should be a minimum of 6 feet 8 inches off the floor so that people won't bump into it. If you want to hang the fixture lower, it is best to place a table under it to prevent friends from conking their heads.

Daylight also should be integrated into the design of an entry, if possible. Use available windows or add windows or skylights to provide some or all of the ambient light during daylight hours. (Look back at Chapter 5 for some application ideas.)

AMBIENT LIGHTING

One option for **ambient lighting** would be to install a pair of wall sconces flanking an art piece or mirror to provide the necessary glow of illumination. Translucent versions may draw too much attention to themselves; opaque sconces (made of metal, bisque, or plaster) will cast light upward, softening the shadows on faces and filling the entry with a pleasing glow of illumination.

Rule of Thumb: Mount opaque wall sconces above eye level, normally 6 to 6 1/2 feet above the finished floor. This applies to 8- or 9-foot ceilings. When you are working with a higher ceiling,

the luminaire can be mounted higher. Do not mount the luminaire closer than 2 feet from the ceiling; otherwise, there'll be a hot spot on the ceiling above the sconce.

A second possible source of ambient lighting is the torchère (see Figure 9.7). If electrical outlets are already available, then an electrician is not needed. Torchères are the quickest and easiest way of adding ambient light to any room. Remember to choose a luminaire with a solid reflector-type shade that provides uplight only; otherwise attention will be drawn away from the other, more interesting aspects of the entry. A half-switched receptacle would allow your clients to turn on the torchère using a wall switch instead of turning it on at the luminaire itself (refer back to Figure 6.1 in Chapter 6).

A more architecturally integrated solution to the question of ambient light would be to install cove lighting (see Figure 9.8). A linear light source can be hidden behind molding details to uplight the ceiling along the perimeter of the entry. In new construction, this is an inexpensive addition to overall building costs. In a remodel situation, this could be the costliest and most labor-intensive of the ambient lighting solutions. Adding a series of opaque wall sconces would create an interesting pattern of light in an entry hall while at the same time being more cost-effective.

Lastly, you could substitute a pendant-hung, opaque or semi-translucent luminaire in place of a traditional chandelier to create the necessary fill light (see Figure 9.9). This would eliminate the source of sparkle, so you could install translucent or candlestick-type wall sconces on either side of the art above a console as the sparkle of light for the entry. Decorative wall sconces are normally mounted at 5 1/2 to 6 feet on-center (centerline of the junction box) above the finished floor.

FIGURE 9.7 (left)
Torchères can also be a good, easy way of adding ambient light. They provide the illumination that people will think comes from the chandelier, which can then be dimmed to an appropriate level.

FIGURE 9.8 (right)
Cove lighting inside the molding detail provides ambient light without glare. Again, the chandelier gives the illusion of providing illumination, but it is dimmed so it will not produce too much distracting brightness.

ACCENT LIGHTING

Now that you have addressed the decorative and ambient light questions, you can tackle the accent lighting. While the common choice for accent lighting is apt to be track lighting, it is generally not the best solution. For some rooms it may be the only feasible choice because of the architecture, construction restrictions, or cost. But track lighting tends to visually intrude into a room and makes people feel as though they're onstage or on display.

When possible, recessed adjustable luminaires that are mounted in the ceiling are the better solution. These can be directed to particular spots that need highlighting, and they are much more low-profile. Even in an existing home, recessed luminaires made especially for remodel can often be installed within a reasonable budget and with a minimum of mess (except in California, where all recessed fixtures must be rated for insulated ceilings). Always hire a professional electrician to get the job done properly. A well-installed job makes the interior designer or lighting designer look good too.

FIGURE 9.9

A pendant-hung indirect luminaire can be substituted for the chandelier to provide the necessary ambient light. Candlestick wall sconces could be added for sparkle.

RECESSED DOWNLIGHTS

Here's the big question: "Is there truly a good place to use downlights?" The answer is, "Hardly ever." Fixed downlights should be installed only over stationary objects, such as sculptures, niches, or planters built into the architecture. The absolute worst place to use downlights is over seating areas. They cast hard, unflattering shadows on people's faces, making them look tired and older than their true age. Who wants that?

The trend we are seeing in the industry is the use of recessed adjustable luminaires that allow people to easily redirect the lighting as art and furniture are moved around. Interiors are no longer as static as they were in the 1950s, 1960s, and 1970s. Both MR16's and MR11's (in halogen or LED versions) can be great sources of flexible accent light.

In designer magazines, we constantly see rooms filled with a series of recessed downlights casting light in circles on the floor. Their intended purpose is to provide ambient illumination. Downlights, no matter what lamp is used, are a poor source of fill light because of the shadows they cast and the absence of light reflected back toward the ceiling. Use other sources, such as wall sconces or cove lighting, for the ambient lighting. Use adjustable downlights for accent lighting.

Avoid specifying fixed downlights. They don't give the flexibility needed to highlight different sizes, shapes, and mounting heights. As mentioned, interiors are not static anymore. With today's modern, on-the-move lifestyle, flexibility is necessary in order to accommodate new

furnishings or new homeowners. A fixed downlight offers very few options and limits your client's choices. On the other hand, don't go crazy with recessed adjustable luminaires and fill the entire ceiling with holes, often referred to as the **planetarium effect** or the **Swiss cheese effect**. Don't feel you have to light everything in a room. Let some art objects fall into secondary importance to be discovered later in the evening. Lighting everything gives all items in the space the same importance, which ends up being not all that interesting visually.

Accent light does not have to be permanently installed. A number of portable luminaires are readily available that will work in temporary, lower-budget, or historical protected homes. In addition, most track lighting companies manufacture weighted bases to accommodate their track heads, allowing them to be used as portable accent lights (see Figure 9.10). There are also stake lights that fit into planter pots to uplight plants and cast intriguing shadow patterns on the ceiling (see Figure 9.11). These quick and nonpermanent fixes can add wonderful texture to a space. Refer to Chapter 4 for other portable options.

• THE BOTTOM LINE

Be sure to hide light sources as much as possible. Let what is being highlighted come into focus, not the luminaires themselves. Use your design know-how and your client's assets, whatever they are, to turn straw into gold. Well-designed lighting can be powerful alchemy in the entry and throughout the rest of the house.

FIGURE 9.10 (left)
Weighted bases are available that can hold track heads, so they can be used as portable accent lights.

FIGURE 9.11 (right)
Stake lights in planters can cast intriguing shadows on the walls and ceilings.

10

Living Rooms—Layering Comfort with Drama

The way we view living rooms today is very different from the way they were often experienced years ago. Then, living rooms seemed to be off-limits. No one would enter unless company came over. It was as if an invisible braided rope kept the family out. It's almost like the way people treat guest towels—as "too nice to use."

Not that it was a place anyone really wanted to go, anyway. The furniture was formal and uncomfortable. Sometimes it had plastic slipcovers that stuck to people's legs in the summertime. Even the lamp shades may have had plastic covers—the kind that looked like big shower caps. That "hands-off" feeling is finally softening a bit. The furniture is getting more comfortable and arrangements more relaxed.

Nowadays, people have reclaimed the living room. It's not just reserved for special occasions anymore. Furniture plans are less static. It used to be that everything stayed in exactly the same place. Now, paintings, sculpture, and plants are rotated around the house to keep the look fresh. The living room is often rearranged at holidays to accommodate a Christmas tree or dancing, or to set up a buffet for a Thanksgiving feast.

Lighting should be as flexible as the rest of the home's components, and it needs to be controllable enough to satisfy a variety of needs. As was mentioned in Chapter 9, straight downlights are too inflexible for the way people live today. Let's reassert here that installing recessed fixtures over a seating area puts people in a very bad light.

Although entertaining at home is very popular, it's still the owners of the house who spend the greatest amount of time there. The designer's first concern is to give them adequate illumination for their day-to-day activities. Then layer that with lighting options for entertaining.

Ask your clients what they plan to do in the living room. Will they read there? Will they watch television? If they have children, will they want to do puzzles on the floor or board games on the coffee table? Getting a picture of how the space will be used will help you decide how to light it.

Ambient Lighting

The first goal is to create adequate ambient light. There are many ways to do this. The typical 8-foot ceiling offers the least number of options. One solution would be the installation of two or four opaque wall sconces in the room (see Figure 10.1), mounting them 2 feet down from the ceiling.

A possible alternative would be to place a pair of torchères flanking the fireplace or a major piece of furniture, although the illumination would be less even than with the four wall sconces (see Figure 10.2). If the room is large, consider using two torchères on a diagonal. Torchères provide excellent ambient light for a room without needing an electrician (as long as there are existing receptacles to plug them into). Their main job is to fill the volume of space with an over-all illumination that softens the shadows on people's faces and shows off the architectural detailing.

If you have a white or light-colored ceiling, the torchère can also provide suitable secondary task lighting for reading, though it should be used only for light reading such as newspapers and magazines. For serious reading, such as books or balancing the checkbook, use pharmacy-type lamps that position the light between your head and the work surface.

In a living room with 9-foot or higher ceilings, you have more open options. In a smaller living room, a single pendant fixture that provides both ambient and decorative illumination is a good possibility. A pair of pendant luminaires with an overall length of 2 feet to 30 inches would work well for a 9- to 12-foot flat ceiling in a room 15 feet wide and 15 feet long (see Figure 10.3). A pitched ceiling would require luminaires adapted for the slope.

A higher ceiling would also work well in conjunction with a cove lighting detail, where the light source is hidden behind a crown molding, valence, or cantilevered detail (see Figure 10.4). Liv-

FIGURE 10.1 (left)
Floor plan: A series of four wall sconces would be a viable solution to provide adequate ambient light for this living room.

FIGURE 10.2 (right)
Two torchères can also provide the room's ambient light, but it will not be as evenly lighted as when four wall sconces are used.

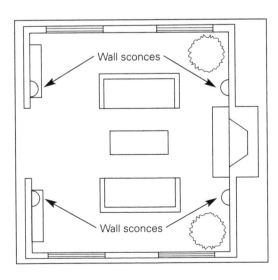

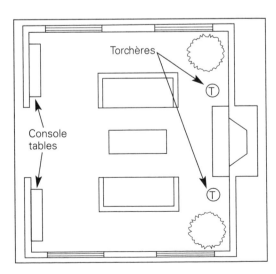

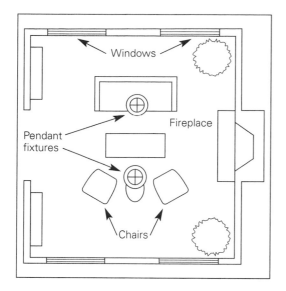 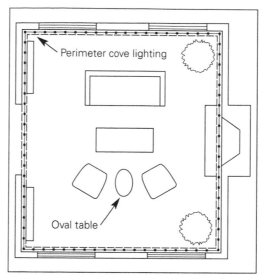

FIGURE 10.3 (left)
Two pendant luminaires would do a great job of providing ambient light, as long as the ceilings are 9-foot or taller. Then add accent lights and task lights for a complete lighting design.

FIGURE 10.4 (right)
Perimeter cove lighting is a very clean, architecturally integrated way of getting ambient light into the living room. This should be used in conjunction with other light sources for better light layering.

ing rooms with gabled ceilings and support beams that are parallel to the floor offer an additional option. In this situation, linear strip lighting can be mounted on top of the beams to provide ambient light from a totally hidden source (see Figure 10.5). This would be a perfect spot to use LED linear lights as the light source.

There are four different methods of installing this linear indirect lighting:

1 Rout a channel in the top of the beam.
2 Place it in a surface channel on top of the beam.
3 Run a length of quarter-round molding along either side of the luminaire.
4 Wrap fascia boards around the beam to create a channel.

Asymmetrically sloped ceilings are common architectural elements in homes built in the 1980s. This results in one very tall wall that often becomes a dead space, because it is too high to hang art. It is a perfect spot to mount a series of wall sconces that fill the room with an abundant amount of ambient illumination (see Figure 10.7). Using a sconce with an **asymmetric reflector** will help throw light out toward the center of the ceiling. For an example of this type of sconce, take a look at the Wedge by Belfer Lighting (www.belfer.com); it comes in a halogen version and a dimmable fluorescent version.

Accent Lighting
Once you have decided what method you'll use to give the living room its fill light, the next step is to decide on accent lighting. The type of luminaire you choose for the source of accent lighting needs to be flexible like it does in all the other rooms. As your clients move furniture and art around, the lighting needs to accommodate each new arrangement.

Remember, when fixed downlights are used for accent lighting, they offer no flexibility at all. If the highlighted object is moved, the clients are left with a circle of light on the floor. If you specify recessed adjustable luminaires, you will provide clients with the adaptability they need. There are both line-voltage and low-voltage versions of these luminaires (refer to Chapter 4 for compar-

FIGURE 10.5

For living rooms with
gabled ceilings and beams
that are parallel to the
floor, you have the option
of locating indirect lighting
on top of the beams.

isons between these two options). One of the advantages of a low-voltage recessed adjustable luminaire is the ability to use a smaller-aperture trim in the ceiling, which draws less attention to the unit itself. Using an LED source will offer both lower maintenance and energy savings.

If you are working on an existing home that already has recessed luminaires, it is possible to leave the housings (the main part of a recessed luminaire installed inside the ceiling) and replace the trims (the visible part of a recessed unit, which is attached to the housing) with line- or low-voltage adjustable versions. In new construction and remodel projects, placement of these accent lights is dependent on what is to be highlighted. That's why it's so important to know the furniture plan before laying out the lighting.

Figure 10.8 shows a living room with furniture centered on a fireplace. Recessed adjustable accent lights are positioned to highlight various parts of the overall design. On the north wall, the sculpture on the table is illuminated with a single recessed adjustable luminaire. On the east and west walls, two pairs of recessed adjustable luminaires **cross-illuminate** the art over

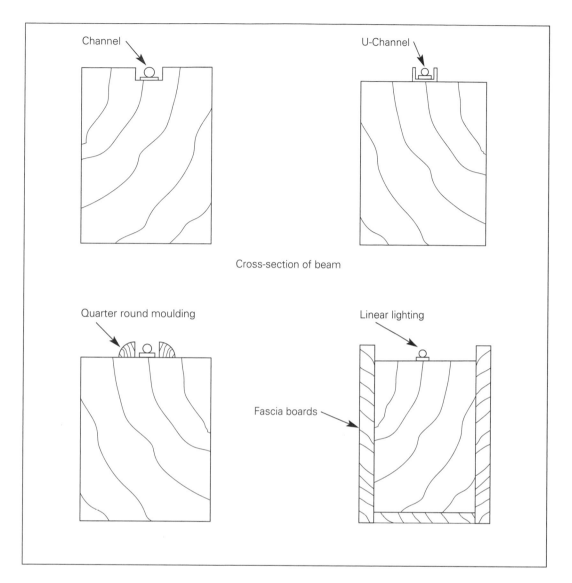

Channel

U-Channel

Cross-section of beam

Quarter round moulding

Linear lighting

Fascia boards

FIGURE 10.6
Here are four methods of masking the linear lights mounted on top of vertical support beams.

the console and the fireplace. It's better to use two luminaires to light a painting that has a glass or Plexiglas® face, because a single accent light centered on the art could simply reflect back into people's eyes. By cross-illuminating, light is directed away from the normal viewing angle. The **angle of reflectance** plays a role whether one, two, or more luminaires are used.

The single recessed adjustable accent light on the south and east walls illuminate objects on a small table, a plant, and a corner sculpture. The luminaire in the center highlights the coffee table. The flexibility of recessed adjustable accent lights allows the coffee table to be illuminated even though the luminaire isn't centered over the table itself.

Track Lighting

Sometimes track lighting ends up being the design choice when other options aren't available. For example, if there is inadequate ceiling depth in which to house recessed luminaires or it is

FIGURE 10.7 (left)
Make use of the tall wall by installing a series of wall sconces for the much-needed ambient illumination.

FIGURE 10.8 (right)
This is a partial lighting plan showing recessed adjustable luminaires used for accent lighting. Alone these would create the "museum effect" where what you own appears to be more important than family and friends.

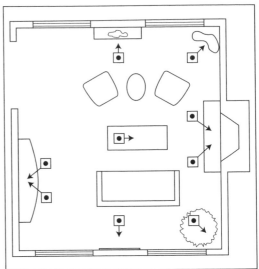

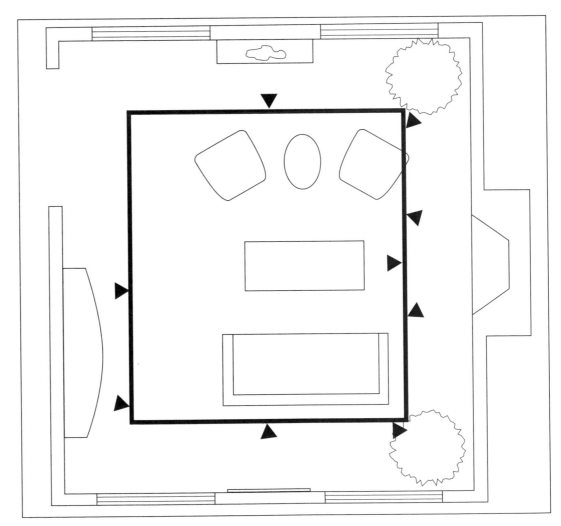

FIGURE 10.9
If recessed luminaires aren't a possibility on a particular project, track lights set up in a perimeter pattern would do an acceptable job.

concrete construction, a surface-mounted system must be used. If track lighting is your choice, a good arrangement in the living room would be to run it around the perimeter (see Figure 10.9). You can make the track seem more architecturally integrated by installing a run of molding on either side of the track (see Figure 10.10). Try to pick out track fixtures that shield the light source from view.

HALOGEN BRIDGE SYSTEMS

An alternative to recessed and track lighting is a more techie-looking product, generically called a **halogen bridge system**, **cable system**, or **rail system**. This is a low-voltage system of two wires or rails strung parallel to each other across a ceiling space. Single-rail systems are available as well. Luminaires, normally using MR16 or MR11 lamps, can be clipped and locked into place along the wires or rail(s) to highlight various objects below (see Figure 10.11). This works especially well in homes where the ceilings are sloped or very high; otherwise, changing the lamps in recessed or track luminaires would be difficult because of their inaccessibility. The rail versions are sturdier than the wire versions. Both can be laid out or bent to follow curving hallways or simply curved to add visual interest.

Even though these luminaires are low in wattage, they are high in **amperage**, requiring a specific **gauge** of wire. Make sure the installing electrician knows this and uses the correct gauge. The high amperage also limits the number of luminaires per transformer. Normally the maximum load is 300 watts, or six 50-watt lamps. The lighting showroom that distributes the cable system or the manufacturer's representative will help you or the electrician to put the correct components together.

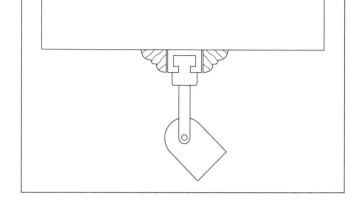

FIGURE 10.10

[Side section]
The addition of moldings on either side of the track run will help it blend in a little more architecturally.

FIGURE 10.11

Using a "halogen bridge" system, running parallel to the floor, lets the luminaires be reached more easily, to change bulbs or readjust the lights.

TASK LIGHTING

The last consideration in the layout of the lighting design is task lighting. The main function of task lighting in the living room is for reading or related activities. Since the best position for a reading light is between one's head and where one's attention is focused, a pharmacy-type luminaire or a tabletop luminaire with an opaque or semi-translucent shade will work very well (check the examples of these type of fixtures in Chapter 4).

If the floor plan has furniture in the middle of the room, it's a good idea to specify **floor plugs** so that cords don't cross the floor to an electrical outlet in the wall. As far as installation goes, crawl space or basement accessibility is a bonus for the electrician in a remodel project.

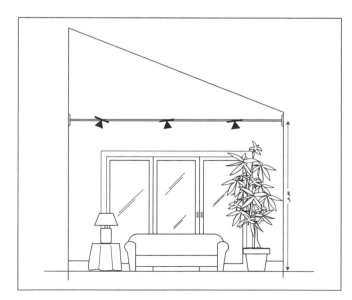

FIGURE 10.12
Switched floor plugs help
keep cords from being
tripped over.

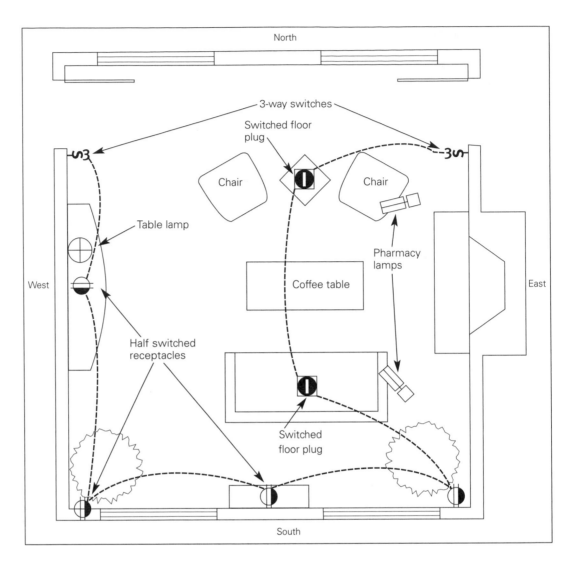

In Figure 10.12, the sofa and the occasional table both have a switched floor receptacle in which to plug the pharmacy lights. These luminaires can be placed on either side of each sofa. The west and south walls have half-switched receptacles (refer back to Figure 6.1 in Chapter 6), so that possible table luminaires and uplights for the plants can come on with the flip of a switch, instead of the homeowner having to go from light to light.

THE BOTTOM LINE

Remember, all the elements of lighting (task, ambient, decorative, and accent) must be considered to create a totally functional and adaptable lighting design. They are the "fantastic four," and they work best as a team.

11

Dining Rooms—The Main Event

Dining rooms used to be the last holdout for a traditional, static furniture arrangement. Now they too have been transformed in some homes into multiple-use spaces. Homeowners have begun to realize how little of their time was spent formally entertaining, and they wanted to reclaim this often underutilized room for additional purposes.

Previously, the dining room table itself was always too big for anything other than a meal for eight or ten people. Today, tables have become more flexible in size, folding down to more intimate seating for four, or able to be divided in two to make a pair of game tables. Even homeowners who have kept their large tables want to be able to push them against a wall for buffet dining. All of these changes created a need for adjustable lighting and required homeowners and designers to rethink the use of a chandelier.

RETHINKING CHANDELIERS

Both chandeliers and sconces can play the important role of decorative lighting in the dining room. They are the visual "jewelry" for the space. Think of the chandelier as the crown and the sconces as the earrings.

For eons, the dining room table has been centered under the chandelier. Many people spent countless hours of their lives making sure that this alignment was just perfectly symmetrical. Dining room tables began to be moved around, as furniture arrangements became more fluid. This meant that the chandelier in the center of the space started getting in the way. For those clients who want a traditional feel but with the flexibility to create a more multifunctional room, there are a good number of choices:

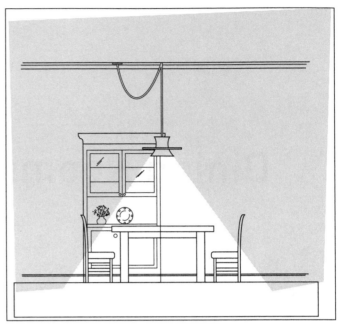

FIGURE 11.1 (left)

A decorative luminaire mounted tightly to the ceiling will be less distracting than a hanging fixture when the table is moved aside.

FIGURE 11.2 (right)

A pendant light on a pulley system can be raised out of the way when the table is moved.

1 Specify a decorative luminaire that hugs the ceiling so that it doesn't look odd when the table isn't in the center of the room (see Figure 11.1). It then visually relates to the ceiling plane rather than the location of the table.

2 Select a pendant light on a pulley system that allows your client to raise or lower the luminaire. There are a good number of European-designed pendants available, primarily contemporary styles (see Figure 11.2). For some modern examples, check out Artemide (www .artemide.us) and Taller Uno (www.talleruno.com).

3 A traditional multi-armed chandelier of bronze or crystal could be hung in a recessed dome or coffer so that it is visually linked to the ceiling configuration rather than to the table location (see Figure 11.3). In a remodel project where it is too expensive or there is inadequate attic space for a dome, a decorative ceiling medallion will create a similar illusion.

The decorative luminaire mounted over the table should be at least 12 inches narrower than the tabletop; and the bottom of the fixture should be 30 to 36 inches from the top of the table. If the ceiling is higher than 8 feet, add 3 inches per foot over the 8-foot height, but this can vary depending on the layout of the room and whether the ceiling slopes. These are just guidelines. The chandeliers normally come with additional lengths of stem, chain, or cable to allow for an on-site adjustment. It really comes down to an aesthetic call.

Many clients in more modern-style homes are forgoing any decorative luminaire at all and are relying instead on recessed adjustable luminaires to provide illumination for the table, no matter where the table is placed (see Figure 11.4). In Figure 11.4, three recessed adjustable luminaires are used. The middle one highlights a flower arrangement in the center of the table.

The two outside luminaires are used to **cross-illuminate** the tabletop itself, adding sparkle to the dishes and silverware. Make sure the two outside luminaires are not pointed straight down.

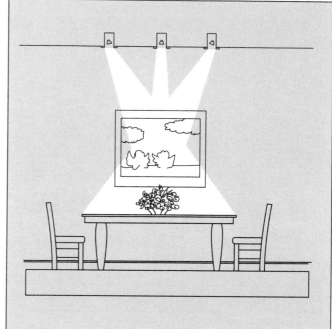

This would cast harsh shadows on the people at both ends of the table and could create glare from glass, lacquer, or a highly polished wood table. Keep these two luminaires pointed at an angle from the ceiling line that is less than 45 degrees. At 45 degrees or more, the light may glare into people's eyes. If luminaires are aimed at an angle less than 45 degrees, light will hit the tabletop first and then bounce back up, giving a soft, more complimentary underlighting of people's faces. Figure 11.5 shows how these same luminaires can be redirected toward the wall when the table is being used for a buffet.

For those clients happy with a traditional setting in their dining rooms, the addition of two recessed adjustable lights on either side of a crystal-style chandelier will help add drama to the table. This allows the chandelier to be dimmed to a pleasing glow while giving the impression of providing the table's illumination (see Figure 11.6). The light from the recessed fixtures, as it passes through the crystals, will help any crystals come to life. For a taste of what is available in traditional and not-so-traditional chandeliers, take a look at Fine Art Lamps (www.fineartlamps.com), Chonbek (www.chonbek.com), and Ingo Maurer (www .ingo-maurer.com).

A large chandelier may require additional support at the junction box. Most standard junction boxes will support up to 50 pounds. Check with the manufacturer to find out what the weight is so that electrical contractor can accommodate it. Large or ornate chandeliers installed in rooms with a high ceiling may require a pulley mechanism that is mounted above the ceiling to lower the chandelier for ease of relamping and cleaning. Companies such as Aladdin Light Lift (www.aladdinlightlift.com) make these pulley systems.

FIGURE 11.3 (left)
A dome detail in the ceiling will allow for a more traditional hanging chandelier without hitting people in the head when the table is relocated.

FIGURE 11.4 (right)
A table with no chandelier makes use of three recessed adjustable luminaires to highlight the table setting as well as the centerpiece.

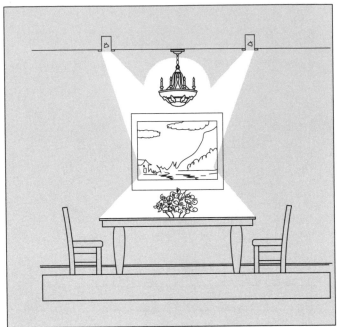

FIGURE 11.5 (left)
Recessed adjustable luminaires located over the dining room table can be redirected to light the table when it is against the wall serving as a buffet.

FIGURE 11.6 (right)
Two recessed adjustable luminaires in combination with a chandelier provide highlighting for the table and let the decorative luminaires take all the credit.

AMBIENT LIGHTING

Whatever solution you choose for table illumination, this alone will not complete the lighting scenario. Ambient light and additional accent lighting should still be considered. While it's true that the decorative luminaires will provide some illumination for the dining room, they can easily overpower the rest of the elements in the space if turned up too bright. This is the same problem that occurs in entrances. Here, as everywhere else in the home, light layering is the best way to illuminate a space effectively.

Adding ambient lighting is relatively straightforward. Many of the options mentioned in previous chapters work here as well: torchères, wall sconces, and cove lighting. If the dining room you are working on has a dome detail, the perimeter can be illuminated with low-profile cove lighting so that fill light is bounced off the dome's interior. If it is a beamed ceiling, channels can be used, as discussed in Chapter 10. Just don't leave it out; otherwise what people own overpowers the people themselves. People deserve to be the stars in their own homes. Well-balanced lighting with a generous layer of ambient light is the key.

ACCENT LIGHTING

The two or three recessed adjustable luminaires located over the dining room table already address accent light for the table itself and the centerpiece. Single downlights integrated into some specially modified chandeliers and pendants may be used to provide accent light for centerpieces as well. Some companies that make these hanging fixtures with a hidden downlight are Progress Lighting (www.progresslighting.com) and Phoenix Day (www.phoenixday.com).

Other areas in need of accent light are the walls, the side table or buffet, and plants. For art on the wall, remember to use cross-illumination when possible to keep the light source from reflecting back into people's eyes. It can be very uncomfortable to have a reflected light glare into your eyes as you are trying to enjoy dinner. It would be like someone shining a flashlight at you as you try to eat.

Also, don't feel that every hanging piece of art has to be illuminated. It's all right to let some of them fall into secondary importance. It lets them be "discovered" as guests take a second look around the room. Do add one or two recessed adjustable luminaires to accent the side table, buffet, or console. A silver tea service will sparkle and a buffet dinner will look even more scrumptious when highlighted.

Playing with Shadows
Potted plants can be uplighted, downlighted, or both. Broad-leaved plants such as fiddle-leaved figs are better illuminated from above or backlighted for a strong silhouette. More airy-leaved

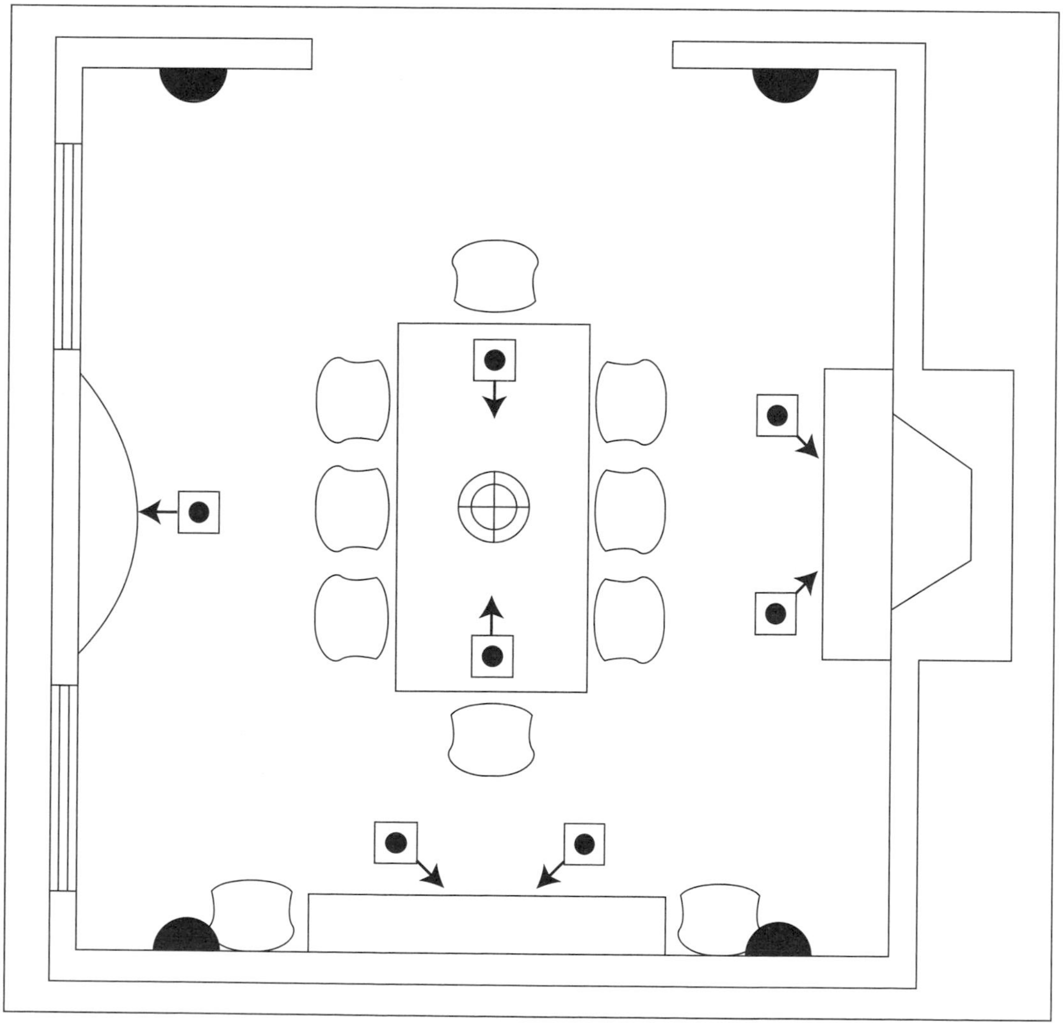

Dining rooms have been transformed in some homes into multi-use spaces. These changes have created a need for adjustable lighting and forced homeowners and designers to rethink the use of a chandelier.

FIGURE 11.7
This is a possible lighting layout for a more traditional dining-room furniture plan.

FIGURE 11.8

This perspective drawing shows what the room looks like when translated from the lighting plan.

plants, such as a ficus tree, can be illuminated from the front, casting leaf patterns on the walls and floor. They can also be uplighted, which creates a shadow pattern on the walls and ceiling. Palms are best shown off when they are lighted both from the top and from below. The sculptural quality of a cactus calls for lighting from the front at a 45-degree angle, preferably off to one side, in order to add dimension. Lighting plants outside can also visually expand the dining room if it has windows that look out onto a yard or balcony and make the outside feel like a part of the inside.

Figures 11.7 and 11.8 illustrate one way a traditional dining room layout can be lighted. Figure 11.8 is what a lighting plan would look like before lines have been drawn in to show what fixtures are connected together and how they will be controlled. Figure 11.7 is a perspective drawing of the same room as people would see in it real life. In time, you will be able to look at a lighting plan and visualize what the final effect will be. The opposite will also be true; once you have decided how you want a space to be illuminated, you will be able to draw up an electrical plan that will produce the layered-lighting effect you want.

PLATE 2.1 (top)

A metal vessel, containing moss, provides a focal point in this entry way. The deep green color is enhanced using a green dichroic filter in the recessed fixture above. The intense green, playing off the vibrant red of the lacquered chest, creates a bold statement.

PLATE 2.2 (bottom left)

Sometimes it is not just interior lighting design alone that will make a space work. In this case an architect was also brought in to be part of the design team. In this kitchen remodel, the main visual problem was the strong diagonal line at the ceiling created by the staircase leading to the upper level. The architect resolved the problem by creating two barrel vaults to conceal the stairway profile. Here you can begin to see the framework installed to form the vaults.

PLATE 2.3 (bottom right)

This "after" shot shows a striking difference. The strong diagonal line of the staircase is totally concealed by a lower barrel vault. A line of pendant fixtures help add a human scale to the narrow galley kitchen. At the entry a translucent paper sculpture and tall candles mark the entry to the kitchen, helping to integrate it into the rest of the space.

PLATE 2.4

This welcoming kitchen uses energy efficient lighting in a very alluring manner. The two pendant fixtures made by Basic Source, uses 3 hard-wired dimmable CFLs to provide both uplighting and decorative illumination to help humanize the space. The pots located inside the niches are up-lit from a linear, dimmable fluorescent source, made by Belfer Lighting. The under-cabinet task lighting uses a Belfer strip fitted with LED festoon lamps, made by Permlight. The four recessed low voltage fixtures located above the center island use LED MR16's.

PLATE 2.5

The corner of this kitchen has both under-cabinet lighting and illumination within the cabinets that make use of LED sources. There is a warm incandescent feel to the illumination, which is dimmable and has an average rated lamp life of 30,000 hours.

PLATE 2.6

A detailed shot, looking below the overhead cabinets, shows the linear strip of LED lighting. The fixture is made by Belfer lighting, and the LED festoon lamps are made by Permlight.

PLATE 2.7
This breakfast room off the main kitchen has a dimmable fluorescent pendant fixture (not seen in the shot), which provides the main source of ambient light. The pair of wall sconces are dimmed to a glow and along with the candles create the illusion of providing the room's illumination.

PLATE 2.8
This master bedroom makes full use of energy efficiency lighting. All the recessed fixtures are LEDs, manufactured by Permlight. The shoji panel doors for the clothes closets are back lit using a fluorescent source, which is mounted on the ceiling. A Noguchi lamp sitting on the tansu uses a screw-in CFL to full advantage.

PLATE 2.9 (left)
A garden court yard features a dancing show of light as underwater fixtures pass through the bubbling fountains. The pattern of light plays off the bold color of the retaining wall. The fixtures are made by Focus Industries.

PLATE 2.10 (right)
The shade of this table lamp appears to float above its glass cylinder base. This decorative element draws people into the space without overpowering the other design elements. Sometimes lighting only needs to offer a glow to be effective.

PLATE 2.11
Here an open plan kitchen is made warm and inviting through the use of ambient light placed on top of the cabinets. Even though it has an incandescent quality, both the indirect lighting and the light for the counter tops is a fluorescent source.

PLATE 2.12

A view of this living room, looking towards the back yard, shows how illumination outside can help expand interior spaces at night. The two pendant fixtures provide both decorative and ambient light, using screw-in dimmable CFLs. Track lighting, running along the apex beam, highlights art and table tops.

PLATE 2.13

Looking at the living room from another direction, shows how the lighting plays an important role to create a welcoming environment. Low voltage picture lights, mounted above the bookcases, accent the books and art objects.

PLATE 2.14 (left)
A three foot tall Japanese mask welcomes visitors into this home. The face is gently illuminated with a 50 watt MR16, but is fitted with a cosmetic filter to help warm up the skin tones.

PLATE 2.15 (right)
A giant tree root becomes an elegant piece of sculpture in this foyer. Two recessed, adjustable, low voltage fixtures help add depth and dimension to the piece.

PLATE 2.16
Using votive candles on the dining room table casts a complimentary glow against people's faces. The flame of a taller candle might keep you from seeing the person sitting across the table.

PLATE 2.17
This image shows the living room side of a wide great room. In the center a tall woven wood floor lamp helps add texture to the space. Recessed adjustable low-voltage fixtures provide focus to the framed photographs and the natural fiber weavings on the wall.

PLATE 2.18
A view of the opposite side of the great room shows a center fireplace that is open on both spaces. Beyond the fireplace is the dining area. Recessed adjustable low-voltage fixtures by Juno Lighting project light onto the art and tabletops.

PLATE 2.19
A close-up of the niche located next to the fireplace, displaying an art glass vase. This piece is illuminated with a single 10-watt puck light by Lucifer Lighting.

PLATE 2.20

Three votive candles offer a quick fix to help get guests safely up and down these exterior steps. There is no fear of fire or them blowing out because they are actually battery operated LEDs, made by Always Something Brilliant.

PLATE 2.21

What we are seeing in this image is the entry-way to a master bedroom. The floating staircase takes on a strong sculptural feel when set against the illuminated foliage. A pair of lanterns from Bali helps lead you into the master bedroom. Three recessed adjustable low-voltage fixtures help add depth and dimension by highlighting the shoji panels, the tansu, and the woven reed cushion.

PLATE 2.22

As you enter the main part of the master bedroom the first thing that you see is a tall French table lamp, covered in a translucent fabric. This is the decorative element for the space. Two recessed adjustable LED fixtures, located above the bed, offer individual reading lights. Additional recessed adjustable low-voltage fixtures show off the painting above the headboard and the objects on the bedside tables. The city view beyond the well-illuminated foreground plantings becomes part of the overall scene, because the black mirror effect has been circumvented.

PLATE 2.23

What we see in this kitchen appears to be standard incandescent lighting, in fact the under-cabinet lighting and the recessed fixtures use LEDs. The recessed fixtures are made by Permlight and have been fitted with a trim from Juno Lighting.

PLATE 2.24

You may be surprised to learn that all the lighting in this very comfortable kitchen comes from fluorescent or LED sources. The two alabaster pendants, made by the Basic Source, use three GU-24 dimmable CFLs (by MaxLite).

The recessed fixtures are dimmable LEDs, made by Cree Lighting, and the undercabinet lighting comes from a series of fluorescent puck lights by Tresco International.

PLATE 2.25

This is probably one of the largest residential kitchens that you will ever see. The space opens up into an equally generous family room. The L-shaped island divides the two spaces. A row of cast glass and metal pendants offers a sense of separation between the two areas. Recessed adjustable low-voltage fixtures project additional light onto the butcher-block table and countertops.

PLATE 2.26

A detail of the pendant fixtures, designed by Christina Spann, showing their hand-forged quality.

PLATE 2.27
Interior designers these days
are creating bathrooms where
design elements continue in
from neighboring spaces. Here
glass block walls allow natural
light to flow into the bathroom.
Now that art is becoming a
standard element in bathroom
spaces, recessed adjustable
low-voltage fixtures specifically
made to be installed in wet
locations can be used to accent
objects in tub and shower
areas.

PLATE 2.28
A close up of the sink area reveals a pair of Frank Lloyd Wright
inspired wall sconces, by George Kovacs; providing excellent
cross illumination at the mirror.

PLATE 2.29
This sumptuous master bath uses two pairs of vanity lights by Boyd
Lighting to illuminate the sinks. Each of these fixtures holds one 36-watt
fluorescent lamp. One recessed adjustable low-voltage fixture draws attention to the raku vessel that is located between the sinks. Another recessed
adjustable low-voltage fixture, rated for wet locations, is installed over the
walk-in shower area. Outside, an impressive shadow pattern shows up on
the frosted glass as light passes through the overhanging branches.

PLATE 2.30

Powder rooms can afford to be more daring than master baths. Here guests need only need to wash their hands or check to see if there is spinach in their teeth, so the light level does not have to be intense. In this particular powder room, wall sconces are mounted on the return walls instead of either side of the mirror, to help make this small space appear a bit larger. Three recessed adjustable low- voltage fixtures show off the stone sink, the Macintosh inspired chair and the Japanese silk screen (as seen reflected in the mirror).

PLATE 2.31 (left)

During the day no one is aware of the lighting element nestled in among the plantings.

PLATE 2.32 (right)

As the sun begins to set, this glass sculpture, illuminated from within, begins to make its presence known.

PLATE 2.33

After night falls, this piece, designed by Pam Morris, becomes a visual icon that helps lead guests to the front door.

PLATE 2.34

In this study many lighting elements are at play. On the wall above the sofa two mica and metal sconces, made by Boyd Lighting, offer the decorative layer of illumination. On the opposite wall (just out of camera range) a pair of torchères provide the much-needed fill light for this space. A directional uplight, sitting on the floor, enhances the form of the wooden sculpture. Recessed adjustable low-voltage fixtures bring attention to the coffee table, the painting, and the low teak console. The images of objects located on the other side of the shoji panel appear as intriguing silhouettes.

PLATE 2.35

Here in this arts and crafts dining room, the hanging fixture over the table, made by Metro Lighting, actually uses screw-in, dimmable compact fluorescent lamps. The glass shades shield the light source.

PLATE 2.36
Brightly colored LEDs, like the ones being used to uplight this glass ball, can be a fun decorative element. However these intense colors should be used sparingly.

PLATE 2.37
This bathroom is not only alluring, it is also completely energy efficient. The plaster wall sconces, made by Phoenix Day Company, use screw-in, dimmable CFLs to provide a lush ambient light (made by Earthtronics).

PLATE 2.38

The ceiling height in this living room goes up to 20 feet. The wrought iron chandelier, with an overall length of 4 feet helps to create a human scale to the room. The flame tip lamps are actually long-life cold athode versions made by TCPI, Inc. They are dimmable, provide a very warm glow and have an average rated lamp life of 10,000 hours, reducing the number of times the home owners have to get up on a tall precarious ladder.

PLATE 2.39

This magnificent mid-century modern home comes to life at night. Recessed adjustable low voltage fixtures by Halo are used to create pools of illumination to help add depth and dimension to this very large living room. A pair of opaque wall sconces (by Sedap), flanking the Kormandel screen, look like modern interpretations of torches. Ambient light comes from linear LED lighting, mounted on top of a cantilever that runs around three-quarters of the room.

PLATE 2.40

After dark, a gently radiant neon sculpture becomes a focal point on the deck, located beyond the bank of floor to ceiling glass doors. A pair of shielded exterior fixtures, mounted in the corners above the door line, cross-illuminate the plantings and pottery. In the upper right corner a hanging lantern uses a single candle to add a touch of romance.

PLATE 2.41

Side-lit fiber optics by Fiberstars are used to create an illuminated handrail. The illuminator, located in a closet off to the left, houses the light source and a color filter. Presently the handrail is lavender but by simply changing the filter in the illuminator, the handrail can become any color of the rainbow.

PLATE 2.42

The red metal sculpture and gentle water feature are fore-lighted from a pair of shielded directional exterior fixtures (by B-K Lighting), mounted on the eave of the house. The stand of three palm trees is illuminated with a pair of additional directional fixtures, mounted behind the low stone wall. The single palm tree in the distance is allowed to fall into silhouette against the evening sky to help enhance the feeling of depth.

PLATE 2.43

This spectacular dining room uses a variety of lighting techniques to produce an aura of suffused radiance. The giant chandelier creates a floating crown of luminosity above the table. A pair of recessed adjustable low-voltage fixtures (located one foot out from each side of the chandelier) gently cross illuminate the Han dynasty figure in the center of the table. The two ornate columns, which flank the French doors leading out onto the deck, are up-lit from below to bring out the impressive detail. Beyond the French doors, a riot of brightly illuminated greenery creates a magnificent background for an unforgettable dining experience.

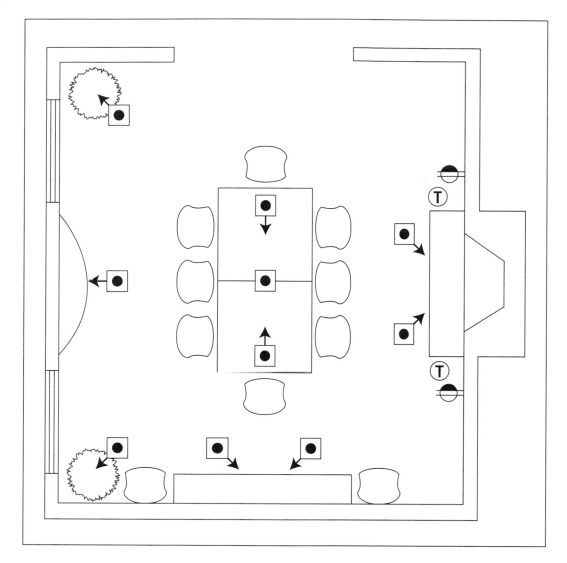

FIGURE 11.9
This is a more nontraditional furniture plan. Note that the table can be separated to make smaller tables.

This particular design used an alabaster pendant that is providing both decorative and ambient light. It is flanked by two recessed adjustable luminaires (as shown in Figure 11.6 but using a more traditional chandelier) to highlight the tabletop. In addition, four semi-opaque wall sconces are being used to provide the ambient light and a bit of decorative light, while five more recessed adjustable luminaires have been installed to highlight the art and tabletops.

Figures 11.9 and 11.10 show how a less traditional dining room might be illuminated. The table is actually two 4-foot square tables that can be separated for smaller family dinners and card games. The use of three recessed adjustable luminaires in this scenario lets the lighting follow the tables wherever they end up in the room. This time, a pair of torchères is located along the right-hand wall to provide the ambient light. Seven additional recessed adjustable luminaires accent the art above the fireplace, the art above the console on the left wall, and the two plants in the corners of the room.

FIGURE 11.10
This perspective drawing shows what the dining room looks like with the lighting and furniture in place (the floor plan with the lighting layout is shown in Figure 11.9).

FIGURE 11.11 (left)
Standard-height candles obstruct your view of the person across the table.

FIGURE 11.12 (right)
A low votive candle provides a soft, complimentary uplighting.

CANDLES DO COUNT

Candles should be used correctly as well. No light source gets overlooked in this book. Typically, at the dinner table you artfully place candlesticks flanking the centerpiece. Then when you and your guests sit down at the table, it puts the candle flame right at eye level. When you look at the flame for a while and then cast your gaze toward the guests, you'll notice that there is a black hole where their heads used to be. This is much like the effect you experience after someone has taken a flash picture of you. To solve this problem, use candles that are either lower or higher than eye level. That way you'll get that soft golden glow, but the candle will not distract you from looking at the person across the table. Reviewing Figures 11.11, 11.12, and 11.13 should give you an idea of what can happen.

• THE BOTTOM LINE

As in the rest of the house, light layering in the dining room is the way to go. The addition of individual dimmers or multiple scenes created by a control system can offer many levels of inviting illumination. Dimming the chandelier down to a glow will help bring out the true beauty of the luminaire. Having control over the accent lights and ambient sources will allow for full brightness when needed to clear the table or work on a puzzle, or provide the proper dimness to complement the other lighting in the room when entertaining. The goal is to create a balanced illumination that allows people to enjoy the space comfortably and enhances the other elements of your design.

FIGURE 11.13

A tall candle adds the romance without the glare.

12

Bedrooms—Private Sanctuaries

Often it's the bedrooms that are thought of as unimportant areas when a lighting plan is being put together. They are usually left with a fixture in the center of the ceiling and a couple of half-switched receptacles (refer back to Chapter 6). Think about how much time we spend in our bedrooms. Statistics show that we spend one-third of our lives sleeping. Many individuals spend that time sleeping with a significant other. People would naturally like to look their best in such an intimate setting.

AMBIENT LIGHTING

This is the one room where ambient light is first and foremost. People are the main event in a bedroom setting. Use indirect lighting to help erase dark circles and soften age lines. Your clients will love you for it.

Quick Fixes

If there is an existing luminaire in the center of the ceiling, an easy upgrade would be to replace it with a pendant-hung or semi-flush indirect fixture (refer back to Chapter 4). This will provide illumination that bounces off the ceiling and walls to create a flattering, shadowless light (see Figures 12.1 and 12.2).

A semi-flush fixture works well for the standard 8-foot ceilings. If you have a 9-foot or higher ceiling, then a pendant-type fixture is a viable option. For examples of semi-flush fixtures that are traditional or transitional in feel, take a look at Murray Feiss (www.feiss.com), Johnson Art Studio (www.johnsonartstudio.com), and Boyd Lighting (www.boydlighting.com). For more modern, European-looking options, check out Estiluz (www.estiluz.com), Artemide (www.artemide.us), and Foscarini (www.foscarini.com).

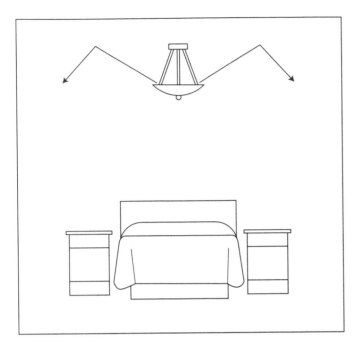

FIGURE 12.1 (left)
Replace the existing ceiling luminaire with a pendant-hung indirect version for a good source of fill light.

FIGURE 12.2 (right)
This beautiful fixture made by Sirmos Lighting appears to be made of alabaster, glass, and metal. In reality, it is made entirely of resin. The semi-opaque quality of the materials allows this fixture to provide both ambient illumination and a dash of decorative light.

While many of these come in fluorescent, they are not usually available in dimmable versions. Here, the better solution would be to use a fixture with a standard socket and use a dimmable screw-in fluorescent, such as those made by Technical Consumer Products (www.tcpi.com). The warm color produced by these fluorescent lamps is so close to incandescent that if people can't see the swirly shape of the lamps, they just assume that it is incandescent.

Sometimes clients are reticent about putting a lot of time and money into architecturally integrated lighting design solutions. For these more cost-conscious customers, a pair of torchères should do the trick. This is a non-electrician-involved solution (see examples in Chapter 4) that is especially good for a fast solution in a smaller bedroom or guest bedroom. Look for luminaires that have an opaque or semi-opaque shade to help hide the light source and project the light upward. Here, too, a dimmable screw-in fluorescent could replace a standard incandescent lamp. For traditional torchères, check out Fine Art Lamps (www.fineartlamps.com), and for more modern versions, take a look at Artemide (www.artemide.us) and Terzani (www.terzani.com). Even Restoration Hardware (www.restorationhardware.com) has some good-looking ones that are reasonably priced.

Also, you could place a halogen indirect light source on top of a tall piece of furniture, such as an armoire (see Figure 12.3). Often there is a recess on the top of these furniture pieces that provides a great hiding spot for an indirect source of illumination. In some homes there is a canopy bed with a solid top; this too can be a great location for a hidden indirect light (refer back to Chapter 4 for an example).

Working with the Architecture

Where it used to be that the high-pitched ceilings were reserved for the living room or great room, these days many homes are now sporting master bedrooms with pitched ceilings as well. Usually there is an apex beam that runs the length of the room. In both new construction and remodel projects, one way to add both ambient light and help humanize the scale of the room is to hang one, two, or even three pendants, depending on the size of the room. For new construction projects, the apex beam can be pre-drilled and electrified before the roof is installed. If it is a remodel project, one way to provide the necessary power is to run a trim board along the underside to the apex beam. This would be routed on the backside to run the wiring. A **pancake junction box** could then be used, from which the fixture would be hung.

If there are support beams that run parallel to the floor, they can also be used to provide ambient light for the bedroom (refer to Chapter 10). This can be done in addition to the use of pendant fixtures.

Quite often now we see many modern homes built with asymmetric sloped ceilings. This leaves the room with one tall wall area, which is often considered a dead space. Mounting a series of two or three wall sconces up there will create great fill light without wasting any of the wall space at the normal viewing heights. Using a fixture with an internal reflector will help push the illumination out into the room. Belfer (www.belfer.com), Visa Lighting (www.visalighting.com), and Elliptipar (www.elliptipar.com) make wedge-shaped fixtures that can visually blend into the architecture.

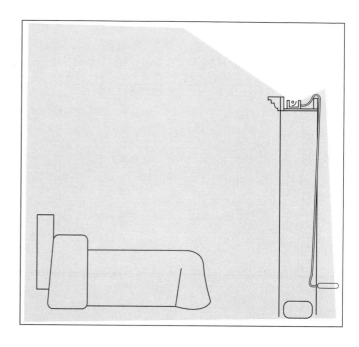

FIGURE 12.3

Atop a tall piece of furniture such as this armoire is a great spot to hide a source of ambient light.

Another way to go on the high wall would be to use a series of luminaires that are actually recessed into the wall. They look like small clerestory windows. Two of the companies who make fixtures like these are the Reflex by Belfer (www.belfer.com) and the Vice Versa and Recto Verso by Delta Lighting (www.deltalight.us). Both styles come in fluorescent versions that will provide a good punch of light for less power consumption and last up to ten times longer than a standard incandescent lamp or five times longer than a halogen source.

The **coffered ceiling** has become more commonplace in bedrooms as well. This consists of a series of beams or deep moldings that intersect to form a grid pattern. It used to be that only the library or maybe the dining room sported a coffered ceiling detail.

A reveal can be created behind a layer of perimeter molding (such as you saw in Chapter 8) to hide an indirect light source, like a series of mini cove lighting details. Illumination from this alone can make the space feel a bit commercial. Installing decorative luminaires that are translucent or semi-translucent in the center of the coffers (or at some of the intersections of the beams) will add the layer of sparkle and additional ambient light for the room to really cozy it up.

Another architectural style challenge is the tray ceiling (see Figure 12.4). It is a little bit of a tired architectural look that seems to be making a comeback, as people are requesting their architects to design faux-chateaux for them. This architectural detail lends itself to a perimeter cove lighting detail, but the lighting can end up being too bright where the ceiling slopes sharply out

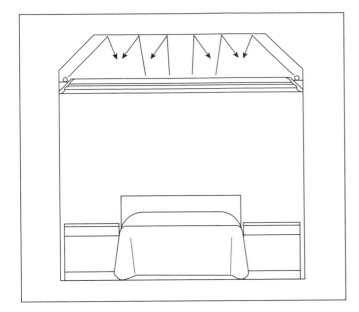

FIGURE 12.4

A "tray-style" ceiling lends itself to a cove lighting detail.

from the wall. If you have the ability, it would be a better look if the sides of the tray ceiling were gently curved to allow the light to more evenly wash up toward the ceiling.

If the clients are unwilling to soften the slope of the tray, another option would be to install a deep crown molding at the point where the wall meets the tray ceiling. Lighting could then be placed behind it to project light up without too much of a hot spot. Adding another layer of crown molding where the sloped sides of the tray detail meet the ceiling will provide a focal point for the indirect lighting. The light helps emphasize the architect's ceiling concept, while filling the bedroom with a glow of perimeter ambient light.

KIDS' ROOMS

Children's rooms get treated a little differently than those of their parents. Kids, right through their teenage years, tend to spend a lot of time on the floor, playing, doing homework, or just hanging out. For this reason an extra dose of ambient light is needed to provide good shadowless light at the floor level and throughout the room. They don't need accent lights. They don't have art hanging in their bedrooms, such as might be in the master bedrooms or guest rooms.

When they are infants they are often on their backs in their cribs or changing tables. Glary recessed or surface-mounted ceiling fixtures are uncomfortable. Gentle light that is bounced off the ceiling is much more comfortable; and parents are less likely to wake the baby when slipping in to check. As the children get older, it is a good idea to make sure that the indirect light sources you choose have some sort of covering at the top like a tempered glass or plastic lens to keep any objects from getting caught inside the fixtures. Face it: kids like to throw things.

This ambient illumination can come from wall sconces or ceiling fixtures that have an opaque or semi-opaque finish. You can specify a fixture that uses a standard incandescent "A" lamp and use screw-in, dimmable CFLs to keep the cost of running these lights at a minimum, which will tend to be on all the time. Although this type of indirect light can come from a torchère, it is not a good idea to have them in toddlers' rooms. Toddlers often use objects to pull themselves up as they learn to walk. They could easily pull over a torchère.

TASK LIGHTING

Ambient light may make people look better, but it is not enough light to read by. This is when task lighting enters the equation. It is another of the *four functions of light* that must be considered. For the bedroom, this is reading light and closet light.

Tabletop Options

For bedside lighting, typically a pair of portable luminaires is placed on the bedside tables. If you choose this approach, there are a few things to consider:

1 Select reading lights that have opaque shades or liners. This will help direct the light down and across the person's work surface. Additionally, the opaque shade helps shield the light from your bedmate (see Figure 12.5). There are more table lamps that can double as bedside lamps out there than any other type of lighting, and listing all the manufacturers would take up the rest of this book. Donghia (www.donghia.com) is one company that offers table lamps that come with opaque shades as a standard option so that you have a taste of what is out there. The rule of thumb is to find a base that you like and then separately find a shade that suits your purposes.

2 Consider a bedside table lamp that has some flexibility in the arm so that it can be positioned to best light your book. Cool euro-style examples of this type of lamp are made by Estiluz (www.estiluz.com); Artemide (www.artemide.us), where you can find the classic Tizio lamp designed by Richard Sapper in 1972; and Luxo (www.luxo.com), which has been around forever and makes versions with built-in magnifiers.

Wall-Mount Options

Wall-mounted swing-arm lamps (see Figure 12.6) are another option. They are a flexible source of illumination that doesn't take up space on the bedside tables. Most of these luminaires are offered with a halogen source that can get pretty hot. For a very cool-looking fluorescent version, take a look at the Metric made by Blauet (www.blauet.com); they make a tabletop version as well.

Mounting these luminaires at the correct height is critical, however. If they are too high, they will be a source of glare, especially for the person sharing the bed. If they are too low, the person may have to slump into an uncomfortable position in order to read. They should be mounted just above shoulder height when the reader is sitting in bed.

The best way to find the correct mounting height is to have your clients get into bed and hunker down against the pillows in their normal reading position. Then measure from the floor to

FIGURE 12.5 (left)

If you choose traditional bedside lamps for reading, specify shades with opaque shades or liners, so that the other person in bed can get some sleep.

FIGURE 12.6 (right)

Swing-arm lamps provide good task light, without taking up space on the bedside table. Mount them at just above your client's shoulder height. (Yes, put them in bed and measure.)

just above their shoulder height. Why? Because the optimum spot to position task lighting is between the person's head and the work surface. Clients sharing a bed may nest in at different heights. Some compromise should be made on both sides so that the reading lights can be mounted at matching heights. Using tension-arm-type lamps, which have the ability to move up and down in addition to in and out, will allow for the maximum flexibility.

Ceiling Options

A third possibility for reading lights is to install a pair of recessed adjustable low-voltage luminaires in the ceiling above the bed (see Figure 12.7). This is what you might call the "airline approach" to providing light for reading. You may have noticed that the reading lights on the airplane are not directly over your seat but actually over the seat of the person sitting next to you. That's because the passenger's own noggin would block the light if it was installed directly overhead.

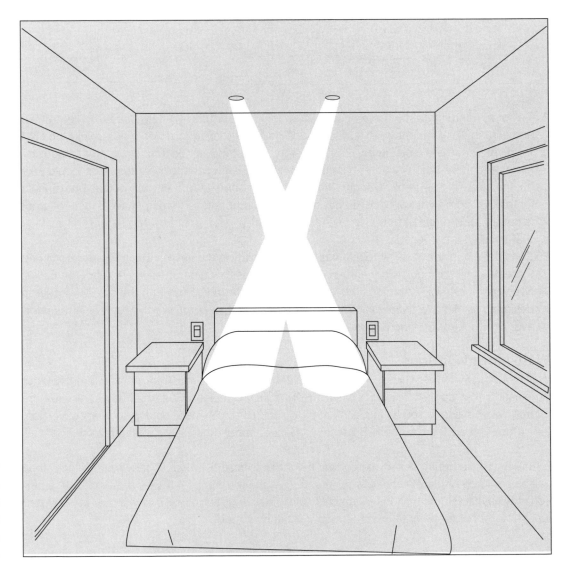

FIGURE 12.7

Cross-illumination above the bed provides "directed" reading light that doesn't disturb the other bed occupant.

The same principle applies in the bedroom. The person on the right controls the recessed adjustable luminaire over his or her partner's side of the bed, and vice versa. By using a lamp with a tight beam spread, such as the MR16 ESX (20-watt spot), the light is confined to a circle of illumination about the size of a magazine. If all the clients read are paperbacks, then you can use an MR16 EZX, which projects a very narrow spot. Since the light does not have to be super-bright, an LED version of the MR lamp can be used very successfully.

These luminaires would be installed in the ceiling a little closer than those that would be lighting art. For recessed reading lights, 18 inches out from the wall is a good distance for normal 8-foot ceilings. If there is also to be art above the bed that will get accent lighting, then all the fixtures can be installed at 24 inches out from the wall.

Using a recessed luminaire with a small aperture helps reduce the possibility of glare. Some recessed adjustable low-voltage lights come with apertures as small as 1.5 inches. It also helps if the luminaire specified has a black-painted interior to further reduce any brightness coming from the light source. Remember to place the dimmers for these reading lights on either side of the bed just above the night tables. Your clients should not have to get out of bed to control the lights.

Closet Lighting

Good lighting in the closet is very important. For most of us the day starts before the sun is up. We run into the closet, flip on the switch, and decide what to wear. Unfortunately, most closet lighting is incandescent. Since incandescent lighting is so yellow, it will dramatically shift your perception of colors. It is impossible to tell navy blue from black under incandescent lighting. Reds will appear orange, and certain shades of blue will appear green. You may end up with two-different colored socks or an outfit that makes you look a little color-blind.

The best type of lighting for color-matching comes from natural daylight. If we could go over to the window to see the true colors, that would be great. But since most of us are getting dressed in the dark, we need to look at artificial light sources as an alternative. A fluorescent source with a color temperature that comes very close to daylight (5,000° K) will be extremely helpful in making good color-matching choices. Like daylight, it is a very cool color of illumination, but this is what you need.

A good option for lighting in the closet would be to have two types of light, both daylight and incandescent. When you are going out at night, most light sources in movie theaters and restaurants are incandescent or incandescent in color anyway, so you have a bit of flexibility. No one will notice that you have black slacks and a navy blue sport coat (see Figure 12.8).

Mounting the fluorescent lighting on the underside of the shelving that is located above the hanging rods will project the light toward the clothing. The brightness of the fluorescent can be hidden with a fascia board. The incandescent light can then be located on or in the ceiling. Put these two light sources on separate controls. A motion sensor or a switched motion sensor will protect you from spending energy unnecessarily, especially if you or a loved one tend to leave lights on (refer back to Chapter 6 on controls). For closets that are not walk-in, install the fluorescent light on the wall space above the door header.

This is the one room where ambient light is first and foremost. People are the main event in a bedroom setting. Help erase dark circles and soften age lines. Your clients will love you for it.

FIGURE 12.8
These shell-shaped pendants by Sirmos Lighting are incandescent while lighting within the casework is fluorescent.

How lighting is incorporated into a space can affect the architecture, the interior design, and the mood of the people in that space. Great lighting happens when all the functions of light are seamlessly blended together. This applies to both interior and exterior spaces.

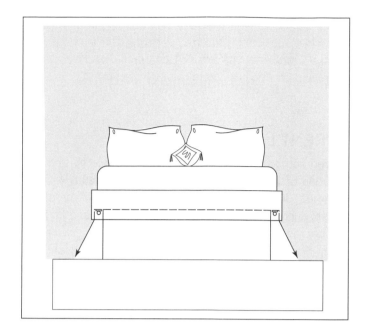

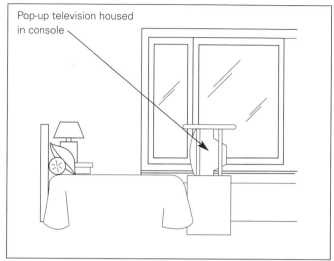

Pop-up television housed in console

Something a Little Special

Some designers like to have lighting running along the underside of a platform bed (see Figure 12.9). This creates the illusion of the bed levitating slightly off the floor. It can also be a great night-light for those people who make frequent trips to the bathroom or occasional trips to the fridge.

Use low-voltage or line-voltage **tube lighting**, using half-watt lamps on 1-inch centers. The tubing is flexible and goes around corners easily. The end effect will be just a gentle glow of light. This lighting can simply be plugged into a switched receptacle or hardwired to a switch or dimmer. Some companies that make these tube lights (also referred to as **rope lights**) are Tivoli Lighting (www.tivolilighting.com) and Starfire Lighting (www.starfirelighting.com). LED versions are available as well through companies like LED Rope Lights and More (www.ledrope-lightsandmore.com).

A TELEVISION TECHNIQUE

One last item to consider doesn't have as much to do with lighting as it does with visibility. Today, new master bedrooms are often quite enormous. The bed will be near one wall and 15 or 20 feet away on the opposite wall will be a flat-screen television mounted on the wall or inside an armoire. That's simply too far away for people to watch without using binoculars. A more practical solution would be to place a console at the end of the bed that houses a pop-up flat-screen TV (see Figure 12.10). The television disappears into the console when not in use.

There are manufacturers who make this device that can rotate as well, so if there is a seating area in the bedroom, the owners don't have to get into bed to watch TV. If the flat-screen television is mounted on the wall, devices are available that allow you to hang a piece of art in front

FIGURE 12.9 (left)
Underlighting the bed gives a sense of hovering, like the bed is about to take off.

FIGURE 12.10 (right)
Do your clients a favor and locate the television at the foot of the bed instead of way across the room. There are consoles available that allow the television to pop up when being watched and then disappear inside when not in use.

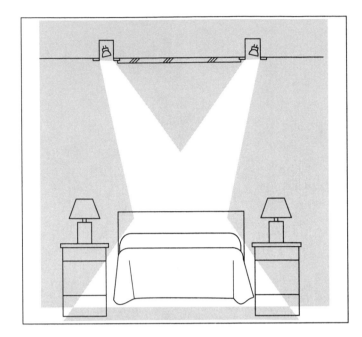

FIGURE 12.11

If you have clients who want a mirror above the bed, then cross-illuminate them with two recessed adjustable lights on each of the long sides of the bed, using lamps with complementary wide beam spreads.

of the screen to hide the TV when it is not in use. These come in manual and motorized versions. Some companies to take a look at online are TV Coverups (www.tvcoverups .com) and Lift-Tech (www.televisionlifts.com).

ACCENT LIGHTING

As bedrooms are becoming more than just places to sleep, the idea of bringing in framed art and sculpture is more common. Just like in the other more public rooms of the house, such as the living room, dining room, and kitchen, the bedrooms benefit from having things to look at and enjoy. Recessed adjustable low-voltage fixtures are the best way to go if there is adequate ceiling depth. Remember that in California, all recessed fixtures must be rated for insulated ceilings and airtight.

Using halogen MR16 lamps with UV filters or LED versions will help protect the art. Using UV-inhibiting glass on the framed art will help protect it from the UV rays coming from natural light. The different types of the lighting in the room should be on separate controls for maximum flexibility. This can be simple switches and dimmers, a preset system, or part of a whole-house system (refer back to Chapter 6 on controls).

THE BOTTOM LINE

Make the bedroom into the oasis of the house. It is a place to find a little escape from the world, and it is that last holdout for romance. Light your clients well in the master bedroom and you will have clients for life.

13

Bathrooms—Functional Luxury

Bathrooms, especially the master baths, are the one place in the home where it is perfectly acceptable to lock the door for a stretch of time and briefly escape from the rest of those who live in the house. They can be the *sanctuary* of the home. Everyone needs a little alone time.

The continuing trend is that people are investing the equity of their homes in remodeling their existing residences rather than moving into the next bigger house as their parents might have done. Homeowners are most willing to invest their money on an updated bath. Kitchens too are in this category. They know that the money they spend can be added almost dollar-for-dollar to the value of the house. Even people that are putting their homes on the market are willing to upgrade bathrooms and kitchens to make their homes more desirable when compared to other homes on the market.

These remodels, along with new construction, are looking at greener design as a part of the selling point. Bathrooms are often a designer's or architect's first foot in the door for a remodel project. So doing a great job can lead to other areas in the home. Getting the lighting right will make help make them dramatic, functional and relaxing.

TASK LIGHTING

Well-designed lighting is of the utmost importance in the bathroom. Yet, more often than not, people are living with inadequate lighting that was installed by the contractor on the project because it is the way it has been done for decades. How many times have we seen a dramatic photograph of a vanity area in an upscale magazine with the recessed downlight directly over the sink? It makes for a great shot, but imagine yourself standing at the mirror with that harsh light hitting the top of your head.

Remember when, as a child, you would hold a flashlight under your chin to create a scary face? With downlights, the same thing happens, only in reverse. Long, dark shadows appear under your eyes, nose, and chin. This is extremely bad lighting for applying makeup or shaving (refer back to Chapter 8). This type of lighting can visually age a person by 10 or 15 years. No one wants to appear older than they actually are, especially first thing in the morning. This is no way to start the day.

Another common installation we see all the time is the use of one light fixture that is surface-mounted above the mirror. This is only slightly better than the recessed downlight. At best, it illuminates the top half of the face, letting the bottom half fall into shadow. This is an especially hard light by which to shave. There are only so many ways you can tilt your head to catch the light (see Figure 13.1). Good task lighting should be effortless; no contortion on the part of the client should be involved.

Many builders and architects also have a propensity for installing fluorescent or incandescent light in soffits, fitted with either acrylic diffusers or egg crate louvers, located over the vanity areas. They too mostly illuminate the top half of a person's face. A white or light-colored counter can help reflect some light from below by bouncing illumination up onto the lower part of the face. You are cross-lighting from top to bottom in this instance. This is not the optimal solution. Consider this only if vertical cross-illumination is impossible to install. Remember, the more stuff that ends up on the counter, such as towels and containers, the less reflective surface there will be.

For the best task lighting, use two translucent luminaires flanking the mirror area above the sink to provide the necessary shadowless cross-illumination (see Figure 13.2). The principle of evenly illuminating the face originated in the theater, where actors applied makeup in front of mirrors surrounded by bare lamps in porcelain sockets. These provided even, complimentary task light for people's faces (refer back to Chapter 8).

Along the lines of this technique, about 30 years ago now, luminaire manufacturers started to put vanity **light bars** on the market. Soon homes everywhere were sporting the now ubiquitous multi-lamp brass, white, or chrome light bars above the mirror. These light bars were, and still are, a low-cost way of getting proper task light, but they tend to be on the glary side and have a very dated look. If you have only 30 bucks to spend, then this is a way to go.

Sometimes for double-sink vanities they ran a bar the entire length of the countertop. The architects loved it because the look integrated itself well into the strong vertical lines of the sink area and didn't interrupt the surface of the mirror. But the homeowners were still not getting the light they needed. Remember, these bars, or one of the hundred of better versions now available on the market, work best when mounted vertically on each side of the mirror. A third one could be mounted above the mirror, but it is not absolutely necessary for good task lighting. A luminaire mounted above the mirror by itself is just not an adequate source of work light.

A more attractive trend in providing cross-illumination is to use translucent luminaires, mounted at eye level on either side of sinks (see Figure 13.3 and 13.4). Good materials to use are white glass, frosted leaded glass, opal acrylic, or resin. These task lights can flank a hanging mirror or be mounted on a full-wall mirror (see Figure 13.4). For inset sink areas, the mirror lights can be

The most important thing to remember in lighting the bathroom is that good illumination for tasks is primary, because looking good is hard work.

FIGURE 13.1

This is typically what we see in a bathroom, one light fixture mounted over the mirror. This provides a perfect light if you are shaving or applying makeup only to your forehead. Two light fixtures flanking the mirror, mounted at eye level, is the proper way to provide shadowless task light at the sink.

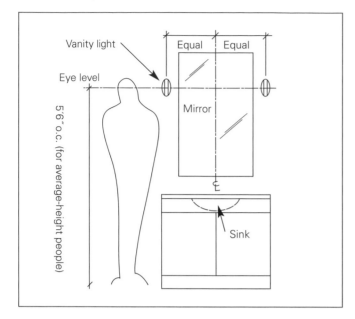

mounted on the return walls (see Figure 13.5). If you feel you must use an incandescent source, the amount of light needed for shaving and applying makeup is 75 to 100 watts on either side of the mirror. In halogen or xenon 50 to 75 watts is needed. In fluorescent only 20 watts to 40 watts is necessary. For smaller baths, such as the powder room where just a pleasant glow of illumination is need, then only 40 to 60 watts of incandescent is needed or 7 to 13 watts of fluorescent.

Many well-designed American and European luminaires are perfect for this application. The Europeans have accepted fluorescent as a viable alternative for many years and offer most of their light fixtures in both incandescent and fluorescent versions.

FIGURE 13.2

Vanity lights are optimally mounted at eye level, flanking the mirror.

The American manufacturers have been a bit slower in offering their higher-end fixtures in fluorescent, but as people are becoming more used to using fluorescents as their lamp of choice, the selection is growing exponentially. Some manufacturers to take a look at online are Artemide (www.artemide.us.com), Basic Source (www.basicsourcelighting.com), Estiluz (www.estiluz.com), FLOS USA (www.flos.net), Johnson Art Studios (www.johnsonartstudio.com), Justice Design Group (www.jdg.com), Thomas Lighting (www.thomaslighting.com), and Visa Lighting (www.visalighting.com), just to name a few (see Figure 13.11).

FIGURE 13.3 (left)

Two sinks mounted too far apart need a pair of light luminaires.

Remember that you can simply replace an incandescent lamp with a screw-in CFL, except in California when it is part of a remodel or new construction. California's Title 24 and its effect on bathroom design will be covered in greater detail later in this chapter.

FIGURE 13.4 (right)

Two sinks mounted closer together can share three light luminaires.

For some remodel projects the owners may not want to go to the expense of having an electrician install two new junction boxes for the proper placement of a pair of vanity lights. A few companies have come up with an innovative solution that makes use of the existing junction box above the mirror. They use it to power up a pair of hanging lights that are attached to a center light. This provides both cross-illumination and lighting from above as well. Take a look

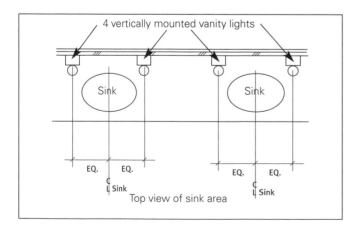

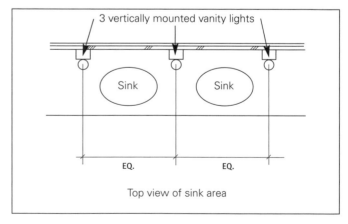

online at those offered by Forecast Lighting (www .forecastltg.com); the F-4810-36 and the F-4820-36.

For a cleaner look, designers and architects may want fixtures that don't project out from the wall or mirror. Several companies offer recessed fluorescent fixtures that are flush with the face of the mirror. This produces a very continuous line that has a more architecturally integrated feel. Using a fluorescent lamp that has a color temperature close to that of incandescent (2,700° K) will help most homeowners stay in their comfort zone. Two companies that offer fixtures like this are Aamsco Lighting Inc. (www.aamsco.com), whose version is called the Mirror-Lux, and Boyd Lighting (www.boydlighting.com), whose version is called the Emanation.

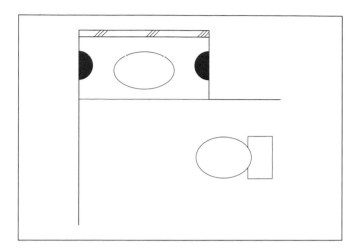

FIGURE 13.5

In small vanity areas, task lights can be mounted on the return walls.

You can also use mini-pendant fixtures that are hung from the ceiling on either side of the sink. These should be mounted 12 to 18 inches out from the wall, and the shade part should hang at eye level (5 feet, 4 inches to 5 feet, 6 inches). This keeps the mirror free of fixtures and allows you to reuse the existing mirror, because the power is being run through the ceiling. For good-looking mini-pendant fixtures that have enough punch, look at the Laia 2 by Taller Uno (www.globallighting.com), the Nite by B.LUX (www.globallighting.com), and the Fusion 2 by LBL Lighting (www.lbl.com).

There are also fixture manufacturers that offer mirrors with the wall sconces built in. These can come in both modern versions and more traditional styles. For examples of the traditional styles, look at Fine Art Lamps (www.fineartlamps.com), and for something more modern, take a look at Robern (www.robern.com).

Another option is to install a mirror that visually floats out from the wall with lighting that runs behind the perimeter. These backlighted mirrors come in round, oval, square, and rectangular versions. They don't have the huge punch of light that might be necessary for the master bath but could work well for children's baths, guest baths, or powder rooms. Some companies to check out for examples are Access Lighting (www.accesslighting.com) and Electric Mirror (www.electricmirror.com). Electric Mirror also makes an illuminated mirror with a built-in television monitor for the ultimate in multitasking at the sink.

There are also illuminated makeup mirrors, some with magnifying capabilities. These illuminated makeup mirrors come in portable versions and wall-mounted versions that are either plug-in or hard-wired (see Figure 13.6). They also come in swing arm versions, scissor arm versions and vertically adjustable versions that slide up & down on a fixed rod. Some companies to check out online for examples are the Baci and Echo by Remcraft (www.remcraft.com or www.bacimirrors.com).

Note: To protect the homeowner from electric shock, luminaires located this close to water should be installed with an instantaneous circuit shutoff, called a **ground fault interrupter (GFI)** (see Figure 13.7).

FIGURE 13.6
This portable illuminated
makeup mirror provides
very good close up task
light for plucking, tweez-
ing, and spackling.

AMBIENT AND GENERAL ILLUMINATION

General illumination is another layer of lighting that really helps make a bathroom work on all levels. One good reason for adding some type of ambient illumination in bathrooms is that they are becoming multifunctional areas. Homeowners now have exercise areas, dressing rooms, lounging areas, and whirlpools. Some bathrooms have become intimate entertaining areas that deserve all the design care that you give to the other main areas in the house.

For a majority of the bathrooms, we are dealing with a standard 8-foot ceiling. A ceiling fixture that is mounted flush to the ceiling can offer some general illumination. It alone cannot do an adequate job of providing light for a bathroom, but it can help be part of the solution. Often someone just wants to run into the bath to do their business or grab something and run back out. Turning on the overhead light is fine.

In a smaller bath with one sink it is best to locate the ceiling fixture in line with the vanity. This provides a complimentary backlighting for the person looking in the mirror. If there are two sinks, then center one ceiling fixture on each of the basins.

Style-wise there are often "families" of fixtures where the vanity lights and the ceiling lights match. This is fine to do, as many homeowners want everything to match—it's just not all that exciting. As long as the fixtures provide the right kind and amount of illumination, you are free to mix things up a bit. In the world of furniture, designers have been mixing styles and periods for years. This is **eclectic** design. Sometimes shaking up what is expected can result in a much more interesting and personal look.

Indirect lighting in a bathroom adds a warm overall glow to the space. Opaque or semitranslucent wall sconces or cove lighting that directs light upward can provide gentle ambient illumination. The linear cove lighting can use warm-colored compact fluorescents, runs of LED strips, or LED festoon lamps in more standard **clip strips**. These fluorescent and LED choices not only comply with tighter energy restrictions but also provide comfortable, low-maintenance light for the entire room. Yes, you can use incandescent sources for the indirect lighting in states other than California, but have you no love for the Earth?

For bathrooms with higher ceilings, close-to-the-ceiling (**semiflush**) or pendant-hung fixtures can also be considered as a source of fill light. These too, come in a great variety of styles. Check out Murray Feiss (www.feiss.com), Metro Lighting & Crafts (www.metrolighting.com) and Hubbardton Forge (www.vtforge.com) for more traditional looks; and for something modern or transitional, look at Foscarini (www.foscarini.com), Boyd Lighting (www.boydlighting.com), and FLOS USA (www.flos.net). For the ultimate in green design, check out a company called Eleek Incorporated (www.eleekinc.com), who make all their lighting and accessories out of recycled materials.

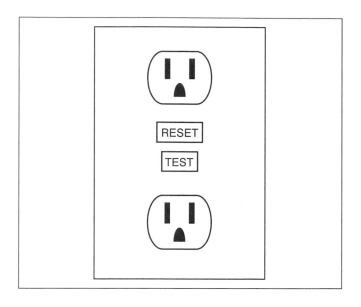

FIGURE 13.7

(right) A GFI (ground fault interrupter) prevents people from being shocked if they touch water and an electrical appliance at the same time.

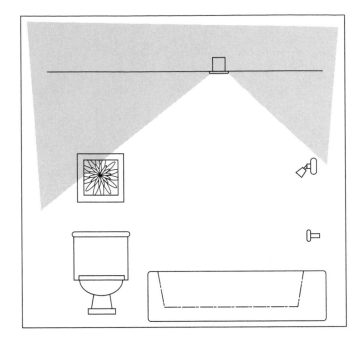

FIGURE 13.8
Recessed downlights may help reduce glare, but the downside is that they aren't adequate sources of fill light. They leave the ceiling in darkness.

Lighting for Tubs and Showers

While the task area at the vanity is the most critical to illuminate correctly, other areas of the bath must be considered as well. Tubs and showers need a good general light. For this purpose, recessed luminaires with white opal diffusers are commonly used and relatively effective. One drawback is that many of the units on the marketplace project approximately 2 inches below the ceiling line and may not be visually comfortable. They also tend to collect dead bugs. Also, these luminaires are usually limited to 60 watts incandescent of light, which is not very much. They use a normal household bulb (**"A" lamp**), which throws as much light back into the fixture as it projects out. This is not very effective—or efficient.

We're all a little sensitive to bright light the first thing in the morning. Fully recessed luminaires with lenses, which are flush or slightly recessed into the ceiling, will render the upper third of the shower or tub area a little more comfortable (see Figure 13.8). These luminaires do a better job at reducing glare and allow the use of energy-efficient bulbs.

A recent development makes lighting wet locations a little more exciting. Some luminaire manufacturers now offer recessed adjustable low-voltage fixtures that are waterproof (rated for wet environments). As designers are specifying interesting tile, plumbing fixtures, and even niches for art, they can install directional fixtures to highlight these exciting elements. Using LED mirror reflector lamps instead of standard incandescent varieties helps make these fixtures both attractive and energy-efficient.

Make sure that all luminaires, whether recessed or surface-mounted, that are to be used in the shower, in the steam room, and over the tub are listed for wet locations by **UL**, **ETL**, or another approved testing laboratory, such as **CSA** for projects in Canada. If Underwriters Laboratories tests them, they will have a blue UL label that indicates they are rated for use in a wet location. Also check to see if these luminaires should be circuited with GFIs for extra safety. Additionally, when specifying a surface-mounted or hanging fixture over a spa or bathtub, make sure that code requirements are checked. The national electric code now requires that the bottom of the luminaire is no lower than 8 feet above the high-water level. This means just below the lip of the tub.

Night Lights

Another great little technique is to add **toe-kick lighting**. This is a subtle band of illumination that is installed at the base of the bath vanity. It is just enough of a glow to allow people in the middle of the night to get in and out of the bathroom safely without having to be assaulted by a bright light. In total darkness it is amazing how just a little bit of gentle light will do the trick. The product to use is a tube light such as Tivoli Lighting (www.tivolilighting.com) or a rope light such as Holiday LEDs (www.holidayleds.com) or American Lighting Inc. (www.americanlighting.com).

Normally the tube lighting is 12-volt and needs a transformer. The rope lighting is normally 120-volt and doesn't require a transformer. Both types come in both incandescent and LED versions. Both are also available in colors, but the excitement of a glowing green or red line of light can get old pretty quickly. It is better to use a source that is in the incandescent color range (2,700 K to 3,000° K).

It also helps to have this light on a motion sensor, so as the person is groggily shuffling into the bathroom, he or she doesn't even have to fumble for a switch. This is also great for guests who would not know exactly where the switches are at midnight—and for kids who are forgetful about turning out the lights when they are done.

TITLE 24 for the BATH

As of October 1, 2005, California's Title 24 was revised to show even stricter requirements for energy-efficient lighting. If you will be working on a new construction project or a remodel project in California, these new requirements will apply to you. Newer versions of Title 24 will continue to be released. The restrictions about the use of incandescent lighting will not get easier in the years to come; they will get tighter. Don't be surprised if incandescent lighting is outlawed altogether in the great state of California.

As you have been made aware, California's Title 24 regulates everything from floors to ceilings to windows. As far as lighting goes, expect significant changes ahead whenever there is work requiring a building permit. The main reason for the existence of Title 24 is to reduce energy consumption. Before, it just concerned the kitchen and bath in regards to lighting. Now it includes utility rooms, bedrooms, dining rooms, and even the front-porch light.

Prior to 2005, the older code required that when a person is entering the bath or kitchen, the first switch had to control fluorescent lighting. The new code requires that 100 percent of the lighting in the bath must be fluorescent or a light source with an efficacy of 40 lumens per watt (some light-emitting diodes are meeting this requirement).

As of October 1, 2005, all hardwired lighting in the bath must be fluorescent or controlled by a manual-on occupant sensor. Every light in the bathroom, powder room, laundry room, and garage will have to be on a motion sensor, if it is not fluorescent. If you read between the lines, this allows that as long as the lighting is on switched motion sensors, it can be incandescent. This means, though, that you would have no dimming capabilities (until someone invents a dimmable switched motion sensor), and it means no energy efficiency (see Figure 13.12).

So there goes relaxing quietly in the tub if you are incandescent insistent, since you will have to flail around a bit to get the lights to come back on if you are lying still for too long. Also, these motion sensors at present only come in white or ivory, which doesn't bode well for the designer who likes to match switches to the color of the room. Watt Stopper (www.wattstopper.com) is one of the companies working on creating a line of designer colors.

Also, all recessed fixtures must be rated for insulated ceilings *and* be certified airtight. They must have electronic ballasts as well. This is not only true for bathrooms but for every room in the house. This means that fixtures using remodel housings are out in California.

Make sure that all luminaires in the shower are listed for wet locations by UL, ETL, or other approved testing laboratory. If they are tested by Underwriters Laboratories, they will have a blue UL label. Also check to see if these luminaires should be circuited with GFIs for extra safety.

FIGURE 13.9
The effect of placing one recessed downlight over the toilet can be very disheartening. Note the long shadows under the rolls of toilet paper and towel and imagine yourself under this same quality of light. A little ambient light in the form of wall sconces or a semiflush ceiling fixture would go a long way toward creating a much more pleasant environment.

Fluorescent in the Bathroom

The fluorescent option is important today. The main reasoning is plain old energy efficiency. As you learned back in Chapter 3, fluorescents are at least three times more energy-efficient than incandescent lamps. Do not put a recessed fluorescent or any recessed fixture of any kind over the toilet. It is a common mistake that creates the most unflattering shadows imaginable (see Figure 13.9). You don't want to look your worst when you are the most vulnerable.

Getting past your client's fear of fluorescent lighting will be the hardest part of the project. Fortunately, the color temperatures of many of today's fluorescent lamps are very flattering to skin tones. In response to color rendition criticism, most manufacturers have introduced recessed and surface-mounted luminaires that use lamps with color-correcting phosphors, including the newer compact fluorescents.

Not only do these lamps have a greatly improved color rendering, but the lumen output is substantial. For example, a 20-watt CFL produces an amount of illumination close to that of a 75-watt incandescent bulb. Many luminaires today use two 13-watt CFLs or a 26-watt quad lamp that puts out as much light as a 120-watt incandescent source for 26 watts of power. Because one of the color temperatures available in the compact fluorescent lamp is close to that of incandescent (2,700° K), both light sources can be used in one's bath without creating disconcerting color variations.

Two drawbacks to some of the older CFLs, as mentioned in Chapter 3, were an inherent hum and the lack of a rapid-start ballast. The latter deficiency causes the lamp to flicker two or three times before stabilizing. Quad versions are much quieter because they use an electronic (solid-state) ballast and have a relatively rapid startup. Dimming of compact fluorescents (both screw-in and hardwired versions) is now a reality.

These advances, along with the improved colors, long life, and quiet operation, make fluorescent lighting worth a second look. (Chapter 3 covers your fluorescent options, including the newer lamps that can be dimmed with an incandescent dimmer instead of the more expensive fluorescent dimmer). Yes, we are drumming the use of fluorescents into you and we will not let up. Make Al Gore proud. Save the polar bears. Feel the guilt.

Exhaust Fans

Windowless interior bathrooms may require an exhaust fan. Bathrooms with operable windows are not required by code to have an exhaust fan, although many homeowners like to have fans to help remove steam and odors. Units are now available with compact fluorescent sources that meet energy conservation requirements. Specifying a combination fan and light is a quick fix, but not an attractive choice. Make sure to specify separate switching for the fan and light, if allowed by code, so that the fan doesn't automatically go on when someone runs into the bathroom to grab a tissue or wash his or her hands.

Skylights

Often skylights are installed to supplement or replace electric lighting during the daytime hours. Clear glass or acrylic skylights project a hard beam of light, shaped like the skylight opening, onto the floor of the bath (as mentioned in Chapter 5). Bronze-colored skylights cast a dimmer version of the same shape, while a white opal acrylic skylight diffuses and softens

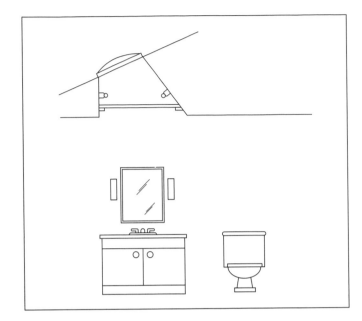

FIGURE 13.10
Lighting can be located within the light well to provide additional illumination at night, instead of becoming a "black hole" at night.

the natural light, producing a more gentle light that fills the bath more completely. Existing clear or bronze skylights can be fitted with a white acrylic panel at or above the ceiling line to soften the light they cast (see Figure 13.10). All specified skylights should have ultraviolet filters to slow the deterioration or fading of materials, caused by the sun's ultraviolet rays.

If the light well is deep enough (covered in Chapter 5), low-maintenance fluorescent luminaires with can be mounted between the acrylic panel and the skylight (see Figure 13.10). These inexpensive lights can be used to keep the skylight from appearing as a dark recess in the ceiling at night.

If fluorescent luminaires are used, dimming ballasts can be specified to allow control over the amount of light being emitted. Although such ballasts are not inexpensive, one of the advantages of dimming fluorescents is that they don't change color temperature significantly when dimmed. In this regard they are unlike incandescent lamps, which become more amber as they are dimmed. The newer breed of screw-in fluorescent, such as those made by Technical Consumer Products (www.tcpi.com), can be dimmed with a standard incandescent dimmer. This offers a low-cost, energy-efficient dimmable option for the lighting within the skylight.

Accent Lighting

Along with this newfound need for ambient illumination comes an opportunity for accent lighting. Plants and art pieces, as well as design and architectural details, can be highlighted. This added layer of accent lighting helps add depth and dimension to the bath. Use recessed adjustable fixtures when possible to help hide the light source. If it is open-beam construction or concrete construction, then you can look at using a track or low-voltage rail system.

The Powder Room

When clients are entertaining, the room most frequently visited by their guests will likely be the powder room. This space can be treated a bit differently than the other bathrooms. No serious tasks are going to be performed by guests. This is a place where people will wash their hands or check their hair and makeup before rejoining the soirée. Choosing the correct size of these fixtures is important. Here lights should be just a flattering glow. Sometimes a pair of translucent luminaires on either side of the mirror with the addition of a fixture in the middle of the ceiling will do the trick.

Some powder rooms do double duty as guest baths for overnight house guests. If this is the case, light the bath as you would a master bath, also making sure to put the various lights on dimmers to allow for flexible control over the illumination levels.

Here are some frequently asked questions by clients about lighting in the bath. Having some astute answers will help make you look like a pro:

How important is lighting to a bathroom design?

Lighting is more important in the bathroom than any other room in the house. This is the place where we all do very detailed and important work such as shaving or applying makeup. It is also the first place we see ourselves in the morning and the last place we see ourselves at night. Don't you want the sight of yourself to always be a positive one?

Bathrooms are often the smallest rooms in a house. What particular challenge does this present in terms of lighting?

Consider the idea of creating a jewel box. A bathroom doesn't have to be big to be effective. Well-selected finishes and bath fixtures, along with well-designed lighting can turn any sized bathroom into a luxurious retreat. It really is the one door in the house that we can shut out the rest of the world for a few quiet moments without feeling guilty.

Often bathrooms lack windows. How does a homeowner compensate for lack of natural light?

Natural light is very good and basically free. Try to incorporate it whenever possible. A room without a source of natural light feels a bit subterranean. The addition of windows or skylights should be a natural part of a remodel.

What's the most common mistake when it comes to bathroom lighting?

It is trying to use one source of light to fulfill all the lighting needs for the space. Anyone who has been in a bathroom with just one fixture in the ceiling or just a light over the mirror knows how bad lighting can be.

Why are bathrooms so often improperly lit?

People tend to repeat what they have known, which was usually a light mounted above the mirror and maybe a recessed shower light above the tub. Contractors will probably have a similar concept, having grown up in the same types of bathrooms. Getting someone in to help with the lighting design will make a world of difference. Cut out pictures of bathrooms you'd like to use as a reference point.

How do you determine how much lighting is needed in a bathroom?

Look at the overall design, review the finishes, evaluate the colors being used, and look at the age of the clientele. Older eyes need a whiter color of light. As our eyes age, they tend to see more yellow. If you combine that with standard incandescent light, which is also yellow, it cuts down on your visual acuity.

How do you determine where to place lighting in a bathroom, especially task lighting?

First you look at the task areas. These are the spots where work is done, such as the mirror over the sink, the tub/shower area, and perhaps a good reading light at the toilet. The best

FIGURE 13.11
This tall linear wall sconce from Boyd Lighting would be a good choice for task illumination, installed on either side of the mirror in a bath or powder room. It is available with a fluorescent socket.

FIGURE 13.12
California's Title 24 states that all the lighting must be high efficacy (40 lumens per watt) or controlled by a switched motion sensor.

task light at the mirror is a pair of fixtures mounted on the wall, flanking the sink. Called "cross-illumination," this provides shadowless task light for your face. Once the task lighting has been addressed, then you can look at other types of lighting that will pull the whole look of the room together.

What are some examples of accent, decorative, and ambient lighting in a bathroom?

Once they have the task lighting picked out, most people think that it is a done deal. However, this is just one component of good lighting. Consider adding art to a bathroom space and illuminating it. This is incorporating accent lighting for visual interest. Having a wonderful fixture or two hanging from the ceiling will dress up the bath and add a layer of luxury. This is decorative lighting. Bouncing some lighting off the ceiling from behind a cove detail adds a layer of ambient light, which softens shadows and can easily take ten years off your appearance. Who wouldn't want that?

Why use zoned lighting and dimmers in a bathroom?

Think about the idea of laying different sources of illumination together to create scenes. One scene could be for getting ready in the morning, another could be for a relaxing soak in the tub, a third scene for getting ready to go out on the town in the evening, and a fourth could be a low level of illumination for those middle-of-the-night trips to the bathroom. California's new Title 24 requirements make the use of a preset four-scene system a bit more challenging, but it can be done. Dimmed sources need to be high efficacy (40 or more lumens per watt); only fluorescents and some LEDs fulfill this requirement. Any incandescent sources must be controlled by manual-on occupancy sensors, which limits the use of a preset multiscene system. Projects located outside of California do not have to conform to Title 24 guidelines.

• THE BOTTOM LINE

Bathrooms and kitchens are the two areas in which people are most willing to invest their money, because a well-done remodel in these two rooms adds immediate value to the home. Clients can normally recoup the money they have invested when the home goes on the market.

The most important thing to remember in lighting the bathroom is that good illumination for tasks is primary, because looking good is hard work.

Home Offices—Work Spaces That Really Work

With the advent of computers, Internet access, digital drawings, and cell phones, an amazing number of people have moved their offices into their homes, either full-time or part-time. These lucky people no longer have to face the aggravation of the commute or, for those who are self-employed, the overhead costs of a separate workspace. Some designers and related professionals find that they spend most of their time with clients at job sites or showrooms anyway, making a separate office unnecessary.

For many more individuals, the home office serves as an important supplement to the main office space. The challenge is, How do you make this office space usable and comfortable for yourself and possibly integrate it subtly into the residential look of the home environment?

Often the office area may be visible from other areas of the house. How do you make it truly work-oriented without creating a commercial-looking office environment? Often these spaces also have to double as guest rooms during visits from family and friends. The trend to humanize office environments has been going on for 15 or so years. The early to mid-1980s were the culmination of years of hard-edged commercial design. Lighting design seemed to follow the same route. The trend was to fill rooms with flat, shadowless, almost hospital-like illumination. Depth and dimension were lost. Softness and texture were eliminated. Finally, people grew tired of it and longed for a more welcoming place to work.

These days designers create a more residential feel for work environments. They gravitate toward color; texture; softer edges; plush carpeting; plants; and warm, comfortable illumination. This design same trend has made its mark as America's workforce is moving back home.

With business now so computer-oriented, a designer's major focus shifts to how lighting affects people working at a computer screen. Since much of our work these days is done on the computer, we have genuine concerns about eye strain, fatigue, and headaches. These can

FIGURE 14.1
A series of recessed luminaires will cause hot spots
of glare to appear on the
monitor.

Designers seek a more
residential feel for
work environments.
They gravitate toward
color; texture; softer
edges; plush carpeting;
plants; and warm, com-
fortable illumination.
This design trend has
made its mark as
America's workforce is
moving back home.

often be caused by contrast and reflection. Glare is an uncomfortable light level or light location that can be increased by contrast and reflection. The screen on the computer will reflect
the light back like a low-reflective mirror, especially if the Web site you are looking at has a dark
background. Recessed fixtures and ceiling-mounted luminaires can create hot spots on the
screen as well. A ceiling filled with recessed luminaires or track lights can create little glare
spots on the mirror-like surface of the screen (see Figure 14.1). If you are using a laptop or a
flat-screen monitor with some adjustability, you can often reposition the screen to help reduce
the glare.

Sometimes even what you wear will affect the reflection. If you are facing a window, a white shirt or blouse will show up on the screen and keep you from seeing areas of the data display when it is on a dark background (see Figure 14.2).

FIGURE 14.2 (left)
Even a light-colored shirt or blouse or clown makeup can cause a reflection on the monitor, obscuring some of the data displayed.

TASK LIGHTING

A common misconception is that the more light there is, the better people can see. If there is too much unshielded light in the room, the monitor becomes difficult to read because of the amount of light hitting the surface of the screen (see Figure 14.3). Also, it is uncomfortable because your eyes are trying to adjust to the glare coming from light sources in the room. As long as the task, ambient, decorative, and accent lighting are on separate controls, you can adjust the lighting to create a more comfortable work environment.

FIGURE 14.3 (right)
Positioning the screen away from the windows or other highly reflective surfaces will help reduce glare on the monitor.

As discussed in previous chapters, the optimum position for task lighting is between your head and your work surface. A desk lamp with an opaque shade and an adjustable arm provides light for the keyboard and papers on the work surface without reflecting onto the screen or glaring into your eyes (see Figure 14.4). For some examples take a look at Estiluz (www.estiluz.com), Artemide (www.artemide.us), and Luxo (www.luxo-lighting). Consider using fluorescent lamps to cut down on heat and energy consumption.

Trying to provide task light from the ceiling can cause two problems. The first is that your head will cast a shadow onto your work surface. Also, you will have the problem of "veiling reflection," where the lighting hitting the white paper reflects glare into your eyes as you try to read (refer back to Chapter 1). This, too, can cause eye fatigue and headaches. It can also create an uncomfortable contrast between the surface brightness of the document and the brightness of the screen itself. Going back and forth from a brightly illuminated document to a more dimly lit

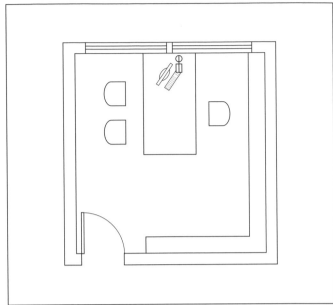

FIGURE 14.4 (left)

Using a flexible tabletop task light provides lighting for the work surface without putting any reflection onto the surface itself.

FIGURE 14.5 (right)

Make good use of the natural light coming in through the windows. Use some type of shade to control the light level when using the computer.

screen can also cause eye fatigue. Try to balance the amount of illumination on the documents with the illumination level of the monitor.

Interior Design Plays a Role

What steps can you take to minimize these problems? A lot of the answers relate to the interior design and space planning as well as the lighting. Step one would be to keep the color contrast between the walls and ceiling to a minimum. Stay away from using glossy finishes that could reflect distractingly onto the screen or into your peripheral vision. Specify work surfaces that aren't highly specular like polished granite.

Another planning consideration is to avoid positioning people with their backs to a window. The image of a bright window can overpower data on the monitor during the day. It is better to position the person so that he or she is sitting perpendicular to the window (see Figure 14.5). Make sure that light coming through the windows is controllable, using some sort of shade or blind.

Ambient Lighting

If recessed or track lighting exists or is being considered, then specify trims that have louvers or baffles that create a visual brightness cutoff at the face of the unit. Instead of using recessed luminaires or track lighting, consider using a source of ambient illumination instead to balance out the task lighting at the keyboard. Torchéres would be a quick and serviceable solution in a home office setting (refer back to Chapter 4). They can produce a soft, relatively even illumination across the ceiling without the typical hot spots created by recessed fixtures or track lighting. Some companies to look at for torchéres that can provide good ambient light without looking too commercial are Foscarini (www.foscarini.com), Phoenix Day (www.phoenixday.com), and Casella Lighting (www.casellalighting.com or www.claruslighting.com).

Another option for ambient light is the use of a single opaque or semi-translucent pendant fixture on the ceiling of a small or square home office space; or a series of opaque or semi-translucent pendant fixtures in a rectangular room can offer even illumination across the ceiling. For examples take a look at JH Lighting (www.jhlighting.com), Stonegate Lighting Designs (www.stonegatedesign.com), Sirmos (www.sirmos.com), and Fine Art Lamps (www.fineartlamps.com). If enough symmetrical wall space is available, a series of opaque or semi-translucent wall sconces can be layered into the design for a source of ambient light. For examples of what is available, check out Justice Design Group (www.jdg.com), Derek Marshall (www.derekmarshall.com), and Belfer (www.belfer.com).

If the ceilings are high enough (9 feet or higher), a crown molding or cantilevered soffit detail can be created to hide indirect perimeter lighting for the room. Any of these sources of ambient illumination can be pumped up more brightly when additional fill light is needed and can be dimmed down to a glow when entertaining. Any of these options for ambient light can use dimmable fluorescent sources for long-lasting, energy-efficient lighting.

FIGURE 14.6
Placing an uplight behind the computer can help lessen the contrast between the screen and the wall color.

If the monitor is in a corner, an uplight positioned behind the screen will help soften the contrast between the screen and the corner walls (see Figure 14.6). This is a quick fix and helps cut down on eye fatigue.

Accent Lighting

In the home office, accent lighting is not as important for the day-to-day tasks of running a business. Where it comes into play is at night when the home office is closed and you are entertaining friends. During the day the accent lights can stay off. Then at night, turning off task lights, dimming down ambient light, and turning on accent lights helps integrate the home office into the rest of the house.

Daylighting

Remember, natural light can be a very usable source of illumination and should be incorporated into the design as much as possible. Daylight is totally free and should be utilized as a viable source of illumination. This can come from windows, glass doors, and skylights, as well as from mirrors that can help bounce natural light back into the room (refer back to Chapter 5 on options for daylighting). As mentioned earlier, try to position the monitor perpendicular to the window in order to avoid reflection on the screen and eye strain (see Figure 14.5). Nothing can compete with the intensity of daylight, so use shade material to help control it.

A common misconception is that the more light there is, the better people can see.

• THE BOTTOM LINE

The main objective is to integrate the office into the rest of the home environment without sacrificing the lighting requirements of a well-appointed workspace.

Exterior Lighting—Expanding Interior Spaces Visually

Homeowners are investing their hard-earned home equity dollars in landscape design. Once the inside of the house is done, they are ready to tackle the outdoor spaces. All the home improvement shows talk about **exterior rooms**. This is the term given to outside spaces that are set up for entertaining, such as *alfresco* dining under a *pergola,* chatting poolside, or resting in a gazebo. People are discovering that they have valuable space outside that they can use. Once landscaping is done, they also want to enjoy it at night. This is where lighting design comes into play.

Many of the same light-layering principles apply outside as they do inside. Decorative lighting would be in the form of lanterns flanking doorways and hanging in the center of the gazebo, pergola, or cabana. Accent lighting would be the use of shielded directional fixtures to highlight plantings, sculpture, and water features. Task lighting would apply to lighting at the barbeque and reading light next to the lounge chairs, and ambient light would come from lighting bouncing off the ceiling of the covered areas or the underside of umbrellas.

When designing interior spaces, you may not feel a need to incorporate exterior lighting as a part of the overall design. In reality, there is a lot interior design expertise needed outside, including outdoor furniture, selection of sun-resistant fabrics for upholstery, sculpture, fountains, decorative lanterns, and accessories.

In addition, the illumination of exterior spaces can be directly related to how the interior areas are perceived. One of the great benefits of exterior lighting is that it can visually expand the interior rooms of a residence. When there is no illumination outside, windows become highly reflective at night. This is known as the **black mirror effect** and should be avoided. The windows end up reflecting the lights within the room, so that all people can see at night is their own reflection instead of the view beyond (see Figure 15.1). Unfortunately, window treatments that are flanking the windows tend to accentuate the problem by framing the black mirror. Closing the draperies only confirms the dimensions of a smaller-sized room.

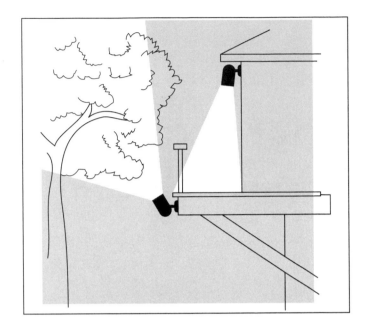

FIGURE 15.1

Fore lighting the deck from under the eaves and uplighting the trees from under the deck will help make the outside feel like part of the interior spaces.

People often feel boxed in at night when they are surrounded by these black mirrors. The room can seem smaller than it actually is. The rule of thumb is to try to balance the amount of light inside and outside the house. This allows the windows to become more transparent, as they are during the day. This exterior light is especially important when people are looking at the outside landscape through the window of an illuminated interior room. Balancing interior and exterior light levels helps keep the windows from becoming black mirrors. The lighting outside needs to be equal to or brighter than the inside lighting in order to be effective.

Psychologically, people also feel safer when they can see out into the yard area around them. They can feel more vulnerable inside the house when there is no lighting outside. You don't have to light up the exterior like the White House. That type of illumination would come under the heading of security lighting.

SECURITY LIGHTING

Security lighting and landscape lighting are two very different things. Yet you will often see people trying to use the same lights to perform both functions. Security lighting is simply a source of illumination that can flood the yard with a good punch of brightness. This is what clients turn on when they hear a noise outside. Security lighting by design is confrontational. The main objective is to provide enough fear-inspiring light so that homeowners can see what is causing the disturbance outside. Landscape lighting is more on the subtle side, as you will begin to understand.

Locations for Security Lighting

Security lights should be mounted as high as possible under the eaves. Specify double-headed fixtures with some adjustability (see Figure 15.2) so that it can be aimed in different directions. Having them angled out and down will provide good yard illumination. Some residential neighborhoods have light pollution (**dark sky**) regulations, requiring fixtures to be shielded or aimed downward to prevent illumination that may disturb the neighbors or the evening sky (see Figure 15.3).

Security lighting is optimally controlled by a **panic switch** located next to the bed in the master bedroom and in the bedroom of another responsible person in the household, such as a grandparent, nanny, or oldest child. A **motion sensor** (see Chapter 6) can also control these security lights, but keep in mind that it might be activated every time the family dog ventures outside. There are some activities that don't need to be highlighted.

Security lights should not come on as part of the landscape lighting. There is nothing worse than driving up to someone's home only to be assaulted by glaring security lights mounted on

the corner of the house. As a guest, you may feel like you've been caught in the middle of a prison break.

LANDSCAPE LIGHTING DEFINED

Sometimes you might have a project where some less-than-welcoming lighting has already been installed. What do you do when you have clients who've installed this confrontational kind of system, thinking they've got landscape lighting? One approach would be to say, "Oh, how wonderful! I see that you've put in an effective security lighting system. Now let's talk about the landscape lighting." This way the clients don't lose face and are possibly more open to ideas on additional exterior lighting concepts.

Landscape lighting needs to be subtle. Attention should be drawn to the plantings, sculpture, water features, and outbuildings, not the luminaires themselves. Decorative exterior luminaires, such as lanterns, can't do the job by themselves. They can easily overpower the facade of the house and the yard area if they are the only source of illumination. Typically you will see two lanterns flanking the front door and maybe a post light at the end of the driveway. These just become disturbing hot spots that leave everything else in silhouette (see Figure 15.4).

Still, decorative fixtures play an important role in the overall lighting design. Their job is to create the illusion that they are providing all of the exterior lighting, when in reality they should provide no more than 25 to 45 watts of illumination each. They serve the same purpose as interior decorative luminaires. Think of them as architectural jewelry for the yard. Visually, they should be more along the lines of a subtle pair of pearl earrings than a diamond-encrusted tiara. Some sample companies to look at for more traditional looking exterior lanterns are Hans Duus Blacksmith (www.hansduusblacksmith.com), Steven Handelman Studios (www.stevenhandelmanstudios.com), Arroyo Craftsman (www.arroyocraftsman.com),

FIGURE 15.2 (left)
Security lighting is best mounted at the roofline along the perimeter of the house.

FIGURE 15.3 (right)
Reasonably priced bullet-shaped luminaires are a good source of security lighting. These are not to come on with the landscape lighting.

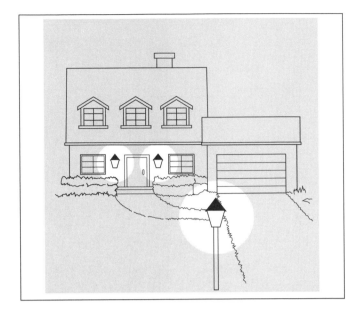

Mica Lamps (www.micalamps.com), Metro Lighting (www.metrolighting.com), and Hubbardton Forge (www.vtforge.com). For modern and retro-modern styles, take a look at FAD Lighting (www.fadlighting.com), Louis Poulsen (www.louispoulsen.com), Bega Lighting (www.bega.com), and Visa Lighting (www.visalighting.com). See Figure 15.5.

Note: In California the lighting fixtures that are installed on the house must be controlled by a motion sensor or hard-wired for fluorescent or LED light sources. Many companies like those listed above offer many of their fixtures with fluorescent sources. One company that offers LED options is Progress Lighting (www.progresslighting.com). While other states may not require the use of energy-efficient sources, it certainly makes sense to consider them.

Dark Sky

More and more, the neighborhoods and cities across the country are requiring exterior fixtures that are approved as "dark sky compliant." Full cut-off luminaires carry the endorsement of the International Dark Sky Association (IDA) for their effectiveness in limiting the detrimental effects of sky glow, also referred to as "light pollution." The IESNA (Illuminating Engineering Society of North America) defines full cut-off as fixtures with

FIGURE 15.4
Decorative luminaires alone become too predominant, leaving the rest of the yard and house in relative darkness.

FIGURE 15.5
This lantern, manufactured by Hans Duus Blacksmith, uses a lightly sandblasted water glass to obscure the CFL inside.

light distributions of 0 percent candela at 90 degrees and 10 percent at 80 degrees.

Glass Options

Another aspect to consider when selecting an exterior lantern is the type of glass. Too often they are chosen with a clear or beveled glass. The result is that at night people only see the lamps inside, instead of the luminaire itself. If you choose a luminaire that has frosted glass, iridescent stained glass, sandblasted "seedy" glass (glass filled with tiny bubbles that resemble seeds), or sandblasted water glass (wavy glass), then you see the volume of the lantern instead of just the lightbulb (see Figure 15.6).

FIGURE 15.6
Selecting a luminaire that has clear or beveled glass will show off only the lightbulb at night. Specifying sandblasted or frosted panels allows the luminaire itself to be the focal point. It also nicely hides a CFL.

Manufacturers normally offer numerous options for the glass in their fixtures. They are normally listed in the back of the printed catalog or usually shown as an option at the bottom of an online catalog page. Some companies go so far as to let you print out a picture of fixture with the glass and finish you want. This way you can show your client exactly what the finished product will look like. Car companies were the first to do this online. They found that car buyers loved the idea of customizing or creating the vehicle of their dreams. A couple of companies that allow you to customize a fixture online are Derek Marshall (www.derekmarshall.com) and Rejuvenation Lamp & Fixture Company (www.rejuvenation.com).

If the fixtures are already on-site and have clear or beveled glass, it is possible to have the glass in the existing lanterns sandblasted. Often mirror companies offer sandblasting as a sideline. Remember to have only the inside sandblasted. If you do the outside, fingerprints will show because of the oil in our skin. Use gloves when handling the sandblasted glass to keep from making marks. If you do happen to touch the sandblasted glass, usually a little rubbing alcohol on a lint-free cloth can remove them.

Correct sizing of exterior fixtures can be tricky. Lanterns displayed in lighting showrooms appear about 25 percent larger than they do when installed on a home. The eye tends to make a visual room out of the surrounding fixtures in the showroom, so the lantern is viewed in a very small space. The result is that people tend to select fixtures that are too diminutive in size. Sometimes a lighting showroom will let you borrow a lantern to try out on a project. If they do, take the size you think is right and the next larger size to help make the right choice.

If you can't get the actual fixture, one low-tech way of determining the correct scale for a particular house is to cut out a piece of cardboard the size of the prospective lantern. Hang it on the house and then back away to view it from the street or driveway. Choosing the correct mounting height is just as important. Take a look at Figure 15.7 to see a strange installation using very expensive luminaires.

Voltage

In designing the landscape lighting, a decision must be made as to which voltage system will be used. The choices are line voltage (120 volts, also known as house current) or low voltage (normally 12-volt or 24-volt systems, although other voltages are sometimes used).

FIGURE 15.7

Determining the correct scale and mounting height of exterior lanterns is extremely important. In this picture you can see how these oversize lanterns mounted 30 inches off the ground make for a rather comical entryway.

In reality, the illumination of exterior spaces can be directly related to how the interior areas are perceived. One of the great benefits of exterior lighting is that it can visually expand the interior rooms of a residence.

One of the determining factors is what already exists on the property. If some exterior lighting has already been done and there is 120-volt current out in the yard, then you are home free. Using one or more transformers, you can branch off from the line voltage and install low-voltage luminaires. Adding additional 120-volt luminaires to the lighting installation of an existing 120-volt system will be expensive and disruptive to the plants due to the trenching that will be required. The electrical code for 120-volt systems requires the wiring to be buried in conduit or directly buried 18 inches or more below the surface of the lawn.

Check local codes for permit requirements. Twelve-volt lighting systems are less restrictive, and installation is relatively easy. Low-voltage 12-gauge cable does not have to be buried, but hiding it under a layer of bark or a shallow layer of dirt is more visually appealing.

Low-voltage systems can use much less power and may not require any additional circuits. Their flexibility makes altering the original lighting design feasible and easy without costly rewiring. Luminaires for 120-volt systems are often larger than those using 12-volt lamps and may visually overpower the yard during the day.

When laying out a 12-volt system, remember to include the location of the transformer as part of the design. **Voltage drop** must be taken into consideration if it is necessary to have a run of over 75 feet from one of the transformers. This refers to the condition where the fixtures that are farthest from the transformer tend to be dimmer than those that are closer to the transformer. Many transformers are available with multi-tap terminals that offer slightly different voltages to help prevent voltage drop.

Often the best landscape lighting comes from a combination of both low-voltage and line-voltage fixtures. The line-voltage luminaires can highlight tall trees and provide an appropriate

 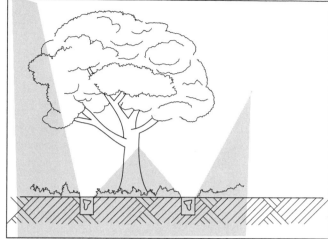

level of fill light for the yard area. Consider using a fluorescent light source in the 120-volt fixtures. A 26-watt CFL can do a very good job of lighting a 30- to 40-foot-tall tree. Some companies that offer fluorescent landscape lights are Kelsey Kane (www.kelsey-kane.com) and Kim Lighting (www.kimlighting.com).

These fluorescent lamps readily come in cooler color temperature choices, which can enhance the color of the plants and trees; whereas incandescent sources tend to make plants look a bit sickly. LEDs are also finding their way into landscape lighting. There are companies that offer landscape lights with built-in LEDs such as BK Lighting (www.bklighting.com), or you can use the LED MR16s in standard-issue low-voltage luminaires. Some good exterior landscape lighting companies to look at in addition to BK Lighting are Lumiere (www.lumiere-lighting.com) and FX Luminaire (www.fxl.com).

Plan Ahead

Save time and construction costs by having power lines or conduit installed under the driveway or patio before paving or bricking. Small plants and trees continue to grow, some slowly and some more rapidly. Plan for maximum growth and install smaller-wattage lamps that can be replaced with higher wattages as the foliage matures.

When working with new construction, it is important to specify a number of outside duplex GFI receptacles for future landscaping or portable luminaires for parties. Planning ahead for switching and transformer locations will save your clients money when the landscaping is started.

LANDSCAPE LIGHTING TECHNIQUES

There are many techniques for landscape lighting from which you can choose. Using a variety of lighting techniques will keep the design interesting. Using only one technique may create a design that looks too commercial. Many lighting showrooms now have landscape displays to help you make an informed choice. Some lighting companies (or their regional reps) have plug-

FIGURE 15.8 (left)
When the lighted object can be viewed from one direction only, above-grade accent lights are the logical choice. To prevent direct glare, fixtures are aimed away from observers. Place the accent lights behind shrubbery to keep a natural looking landscape. *Used by permission of Kim Lighting.*

FIGURE 15.9 (right)
If the lighted object may be viewed from any direction, well lights are the ideal solution. These below-grade (well light) luminaires are louvered to further reduce the potential for glare. Use the optional directional louver to gain efficiency when the lamp must be tilted within the well. *Used by permission of Kim Lighting.*

in-type kits that you can borrow to set up a temporary landscape lighting layout. This will help show your clients how their exterior spaces can be transformed at night.

The following are some options to consider.

Uplighting

This can be a very dramatic way of lighting trees that have a sculptural quality to them (see Figures 15.8 and 15.9). The luminaires can be ground-mounted (see Figure 15.12) or actually installed below grade. These buried luminaires are known as **well lights** (see Figure 15.11). Well lights have little or no adjustability, so they work best for mature trees.

Above-ground directional luminaires have a much greater flexibility and therefore do a better job of lighting younger trees as they mature. Use shrubbery or rocks to help conceal the light source from view (see Figure 15.10). A **below-grade junction box** for a line-voltage fixture will allow the luminaire to be situated closer to ground level. Low-voltage accent lights use stakes to help affix them to the ground. These are easily movable as the garden matures. Have the electrician leave an extra length of wiring per fixture (2 to 3 feet) to allow for some adjustment later on in the life of the garden.

Silhouetting or Backlighting

Silhouetting or backlighting, done by lighting the wall behind the feature to be highlighted, can be a very effective landscape lighting technique. Solid objects can be more dramatic when illuminated from behind or used to project a strong shadow pattern (see Figure 15.13). This can

Some areas have "light pollution" regulations requiring fixtures to be shielded or aimed to prevent illumination that may disturb the neighbors.

FIGURE 15.10
This ground-mounted exterior fixture, manufactured by Kim Lighting, sticks out like a sore thumb in the center of this flat grassy area. Landscaping lighting is meant to be subtle, and fixtures should be integrated into the plantings.

FIGURE 15.11
Here we see an example of a well light, an exterior fixture mounted below grade and fitted with a louvered face that keeps leaves and other debris out of the fixture. Diligence must be used in trimming back vegetation that could cover the face of the fixture; otherwise, the effect of the lighting will be lost.

FIGURE 15.12
This directional uplight, by Kim Lighting, is nestled among low-level plantings to help it visually disappear. Its weathered copper (or verdigris) finish also helps the fixture blend into the foliage.

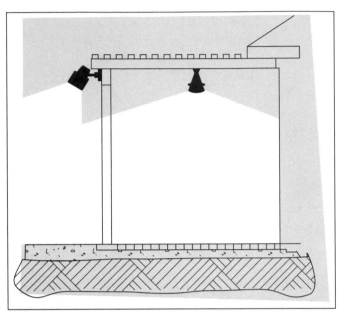

FIGURE 15.13 (left)
Trees and shrubs with interesting branch structure are dramatic when silhouetted against a wall or building facade, especially in winter. This combination of landscape and facade lighting provides additional security near the building. *Used by permission of Kim Lighting.*

FIGURE 15.14 (right)
Downlighting—For outdoor activity areas, luminaires placed above eye level provide efficient lighting for recreation, safety, and security. Overlapping light patterns will soften shadows and create a more uniform lighting effect. Mount to trellises, gazebos, facades, eaves, or trees. *Used by permission of Kim Lighting.*

work inside as well. This is also a good application for fluorescent luminaires. They do a good job of wall washing, consuming a smaller amount of power and having a longer lamp life than incandescent sources.

Remember to specify a fluorescent ballast and luminaire that is designed for freezing temperatures if your project is located in a cold part of the country. Some designers are using color-changing LEDs for backlighting so that they can throw a wash of intense color for a more festive look. One company that makes color-changing LEDs luminaires for exterior use is Color Kinetics (www.colorkinetics.com).

Downlighting

This type of lighting is used primarily for outdoor activity areas. It's best to overlap the spreads of illumination to help reduce shadowing. The luminaires can be mounted on poles, fences, under eaves (see Figure 15.14), and sometimes on the branches of mature trees (see Figure 15.15). This helps light up grassy areas or tennis courts for group sporting activities. This is one of the few places where an HID source could be used for a residential setting.

Spotlighting

Use spotlighting sparingly. While water features, sculpture, or specimen plants do deserve to be highlighted (see Figure 15.16), they will tend to dominate the view as people look outside if they are the only source of illumination. Spotlights should be shielded to avoid glare from the light source. If they are ground-mounted within planting areas, then they should be mounted on tall stakes if the surrounding plantings might cover them (see Figure 15.17). Layer this type of lighting with some of the other techniques to keep the landscaping from looking too spotty. On the other hand, having one feature more brightly lit than all the other areas of the yard can help create a focal destination, leading guests to a particular part of the yard.

FIGURE 15.15
An exterior directional fixture, manufactured by BK Lighting, is affixed to a tree branch using a nylon strap. The strap can be adjusted as the diameter of the branch increases so that the tree is not harmed.

If the lanterns already exist, it is possible to have the glass in them sandblasted. This helps obscure the view of the lightbulb within.

FIGURE 15.16
Spotlighting—Special objects such as statues, sculpture, or specimen shrubs should be lighted with luminaires that provide good shielding of the lamp. Mounting lights overhead on eaves or trellises helps reduce glare. If ground-mounted luminaires are used, conceal them with shrubbery. *Used by permission of Kim Lighting.*

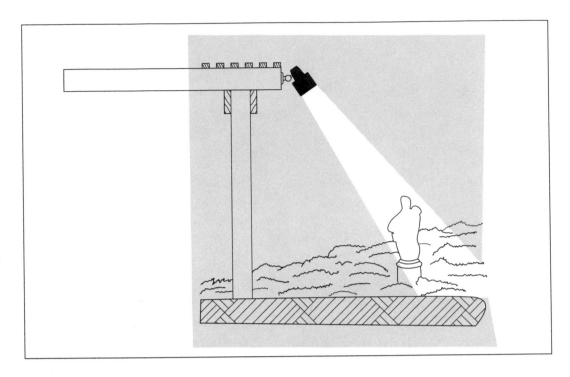

Voltage drop—a loss of electrical current due to overload or long runs (usually over 100 feet), causes lamps at the end of the run to produce a dimmer light than those at the beginning of the run.

Path Lighting

This is one lighting technique that needs to be done judiciously. Too often we see walkways or driveways flanked with rows of **pagoda lights**, used as the only source of exterior illumination. This tends to look like an airport runway. When a pathway light is needed, consider using an opaque **mushroom light** (a path light with a shielded light source) or a downward-facing directional fixture that projects light down without drawing attention to it (see Figures 15.18 and 15.19). Solar versions of these fixtures are readily available on the market in both incandescent and LED options. Most need at least six hours of constant sunlight to work well at night. The fixtures that are installed under trees or in the shadow of buildings simply don't get enough light to charge the photo cells. For a more artistic way to path lighting look at www.attractionlights.com.

Path lights should not exceed 14 inches in height. Otherwise, they will be too visually interruptive during the day. Spacing of path lights will depend on the style of the luminaire and lamp options. This type of lighting technique must be used in combination with additional lighting sources to help create a comfortable exterior environment. Alone, they will only invite UFOs.

Step or Stair Lighting

Step lighting fixtures can be recessed in the sidewalls of a stairway or the risers of steps to illuminate the treads. Step lights with louvered or shielded faced plates offer lighting that is less glary than fixtures with glass faceplates that are unshielded. You can also use a tube light or rope light that runs along the front edge of the steps. These work best when hidden behind a channel or nosing. Many companies, such as Roberts Step-Light System (www.robertssteplite .com) offer a variety of channels to fit many types of stairs including wood, metal, and concrete. This will provide safety as well as background fill illumination for the landscape design (see Figure 15.20). Path lighting is most important at stairs or any change in elevation so that a stroller is warned ahead of time and is spared a possible fall.

FIGURE 15.17
This accent light, manufactured by Lumiere, is used to uplight the plants or sculpture. Note that it is mounted on a tall stake to keep it from being covered by the plantings.

Please note that GFIs (ground fault interrupters) are required on all outdoor circuits in some areas. Local codes should be checked prior to installing the system.

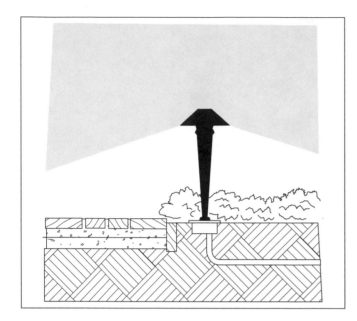

FIGURE 15.18 (left)

Fully shielded mushroom-type lights highlight pathways and ground cover without drawing attention to them. *Used by permission of Kim Lighting.*

FIGURE 15.19 (right)

Partially shielded path lights, like this pagoda-style fixture, create a glare. A fully shielded fixture is a better choice. *Used by permission of Kim Lighting.*

Moon Lighting

This is the most naturalistic way of lighting an exterior space. The effect is as if the area were being illuminated by a full moon. The end result is the creation of a dappled pattern of light and shadow, which is projected onto pathways, water features, statuary, and low-level plantings (see Figure 15.21). This is accomplished by mounting luminaires in the mid-branches of mature trees. Some of these fixtures will be pointed down to create the patterned effect as the light passes through the lower branches, and some pointed up to highlight the canopy of foliage (see Figure 15.22). Whole gardens can be done using this technique to provide both path lighting and accent lighting if there are mature trees on the property. These lights can also be installed on trellises, pergolas, arbors, and under eaves when tall trees are not available. Adding a layer of decorative and ambient light will complete the scenario.

Controls

Simple switching through the use of a timer, home control system, or a photo cell to turn the lights off and on in the garden is the best way to go. It's best not to dim exterior lighting. As mentioned earlier, many outdoor luminaires use incandescent sources. When incandescent lamps are dimmed, the light becomes more amber, and the yellow cast makes the plantings look unhealthy. The whiter the light, the healthier the plants look. Fluorescents and LEDs have cooler color temperature options that offer a more plant-enhancing illumination as well as energy efficiency and long lamp life.

You can, though, divide the lights into different switching groups if you want. A typical arrangement would be to have the decorative exterior lights on one switching group, possibly on a timer that would come on and go off even if your clients aren't home. The second group could be the accent lighting throughout the yard, the third would be ambient lighting, and the fourth would be the security lighting. As mentioned earlier in this chapter, make sure to have additional switches (panic switches) that control the security lighting at key locations inside the home.

Note that GFIs (ground fault interrupters) are required on all outdoor circuits in some areas of the country. Local codes should be checked prior to installing the system. If your client insists on dimming the outside lighting, it is possible for the GFIs to be tripped erroneously if the lights are dimmed with phase-controlled dimmers. It is better to keep the lights at full capacity and use the right-wattage lamps to produce the effect you want.

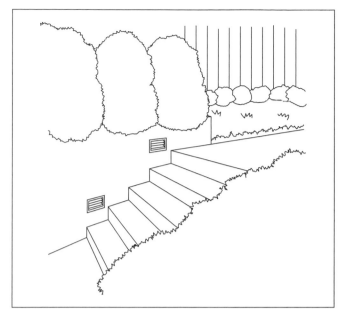

Filters

It's best to stay away from most colored filters. They tend to change the look of plants to an unrealistic color. When you are designing with incandescent sources, one filter to consider is a **daylight-blue filter**. It filters out the amber hue of incandescent light to produce a blue-white light that is very complimentary to plants, making them look lush and green. Many manufacturers offer daylight-blue filters (sometimes called "ice-blue" or "color correction" filters) as an accessory. This small addition can make a huge difference in the overall look of the landscape lighting if incandescent lamps are used. For more information, refer back to Chapter 2's section on color temperature and plants and Chapter 4's section on color filters. Blue light is also better for pools and fountains. Yellow water tends not to be very inviting.

FIGURE 15.20
Step lights can be mounted in the side walls of the stairway to provide safe pathway illumination.

Light color is also a factor when considering the insect population of your clients' gardens or exterior spaces. Insects are attracted to blue light, which is why bug zappers have blue lights.

FIGURE 15.21
Low-voltage lighting mounted in the overhead branches of a tree creates an intriguing shadow pattern on this lion head fountain.

FIGURE 15.22
Moon lighting—The effect
of moonlight filtering
through trees is another
pleasing and functional
outdoor lighting technique.
Both uplighting and down-
lighting are used to create
this effect. With luminaires
properly placed in trees,
both the trees and ground
are beautifully illuminated.
Ground lighting provides
security, and is accented
by shadows from leaves
and branches. *Used by permission of Kim Lighting.*

Bug lights, which repel insects, are yellow. In order to help keep bugs away from family and guests, locate the bug zapper in the far corner of the yard, or make a gift of blue light to a neighbor.

HID AND FLUORESCENT SOURCES FOR LANDSCAPE LIGHTING

There are many more exterior luminaires now available, using fluorescent and HID sources that are suitable for residential installations. Some mercury vapor and metal halide lamps, as well as the cooler-colored fluorescent sources, can do a wonderful job of providing a crisp white light. These work best for illumination of very tall trees and building facades. They have a long lamp life and are very energy-efficient, although many of the HID sources can shift in color over time. If an HID source is selected, it is best to replace the lamp halfway through its average rated lamp life in order to keep the light color consistent.

• THE BOTTOM LINE

Don't limit your design work to interior spaces. There is a ton of money to be made creating out-door rooms. This is the last frontier for design, and you'd better jump on the bandwagon or you will be left behind in the dust.

Applying Lighting Techniques

This section allows you to hone your lighting design skills. It is a chance to combine what you may already know with the information and ideas put forth in this book.

Part A shows guidelines for drawing an easy-to-follow lighting plan.

Part B provides guidelines for writing lighting specifications clearly and completely.

Part C is a questionnaire form that you can give to clients to get them thinking about lighting and the various functions it serves. The more they understand the importance of well-integrated lighting, the more they may be willing to invest.

Part D is a sample lighting project on which you will provide the lighting layout for a condominium project. A sample layout is provided in Appendix Two.

Part E is a review exam covering much of the information covered in Chapters 1 through 15 to test your knowledge and understanding of lighting. Sample answers are provided in Appendix Two.

PART A—GUIDELINES FOR DRAWING AN EASY-TO-FOLLOW LIGHTING PLAN

Everyone has different styles of presentation. The important thing is to get information across clearly and concisely. Remember, your lighting plan must be read and understood by a team of people who aren't intimately familiar with your design like you; they might include architects,

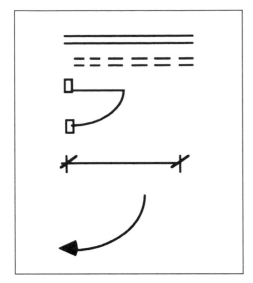

FIGURE 16.1
Make your lighting plan as clear as possible. The more information you provide, the less time you will spend on the phone or at the site explaining what you want done.

interior designers, kitchen and bath designers, sound system engineers, contractors, landscape designers, and, of course, the clients.

A concise lighting plan is often a combination of a floor plan (base plan) and a reflected ceiling plan (RCP). A reflected ceiling plan shows what is happening architecturally at the ceiling plane, including what is on or in the ceiling such as slopes, coffers, beams, skylights, speakers, vents, smoke detectors, or soffits, which will have an impact on where your lighting can go. At the same time the layout of the furniture also plays a critical roll.

It is also important to study the **elevations** in all the rooms. These will show ceiling heights, how the cabinets in the kitchen are laid out (and where task and ambient lighting might be installed), how tall the mirrors are in the bathrooms, how far off the floor the windows are located (for possible placement of furniture below them), and how steep the angle is in a room with a sloped ceiling. All of this information is part of the puzzle and will help you create a lighting design that is well integrated into the architecture of the house.

Sometimes you will come in on a project where the architect has already produced a schematic lighting plan as part of the plan set. This is often referred to as a **generic lighting plan**

Many times, in order for the architect to submit plans for permit approval, the city or county needs to see that the basic lighting requirements have been covered on the plan. This generic lighting plan may consist of a ceiling fixture in the center of each room and wall outlets. There is usually a basic legend that calls out the fixtures and components in broad terms, like "recessed fixture," "surface-mounted fixture," and "switch."

This schematic plan is not a complete lighting design by any stretch of the imagination. You can start from scratch to create a proper lighting plan. The revised and detailed plans that you will create do not have to be resubmitted for permit approval, as significant changes to the architectural plans would. The only thing that may occur is an up-charge in the cost of the electrical permit, based on the number of fixtures and outlets that are installed as part of the final lighting layout.

1. Create an Architectural Background

Start with the base plan of the building (or room) in CAD, with all walls and door swings as background (in a gray-tone or half-tone). Normally the base plan comes from the project architect or the builder. This enables everyone to see the walls and building envelope without them visually competing with the lighting layout. Layer onto it (in dashed lines) all ceiling features, overhangs, skylights, columns, and beams from the RCP that have a bearing on your lighting design (see Figure 16.1).

2. Place the Furniture in Each Room

The next step is to lay out the furniture. This is very important. You cannot make a viable lighting design without knowing where the furniture is placed. An empty room gives no concrete indication of how people will flow through the space or how the room will be used. For example, Will a specific area on the plan act as a guest room or a home office or a combination of both? Also, knowing which wall the bed goes on in all the bedrooms helps determine where switches will be located.

Without knowing where the major furniture pieces are being positioned, it is impossible to locate the correct placement for the floor plugs, wall sconces, recessed fixtures, and hanging fixtures. A seating arrangement may end up "floating" in the center of a room and may need floor plugs for table lamps and reading lights (refer back to Figure 4.42 in Chapter 4). For another example, consider the placement of the dining room table. If you install a chandelier in the center of the ceiling, you are assuming that the dining room table will be centered in the room. Then perhaps a buffet or china cabinet is placed on one wall, and the table ends up being placed off-center. This leaves the chandelier out of alignment with the tables. You don't have to pick the style or fabric for the furniture, just size and placement. All the finish details can come later.

Selecting which walls will be used for hanging art is also an important consideration. This helps determine the number of accent lights you will need. The art placement often relates to the furniture placement. Certain walls will be taken up by tall pieces of furniture, built-in cabinets, or mirrors. The walls that are left will be the ones that may get art. What art goes where is not as critical as simply deciding which walls will get art in the future. Many times it is the size of the wall that helps determine the size of the art it can accommodate.

Hallways are good spots for art because they are often too narrow for furniture. Sometimes they may be even too narrow for art. If you have a tight hallway, one option is to hang the art opposite from the doors that lead into bedrooms or bathrooms. This way, as people are leaving one of these rooms, they are far enough back from the art to appreciate it, instead of simply passing by it.

You can start the design process by creating a **red-line**. This is a hand-drawn layout of the lighting and switching locations that can be used to communicate your design concepts to the clients and the other members of the team prior to inputting it into CAD. That provides the opportunity for the team members to give feedback, so that the lighting is well integrated into the other aspects of the design. It also gives you a chance to verbally walk through the lighting design so that the clients and other team members have a clearer understanding of your concepts.

3. Create a Library of Symbols

Create a library of consistent lighting symbols, along with clear symbols for related components such as switches, dimmers, and floor plugs. CAD programs come with standardized symbols, but they are often too generic to be effective. Customize the symbols in a logical and concise way to make sure that the lighting plan is easy to read and can be used as a guide to install the lighting like you want it. These symbols will become a part of the **legend** (symbol list) and part of the plan set. If you have any unusual luminaires, try to use a simple symbol that suggests that luminaire. This simplicity saves drawing time and is less confusing or distracting to the reader of the drawings (see Figure 16.2 for symbols that are a step above the generic free-with-purchase symbols that come with your drafting software).

Decorative luminaires are usually selected by committee. The project interior designer, the architect, and the homeowners will all have their respective opinions. In order to keep the project moving forward, you can refrain from specifying the decorative luminaires on the legend and use the note, "to be specified by interior designer or homeowners" (see Figure 16.2, under "Decorative"). This gives the design team time to select luminaires at a later date, while allowing you to complete the lighting legend for the lighting design package. You may need to provide the voltage and estimated wattage for the decorative fixtures so that the controls can handle the total **load** on a specific switching group. Also, if a chandelier is being selected that is particularly heavy, it is good to get this information as soon as possible to the contractor or the electrician so that he or she can add extra bracing to reinforce the **junction box** (power feed).

4. Don't Be Stingy with the Information

On your plans, be sure to provide dimensions (distances from the wall and spacing in between fixtures), along with mounting heights for wall sconces and hanging fixtures. The location of the luminaire is critical to your design. In most cases, lighting symbols are larger than the actual luminaires you specify, so the dimensioning is critical to a proper installation.

Because the lighting symbols are not to scale, it may not be safe to allow the installers to take measurements off the plan for luminaire locations. Show dimensions to be sure they have the information they need (see Figure 16.1). Also, the electrician will want to kill you if he or she has to use an architectural scale to measure every fixture location. On CAD drawings use a fine/light pen weight to give the dimensions. This allows the lighting symbols to be the boldest line weight on the plans so they stand out. The background of architectural details and furniture should be the lightest of the three line weights.

The plans can either be printed out for distribution or sent as an e-mail attachment in the form of a **PDF** (portable document format) to all the people on the team. It is a good idea not to send a **DWG** version that could be changed by another team member or subcontractor without consulting you first.

There Will Be Changes

The lighting layout will change as architectural changes occur during the installation. Homeowners will often see the possibility of an additional window or a sloped ceiling instead of a flat one when they see that there is available room under the roofline. This kind of stuff isn't always apparent on the plans and only comes up as an opportunity for change when a walk-through is being done during construction. Just assume that this will happen, and add a certain number of hours to your bid for revisions. The best approach is to give a specific number of hours. Some clients will make many, many changes and eat up a lot of your time that could be spent earning money on another project.

THE BOTTOM LINE

The more information you provide, the fewer questions will arise during the bidding and installation phases. Having to answer the phone fewer times while working on a particular project allows you to work on something else that makes you money.

PART B—GUIDELINES FOR WRITING LIGHTING SPECIFICATIONS

A **specification** (or "spec") is a detailed description of the lighting equipment and components you have chosen for your project. This is a document that will be used by contractors, distributors, and manufacturers who want to bid on the project. Don't be generic. A specification that just says "recessed adjustable low-voltage downlight" is open to a lot of interpretation. Take special care to indicate exactly what you want or risk getting something you don't want. Without clear and concise specifications, you may end up with inferior luminaires installed on the job. The finishes may be different than you wanted and won't blend with the room and may look awkward. Plus, you want to be able to make sure that the fixtures you specify meet all the local or state code requirements.

A good example is California, where all recessed fixtures used in new construction or on remodel projects that involve 50 percent or more of the area being remodeled must be both rated for insulated ceilings and airtight. Don't just assume that the electrician knows this. He or she could have recently moved from another state where such a code doesn't exist. Lighting designers or whoever is doing the lighting design in California must fill out a form showing that the kitchen meets Title 24 requirements. The form is called WS-5R and is available online. (See Figure 16.2 for one that has been filled out.)

Just because a luminaire, made by another manufacturer, may look like the one you have specified, it may not distribute the light in the way you intended. Giving full and complete specifications, including manufacturers' names and the catalog number of the fixtures, helps keep contractors from substituting inferior or inappropriate luminaires simply because they look similar. Put a note on the plans that states that "any substitutions need to be approved of by the designer [you]."

Cover the Following Factors in Your Legend or on Your Plans

1 Description of the luminaire in generic terms (such as: opaque sconce)
2 Where the luminaire is located (such as: Dining Room 122)
3 Orientation of the luminaire (recessed, surface, wall-mounted, etc.)
4 Finish of the luminaire (white, chrome, gloss, matte, etc.)
5 Luminaire mounting height or suspension length (such as: 6'6" OC, AFF)
6 Type of lens, louver, or baffle, if appropriate (such as: daylight-blue filter)
7 Luminaire light distribution characteristics (e.g., asymmetric forward throw), if there is an option on the luminaire
8 Number of lamps (bulbs) per luminaire, lamp types, and color temperature (degrees Kelvin) for fluorescent, LED, or HID sources; number of beam spreads and voltages (such as: 2-100 Watt A 19 IF 120 Volt)
9 Ballast characteristics, such as dimming capabilities and voltage (such as: With Lutron Hi-Lume electronic dimming ballast 120 Volt)

Set Up, in Order of Appearance, the Following on the Legend

1 Generic description of luminaire or component (such as: opaque wall sconce)
2 Location
3 Manufacturer's name and catalog number (such as: Justice Design Group "Large Ambis" 1950)

Recessed

 Arrow on recessed adjustable fixtures indicates which way they are directed. no arrow indicates down light position.

 Recessed adjustable low voltage integral transformer fixture rated for insulated ceilings (throughout). Lucifer DHI-M-120 DL2RX-W W/I50W MR16 EXN 12 Volts.

 Recessed adjustable low voltage integral transformer fixture rated for insulated ceilings and wet locations (showers). Lucifer DHI-M-120 DL2RX-W w/I50W MR16 EXN 12 Volts.

 Recessed adjustable low voltage integral transformer fixture rated for non-insulated ceilings (exterior). Lucifer DHX-M-120 DL2RX-W w/I50W MR16 EXN 12 Volts.

 Recessed dimmable fluorescent fixture (kitchen). IRIS 5/32T SR/H w/Lutron dimming ballast w/1-32W 4-PIN CFL 35K 120 volts.

Decorative Decorative fixtures are specified by the project interior designer or homeowners.

 Ceiling mounted light (throughout) to be specified by interior designer or homeowners.

 Wall sconce (throughout) to be specified by interior designer or homeowners.

 Table lamps (throughout) to be specified by interior designer or homeowners.

 Vanity light (bathrooms, new walk-in) to be specified by interior designer or homeowners.

 Mini pendant fixtures (kitchen) to be supplied by homeowners. Mount 30" above counter height, Confirm with owners prior to installation.

 Pharmacy lamps (throughout) to be specified by interior designer or homeowners.

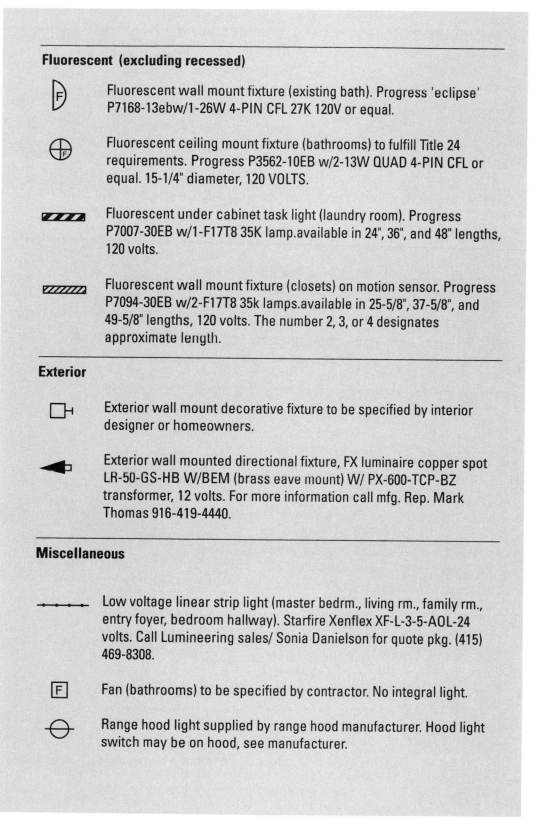

Fluorescent (excluding recessed)

Fluorescent wall mount fixture (existing bath). Progress 'eclipse' P7168-13ebw/1-26W 4-PIN CFL 27K 120V or equal.

Fluorescent ceiling mount fixture (bathrooms) to fulfill Title 24 requirements. Progress P3562-10EB w/2-13W QUAD 4-PIN CFL or equal. 15-1/4" diameter, 120 VOLTS.

Fluorescent under cabinet task light (laundry room). Progress P7007-30EB w/1-F17T8 35K lamp.available in 24", 36", and 48" lengths, 120 volts.

Fluorescent wall mount fixture (closets) on motion sensor. Progress P7094-30EB w/2-F17T8 35k lamps.available in 25-5/8", 37-5/8", and 49-5/8" lengths, 120 volts. The number 2, 3, or 4 designates approximate length.

Exterior

Exterior wall mount decorative fixture to be specified by interior designer or homeowners.

Exterior wall mounted directional fixture, FX luminaire copper spot LR-50-GS-HB W/BEM (brass eave mount) W/ PX-600-TCP-BZ transformer, 12 volts. For more information call mfg. Rep. Mark Thomas 916-419-4440.

Miscellaneous

Low voltage linear strip light (master bedrm., living rm., family rm., entry foyer, bedroom hallway). Starfire Xenflex XF-L-3-5-AOL-24 volts. Call Lumineering sales/ Sonia Danielson for quote pkg. (415) 469-8308.

Fan (bathrooms) to be specified by contractor. No integral light.

Range hood light supplied by range hood manufacturer. Hood light switch may be on hood, see manufacturer.

FIGURE 16.2 (continued)

Power Outlets

Note: we recommend that switch plate receptacle covers all match throughout the house in style and color. Color and finish should be approved of by owners prior to ordering.

Duplex receptacle outlet, to match Lutron Claro series

Quadraplex receptacle outlet, to match Lutron Claro series

1/2 hot switched outlet, to match Lutron Claro series

Ground fault interrupter receptacle

Weather proof duplex receptacle outlet

Switched weather proof duplex outlet for holiday lights

220 volt outlet

Switched floor receptacle, to be specified by contractor

Junction box (stub-out for future landscape lighting)

FIGURE 16.2 (continued)

Switching/Dimming

Note: the color/finish of the following Lutron switches, dimmers, and controls need to be selected by the owners/design team before ordering.

 4 scene preset dimming system Lutron Grafik Eye GRX 3104-color/finish 4 zones. Verify component package with mfg's rep Greg Stewart (510)638-3800 ext. 133, or David Garibay ext. 139.

 4 scene preset dimming system Lutron Grafik Eye GRX 3104-color/finish 6 zones. Verify component package with mfg's rep Greg Stewart (510)638-3800 ext. 133, or David Garibay ext. 139.

 Auxiliary master control, Lutron NTGX-4S-color/finish

 Single pole switch, to match Lutron Diva Series Claro CA-1PSH-color/finish

 3-way switch, to match Lutron Diva Series Claro CA-1PSH-color/finish

 Weatherproof switch

Incandescent dimmer - Lutron Diva Series DV600P-color/finish

Incandescent 3 way dimmer - Lutron Diva Series DV603P-color/finish

FIGURE 16.2 (continued)

Switching/Dimming (continued)

Low voltage dimmer - Lutron Diva Series DV600P-color/finish

Low voltage 3 way dimmer - Lutron Diva Series DV603P-color/finish

Switching group - denotes which fixtures are controlled together

Motion sensor (closets) such as Wattstopper WA-100 or equal

Control switch for ceiling fan

Other Symbols

Smoke detector

Ceiling fan

Television cable inlet

Doorbell

FIGURE 16.2 (continued)

Other Symbols (continued)

(SL)   Tubular skylight, 10" 'Solatube' or equal

FAU   Forced air unit

(WH)   Water heater

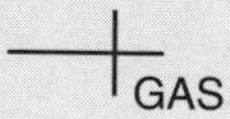

GAS   Gas inlet

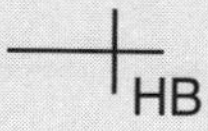

HB   Hose bib

▪▪▪▪▪▪▪   Dryer exhaust duct

HVAC register

Floor register at toe space

Push button switch

External operated disconnect switch

4 Finish (such as: Bisque)

5 Lamping, plus louver or other attachments, if needed (such as: 1- 13 Watt CFL quad, 2700 degrees Kelvin, and a glass diffuser)

6 Voltage (120 Volt, 12 Volt, etc.)

7 Special notes (such as: For additional information on this product, please contact the regional manufacturer's rep: Gregor Stewart, Associated Lighting Representatives, 510-638-3800)

Examples of Complete Specifications

Wall sconce (Master Bedroom #301), Boyd Lighting "Stripes 111," with 3-16 1/2 40-watt lamps, Orange Glass and Cinnamon Bronze finish, 120V. (For other color options and mounting information, contact the regional manufacturer's rep: Kymalisa Froelich, 415-778-4300, or go online at www.boydlighting.com.)

Exterior wall-mounted directional luminaire (Building Facade), BK Lighting "Nite Star 11" N/S-8-BZP-9-11 with 1- 50-watt MR16 EXN (included), 12 Volt (remote transformer required). (For additional information, contact the regional rep: Kathy Schultz, 415-387-4857, or go online at www.bklighting.com.)

Recessed adjustable low-voltage integral transformer luminaire rated for insulated ceilings (throughout house), Lucifer Lighting DHI/ZF-120-E-DL24Z-2SW, with 50-watt MR16 EXN, 12V. (For additional information, contact the regional rep Ray Anderson, Advantage Technologies, 925-806-0501, ext. 222, or go online at www.luciferlighting.com.)

Dealing with Multiples of Fixture Types

You will notice in the sample legend (Figure 16.2) that a gun-sight-type symbol always represents a wall sconce. If you have more than one style, designate each type with a number that corresponds to the room where it will be installed.

Recessed luminaires in the sample legend are represented by circles or squares within squares. For example, a ⊡ represents a recessed, adjustable, low-voltage luminaire, while ⒡ represents a fluorescent downlight. Adding WP next to the symbol indicates that this downlight is wet-location rated for a shower, over a tub, or for an exterior area.

Store Your Symbol Library on Your Computer

These symbols, along with the names of the manufacturers you use most often, can be entered into your computer to generate clear, explicit legends for each of the projects that include lighting. Building a database of frequently used symbols and specifications will save you time on future jobs. The legend should be printed on a separate sheet as part of the plan set. Use a large enough font that is easy to read.

Specification/Submittal Books

Assemble a specification book that has printouts of all the lighting fixtures and related components to be used on the job (these can normally be downloaded as PDFs off the manufacturer's Web site). This will further clarify for the clients and contractors what you intend to have installed. A clear picture will answer a lot of questions in advance. It's also a good idea to insert the corresponding symbols at the top right-hand corner of each specification sheet to match the legend to the actual luminaire being specified. See samples in Figures 16.3 and 16.4.

Cut Sheets

Circle or highlight the manufacturer's name on the catalog **cut sheet** (pages) or spec sheet, along with the catalog number and any other pertinent information. As mentioned above, you could also insert the corresponding symbol in the upper right-hand corner.

Most manufacturers have their entire catalogs online. Each fixture or family of fixtures has its own page, formatted to print onto an 8½ x 11 sheet of paper. These PDFs are great because they are formatted to print right from your computer. It's great to just click "8 copies," instead of trying to make eight usable cut sheets from pages out of various catalogs. Also, many manufacturers have their catalogs on discs to keep in your office and slip into your computer. Usually these can be obtained from the manufacturer's rep or directly from the manufacturer. But they, like printed catalogs, may often contain fixtures that have been discontinued or retooled. Usually it is best to go the Web site for the most up-to-date information. The manufacturers work very hard to keep their online catalogs current. They will often have a link to any new products in their lines on the home page of their sites.

For printed versions of the submittal books, put all the cut sheets in a binder or booklet for each of the players. Place a copy of the legend, resized to fit one or more 8½ x 11-inch sheets at the front. Add a cover sheet with the following information:

Lighting Submittals (This tells us what is in the binder.)

Jones Project (This tells us what project it is for.)

Saratoga, California (This identifies the project location.)

Contractor's Copy (This identifies which particular team member the binder belongs to.)

Print out copies for the submittal booklet for the architect, interior designer, contractor, electrician, lighting designer, and the owners. It's a good idea to make one or two spare booklets and keep them in the client file. One of the players is always losing his or her copy, and it will save you a lot of reprinting all the cut sheets again. These PDFs can be assembled in a file on your computer and sent as an attachment to all the players. This will save time, postage, and paper.

FIGURE 16.3

This sample catalog sheet marks which is the specified luminaire, along with the corresponding symbol. Used by permission of Lutron.

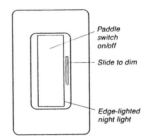

Ordering Guide

Use the table below to select the appropriate model number for Diva:

1. Determine the type of light.
2. Determine type of control.
3. Select the appropriate capacity.
4. Add your choice of color.

Type of Light	Type of Control	Model Code	Capacity 600W*	Capacity 1000W**	Color	
Incandescent	Single-pole	DV-	600P-	10P-	WH	White
	3-way	DV-	603P-	103P-	IV	Ivory
			600VA**	1000VA**	AL	Almond
					GR	Gray
Low-Voltage	Single-pole	DVLV-	600P-	10P-	BR	Brown
	3-way	DVLV-	603P-	103P-	BL	Black

Example: The model number for a low-voltage, 3-way, 600VA Diva dimmer in white is: DVLV-603P-WH.

*Available 4/30/92
**Available 5/29/92

Wallplate Options

Use Diva with Lutron SkyLine™ screwless wallplates or with any standard designer-style wallplate. Both styles are available through your local electrical distributor in colors to match Symphony Series controls. Wallplates are not included with Symphony Series controls.

Worldwide Technical and Sales Assistance

For help with applications, systems layout, or installation, call the toll-free *Lutron Hotline*:
(800) 523-9466 (U.S.A.)
Outside the U.S.A., call (215) 282-3800
FAX: (215) 282-3090

SkyLine screwless wallplate

Standard designer-style wallplate

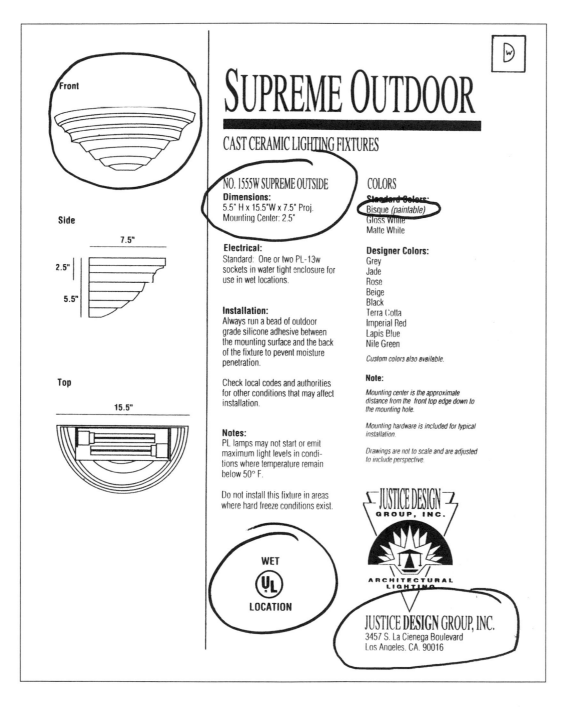

SUPREME OUTDOOR

CAST CERAMIC LIGHTING FIXTURES

NO. 1555W SUPREME OUTSIDE

Dimensions:
5.5" H x 15.5"W x 7.5" Proj.
Mounting Center: 2.5"

Electrical:
Standard: One or two PL-13w sockets in water tight enclosure for use in wet locations.

Installation:
Always run a bead of outdoor grade silicone adhesive between the mounting surface and the back of the fixture to pevent moisture penetration.

Check local codes and authorities for other conditions that may affect installation.

Notes:
PL lamps may not start or emit maximum light levels in conditions where temperature remain below 50° F.

Do not install this fixture in areas where hard freeze conditions exist.

COLORS

Standard Colors:
Bisque *(paintable)*
Gloss White
Matte White

Designer Colors:
Grey
Jade
Rose
Beige
Black
Terra Cotta
Imperial Red
Lapis Blue
Nile Green

Custom colors also available.

Note:

Mounting center is the approximate distance from the front top edge down to the mounting hole.

Mounting hardware is included for typical installation.

Drawings are not to scale and are adjusted to include perspective.

Front

Side

7.5"

2.5"

5.5"

Top

15.5"

WET UL **LOCATION**

JUSTICE DESIGN GROUP, INC.

ARCHITECTURAL LIGHTING

JUSTICE DESIGN GROUP, INC.
3457 S. La Cienega Boulevard
Los Angeles, CA. 90016

FIGURE 16.4

This is an additional sample catalog page with the specified luminaire highlighted and the corresponding symbol added to the page. Used by permission of Justice Design Group.

PART C—LIGHTING QUESTIONNAIRE

The following questionnaire is a good starting point when you are meeting with your clients to discuss lighting. Getting these questions answered will help you create a design that suits the project. Note that this is a one-room project. If your project encompasses an entire house, then the same questions will apply to each room. Send this out digitally to the clients prior to the meeting so that they will have done their homework before meeting with you.

To Our Clients

There are many factors that affect the way a room is lighted. By answering the following questions, we will be able to give you the lighting design advice that best suits your needs.

Project Plans—Please send a bound copy of the plans or a digital file so that we can study the project prior to meeting with you. Sometimes the plans were hand-drawn. If this is the case, get a full-size set (preferably 1/4-inch-scale) photocopied and sent to us.

1 New construction or remodel? (circle one)
   If it is a remodel project, where are the existing lights located? (Mark them on the plan if there is no lighting plan in the set or take digital photographs and forward them to us. Make sure to label which room.)
2 Ceiling height _____ Sloped or flat? (circle one)
   Hopefully the plan set has sections to show ceiling height and any slopes. If only floor plans exist, please indicate the ceiling heights and other details such as sloped ceilings, beams, or coffers. Digital photos of the ceilings can be very helpful as well.
3 Is there enough ceiling depth to consider recessed fixtures as an option? ____Yes ____No
   Usually any existing recessed fixtures for a remodel project are a good indication. New construction will show ceiling depths in the section drawings.
4 Are there skylights being considered? ____Yes ____No ____To be added
   Daylighting is a really great way to make use of natural light.
5 If you have, or want, skylights, are they clear, bronze, or white? (circle one)
6 Do you have a budget in mind? ____Yes ____No
7 What colors are the walls and ceilings to be painted? (Provide samples if possible).

   _____
   _____
   _____
   _____

8 What do the windows look out onto? Is landscape lighting to be part of the overall design?

   _____
   _____
   _____
   _____

PART D—CONDOMINIUM PROJECT

Your Assignment: You have been asked to design the lighting concepts for a new condo. The clients want you to tell them where to put lights and what type of luminaires you recommend (see Figure 16.5).

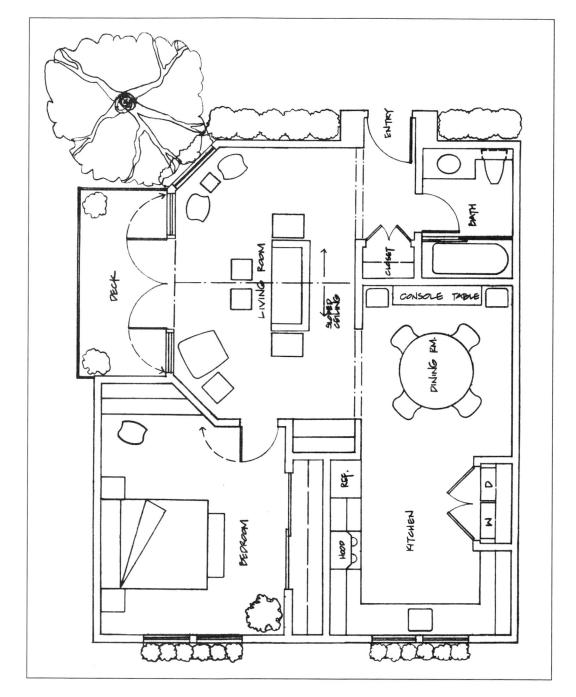

FIGURE 16.5
Condo Project. Photocopy this page and try your hand at developing a lighting plan based on the given client information.

You are to use the sample list of symbols provided (see Figure 16.2) to designate the type of luminaires to be installed. If a symbol is not listed for a luminaire you would like to use, create one and identify it on the legend.

The reason to start using distinct symbols is to make the lighting plans easy to read. The norm in the industry for way too many years was to use the same symbol to represent almost everything: ceiling-mounted luminaires, wall-mounted luminaires, recessed luminaires, even table lamps. This is confusing to read and can lead to mistakes during the counting of each fixture needed, as well at installation.

What you know about the clients:

1 They are a married couple, 30-year olds, without children. The walls and ceilings are white and the floors are light oak.
2 You have already worked out the furniture plan and location of art with these clients. That furniture layout is shown on the plan.
3 They have enough money from their dual incomes and a home improvement loan to do whatever you recommend. You are not limited by budget.
4 There will be 9-foot ceilings throughout, except for the living room, which has a pitched ceiling that is 12 feet high at the apex (center) beam.
5 There is adequate space available for recessed luminaires.
6 The condo complex is located in Baton Rouge, Louisiana, and their unit is on the first floor.

What to include in your lighting design:

Throughout the project, make sure you provide adequate lighting for task, ambient, and accent illumination. Don't forget to consider exterior lighting as well.

Solution: There are as many possible solutions as there are different designers. It is a good look at what a finished lighting plan looks like. See if you can "read" it and understand what the lighting designer intended.

PART E—REVIEW EXAMINATION— RESIDENTIAL/LANDSCAPE LIGHTING

1. What is meant by layering light? Explain and give four types.

_____

_____

_____

_____

2. What is meant by humanizing light?

_____

_____

_____

_____

3. What do the terms color temperature and CRI mean? How would you use them to choose a lamp for a specific space?

_____

_____

_____

_____

_____

4. How do finishes and light sources interact in a space? Explain by giving examples.

_____

_____

_____

_____

5. What are some of the things to consider in specifying a fluorescent luminaire? How can you help a client become comfortable with using fluorescent?

_____

_____

_____

_____

6. If you were setting the scenes for a four-scene preset dimmer system, what scenes might you use? How would the four scenes differ?

_____

_____

_____

_____

7. How does Title 24 affect kitchen and bath lighting in California?

_____

_____

_____

_____

8. What are some of the considerations (other than Title 24) used when designing lighting for kitchens? Explain.

_____

_____

_____

_____

_____

9. When lighting landscapes, safety, security, and beauty are to be considered. Choose one of these and describe some of the techniques used to accomplish this.

_____

_____

_____

_____

_____

10. Why is it important to know which plant materials are being used when doing landscape lighting?

_____

_____

_____

_____

11. What are some of the architectural constraints one must deal with in doing lighting design? Give an example.

_____
_____
_____
_____
_____

12. Describe the steps you would take in executing a lighting design from start to finish.

_____
_____
_____
_____

13. Color temperature is measured in degrees of _____

14. Do green plants look better under a cooler or a warmer color temperature?

_____

15. Name two benefits of ambient light.

1. _____
_____
2. _____
_____

16. Give two examples of task lighting in each of the following:

A home office:

1. _____
2. _____

A kitchen:

1. _____
2. _____

17. How would you improve on the lighting in a dining room that is lighted only by a chandelier?

_____
_____
_____
_____

18. What does the "MR" stand for in an MR16 lamp? (Hint: The answer is not "mister.")

_____

_____

_____

_____

19. What is the diameter of an MR16 lamp? _____

_____

20. To dim a quartz (tungsten halogen) lamp without significantly shortening its life, what percentage of the time must it be burning at full capacity?

_____

21. Why are clients afraid of fluorescent and LED sources? What can you do to "enlighten" them?

_____

_____

_____

_____

22. For task lighting at a vanity, where is the best place to locate the luminaires?

_____

_____

_____

_____

23. HID stands for_____

24. Mercury vapor lamps produce what color light?

_____

_____

25. High-pressure sodium lamps produce what color light? _____

26. People tend to look rather unattractive under high-pressure sodium light. What might look good under this light?

_____

_____

27. Is "daylight" a warm color or a cool color temperature?_____

28. What does the R stand for in a 75PAR20 lamp? _____

29. Name two disadvantages of the compact fluorescent.

1. _____
2. _____

30. The four lamp categories are incandescent, fluorescent, LED, and HID. Which category does a halogen lamp fit into?_____

31. What are two advantages of fluorescent over incandescent?

1. _____
2. _____

32. Describe the "black-mirror" effect.

_____
_____
_____
_____

33. Describe the "moonlighting" effect.

_____
_____
_____
_____

34. Why is it necessary to light the clients in addition to the art and architecture in a home?

_____
_____
_____
_____

35. If you were glowing from within, what color light would you emit to attract bugs?

_____

36. Give three advantages of low-voltage lighting.

1. _____
2. _____
3. _____

37. Give three disadvantages of low-voltage lighting.

1. _____
2. _____
3. _____

38. "Pagoda lights" alone in a landscape design create what kind of effect?

_____

_____

39. Describe the term "veiling reflection."

_____

_____

_____

_____

40. What does not change significantly when you dim fluorescent?

_____

_____

_____

_____

41. What is the best way to light a piece of art with a reflective face (such as glass or Plex-iglas™)?

_____

_____

_____

_____

42. When a client says, "How much light do I need for this room?" list at least three questions you need to ask the clients about the space.

1. _____
2. _____
3. _____
4. _____
5. _____

43. What is a "panic switch" and where is it best located in a home?

_____

_____

44. What is the most important element of any design project?

_____

_____

_____

_____

Resources: How to Use Them

Compared to architecture and interior design, lighting design is a relatively new and emerging field that had its beginnings around 1974. A basic lighting course or this text cannot cover all aspects of lighting design. It is important that you feel comfortable utilizing all the resources available to you.

THE INTERNET

If you have a question, a search online is the first line of defense. If you need to know more about LEDs, then find companies that make them. Look for studies or existing research on areas where you have questions. Thousands of articles have been archived on lighting design. Professional lighting organizations like those below will have a library of related articles. Also, magazines that specialize in lighting and design have lots of articles available from a search off their home pages. Some of these publications include *Architectural Lighting* (www.archlighting.com), *Residential Lighting* (www.residentiallighting.com), *Lighting Design & Application* (*LD&A*, www.iesna.org/LDA/article_indices.cfm), *Kitchen & Bath Design News* (www.kitchenbathdesign.com), and the *New York Times* Home & Garden section (www.nytimes.com/pages/garden).

ORGANIZATIONS

Please take advantage of the opportunities to expand your education. Listed below are associations that host classes or seminars around the country on all aspects of lighting design. The American Lighting Association (ALA, www.americanlightingassoc.com), Illuminating Engineering Society (IES, www.iesna.edu), and American Society of Interior Designers (ASID, www.asid.org) are all open to design professionals and students.

HANDS-ON

Take time to visit your local lighting showrooms; investigate and learn how to use their lighting labs. Most showrooms now have recessed, track, and outdoor labs of some sort, along with full displays of dimming options.

Interior design market centers put on seminars in conjunction with their annual, or semiannual, market events. Get on their mailing lists to find out in advance what programs are coming up.

GETTING WORK EXPERIENCE

Intern with or try to work with a particular individual or lighting design company that is knowledgeable and willing to teach in a real-life situation. The International Association of Lighting Designers (IALD, www.iald.org) has a listing of positions available. Working at a lighting showroom will give you hands-on experience.

ACCREDITATION

Many lighting showrooms belong to the ALA, which offers lighting classes for employees that can enable them to become a Certified Lighting Consultant as part of their organization. The IES has a program in place for Certificates of Technical Knowledge.

CODE REQUIREMENTS

Check with your local building department to verify local and state code requirements. Most have handbooks available at your library. It is far better to ask questions than to have to replace a ceiling because you specified the wrong placement of recessed fixtures.

PROFESSIONAL ORGANIZATIONS

International Association of Lighting Designers (IALD)
Suite 9-104
The Merchandise Mart
Chicago, IL 60654
312-527-3677
312-527-3680 (fax)
www.iald.org

Illuminating Engineering Society of North America (IES)
345 E. 47th Street
New York, NY 10017
www.iesna.org

American Lighting Association (ALA)
P.O. Box 420288
Dallas, TX 75342
800-274-4484
www.americanlightingassoc.com

American Society of Interior Designers (ASID)
608 Massachusetts Ave., NE
Washington, DC 20002-6006
202-546-3480
202-546-3240 (fax)
www.asid.org

LightFair International (Annual Lighting Conference)
Produced by AMC, Inc.
240 Peachtree Street, NW
Atlanta, GA 30303
404-220-2221
404-220-2442 (fax)
www.lightfair.com

THE BOTTOM LINE

You can never know too much, so take advantage of all the information that is out there. New and improved lamps are rapidly being developed; and keeping up with the green side of the technology is as important as knowing new fashion styles or colors.

Sample Answers and Layout

The following are sample answers to the review examination given in Chapter 16:

1 *What is meant by layering light? Explain and give examples.*

The use of a combination of luminaires to create a cohesive overall lighting design, which is a blend of task, ambient, accent, and decorative sources.

2 *What is meant by humanizing light?*

Making people look their best and feel comfortable.

3 *What do the terms color temperature and CRI mean? How would you use them to choose a lamp for a specific site?*

Color temperature measures in degrees of Kelvin, the color quality of a lamp. The CRI (color rendering index) compares the lamp source to daylight and its ability to mimic daylight. Warmer paint and fabric colors are complimented by a warmer color temperature of 2700 to 3500 degrees Kelvin. Cooler-colored materials in the blue and green range look better with 4000- to 6500-degree illumination. All colors are better with a higher CRI.

4 *How do finishes and light sources interact in a space? Explain by giving examples.*

Lamps and luminaires must be selected based on the finishes in a particular space. Dark surfaces absorb light, while light-colored surfaces reflect light, so deeply hued rooms need more light.

5 *What are some of the things to consider in specifying a fluorescent luminaire? How can you help a client become comfortable with using fluorescent?*

Some people are sensitive to hum, so specifying a fixture with an electronic ballast will eliminate that problem, whereas fixtures with magnetic ballasts have an inherent noise factor. Another thing to take into consideration is the colors in the space being illuminated, making sure that the color temperature of the lamp compliments those colors. Also, some people are turned off simply by the sight of a CFL and using a luminaire that has a lens or shade to hide the light source will alleviate that visceral response. Consider using an electronic ballast, so that the luminaire is as quiet as possible. A dimming ballast would allow for varying light levels.

6 *If you were setting the scenes for a four-scene preset dimmer system, what scenes might you use? How would the four scenes differ?*

Scene One: Normal—For everyday setting.
Scene Two: Pass through—A low light level; enough to see.
Scene Three: Party—A little more accent and less ambient.
Scene Four: Cleanup—All lights up to full.

7 *How does Title 24 affect kitchen and bath lighting in California?*

Half (50%) of the wattage for the luminaires in a kitchen must use energy efficient lamping (fluorescent or LED sources) and all of the fixtures in a bathroom must be energy efficient or placed on a motion sensor that has an automatic off function when there is no motion in the room.

8 *What are some of the considerations (other than Title 24) used when designing lighting for kitchens? Explain.*

Provide good general illumination to help reduce shadowing. Locate task lighting between your head and your work surface, such as under-cabinet lighting. If entertaining includes the kitchen area, make the lighting as comfortable and controllable as the rest of the public spaces.

9 *When lighting landscapes, safety, security, and beauty are to be considered. Choose one of these and describe some of the techniques used to accomplish this.*

Where beauty is concerned, work on lighting the plantings without drawing attention to the luminaires themselves. Let the decorative lanterns just be a glow and give the illusion that they are providing the light.

10 *Why is it important to know which plant materials are being used when doing landscape lighting?*

Trees that lose their leaves may be lighted differently than evergreens. Fast-growing plants may overtake a luminaire; extra lengths of cable would allow the luminaire to be moved as the plants mature.

11 *What are some of the architectural constraints one must deal with in doing lighting design? Give an example.*

Existing structures can dictate whether recessed or surface mounted fixtures can be used in the ceiling. Some structures can take advantage of luminaires made especially for remodel, but make sure that there is enough ceiling depth to accommodate a recessed can. California does not allow the use of remodel cans. While 8' is a standard ceiling height, some ceilings can be as low as 7'6", making it important to look at the depth of any surface-mounted ceiling fixtures to make sure there is head clearance.

12 *Describe the steps you would take in executing a lighting design from start to finish.*

1. Sit with the clients to talk about their needs and their budget.
2. Draw up a furniture plan.
3. Draw up a preliminary lighting plan and specifications to review with the clients.
4. Draw up the finished plan and specifications.
5. Review with the installing contractor.

13 *Color temperature is measured in degrees of*

Kelvin

14 *Do green plants look better under a cooler or a warmer color temperature?*

Cooler

15 *Name two benefits of ambient light.*

1. Softens shadows on people's faces so that they look their best.
2. Fills the volume of a space to make it seem larger and more inviting.

16 *Give two examples of task lighting in each of the following:*

A home office:

1. A desk lamp directed toward the keyboard of a computer.
2. A ceiling-mounted luminaire in the supply room.

A kitchen:

1. Lighting under the overhead cabinets.
2. A ceiling-mounted luminaire in the pantry.

17 *How would you improve on the lighting in a dining room that is lighted only by a chandelier?*

Add a recessed adjustable fixture on either side of the chandelier to cross-illuminate the table. Install wall sconces or torchères to provide the much-needed ambient illumination.

18 *What does the "MR" stand for in an MR16 lamp? (Hint: The answer is not "mister.")*

Mirror reflector

19 *What is the diameter of an MR16 lamp?*

2 inches (16 eighths of an inch)

20 *To dim a quartz (tungsten halogen) lamp without significantly shortening its life, what percentage of the time must it be burning at full capacity?*

20 percent

21 *Why are clients afraid of fluorescent and LED sources? What can you do to enlighten them?*

Fluorescents come in many wonderful colors and give three to five times more light than comparable-wattage incandescents. Fluorescents last 10 to 30 times longer than standard incandescents. LED sources are relatively new even though they have been in the public eye since the 1960's, used in signage and street lights. They were first developed in colors and are now being made in incandescent color qualities that can be used comfortably in the home. Their lifespan is listed as 50,000 to 100,000 hours, making them a good choice for hard-to-get-at locations.

22 *For task lighting at a vanity, where is the best place to locate the luminaires?*

Flanking the mirror, mounted at eye level

23 *HID stands for*

High-intensity discharge

24 *Mercury vapor lamps produce what color light?*

Bluish-green

25 *High-pressure sodium lamps produce what color light?*

Yellow-orange

26 *People tend to look rather unattractive under high-pressure sodium light. What might look good under this light?*

Brick, sandstone, the Golden Gate Bridge

27 *Is "daylight" a warm-color or a cool-color temperature?*

Cool

28 *What does the* R *stand for in a 75PAR30 lamp?*

Reflector

29 *Name two disadvantages of the compact fluorescent.*

1. Some hum.
2. Some don't have rapid-start ballasts.

30 *The four lamp categories are incandescent, fluorescent, LED, and HID. Which category does a halogen lamp fit into?*

Incandescent

31 *What are two advantages of fluorescent over incandescent?*

1. Longer life
2. Greater variety of colors

32 *Describe the "black-mirror" effect.*

When a lighting design has neglected to light the exterior spaces, windows can become "black mirrors" at night. Exterior lighting helps eliminate this problem.

33 *Describe the "moonlighting" effect.*

Positioning exterior fixtures so that they filter through the branches of the trees creates an effect similar to light cast by the moon.

34 *Why is it necessary to light the clients in addition to the art and architecture in a home?*

The space needs to be humanized so that the homeowners can feel comfortable in the space. Lighting the people in a space helps them look and feel their best.

35 *If you were glowing from within, what color light would you emit to attract bugs?*

Blue-white

36 *Give three advantages of low-voltage lighting?*

1. Compact lamps
2. Tight beam spreads
3. Energy-efficient

37 *Give three disadvantages of low-voltage lighting?*

1. Hum
2. Voltage drop
3. Limited wattage

38 *"Pagoda lights" alone in a landscape design create what kind of effect?*

They create the appearance of an airport runway. The small circles of light only draw attention to the fixtures and do not show off the plantings or the facade of the house.

39 *Describe the term "veiling reflection."*

The mirror-like reflection of a light source on a shiny surface when light comes from the ceiling directly in front of you, hitting the paper at such an angle that the glare is reflected directly into your eyes, as if you are trying to read through a veil.

40 *What does not change significantly when you dim fluorescent?*

The color temperature

41 *What is the best way to light a piece of art with a reflective face (such as glass or Plexiglas™)?*

Add an adjustable recessed fixture on either side of the art to cross illuminate the area in front of the art

42 *When a client says, "How much light do I need for this room?," list at least three questions you need to ask the clients about the space.*

1. What color will the walls and ceilings be painted?
2. Will they be doing tasks, such as reading, in the space?
3. Will they be entertaining in the space?
4. Are there skylights?
5. What is the finish or trim?

43 *What is a "panic switch" and where is it best located in a home?*

A switch located in a convenient place to turn on the exterior lights. In a home, it is best located next to the bed.

44 *What is the most important element of any design project?*

You may think that lighting is the correct answer, but in the end money is the true deciding factor. It is necessary to determine the budget and work within it. Sometimes the best design ideas spring from a limited amount of cash.

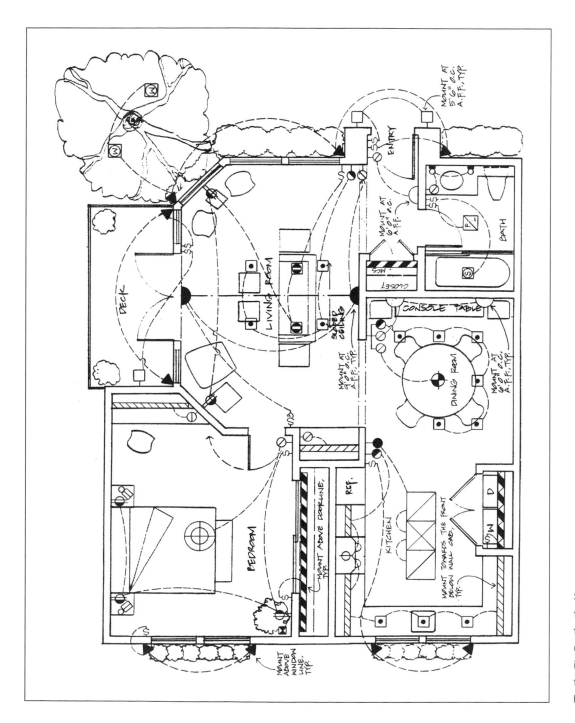

Sample lighting layout for the condo project in Chapter 16. Check the symbols used with the ones listed in Figure 16.5 to get a better understanding of what has been designed.

Here is a quick reference guide for terms that are commonly used in lighting design. They have been put in layperson's terms so that you can effectively explain them to your clients.

A lamp—Refers to the shape of a standard household bulb. The *A* stands for "arbitrary."

Absorption—Refers to a measure of the amount of light absorbed by an object, instead of being reflected. Dark-colored and matte surfaces are least likely to reflect light.

Accent lighting—Lighting directed at a particular object in order to focus attention upon it.

AFF—An abbreviation for above the finished floor. A term used to provide the mounting height on a wall.

Alabaster—A stone with translucent qualities, used on decorative fixtures.

Ambient lighting—The soft, indirect light that fills the volume of a room with illumination. It softens shadows on people's faces and creates an inviting glow in the room.

American National Standards Institute–See ANSI.

Amperage—The amount of electrical current through a conductive source. Low voltage has more amperage than line voltage.

Angle of reflectance—The angle at which a light source hits a specular reflective surface is the same as the angle at which the resulting glare is reflected back.

ANSI— American National Standards Institute has established a five-digit numbering system, in national use, for designating lamp types.

Architectural lighting—Luminaires that are recessed into ceilings or installed permanently on walls or in floors.

Argon—The most abundant noble gas, used in combination with other gases in fluorescent and neon illumination and in mercury vapor lamps. It is a source of ultraviolet light giving a deep blue color.

Asymmetric reflector—A reflector designed to project light forward and away from the luminaire.

Average rated life—The average life is determined by illuminating a number of lamps and noting when 50% of them have burned out.

Ballast—A device that transforms electrical energy. It is used by fluorescent, mercury vapor, high- and low-pressure sodium, and metal halide lamps so that the proper amount of power is provided to the lamp.

Banker's lamp—A desktop task light, usually fitted with a green-cased glass shade.

Bar hangers—Metallic arms that are used to suspend a recessed fixture in between joists.

Bayonet—A lamp base using one or more pins to connect to the socket that, in addition, is designed to lock in place by turning. Used commonly in some countries and where vibration might loosen conventional lamps, such as in automotive applications.

Beam spread—The diameter of the pattern of light produced by a lamp, or lamp and luminaire together.

Below-grade—Recessed below ground level.

Black holes—The effect you get when looking into a non-illuminated skylight at night.

Black mirror—Refers to a glass door or window in a room that reflects the viewer's image and the light in the room around that person at night instead of seeing the objects or view beyond.

Bi-pin—The base of the lamp is designed to connect the socket using 2 pins (sometimes 4 pins) instead of a screw-in base.

Bouillotte lamp—A portable luminaire with an opaque shade used for reading. Originally designed with real candles, it now uses electrified candles.

Bridge system—Two-wire low-voltage cable or rod system.

Cable system—A one- or two-wire low-voltage cable system.

Candela—The intensity of luminosity that one candle emits as light.

Candelabra base—A small-diameter base for a lamp that comes in different configurations such as screw-in or 2-pin. The socket of the fixture determines which lamp base is to be used.

Catalog sheet—See Cut sheet.

CFL—Compact fluorescent lamp. A small lamp, with an integral ballast, designed with a screw-in base or a non-integral ballast with a 2-pin or 4-pin base. A screw-in-base CFL can be used to replace a standard Edison A-19 lamp.

Chandelier—A hanging decorative luminaire.

Chroma therapy—A practice of using light of varying colors to affect the emotional system.

Clerestory—A line of windows that runs at the top of a wall where it meets the ceiling.

Clip strips—A run of linear light using low-voltage festoon lamps to create task or indirect lighting.

Cloudy-day effect—Where the lighting in a space is so even that there is no depth or dimension.

Code—Electrical guidelines that must be followed in order to ensure a safe electrical installation. These can be national, state, or city regulated.

Coffered ceiling—A pattern of intersecting beams on a ceiling.

Cold cathode—A neon-like electric-discharge light source primarily used for illumination. Cold cathode can sometimes be used where fluorescent tubes would be too large or too hard to relamp.

Color boxes—A series of cubicles that allows for the comparison of lamps of various color temperatures, side by side.

Color-corrected—The addition of phosphors in a lamp to create better color rendering.

Color-correcting filter—Color-altering lens placed in front of a light source to reproduce colors faithfully or give them a dramatic flare.

Color Rendering Index (CRI)—A scale used to measure how well a lamp illuminates an object's color tones as compared with the color of daylight.

Color spectrum—The range of colors that can be achieved using artificial light or natural light.

Color temperature—The color of light measured in degrees of Kelvin.

Compact fluorescent lamp (CFL)—See CFL.

Cosmetic filters—Lenses that have a peach hue to improve skin tone.

Cove lighting—Indirect perimeter lighting behind a linear architectural detail.

Cross-illumination—The use of a pair of fixtures to project illumination onto a piece of art or tabletop from two directions. This helps redirect glare.

CSA—Canada Standards Association, Canada's version of UL.

Cut sheet— A page out of a catalogue that describes a lighting device or component. Also known as a catalog sheet.

Dark sky ordinance—IDA (International Dark Sky Association) guidelines to limit light pollution in the night sky.

Daylight—The mix of skylight and sunlight.

Daylight-blue filter—A light-blue lens that reduces the amber hue of incandescent light.

Daylight fluorescent—An artificial source imitating the Kelvin temperature of daylight.

De-buzzing coils—Sound-dampening devices used to reduce the hum coming from dimmers or low-voltage fixtures.

Decorative luminaire—A light fixture that is designed to please the eye and provide focal illumination.

De-rating—The reduction of the amount of wattage used to prevent overheating. Related to ganging of dimmers. The more dimmers that are located in the same box, the less wattage they can control.

Dichroic—Accurate color filters characterized by the color(s) of light that they reflect, rather than the color(s) they pass.

Diffusion filters—Glass lenses used to widen and soften light output.

Dimmer—A control that regulates light levels.

Dimming ballast—A device used with fluorescent lamps to control the light level. May also apply to HID sources.

Diode—The simplest sort of semiconductor, which is a material with a varying ability to produce light.

Double-envelope halogen—Denotes a second shell that allows you to safely handle the lamp with your bare hands when installing.

Downlight—A luminaire that is used to project light toward the ground.

Downlighting—A technique that uses a luminaire to project light downward.

DWG—An abbreviation for a CAD (computer assisted drafting) format to store 2- or 3-dimensional design data that can be digitally changed.

Eclectic—A mix of styles used in interior design.

Efficacy—A measurement of the efficiency of a light source.

Electronic dimming ballasts—An electronic ballast that uses high-frequency oscillations of power to eliminate flicker and hum that is often associated with fluorescent fixtures.

Electronic transformer—Converts voltage from one level to another (e.g., 120 volt to 12 volt) with no sound, as the frequencies are higher than in magnetic transformers.

Elevations—Height of an architectural element above a fixed point, showing correct proportions of all the components.

ETL—An independent testing facility, similar to UL.

Exterior rooms—Spaces used for outdoor entertaining.

Fade rate—The rate at which light levels decrease.

Fascia—A wood trim or mounding mounted at the top or bottom of cabinetry or furniture often used to hide a light source.

Festoon—A tubular lamp with bullet-shaped metal end caps connecting it to the electrical supply.

Fiber optics—An illuminating system composed of a lamp source, fiber, and output optics used to remotely light an area or object.

Filters—A glass or metal accessory used to alter beam patterns.

Fish tape—A device used to pull wires through tight spaces or conduits.

Floor plug—An electrical outlet recessed into the flooring of a room

Fluorescent lamp—A very energy-efficient type of lamp that produces light through the activation of the phosphor coating on the inside surface of a glass envelope. These lamps come in many shapes, wattages, and colors.

Foot-candle—The light that falls on a given surface measured as a unit of illumination equal to 1 lumen per square foot.

Framing projector—A luminaire that can be adjusted to precisely frame an object with light.

Ganging—The grouping of two or more controls in one enclosure.

Gauge—Thickness of wire that transmits varying degrees of electric current.

Generic lighting plan—A drawing showing the basic symbols for types of lighting that might be installed, without the dimensional details or exact specifications.

GFI (ground fault interrupter)—An instantaneous disconnect device that turns off an electrical appliance or circuit when it comes in contact with water, in order to prevent electric shock.

Glare bomb—A source of uncomfortably bright light that becomes the focus of attention rather than what it was meant to illuminate.

Glass block/glass brick—A transparent or translucent building material.

Great room—A large space in a house that often includes the living room, dining room, and kitchen.

Ground fault interrupter—See GFI.

Halogen—An incandescent lamp containing halogen gas that recycles the tungsten. It is whiter in color than standard incandescent lamps but becomes more yellow when dimmed.

Halogen bridge system—See Bridge system

Hardwire—A method of luminaire installation using a junction box.

High-intensity discharge (HID) lamp—A category of lamp that emits light by electrically activating pressurized gas in a bulb. Mercury vapor, metal halide, and high- and low-pressure sodium lamps are all HID sources. They are bright and energy-efficient light sources, used mainly in exterior environments.

High-pressure sodium—An HID lamp that uses sodium vapor as the light-producing element. It produces a yellow-orange light.

Hole saw—A drill bit used to cut very clean holes in doors, walls, floors, and ceilings.

Housing—An enclosure for recessed sockets and trim installed above the ceiling line.

IC cans—Recessed fixtures designed to be in direct contact with insulation.

Ice-blue filter—Alternative name for a daylight-blue filter that reduces the amber hue of incandescent light.

Illuminator—Part of a fiber-optic system, a box that houses the light source, fan, and coupler for a fiber-optic run.

Incandescent lamp—The traditional type of lightbulb that produces light through electricity, causing a filament to glow. It is a very inefficient source of illumination.

Junction box—An enclosure for joining wires behind walls or ceilings.

Kelvin—In lighting design, a measure of color temperature.

Lamp—What the lighting industry calls a lightbulb; a glass envelope with gas, coating, or filament that glows when electricity is applied. Also a common word for a portable light fixture but not used in the professional lighting community in this sense.

LCD—An abbreviation for liquid crystal display, which is a thin, flat display device made up of any number of pixels in front of a light source.

LED—An abbreviation for light-emitting diode, which is the fourth technology discovered to produce light from energy, the first three being incandescent, fluorescent, and HID. This newly rediscovered light source is the most energy-efficient technology and came out of the silicon chip revolution.

Legend—A list of symbols that relate to lighting and electrical components used on a lighting plan.

Light bar—Bare lightbulbs mounted to a housing that are used for low-cost task light at the vanity.

Light boxes—See Color boxes.

Light-emitting diode—See LED.

Light layering—Using the four functions of light (task, ambient, accent, and decorative) together in order to create a cohesive design.

Line voltage—120-volt household current, standard in North American homes.

Liquid crystal display—See LCD.

Load—The total number of watts calculated to run on a circuit.

Louver—A metal or plastic accessory used on a luminaire to help prevent glare.

Low-pressure sodium—A discharge lamp that uses sodium vapor as the light-producing element. It produces an orange-gray light.

Low-voltage lighting—A system that uses a current of less than 50 volts (commonly 12 volts) instead of 120 volts, the standard household current in the United States. A transformer is used to convert the electrical power to the appropriate voltage.

Lumen—A unit of light power from a light source: the rate at which light falls on 1 square foot of surface area 1 foot away from a light source at 1 candlepower or 1 candela.

Luminaire—The complete light luminaire with all lamps (bulbs) and parts necessary for positioning and obtaining power supply.

Lux—Conveys the light cast on a surface by a 1-candela source one foot away. Lux and foot-candles are different units of the same quantity, and it is valid to convert foot-candles to lux and vice versa.

Magnetic dimming ballast—A magnetic ballast does not use high-frequency oscillations, as the electronic ballasts; and it has moving parts that result in an audible hum.

Magnetic transformer—A device that converts electricity from one voltage to another. A magnetic transformer has moving parts that causes an inherent hum.

Mass-relamping—Replacing all the lamps in a group of fixtures when they start to burn out, rather than one by one.

Mercury vapor lamp—An HID lamp where the light emission is radiated mainly from mercury. It can be clear, phosphor-coated, or self-ballasted. It produces a bluish-green light.

Metal halide lamp—An HID lamp where the light comes from radiation from metal halide. It produces the whitest light of the HID sources.

Mica—A naturally occurring, flame-resistant, silicate mineral that can be cut into thin sheets and used to make shades for fixtures to give a warm glow of yellow-orange light.

Mirror reflector (MR16 and MR11)—Miniature tungsten-halogen lamps with a variety of beam spreads and wattages, controlled by mirrored facets positioned in the reflector. Now also available in LED versions.

Moonlighting effect—The dappled pattern of light and shadow that mimics the effects of natural moonlight.

Motion sensor—A control that activates luminaires when movement occurs.

MR11—A mirror reflector lamp that is 1⅜ inch in diameter.

MR16—A mirror reflector lamp that is 2 inches in diameter.

Museum effect—An environment with only accent lighting that makes the art seem more important than the people in the space.

Mushroom light—An exterior pathway and garden luminaire whose shape resembles that of a mushroom.

National Electric Code—See NEC.

NEC (National Electric Code)—The rules for electrical installations that must be followed to ensure a safe installation, used throughout the United States.

Neon—A glass vacuum tube filled with neon gas and phosphors that can be formed into signs, letters, or shapes.

Non-specular—Not reflective.

OC—An abbreviation for on center, which is a drafting term to show the placement of a component equidistant between 2 points.

Opaque—Solid, permitting no light to pass through.

Open-hearth effect—Lighting that creates the feeling of a glowing fire.

Open plan—An architectural design where rooms flow from one to another without doors.

Optical framing projectors—See Framing projector.

Pagoda light—An exterior pathway luminaire that resembles a pagoda.

Pancake junction box—A shallow junction box, approximately 1/4" deep.

Panic switch—An on–off switch to activate security lighting, usually located by the bed for emergencies.

PAR lamps—Lightbulbs with parabolic aluminized reflectors that give exacting beam control. There are a number of beam patterns to choose from, ranging from wide flood to very narrow spot. PAR lamps can be used outdoors due to their thick glass, which holds up in severe weather conditions. PAR stands for "parabolic aluminized reflector."

PDF—An abbreviation for a CAD-format document to store 2- or 3-dimensional design data that cannot be digitally changed.

Pendant—A luminaire that is suspended from the ceiling by wires, chains, or metal rods.

Pharmacy-type luminaire—A portable floor or tabletop luminaire that is used for reading. It normally has an opaque shade.

Phosphor—A substance that glows (phosphorescence) after exposure to energized particles, in particular electron flow in fluorescent lamps. A mixture of phosphors are used to give fluorescent light different-colored hues.

Photo-pigment bleaching—The mirror-like reflection of the sun on a shiny surface, causing glare.

Photosensor—A control device that activates luminaires depending on surrounding light levels.

Planetarium effect—The look of too many holes in the ceiling resulting from an overabundance of recessed fixtures.

Portable tabletop luminaires—Table lamps that are decorative or used for task lighting.

Preheat—To burn fluorescent lamps at their full capacity for a specified time before dimming them in order to ensure full lamp life, specifically fluorescent lamps with dimming ballasts.

Puck light/puk light—A very shallow luminaire in the shape of a small hockey puck.

Quartz—The most abundant element on Earth; part of many compounds.

R lamp—An incandescent source with a built-in reflecting surface.

Rail system—Similar to a bridge system that uses rigid rails or rods to run the electricity.

Rapid-start—Fluorescent lamps equipped with ballasts designed to have them turn on immediately, without a brief warm-up time or flicker.

Receptacle—A point of access for electrical power.

Recessed adjustable fixtures—An architectural luminaire that has a flexibility of movement to direct the light.

Red-line—A hand-drawn layout of the lighting and switching locations, in red pencil, that can be used to communicate your design concepts to the clients and the other members of the team prior to inputting it into CAD.

Reflectance—The ratio of light reflected from a surface.

Reflected ceiling plan—A lighting or architectural plan drawn as if you are lying on the floor looking up at the ceiling.

Relamping—The process of replacing a light bulb.

Reveal—A space behind which a light source can be hidden.

RLM—Stands for reflector light microscopy which is a luminaire designed to reflect light down and prevent upward light transmission.

Rope lights—Flexible lights encased in a plastic tubing that can be 12 volt or 120 volt.

Rough service—Industrial-grade lamps that hold up to extreme temperatures and vibration.

Scone—Something that you eat with tea. This is not a wall-mounted decorative luminaire but often accidentally used by people in the place of "sconce" (see below).

Sconce—A wall-mounted decorative or architecturally integrated luminaire.

Security lighting—Exterior illumination intended to flood the property with bright light.

Semi-flush—Close to the ceiling.

Silhouetting—The backlighting of an object.

Silver bowl reflector lamp—A lightbulb that has a silvered head used to direct light back to the base.

Smart house—A home control system.

Snoot—A metal baffle used to shield glare.

Socket—The receptacle that a lamp base connects to.

Socket dimmer—A dimmer that screws into a socket and into which a lamp is then screwed.

Solid-state ballasts—Electronic solid-state ballasts that operate at a much higher frequency (25,000Hz versus 60Hz) eliminating the flicker and hum associated with a magnetic ballast.

Specification—A detailed description of the lighting equipment and components chosen for the project. Often shortened to "spec."

Spotlighting—Using a focused beam of illumination to draw attention to an object.

Spread lens—A glass lens accessory used to diffuse and widen beam patterns.

Stake light—A luminaire mounted on a stake to go into the ground or a planter.

Step light—A luminaire used to illuminate steps or pathways.

Stud finder—A device that detects the location of joists behind walls and ceilings by measuring differences in density or the presence of metal nails.

Submittal booklets—A collection of catalog sheets showing what fixtures are to be used on a project.

Swags—Chain-hung fixtures.

Swiss cheese effect—The look resulting from too many holes in the ceiling resulting from an overabundance of recessed fixtures.

Switch—The control for electrical device.

Switched motion sensor—A switch that has a manual on and automatic off sensor that turns the lights off when nothing in the room is moving.

Task lighting—Illumination designed for a work surface so that good light, free of shadows and glare, is created.

Timers—Control devices to activate luminaires at timed intervals.

Toe-kick lighting—Lighting located at the base of a vanity or counter.

Torchère—A standing portable floor lamp that directs light up.

Track lighting—An electrified metal channel onto which individual luminaires are attached.

Transformer—A device that can raise or lower electrical voltage, generally used for low-voltage lights and neon.

Trim—The part of a recessed fixture seen at the ceiling line.

Translucent—Semi-transparent, allowing some light to pass through.

Transparent—Clear, allowing light to pass through.

Tube lighting—Similar to rope lighting but usually involves a hollow plastic tube with miniature lamps spaced at regular intervals.

Tungsten-halogen—A tungsten incandescent lamp (bulb) that contains gases and burns hotter and brighter than standard incandescent lamps.

UL—An independent testing company, Underwriters Laboratories.

Underwriters Laboratories—See UL.

Uplight—A portable luminaire used to project light toward the ceiling.

Uplighting—Illumination projected toward the ceiling.

UV—Stands for ultraviolet light, which has a wavelength shorter than visible light. It fades colors and thus art should not be exposed to strong UV light for extended periods. Sources of UV rays are sunlight as well as incandescent and fluorescent lamping. LED sources of light are a safe light because they emit no UV.

UV filter—A coating or lens that reduces ultraviolet emissions in order to reduce sun damage or damage caused by artificial light sources.

Veiling reflection—A mirror-like reflection of a bright source on a shiny surface. This causes a difficulty in reading, as if looking through a veil.

Voltage—A measurement of the pressure of electricity going through a wire.

Voltage drop—The decrease of light output in fixtures farther from the transformer in low-voltage lighting systems.

Well light—A fixture that is recessed into the ground.

White light—Usually refers to light with a color temperature between 5,000 and 6,250 degrees Kelvin and composed of the whole visible light spectrum. This light allows all colors in the spectrum on an object's surface to be reflected, providing good color-rendering qualities. Daylight is the most commonly referred-to source of white light. This is not a good color for skin tones.

Whole house—Home control system.

Xenon—An inert gas used as a component in certain lamps to produce a cooler color temperature than standard incandescent. It is often used in applications where halogen may normally be specified, because of a longer lamp life.